CQ GUIDE TO

CURRENT AMERICAN
GOVERNMENT

Fall 2005

CQ PRESS

A Division of Congressional Quarterly Inc.

Washington, D.C.

342.73
C882
Fall 2005

Congressional Quarterly Inc.

Congressional Quarterly Inc., an editorial research service and publishing company, serves clients in the fields of news, education, business and government. It provides comprehensive and nonpartisan reporting on Congress, government and politics.

Under the CQ Press imprint, Congressional Quarterly also publishes college political science textbooks and public affairs paperbacks on developing issues and events; information directories; and reference books on the federal government, national elections and politics. Titles include the *Guide to the Presidency,* the *Guide to Congress,* the *Guide to the U.S. Supreme Court,* the *Guide to U.S. Elections* and *Politics in America.* CQ Press' American Government A to Z collection is a reference series that provides essential information about Congress, the presidency, the Supreme Court and the electoral process. *Congress and the Nation,* a record of government for each presidential term, is published every four years. CQ Press also publishes *The CQ Researcher,* a weekly print periodical and online reference database covering today's most debated social and political issues.

CQ publishes *CQ Today* (formerly the *Daily Monitor*), a report on the current and future activities of congressional committees. The *CQ Almanac,* a compendium of legislation for each session of Congress, is published annually. An online information system, CQ.com on Congress, provides immediate access to CQ's databases of legislative action, votes, schedules, profiles and analyses. Visit www.cq.com for more information.

CQ Press
1255 22nd Street, NW, Suite 400
Washington, DC 20037

Phone, 202-729-1900; toll-free, 1-866-427-7737 (1-866-4CQ-PRESS)

Web: www.cqpress.com

Copyright © 2005 by CQ Press, a division of Congressional Quarterly Inc.

All rights reserved. No part of this publication may be reproduced or transmitted in any form or by any means, electronic or mechanical, including photocopy, recording, or any information storage and retrieval system, without permission in writing from the publisher.

Cover photos: Scott J. Ferrell, Congressional Quarterly
Cover design: Paul P. Pressau

♾ The paper used in this publication exceeds the requirements of the American National Standard for Information Sciences—Permanence of Paper for Printed Library Materials, ANSI Z39.48-1992.

Printed and bound in the United States of America
09 08 07 06 05   1 2 3 4 5

ISBN 1-56802-988-8
ISSN 0196-612-X

Contents

CONTENTS

Introduction

Guide to Current American Government is a collection of articles from the *CQ Weekly*, a trusted source for in-depth, nonpartisan reporting and analyses of congressional action, presidential activities, policy debates and other news and developments in Washington, D.C. Beginning in January 2005, *CQ Weekly* expanded its coverage of the intersection of government and commerce, and several of the articles examine this dynamism in American government. All the articles, selected to complement introductory American government texts with up-to-date examinations of current issues and controversies, are divided into four sections.

Foundations of American Government. This section examines issues and events that involve interpretation of the U.S. Constitution, foundational principles such as federalism and democracy, and political ideologies and political culture in the United States. This edition of the *Guide* includes the transcript of President George W. Bush's second inaugural address, an examination of the changes in the American conservative movement wrought by its greater control over the levers of federal power and a series of articles highlighting the stress points between the federal and state governments.

Political Participation. This section examines current issues in electoral and party politics, voting behavior and public opinion. The articles in this edition analyze the outcomes of the 2004 elections (including an examination of the "red states" vs. "blue states" construct), explore the 2006 midterm election cycle, examine the prominent role now played by "religious voters" in campaigns and elections and look at how the traditional, once-a-decade redistricting cycle is now shifting into a never-ending fight for partisan advantage.

Government Institutions. This section explores the inner workings of Congress, the presidency and the federal courts. In this edition of the *Guide,* the articles discuss the composition of the 109th Congress, reorganization of the powerful congressional appropriations committees, efforts by the White House and congressional Republicans to scale back government regulations, President Bush's prospects for setting the domestic policy agenda in his second term and the challenges he faces in advancing his goals for Social Security. This section closes with an article that considers how the expected resignation of Chief Justice William H. Rehnquist affects the confirmation of the president's judicial nominees, given the bitter partisan division in the Congress.

Politics and Public Policy. This section profiles the major policy issues of today. The articles focus on a range of topics: restructuring the military, managing the ballooning federal deficit, reforming the nation's tax policies, regulating the pharmaceutical industry, addressing digital file-sharing technology's effect on copyright protection, dealing with a growing reliance on an illegal immigrant workforce and resolving the financial crisis that clouds the future of Medicare. This section also examines Congress' new activism in the arena of family law (as in the case of Terri Schiavo, who died on March 31, 2005) and the congressional hearings on steroid use in major league baseball.

Foundations of American Government

This section highlights current issues and themes in American politics that involve the foundations of U.S. government: core principles such as democracy, individual rights and liberties, the role of government, federalism and elements of political ideologies and American political culture. These foundations help frame the attitudes, interests and institutions that dictate political choices and outcomes.

The first article examines the path of American conservatism through the prism of the Terri Schiavo controversy and the highly unusual, if ultimately unsuccessful, actions taken by Congress and the president to intervene in this state court case. Conservatism has long been a movement stressing respect for traditions and institutions, holding social activism and expansive uses of public authority in disdain, and focusing more on means than ends. Some social conservatives' new appetite for activism and for achieving particular results, motivated in part by anger at the decisions made by judges, has turned this tradition on its head. These conservatives now control the leadership of the party that occupies the White House and comprise a majority in both chambers of Congress. With its greater control over the levers of power, the conservative movement now seems willing to use federal power more aggressively to achieve its ends and intrude in matters that in the past were left to the states.

The second selection is a transcript of President George W. Bush's second inaugural address, which incorporates themes of fostering the spread of democracy and liberty around the world in opposition to tyranny and oppression. These themes are now classic elements in American political rhetoric, flowing from the nation's engagement in two world wars and the Cold War conflict with totalitarian state socialism. Bush's contribution to this rhetoric of a broad national purpose reflects his administration's approach to the challenges to domestic security presented by terrorism: "The survival of liberty in our land increasingly depends on the success of liberty in other lands."

The last four articles in this section examine the ongoing tensions between the national and the state governments over public policy domains and political control. The federal system divides sovereignty and power in a fluid formula that pits centralized authority against decentralized authority. The stark reality of this tension is reflected in the experiences of former federal government officials who have returned to their states to take the reins of state government. As the states struggle to cope with their fiscal woes and the prospect of more unfunded federal mandates coupled with dwindling federal aid, more and more state leaders are bucking the national tax-cutting trend and raising state taxes. State and local leaders are aggressively lobbying federal officials to keep the federal grant money flowing despite the growing federal deficit. State leaders are also filling in the gaps and waning momentum in federal education initiatives by championing deeper reforms in educational standards, especially for high schools. The final selection in this section demonstrates the vitality of the "laboratory theory" of federalism, as some states are encouraging stem cell research despite the prohibition on federal funding for new stem cell lines.

A Classic Creed

The Schiavo case highlights the growing readiness of conservatives to rewrite fundamental principles in pursuit of an active social agenda that was never envisioned by the movement's leading lights

TOM DELAY RARELY LEAVES any doubt whose side he's on. On March 19, though, the combative House majority leader was blunter than usual. At a nationally televised news conference, he personally attacked Michael Schiavo for insisting that his wife — the tragically incapacitated Terri Schiavo — would have wanted her feeding tube removed so that she could die.

CQ Weekly March 28, 2005

"What kind of man is he?" DeLay demanded.

But the decision by DeLay and other powerful leaders of Congress, backed by President Bush, to intervene directly in what was at heart a family dispute, wrenching the case out of the Florida courts and practically ordering federal judges to keep Schiavo alive, raised a larger question: What kind of conservatives are these?

"Definitions of conservatism now have to be entirely rewritten," says Lewis L. Gould, a professor emeritus of history at the University of Texas at Austin and author of "Grand Old Party: A History of the Republicans."

Indeed, the word itself might be obsolete. The cultural conservatives who have risen to prominence in the past decade are more aggressive and energetic, more interested in morals than economics. They have become the dominant force in the Republican Party and are as intent on re-engineering the country in their own image as Johnson-era liberals were, but to distinctly different ends. Their

Supplanted

methods are far removed from the ideals of Edmund Burke, the 18th century British statesman whose notions of tradition and personal freedom inspired the American conservative movement.

DeLay and his colleagues didn't just take sides in the Schiavo case, they aggressively took sides, shouldering aside the state courts in an effort to keep the woman alive by reinstating her feeding tube, which had been removed March 18 at the direction of a Florida judge.

Their tactic didn't work. One by one, the federal courts refused to second-guess the state court. Moreover, the public seemed appalled: Between 70 and 82 percent of those polled for ABC and CBS news said Congress should have stayed out of the case.

But by intervening in such a private matter, Bush and the Republicans who control Congress provided the most vivid example yet of how completely the conservative movement has changed. Under the most conservative federal government in modern times, some former lawmakers and movement historians say, Republicans are using their power in ways that aren't conservative at all, in the classic sense of the word. A movement that began as the voice of caution — respectful of traditions and institutions, and more interested in means than ends — is now interested mainly in the results, and is willing to use federal power aggressively to achieve them.

This is not their first departure from the original ideas of conservatism. Bush's foreign policy is run by neoconservatives who favor an assertive Wilsonian interventionism, a contradiction of traditional conservatives' belief that the United States should not try to force the world to follow its example. And fiscal conservatives have seen little they recognize in the tax cuts and spending policies of Bush and the GOP Congress, which have added to an already swelling federal deficit.

Now, however, Bush and congressional Republicans have so strongly entered the culture wars on issues such as abortion and same-sex marriage that they have abandoned all caution about using federal power to achieve the goals of religious conservatives.

"You can't go that way if you want to stand true to fundamental conservative principles of government," said former Rep. Bob Barr, a conservative Republican from Georgia notably wary of federal power. "I think in quieter, less emotional moments, people will start to realize that."

Even among some conservatives who think Congress made the right decision by intervening in the Schiavo case, it was a troubling development. "I think on balance, what Congress did was probably the right thing," said David A. Keene, chairman of the American Conservative Union. But "any time the Congress, for the most valid of reasons, does what it did — which was to interfere with the state judicial process — it's a matter for some concern."

TRIUMPH OF THE CULTURE WARS

What's driving this apparent transformation in the conservative creed? The largest factor, say some political experts, is the anger many conservatives feel over cultural and social issues, such as abortion and gay marriage. And that anger is fueled in part by a feeling that unelected judges have been trampling conservative sensibilities on these issues from the bench, their jobs protected from any public backlash or demands for accountability.

Indeed, many conservative legal experts say it was judges who first injected the federal government into areas such as family law, and social conservatives are now merely fighting on this new turf. "Like it or not," says Lynn Wardle, Brigham Young University law professor, "these areas have been federalized."

Historian George H. Nash, author of "The Conservative Intellectual Movement in America Since 1945," says the top concern now of grass-roots conservatives is the power of the judiciary, not the reach of the White House or Congress. Nash disputes the idea that Bush and the Republican Congress abandoned conservative principles by intervening in the Schiavo case. Instead, he argues that they were simply trying to rein in what they see as an out-of-control judiciary.

"What they see is that an unelected judiciary that isn't particularly sympathetic with 'red' America is now literally making decisions of life and death," says Nash. "It brings the whole issue of the judiciary to a higher level of public consciousness."

But it is apparent that the conservative philosophy guiding Republicans today is not the same philosophy that guided the party throughout the half-century following World War II. It seems to boil down to a preoccupation with protecting the sanctity of life, even if that means actions that traditional conserva-

EMOTIONAL APPEALS: Demonstrators in Florida opposed to removing a feeding tube from brain-damaged Terri Schiavo wore tape they said symbolized her inability to speak for herself. Others rallied to support her husband, Michael, who has said removing the tube would accord with Terri's wishes.

AP PHOTO / CHRIS OMEARA

"A disposition to preserve, and an ability to improve, taken together, would be my standard of a statesman."

— Edmund Burke, 18th century British statesman

tives would have considered dangerous governmental meddling into the private affairs of citizens.

In doing so, legal experts and political analysts say, Republicans have created a brand of conservatism that Barry Goldwater — the party's 1964 presidential standard-bearer and exemplar of traditional conservatism — wouldn't recognize. As University of Baltimore law professor Charles Tiefer puts it: "Barry Goldwater would turn over in his grave to see his party dictate from Washington, D.C., the outcomes in family matters hundreds or thousands of miles away."

But DeLay sees it differently. "Our values must define our laws, not the other way around," he declared in a March 22 op-ed article in USA Today. "If our laws don't prevent a helpless, disabled woman, capable of rehabilitation, from being starved and parched to death by an estranged husband with a clear, personal conflict of interest, then our laws are meaningless."

What's noteworthy about this is that the congressional debate that unfolded the weekend of March 19-20 was as lopsided in favor of federal intervention as the later public opinion polls were lopsided against it. Few House Republicans spoke up against congressional intervention, and only five voted against the legislation. The traditional conservative arguments ended up more in the rhetoric of Democrats, notably Massachusetts Rep. Barney Frank, who led the floor fight against intervention.

That led The Wall Street Journal editorial page, a bastion of the new social conservatism, to dismiss the Democratic arguments as essentially disingenuous. "We'd have more sympathy for this argument if the same liberals who are complaining about the possibility of the federal courts reviewing Mrs. Schiavo's case felt as strongly about restraining the federal judiciary when it comes to abortion, homosexuality, and other social issues they don't want to trust to local communities," the Journal wrote in a March 21 editorial.

That underscores a broader political development in America that goes beyond the decline of traditional conservatism in the Republican Party. Just as social conservatives are abandoning states' rights, for example, in order to battle for their cultural vision for America, so are some social liberals embracing states' rights in behalf of their more liberal vision for the country.

Throughout American history, it has usually been the minority power in Washington that becomes the champion of states' rights, only to abandon it once it seizes the levers of power. "It's so tempting when you've captured both houses of Congress, the presidency and the Supreme Court to throw your weight around a little bit," said Roderick Hills Jr., a University of Michigan law professor.

Meanwhile, the few Republicans who opposed the intervention were mainly moderates, such as Rep. Christopher Shays of Connecticut, and institutionalists such as Sen. John W. Warner of Virginia. Warner did not block the bill in the Senate, but he delivered an anguished floor speech March 20 declaring that the measure was a violation of the 10th Amendment, which gives the states and the people any powers not specifically granted to the federal government.

"It is not easy to be in opposition to this legislation," Warner said, "but I have a duty to state my views in keeping with my oath to support the Constitution as I interpret it."

FALLING IN LINE

But what was most striking about that floor debate was the strong support for the bill, even from some Republicans who usually express concerns about Washington trampling on the rights of states.

Take House Judiciary Committee Chairman F. James Sensenbrenner Jr. of Wisconsin, who last year stubbornly refused to take up a bill, ultimately passed, allowing off-duty and retired police to carry concealed handguns anywhere in the country. Republican leaders had to go around him even to get the bill considered on the floor, but last week it was Sensenbrenner who was one of the loudest advocates for intervention in the Schiavo case.

And then there was Rep. Christopher Cox of California, who voted against a proposed constitutional amendment banning same-sex marriage in 2004 based on federalist concerns. For Republicans who believe in federalism, Cox wrote at the time in a column addressed to his constituents, the amendment "is an uncomfortable fit." Keeping the federal government from grabbing too much power from the states, he wrote, was a principle that "must be observed if our system of government is to function properly."

Such concerns, however, did not keep Cox from voting for the Schiavo bill.

Not everyone believes that Bush and Congress violated conservative principles by intervening. For advocates of limited government, the key question was whether the Schiavo case would set a precedent for future congressional interventions. Many said the Schiavo case was unique — involving a rare public dispute between family members and questions over the motives of the husband and the state courts — and hence it is unlikely to be repeated.

"Does this keep me up at night worrying that this is going to be happening on a regular basis? No. It's not going to be happening on a regular basis," said Grover Norquist, president of Americans for Tax Reform, who has fought to limit the size and scope of the federal government. People should be reassured, he said, by the fact that, of all the people who die every year in a vegetative state, the Schiavo case is the only one that has risen to the national consciousness.

Even intervening so strongly in one case "is so less frightening than the government saying, 'Here is the new rule for all people for all times,' " Norquist said.

To some law professors and political analysts, however, the Schiavo case was the most definitive proof yet that the religious right now dominates the entire conservative movement, to the point that other factions' concerns are brushed aside.

When Bush was re-elected last year, it was clear that social conservatives would demand a stronger voice, based on the strength of their turnout at the polls. They have yet to win outright victories on issues such as abortion and gay marriage. But now, political analysts say, they have demonstrated their power by forcing Congress to intervene in one person's well-publicized struggle.

"This is a Congress that can't deliver much to the religious right, but they can deliver on a symbolic issue," says Marshall Wittmann, a former aide to Arizona Republican Sen. John McCain and currently a senior fellow at the centrist Democratic Leadership Council.

That bothers Republicans who believe such matters should remain private. "You don't get into this game. It's totally personal," said former Republican Sen. Alan K. Simpson of Wyoming. "In my mind, taking it to the Congress is a troublesome feature that will come back to clobber it. If you take one of these on, you're going to get a lot of them."

Libertarians — who believe in personal freedom as well as limited government and have given the Republican Party some of its strongest support — were alarmed as well. "This is not a federal issue. It's always been handled at the state level," says David Boaz, executive vice president of the Cato Institute. "A party that claims to believe in federalism should not be intruding the federal government into issues that are handled by the states."

THE ROOTS OF CONSERVATISM

If traditional American conservatism was built on anything, it was a resistance to activism to achieve particular goals.

That was the guiding principle of Burke, who was a champion of classical liberalism — not the activist ideas of modern American liberals, but the limited-government ideas that launched the American conservative movement. Burke resisted the concentration of power and believed in the wisdom of existing institutions, arguing that checks and balances were needed to prevent any one person or faction from trying to accomplish sweeping political changes.

Burke inspired some of the most influential American conservatives — including Russell Kirk, author of "The Conservative Mind" and a longtime columnist for National Review — with his suspicion of grand designs or an active government that pursued utopian goals.

"We cannot make a heaven on earth, though we may make a hell. We are all creatures of mingled good and evil," Kirk wrote in 1957. Because power is inherently dangerous, he wrote, "so far as possible, political power ought to be kept in the hands of private persons and local institutions. Centralization is ordinarily a sign of social decadence."

By 1965, James Burnham, in "Congress and the American Tradition," wrote that conserva-

Measures of Disapproval

Polls showed most Americans thought Congress should have stayed out of the Terri Schiavo case.

Results from a CBS News poll of 737 adults, conducted March 21-22:

Q. Congress has passed a bill that would require Terri Schiavo's case to be heard in U.S. federal court. Do you think Congress passed this bill because they really care about what happens in this case, or do you think they passed the bill to advance a political agenda?

Really care	Advance political agenda	Both 3%	Neither 1%	Don't know / not applicable
13%	74%			9%

Q. Do you think that Congress' actions in this case would make it easier for Congress to intervene in the lives of individual Americans in the future? IF YES: Are you concerned about that, or not?

Yes, concerned	Yes, not concerned	No, not concerned	Don't know / not applicable
68%	9%	17%	6%

NOTE: Margin of error + / - 4 percentage points. Figures are rounded.

Results from an ABC News poll of 501 adults, conducted March 20:

Q. Florida state courts have heard the Schiavo case. Federal courts have said they don't have jurisdiction because it involves Florida law only. Would you support or oppose a new federal law requiring the federal courts to review the Schiavo case? This probably would mean reinserting the feeding tube until the case goes through the federal courts.

	Support	Oppose	No opinion
ALL	35%	60%	5%
Protestant, non-evangelical	26%	71%	3%
Protestant, evangelical	44%	50%	5%
Catholic	38%	56%	6%
Liberals	34%	62%	4%
Moderates	29%	67%	5%
Conservatives	48%	49%	3%
Democrats	34%	63%	2%
Independents	31%	61%	8%
Republicans	39%	58%	3%
Conservative Republicans	41%	57%	2%

NOTE: Margin of error + / - 4.5 percentage points. Figures are rounded.

tives believe in "the diffusion of sovereignty" and "the diffusion of power," as well as "the retention by the states of an effective share in the sovereignty."

By the time Barry Goldwater ran for president in 1964 as a true conservative, some of those views could be self-defeating. He opposed the Civil Rights Act of 1964 on the grounds that it violated states' rights. "Goldwater had been a racial progressive in the Senate and in his business," said Boaz. But by using his views on government to oppose a law that most

Americans considered a moral imperative, he helped seal his defeat in the election.

When Ronald Reagan was elected president in 1980, he shared Goldwater's passion for limiting the role of the federal government. Everyone remembers the most famous line from his first inaugural address — "government is the problem" — but there was also a less-remembered commitment to federalism. "All of us need to be reminded," Reagan said, "that the federal government did not create the states; the states created the federal government."

In practice, though, Reagan did little to transfer power back to the states. And Bush — who, like most modern Republicans, considers Reagan a conservative icon — has used federal power to achieve ideological goals. He prodded Congress to bolster the federal role in education with the No Child Left Behind Act, a law he is trying to expand this year, and has called for a constitutional amendment banning same-sex marriage.

Bush also has embraced the foreign policy views of the neoconservatives, who have championed the Iraq War as a way to give democracy a foothold in the Middle East. That view would hardly be recognizable to Kirk, who wrote that "the American conservative feels that his country ought to set an example to the world, but ought not to try to remake the world in its image."

THE SOCIAL CONSERVATIVES

The most serious split in the conservative movement, however, has been between social conservatives and libertarians. Social conservatives are far more willing to use federal power to protect life and their image of the American family, and their dominance — backed by deeply felt beliefs about morality and right vs. wrong — has crowded out the views of other conservatives who cling to their belief in limited government.

"The Schiavo case shows the extreme triumph of the cultural conservative element of the Republican Party over the libertarian element, which had stood by federalism because it hated to see Congress coming into the hospital room and the bedroom around the country," said Tiefer of the University of Baltimore.

The argument of cultural conservatives — that Schiavo deserved one more level of appeal

CQ GRAPHIC / JAMIE BAYLIS AND JACOB FREEDMAN

Congress and The Rule of Law

THE TERRI SCHIAVO CASE HAS exacerbated tensions between the courts and congressional Republicans, who already consider the federal bench a handicap to conservative policy on such issues as abortion, the definition of marriage, or the separation of church and state.

Senate debate on President Bush's judicial nominees, bound to be contentious, will only become more so as cases such as Schiavo's raise the political stakes for Republicans and Democrats.

"One of the first tasks we will have is this whole confirmation of judges," Senate Majority Leader Bill Frist of Tennessee told members of the conservative Family Research Council last week. "These activist judges are not interpreting the Constitution. They're rewriting it, and that's wrong."

Republican leaders intervened in the Schiavo case and shifted jurisdiction to the federal courts hoping they would order her feeding tube reinserted. They did not. A U.S. District Court judge in Florida and the 11th Circuit Court of Appeals in Atlanta declined to overturn the state court decision, and the Supreme Court refused to get involved. Congressional conservatives said the decisions were another instance of the judiciary thumbing its nose at Congress and the popular will.

Not only did Republicans not get what they wanted from the courts, they got embarrassed. Opinion polls showed an overwhelming majority of the public thought Congress had no business getting involved in the case. Even half of evangelical Christians had qualms about the legislation, according to one poll.

Conservative lawmakers were furious. "The judiciary has circled their wagons, not around the Constitution, not around the law, not around justice or jurisprudence, but around themselves, defying the Constitution and the will of the people," said Iowa Republican Steve King, a member of the House Judiciary Committee. "They are unanswerable to any force."

In recent years, Republicans such as King have been willing to

TROUBLE IN COURT: Frist, left, with Florida Sen. Mel Martinez on March 20, pledged to confirm more conservative federal judges.

adjust the judicial system, for instance by trying to take away federal court jurisdiction on some social policy questions where they believe courts are legislating rather than judging. They pushed bills to strip federal courts of jurisdiction over gay marriage legislation and the Pledge of Allegiance, for instance, but were not successful.

Ironically, in the Schiavo case, Congress did the opposite, expanding the jurisdiction of the federal courts to hear the Schiavo appeal in an area of law — family law — long reserved to state legislatures and courts. Critics say the Florida case, like the legislation to adjust court jurisdictions and the battle over judicial nominees, shows that Congress' main interest is in guaranteeing a particular policy outcome.

"What they have been asking [federal courts] to do is exactly what they always denounced: asking judges to make it up based on political predilections," said David J. Garrow, a professor at the Emory University School of Law.

Congress clearly had a policy outcome in mind earlier this year when it passed, and Bush eagerly signed, legislation making it easier to shift class action lawsuits from state courts to federal courts. Business lobbyists argued that the law was needed to curb "forum shopping," in which lawyers troll states and in some case the whole country for sympathetic judges and juries for their class action

because the state of Florida did not give her due process — resonated with congressional Republicans of all persuasions. Rep. David Dreier of California called himself "a Republican who believes passionately in states' rights," but explained his support for the Schiavo bill by quoting Thomas Jefferson, who called for a "wise and a frugal government, which shall restrain men from injuring one another."

And Rep. Mike Pence of Indiana, chairman of the Republican Study Committee and one of the most outspoken advocates of limited government in Congress, threw his support behind the Schiavo bill because of the "disregard of innocent human life" he saw in the case.

"It is a moral issue. It's not just a legal

issue," said Janice Shaw Crouse, executive director of the Beverly LaHaye Institute, the research arm of Concerned Women for America, a Christian advocacy group. "You cannot have representative government and not have them respond when so much of the population was outraged. . . . Congress had no choice but to intervene."

Such a view would be a surprise to conservative scholars such as Burnham, who wrote in 1965 that conservatives saw no great need for lightning-quick actions by Congress: "When the legislative function is limited, as it normally should be, to issues of principle and broad policy, there is seldom any real need for immediate action."

The conservative movement has been

undergoing a profound transformation for at least three decades, long before the Schiavo case, and it is not clear that many, if any, Republicans in Congress today would really consider themselves Edmund Burke conservatives. "Give me a week and I can think of one," says Lee Edwards, a historian of the conservative movement and a fellow at the Heritage Foundation.

But Edwards does not think conservative thinkers such as Kirk would feel betrayed by the Schiavo intervention. "He would say, I think, that there is a communitarian responsibility here — that not just the family, but the larger community has a responsibility to act, and it should act," Edwards says.

Even traditional conservatives, historians

AP PHOTO / LAWRENCE JACKSON

> **❝It's very disconcerting to me that we have a judiciary, both on the state level and on the federal level, that seem to have no qualms at all about causing the death of a person by means of starvation and dehydration.❞**
>
> — Rep. **John Hostettler**, R-Ind.

claims. The legislation is aimed at reducing the number and cost to business of class action suits on the presumption that federal courts will not be as generous.

CONGRESSIONAL ACTIVISM

Whether or not Congress should micromanage the courts, there is little dispute that they can. Under the Constitution, Congress has the power to establish federal courts below the Supreme Court and define their jurisdiction. Congress also has the authority to define the jurisdiction of the Supreme Court in all but a few types of cases.

The legislation Congress passed on March 21 expressly gave the U.S. District Court for the Middle District of Florida jurisdiction to consider a lawsuit by Terri Schiavo's parents alleging violations of her rights under constitutional or federal law.

More often than not, social conservatives write bills to take issues out of the hands of federal judges. For instance, the Supreme Court's 2003 decision in *Lawrence v. Texas* invalidating that state's anti-sodomy law convinced social conservatives that the high court eventually will void a 1996 federal law, the Defense of Marriage Act, that bans same-sex marriage. Republicans have moved to defend the marriage law with a proposed constitutional amendment to bar gay marriage and a bill by Indiana Republican John Hostettler that would simply remove federal court jurisdiction over challenges to the 1996 law. They passed the House but not the Senate.

A 2002 decision by a federal court of appeals in California that the phrase "under God" did not belong in the Pledge of Allegiance led the House last year to pass legislation that would have barred federal courts from hearing such challenges to the wording of the pledge. The Senate did not act on the measure. Social conservatives were not through with the 9th Circuit Court, which ruled in the case. Last fall, the House passed an amendment to a bill to carve it into three separate appellate courts, but that did not become law either.

Some legal experts say that if Congress does start blocking the courts from reviewing their actions, it might have unintended consequences. "This kind of pinpoint correction of judicial outcomes by specially tailored laws may have the long-term effect of eroding respect for the rule of law," said Anthony Sebok, a law professor at Brooklyn Law School.

RULING ON THE LAW

Sometimes, lawmakers who seek to preordain legal outcomes sabotage themselves in drafting their bills. The Schiavo legislation contained a flaw that allowed federal judges enough leeway to effectively deny a new legal bid to Terri Schiavo's parents, Bob and Mary Schindler. While the law mandated federal court review of the Schindlers' challenge, it did not expressly require that a federal judge issue an order immediately to reinsert the feeding tube. That allowed U.S. District Judge James D. Whittemore to use the pre-existing legal threshold for granting the Schindlers' motion for a temporary restraining order. He ruled that although the new law might allow the Schindlers to bring their lawsuit, he would not issue the restraining order because the Schindlers had not demonstrated a "substantial likelihood" that they would prevail on their claims.

The series of defeats have led conservative critics to renew their contentions that federal judges are too quick to ignore the will of the people. "It's very disconcerting to me that we have a judiciary, both on the state level and on the federal level, that seems to have no qualms at all about causing the death of a person by means of starvation and dehydration," Hostettler said.,

But conservative lawmakers are unlikely to use the case to pursue broader attempts to change the jurisdiction of the federal courts. "It's very short-term politics," said Joseph L. Smith, a political science professor at the University of Alabama. "I don't think they have a real revolution in federal jurisdiction in mind."

say, would have made exceptions for extraordinary cases such as Schiavo's, where the consequences of acting on principle may be worse than the consequences of government intervention. "I don't think the grass-roots types are looking at this as a matter of who gains politically or constitutional interpretation. They're looking at this as a moral issue," says Nash.

The Bush administration and Congress have been increasingly willing to pre-empt the states on policy issues. A law enacted last year pre-empted state laws by allowing off-duty and retired police officers to carry concealed firearms wherever they travel. This year, the first Republican legislative victory was a law that shifts more class action lawsuits from state to federal courts, a priority for economic rather than social conservatives.

But nowhere is the new conservative paradigm more striking than in domestic relations, a subject that ranges from adoption and child custody to visitation rights and medical decisions. It is an area of law long considered the domain of states and localities.

Since the 1980s, Congress has mandated national standards for child support payments and medical treatment for severely disabled newborns, binding states to federal guidelines through the power of the purse. But until recently, it has shied away from inserting itself into deeply personal decisions surrounding marriage or the end of life. Now, congressional conservatives have worked at banning late-term abortion procedures and gay marriage.

"We really haven't seen that before. Congress never thought it was their domain," said Jennifer L. Rosato, a Brooklyn Law School professor. "They want to make sure that all the legislation around the country reflects a culture of life."

Wardle, the Brigham Young University law professor, said federal intervention such as in the Schiavo case is consistent with the ultimate aim of federalism: curbing the abuse and concentration of power, which he argues has been amassed by federal courts. "Power centers have shifted, so federalism needs to adjust," said Wardle.

Some Democrats in Congress say Republicans have hypocritically discarded federalism when it was inconvenient.

"The concept of a Jeffersonian democracy as envisioned by the founders and the states as 'laboratories of democracy' . . . will lie in tatters," Rep. John Conyers Jr. of Michigan, the ranking Democrat on the House Judiciary Committee, warned during the March 20 floor debate on the Schiavo bill.

But their views did not represent the entire party: 47 House Democrats voted for the Schiavo bill, and Democrats allowed it to pass unopposed in the Senate.

In reality, neither party has particularly distinguished itself as a consistent defender of federalism. That was a point Goldwater made in his 1960 book, "The Conscience of a Conservative," considered an ideological pillar of the modern conservative movement. Goldwater observed that "the Republican Party, like the Democratic Party, summons the coercive power of the federal government whenever national leaders conclude that the states are not performing satisfactorily."

But there is another factor at work in the Schiavo case. The price of acting on principle, and keeping Congress out of the case, would have guaranteed Schiavo's death. It's rare that such abstract notions about the role of government are put to such a personalized, and painful, test.

"One of the tests of federalism is that you have to support it even when you know it's going to produce results you don't like," says Boaz of the Cato Institute. "The Republican majority has failed this test. But the Democrats have been failing the test all along."

THE AFTERMATH

In writing the Schiavo bill, lawmakers were careful to specify that the measure does not set a precedent for future legislation. But family law experts and even social conservatives who supported the bill say lawmakers are kidding themselves if they believe that.

"I think there's no way to avoid having it set a precedent," says Crouse. "If a similar circumstance comes along, they'll have to act as well. . . . Congress may wish otherwise, and it can try to confine its involvement to this case, but I don't think it will have any choice."

Family law experts fear that families who until now might have been willing to sort out end-of-life decisions with a social worker or hospital counselor may now look to legislative intervention. "I think there's terrifying precedent value," said Harvard Law School professor Elizabeth Bartholet.

That is exactly the scenario Warner had in mind. "Who can say there are not other tragic situations across our land today; who can predict what the future may inflict by way of personal hardship upon our citizens?" he asked in his floor speech. "I fear the door has opened, and Congress . . . will again and again be petitioned to deal with personal situations which are the responsibility of the several states."

Such fears may be overblown, particularly after a string of federal court judges from Florida to Atlanta and the Supreme Court in Washington quickly rejected bids to reinsert Schiavo's feeding tube. And some independent analysts agreed with Norquist that the case was unique and therefore unlikely to be repeated. "I think it's the facts of the case that make this a special one, and one that is riv-

eting and wrenching for many people," says Nash.

But the federal courts' decisions brushing aside Congress' attempts at intervention may also provide new ammunition for social conservatives angry at what they view as an arrogant judiciary that flouts the popular will.

The political fallout is unclear. As broadly unpopular as the move was, congressional redistricting has made most House seats safe for incumbents. Even in districts where most voters cast their ballots for Democrat John Kerry in last year's presidential residential race, many of the House Republicans who voted for the bill won by healthy margins.

In the Senate, even though the GOP holds a 55-seat majority, Democrats will be defending more seats in 2006. Seventeen Democrats and independent James M. Jeffords of Vermont, who often votes with them, will be up for re-election, compared with just 15 Republicans.

But it will be hard for lawmakers to ignore the polls showing such overwhelming opposition to the move. "I think both parties really didn't see how big the issue was," says Gould. "It's like the Constitution is Play-Doh, and you can reshape it every day. . . . Is it proper, when you don't like the results, to just erase the blackboard and start over?"

And by getting the federal government involved in such a private matter, supporters of the Schiavo bill will add to the cynicism about Congress, says Barr. Lawmakers are "paid, first and foremost, to uphold the Constitution, particularly as conservatives. . . . To me, it's not even a close call." For conservatives in Congress, it may be a closer call next time. ∎

Bush's Second Inaugural Address

'The survival of liberty in our land increasingly depends on the success of liberty in other lands.'

Following is the CQ Transcriptions transcript of George W. Bush's address from the West Front of the Capitol on Jan. 20, delivered just after he took the oath of office for his second term as president.

VICE PRESIDENT CHENEY, Mr. Chief Justice, President Carter, President Bush, President Clinton, members of the United States Congress, Reverend, clergy, distinguished guests, fellow citizens:

On this day, prescribed by law and marked by ceremony, we celebrate the durable wisdom of our Constitution and recall the deep commitments that unite our country.

I am grateful for the honor of this hour, mindful of the consequential times in which we live and determined to fulfill the oath that I have sworn and you have witnessed.

At this second gathering, our duties are defined not by the words I use, but by the history we have seen together.

For a half a century, America defended our own freedom by standing watch on distant borders. After the shipwreck of communism came years of relative quiet, years of repose, years of sabbatical. And then there came a day of fire. We have seen our vulnerability and we have seen its deepest source.

For as long as whole regions of the world simmer in resentment and tyranny, prone to ideologies that feed hatred and excuse murder, violence will gather and multiply in destructive power and cross the most defended borders and raise a mortal threat.

There is only one force of history that can break the reign of hatred and resentment and expose the pretensions of tyrants and reward the hopes of the decent and tolerant, and that is the force of human freedom.

We are led, by events and common sense, to one conclusion: The survival of liberty in our land increasingly depends on the success of liberty in other lands. The best hope for peace in our world is the expansion of freedom in all the world.

America's vital interests and our deepest beliefs are now one. From the day of our founding, we have proclaimed that every man and woman on this earth has rights and dignity and matchless value, because they bear the

ATTENTIVE AUDIENCE: Near Bush as he delivered his address were several presidential aspirants past and future — among them the president's 2004 Democratic challenger, Sen. John Kerry of Massachusetts, far left.

image of the maker of heaven and Earth.

Across the generations, we have proclaimed the imperative of self-government, because no one is fit to be a master and no one deserves to be a slave.

ENDING TYRANNY

Fancying these ideals is the mission that created our nation. It is the honorable achievement of our fathers. Now it is the urgent requirement of our nation's security and the calling of our time.

So it is the policy of the United States to seek and support the growth of democratic movements and institutions in every nation and culture, with the ultimate goal of ending tyranny in our world. This is not primarily the task of arms, though we will defend ourselves and our friends by force of arms when necessary.

Freedom, by its nature, must be chosen and defended by citizens and sustained by the rule of law and the protection of minorities. And when the soul of a nation finally speaks, the institutions that arise may reflect customs and traditions very different from our own.

America will not impose our own style of government on the unwilling. Our goal, instead, is to help others find their own voice, attain their own freedom and make their own way.

The great objective of ending tyranny is the concentrated work of generations. The difficulty of the task is no excuse for avoiding it.

America's influence is not unlimited. But, fortunately for the oppressed, America's influence is considerable, and we will use it confidently in freedom's cause.

My most solemn duty is to protect this nation and its people from further attacks and emerging threats. Some have unwisely chosen to test America's resolve and have found it firm. We will persistently clarify the choice before every ruler and every nation: the moral choice between oppression, which is always wrong, and freedom, which is eternally right.

America will not pretend that jailed dissidents prefer their chains, or that women welcome humiliation and servitude, or that any human being aspires to live at the mercy of bullies. We will encourage reform in other governments by making clear that success in our relations will require the decent treatment of their own people.

America's belief in human dignity will guide our policies, yet rights must be more than the grudging concessions of dictators. They are secured by free dissent and the participation of the governed.

In the long run, there is no justice without

CQ PHOTO / SCOTT J. FERRELL

freedom, and there can be no human rights without human liberty.

Some, I know, have questioned the global appeal of liberty — though this time in history, four decades defined by the swiftest advance of freedom ever seen, is an odd time for doubt.

Americans, of all people, should never be surprised by the power of our ideals.

Eventually, the call of freedom comes to every mind and every soul. We do not accept the existence of permanent tyranny because we do not accept the possibility of permanent slavery. Liberty will come to those who love it.

Today, America speaks anew to the peoples of the world. All who live in tyranny and hopelessness can know the United States will not ignore your oppression, or excuse your oppressors. When you stand for your liberty, we will stand with you.

Democratic reformers facing repression, prison or exile can know America sees you for who you are, the future leaders of your free country.

The rulers of outlaw regimes can know that we still believe as Abraham Lincoln did: "Those who deny freedom to others deserve it not for themselves; and, under the rule of a just God, cannot long retain it."

The leaders of governments with long habits of control need to know: To serve your people you must learn to trust them. Start on this journey of progress and justice, and America will walk at your side.

And all the allies of the United States can know: We honor your friendship, we rely on your counsel and we depend on your help.

Division among free nations is a primary goal of freedom's enemies. The concerted effort of free nations to promote democracy is a prelude to our enemies' defeat.

Today, I also speak anew to my fellow citizens. From all of you, I have asked patience in the hard task of securing America, which you have granted in good measure.

Our country has accepted obligations that are difficult to fulfill and would be dishonorable to abandon. Yet because we have acted in the great liberating tradition of this nation, tens of millions have achieved their freedom. And as hope kindles hope, millions more will find it.

By our efforts we have lit a fire as well — a fire in the minds of men. It warms those who feel its power. It burns those who fight its progress. And one day this untamed fire of freedom will reach the darkest corners of our world.

A few Americans have accepted the hardest

duties in this cause. In the quiet work of intelligence and diplomacy, the idealistic work of helping raise up free governments, the dangerous and necessary work of fighting our enemies, some have shown their devotion to our country in deaths that honored their whole lives. And we will always honor their names and their sacrifice.

All Americans have witnessed this idealism, and some for the first time. I ask our youngest citizens to believe the evidence of your eyes.

You have seen duty and allegiance in the determined faces of our soldiers. You have seen that life is fragile, and evil is real, and courage triumphs. Make the choice to serve in a cause larger than your wants, larger than yourself, and in your days you will add not just to the wealth of our country, but to its character.

FREEDOM AT HOME

America has need of idealism and courage, because we have essential work at home: the unfinished work of American freedom.

In a world moving toward liberty, we are determined to show the meaning and promise of liberty.

In America's ideal of freedom, citizens find the dignity and security of economic independence, instead of laboring on the edge of subsistence. This is the broader definition of liberty that motivated the Homestead Act, the Social Security Act and the G.I. Bill of Rights.

And now we will extend this vision by reforming great institutions to serve the needs of our time.

To give every American a stake in the promise and future of our country, we will bring the highest standards to our schools and build an ownership society.

We will widen the ownership of homes and businesses, retirement savings and health insurance, preparing our people for the challenges of life in a free society.

By making every citizen an agent of his or her own destiny, we will give our fellow Americans greater freedom from want and fear, and make our society more prosperous and just and equal.

In America's ideal of freedom, the public interest depends on private character, on integrity, and tolerance toward others, and the rule of conscience in our own lives. Self-government relies, in the end, on the governing of the self.

That edifice of character is built in families, supported by communities with standards, and sustained in our national life by the truths of Sinai,

FINAL APPEARANCES?: For the fifth and very likely the last time, Chief Justice William H. Rehnquist, who is ill with thyroid cancer, administered the oath. Colin L. Powell, the outgoing Secretary of State, used his cell phone to capture a glimpse of Bush after his address.

CQ PHOTOS / SCOTT J. FERRELL

the Sermon on the Mount, the words of the Koran, and the varied faiths of our people.

Americans move forward in every generation by reaffirming all that is good and true that came before: ideals of justice and conduct that are the same yesterday, today and forever.

In America's ideal of freedom, the exercise of rights is ennobled by service and mercy and a heart for the weak.

Liberty for all does not mean independence from one another. Our nation relies on men and women who look after a neighbor and surround the lost with love.

Americans at our best value the life we see in one another and must always remember that even the unwanted have worth.

And our country must abandon all the habits of racism because we cannot carry the message of freedom and the baggage of bigotry at the same time.

From the perspective of a single day, including this day of dedication, the issues and questions before our country are many.

From the viewpoint of centuries, the questions that come to us are narrowed and few. Did our generation advance the cause of freedom? And did our character bring credit to that cause?

These questions that judge us also unite us, because Americans of every party and background — Americans by choice and by birth — are bound to one another in the cause of freedom.

HEALING DIVISIONS

We have known divisions, which must be healed to move forward in great purposes. And I will strive in good faith to heal them. Yet those divisions do not define America.

> **❝All who live in tyranny and hopelessness can know: The United States will not ignore your oppression or excuse your oppressors.❞**

We felt the unity and fellowship of our nation when freedom came under attack, and our response came like a single hand over a single heart. And we can feel that same unity and pride whenever America acts for good, and the victims of disaster are given hope, and the unjust encounter justice, and the captives are set free.

We go forward with complete confidence in the eventual triumph of freedom. Not because history runs on the wheels of inevitability; it is human choices that move events. Not because we consider ourselves a chosen nation; God moves and chooses as he wills.

We have confidence because freedom is the permanent hope of mankind, the hunger in dark places, the longing of the soul.

When our founders declared a new order of the ages, when soldiers died in wave upon wave for a union based on liberty, when citizens marched in peaceful outrage under the banner "Freedom Now," they were acting on an ancient hope that is meant to be fulfilled.

History has an ebb and flow of justice, but history also has a visible direction, set by liberty and the author of liberty.

When the Declaration of Independence was first read in public and the Liberty Bell was sounded in celebration, a witness said: "It rang as if it meant something." In our time it means something still.

America, in this young century, proclaims liberty throughout all the world and to all the inhabitants thereof. Renewed in our strength, tested but not weary, we are ready for the greatest achievements in the history of freedom.

May God bless you, and may he watch over the United States of America. ∎

The Federalist Divide

The distance and dissonance between Washington and state capitals grows more pronounced

SOMETHING FASCINATING is going on in Indiana. Another conservative Republican with Washington experience has gone home to run a state and found that having to govern in the real world is intruding on his ideology. It's becoming something of a pattern, one which we may see more often as Washington tries to offload its deficit onto the states.

In the first 30 months of the Bush administration, Mitch Daniels served as director of the Office of Management and Budget, said by some — including his own biography — to be the second most powerful job in the federal government.

Daniels' conservative credentials are impeccable. He was a top aide to Sen. Richard G. Lugar, R-Ind., then worked in the Reagan White House. He returned home to Indianapolis to run the Hudson Institute, a prestigious conservative think tank, then moved to top executive positions with the pharmaceutical giant, Eli Lilly and Co.

At OMB, Daniels presided over the administration's strategy to stimulate a mildly depressed economy with tax cuts for higher-income citizens, while accelerating spending to levels not seen since the Great Society days of the 1960s. After he left to run for governor of Indiana, the administration began to apply the brakes on spending gently but held the line on taxes. Although federal spending had soared, revenue as a share of the national economy was at a level dating back to the 1950s. The difference, of course, was a staggering deficit.

So Daniels left a White House that had enjoyed surprising success in achieving its goals, to go home to campaign in a state that, like many others, was in fiscal distress.

Then the man whom President Bush nicknamed "The Blade" for his skill in cutting both budget requests and taxes did something that stunned most everyone. He took a look at Indiana's books, declared that the state had a structural deficit and proposed an increase in the income tax for wealthier Hoosiers. It would be just a temporary hike, for sure, on those making more than $100,000.

But conservatives both in the state and elsewhere were not pleased. The Wall Street Journal fumed. Grover Norquist, head of the anti-tax Americans for Tax Reform, declared that Daniels had "folded under the pressure of big-spending interests" faster than any "governor claiming to be a Reagan Republican" he had ever seen.

> **Now the concern among governors ... is that the Bush administration and Congress ... are preparing to export their own fiscal problems to the states.**

It may have been faster, but it was hardly unique. During his three terms in the U.S. House, Bob Riley compiled one of the chamber's most conservative voting records. But when he became governor of Alabama, he managed to push the largest tax increase in the state's history through the legislature, only to see it clobbered by voters in a referendum. Other Republican governors in conservative states such as Arkansas, Idaho, Nevada and Ohio had more success — increasing taxes during what had become the worst fiscal downturn in 60 years.

HARD LESSONS

Now the concern among governors of both parties is that the Bush administration and Congress, facing annual deficits that are almost as large as spending on all discretionary domestic programs, are preparing, in effect, to export their own fiscal problems down to the states. The best early estimate of the administration's fiscal 2006 budget proposal for the next five years shows a loss of $214 billion in funding for education, health care, housing, transportation, parks, law enforcement and other programs in states and localities.

What's more, the states' own ability to raise revenue is being crimped while the feds are mandating that they do more, without providing the resources. Congress has imposed a moratorium on Internet access taxes. Changes in the telecommunications industry are threatening revenues that both states and localities have relied on for decades. And programs such as No Child Left Behind or the special education law may have noble goals, but Congress never has been willing to provide the funding that was promised, leaving the states to pick up much of the bill.

That's why people such as Daniels, Riley and Dirk Kempthorne, a former U.S. senator and now Republican governor of Idaho, change their behavior when they move from Washington to their state capitals. It's one thing to administer a budget process or cast votes in Congress. It's quite another to run a government that delivers direct services; at some point the books have to be balanced.

David M. Walker, the U.S. comptroller general, is the official who audits the federal government's annual financial statement. He is one of the few outspoken critics against the culture of debt that not only defines government, but also the society as a whole.

In making his argument for reforms in federal budgeting, Walker recently said that "we should look to the states. In some ways the states are way ahead of the federal government in dealing with their fiscal imbalances. They have made hard choices in the past — partly driven by their state constitutions, partly by their inability to print money and partly by their sensitivity to their bond ratings."

Walker is doing his job. And though Mitch Daniels may not be the most popular guy either in Indiana or Washington right now, he is, too. ■

CQ Weekly March 7, 2005

Grant Program's Fight for Life

White House move to cut community development grants meets heavy resistance from local officials

CLARKSVILLE, A SMALL CITY of about 108,000 residents northwest of Nashville, appears prosperous. It has a poverty rate a bit lower than the national average and a much lower unemployment rate — and wouldn't appear plagued by big-city problems.

But Mayor Don Trotter says his city has a worsening problem with homeless veterans discharged from nearby Fort Campbell, home of the Army's 101st Airborne Division. Former junior-level enlisted personnel have difficulty finding jobs that enable them to afford Clarksville's rising cost of housing.

So Trotter and nine other Tennessee officials came to Washington the week of March 14 to combat President Bush's proposal to eliminate the Community Development Block Grant (CDBG) program, which Clarksville is using to help finance more low-cost housing.

He told members of the state's congressional delegation that a loss of CDBG aid, "could cause problems for a lot of people who just can't help themselves," he said.

Trotter is one foot soldier in a legislative battle that could redefine the federal government's role in assisting financially strapped communities. The CDBG program has been the centerpiece of that effort over the past three decades.

Swift, negative reaction from local elected officials and their allies on Capitol Hill gave supporters of the program symbolic victories during House and Senate debates over the fiscal 2006 budget resolution. But over the next few weeks, the administration intends to intensify its offensive to win congressional support for overhauling CDBG and other programs that provide local economic development aid.

The president proposes ending the Housing and Urban Development Department's role

Dollars Decline

CDBG's appropriation for fiscal 2005 is $4.1 billion, down 8 percent from a current dollar peak a decade ago. When adjusted for inflation, spending on CDBG is at its lowest point ever, less than half the fiscal 1978 funding level.

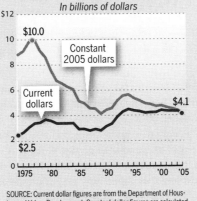

In billions of dollars

SOURCE: Current dollar figures are from the Department of Housing and Urban Development. Constant dollar figures are calculated using the consumer price index.

in the CDBG program. It would consolidate that program's functions, along with those of 17 smaller grant programs, in the Commerce Department, creating what Bush calls a Strengthening America's Communities Initiative, with a budget of $3.7 billion.

That's 30 percent less than the $5.3 billion appropriated this year for the 18 programs combined, and $400 million less than was appropriated for CDBG alone in fiscal 2005.

The initiative would also absorb the Economic Development Administration in Commerce, the Community Services Block Grant program at the Department of Health and Human Services and some rural development programs divided between the Agriculture and Housing departments. But it is the bid to eliminate the CDBG program that has drawn the most passionate resistance.

"It's been working well," Trotter said. "Why, when you find a federal program that works well, do you want to mess with it?"

The Bush proposal is more than a simple consolidation or cost-cutting move. The administration aims to fundamentally change the direction of urban and rural anti-poverty policy by more directly focusing federal efforts on boosting private enterprise and away from the diffuse aid programs that currently serve low-income people and communities.

The intent of the plan is to promote sustained growth, "thereby reducing a community's reliance on perpetual federal assistance," said David A. Sampson, assistant Commerce secretary for economic development, at a regional economic development conference in St. Louis in February. "The job of government is to remove barriers to growth, create a positive business environment, be accountable for taxpayer dollars and to ensure results for programs aimed at helping people."

"Outraged and appalled" is how Don Plusquellic, the Democratic mayor of Akron, Ohio, and president of the U.S. Conference of Mayors, summed up the reaction of fellow mayors, other local officials and development organizations. The plan "will have a devastating economic impact on communities across this country," he said shortly after the administration unveiled its proposal.

The danger, say supporters of the existing network of programs, is the potential loss of what "community development" means — not just more jobs and more profitable businesses, but an overall improvement in the well-being of the people who make up a community.

"It will lose its essence," said Rita Arancibia, community development manager for Clarksville. Community development efforts, such as

CQ GRAPHIC / MARILYN GATES-DAVIS

the town's full-court press to reduce home-lessness and increase the amount of low-cost housing, "will be swallowed by the economic development side of it and it will lose the people side."

BUDGET BATTLE

Trotter and his group were among dozens of mayors and other local elected officials swarming the Capitol the week of March 14, wearing "Save CDBG" buttons and talking to lawmakers as both chambers of Congress debated the fiscal 2006 budget resolution. Face-to-face encounters were reinforced by a flood of e-mails and phone calls to congressional offices.

The effort paid off, according to officials at Washington associations representing local elected officials. Fifty-five senators signed a letter in March praising the CDBG program and warning that moving its functions to the Commerce Department "would result in inefficiencies, greater complexity and less aid to fewer cities, an approach which does not serve America's communities or taxpayers." A similar House letter drew 181 signatures.

The House budget resolution added $1.1 billion to the administration's budget request for all community development programs — for a total of $14.2 billion — and said it "makes no assumption regarding implementation" of the administration's consolidation program.

The Senate went even further, allocating $15.2 billion and adopting, 68-31, an amendment by Sen. Norm Coleman, R-Minn., that would restore funding for CDBG grants and some other programs to fiscal 2005 levels.

"We successfully got their attention on CDBG," said Chandra Western, executive director of the National Community Development Association, which represents CDBG grantees and helped lead the mobilization. She acknowledged that her allies had an advantage: By law, portions of CDBG funds are distributed broadly by formula to communities in every state. "Every member of Congress gets a piece of CDBG," she said.

A review this year by the Office of Management and Budget (OMB) assailed the CDBG program for not having "a clear and unambiguous mission," and for being "unable to demonstrate its effectiveness" in revitalizing communities. The administration gave the program an overall rating of "ineffective."

"The CDBG has certainly morphed into something other than its original creation, which is a do-gooder, help-the-poor, help-the-depressed-communities-to-revitalize program,"

said Ron Utt, senior research fellow at the Heritage Foundation. "Now it is a general grab bag of budgetary supplements for governments throughout the country."

In the fight to overhaul community development spending, the White House has a chance to regain the upper hand when it submits authorizing legislation for its proposal. Commerce Department officials say that might happen as soon as mid-April.

Savings expected through the administration's proposal would come from directing funds to the neediest communities, said Sandy Baruah, chief of staff for the Economic Development Administration (EDA). Not only would some communities end up with more money, but funding for some activities, such as housing, would increase, he said.

Consolidating the programs in the Commerce Department isn't a signal that they are being abandoned, Baruah said. "Successful economic development is a holistic approach to ensuring good jobs and a higher, rising standard of living for people."

Communities that receive funds under the administration's program would have broad discretion on how to spend the money, he said. "What we're saying is that the local priorities will be addressed through local control."

OMB's critique also said CDBG is rarely the only financing source for economic development projects and that several CDBG-funded activities duplicate other programs. Local governments spend thousands or even millions of dollars just tapping into those various revenue streams, Baruah said.

Visits to economic development projects in 32 states have made him a believer in what the administration is proposing, he said, noting that local governments often cobble together grants from CDBG, EDA and other government agencies for one project.

"One grant is helping to build the street,

another is helping to build the sidewalk, another is helping to build the business incubator that the street and the sidewalk runs in front of. And probably somebody else is helping with the sewer lines underneath the street and the sidewalk," Baruah said.

Some supporters of CDBG concede that he may have a point about the program maze, and agree that HUD needed to work with grant recipients to better document CDBG accomplishments. Western, from the National Community Development Association, said a cross-section of interest groups were working with HUD and OMB to design new perform-

"It will have a devastating economic impact on communities across the country."

— **Don Plusquellic**, Akron, Ohio mayor.

ance yardsticks, and believed last November they had reached a consensus on a way to report how CDBG funds were being used.

"We were putting forth a good faith effort to work with OMB to address their concerns about the reporting," she said, and the group was stunned to learn that the administration had decided to kill the program. "We were all caught blindsided."

Harvey Johnson Jr., mayor of Jackson, Miss., has been working with the CDBG program since its inception, starting as a founder of the Mississippi Institute for Small Towns, where he used CDBG grants to pay for sewer services in small towns where even in the mid-1970s "you literally had raw sewage running into ditches and children playing in those ditches."

He said he is proud of using CDBG money to buy dilapidated houses to be demolished to make room for new homes for low-income buyers. "These people looked forward to home ownership, and a lot of them never thought in their wildest dreams they would have that kind of economic empowerment."

Johnson said he has worked productively with EDA, but the two programs ought not be merged into a single entity. "HUD has over the years proven itself to be the kind of organization that has the tentacles in the

AKRON MAYOR'S OFFICE

community to make CDBG go," he said, noting that while HUD has a field office in Jackson, EDA doesn't have an office anywhere in Mississippi.

One key member of Mississippi's congressional delegation is supporting the president's proposal, however. "I support what CDBG does," said Republican Sen. Trent Lott, who nonetheless voted against the budget resolution amendment that called for restoring CDBG funding. "It doesn't make a difference where the funds are and what the name of the program is as long as the funds are available."

Lott said he has told local officials that Bush's plan might mean more money, not less, for local revitalization if administrative overhead and duplication are eliminated.

"Mayor Johnson needs to just relax," Lott said. "Jackson is doing very fine, thank you, and will continue to get a significant share of federal money."

Ironically, CDBG was itself born of a consolidation of urban revitalization programs that had little support in the administration of President Richard Nixon. About a decade later, the EDA was placed on the chopping block by another Republican president, Ronald Reagan, only to be saved by Congress.

"I understand that Republicans generally

> # "It doesn't make a difference where the funds are . . . as long as the funds are available."
>
> — Sen. **Trent Lott**, R-Miss.

get a bad rap on development programs," Baruah said. But he said Bush sincerely wants to revolutionize urban and rural aid programs, not gut them. "This president has made it clear that there is a legitimate federal role and an important federal role in community and economic development." He said Bush's support for reauthorizing EDA in 2004 "demonstrates a commitment to programs that work."

CDBG supporters organized local Community Development Week activities the week of March 27, timed to coincide with the congressional recess so members could attend events touting success stories. They are hoping lawmakers will remember those stories when they decide the fate of the CDBG consolidation and put the final touches on the budget.

While the administration's broad outline has won some support from congressional leaders, the program's advocates are trying to win rank-and-file support by pointing to what they do with the money.

Mayor Johnson, for one, has a run-down, 78-year-old building in downtown Jackson that is being converted into a mixed-use office-retail-residential complex with CDBG funds. Mayor Trotter is working to have low-cost housing ready for an influx of Army families he is expecting in the next few years.

If the administration is to succeed in overhauling community development spending, lawmakers will probably have to be convinced that projects like these won't be forgotten. ∎

States Eager to Retake Lead in School Policy

As Bush's plan to expand No Child Left Behind fails to ignite, governors step up with their own proposals

FOUR YEARS AGO, the Bush administration and Congress decided that the federal government should exert more influence over public school policy and passed a landmark law that limited state and local governments' ability to set academic standards for elementary and secondary school students.

But this year, many of the nation's governors are reasserting themselves by attempting to raise standards in an area the 2001 law did not specifically address — high schools. The governors, convinced that academic progress will translate into economic growth, are weighing in just as a divided Congress begins contemplating another Bush initiative to expand the 2001 law to students through the 11th grade.

Bush is asking for $1.5 billion to broaden the law through initiatives such as college preparation courses and programs aimed at preventing students from dropping out of school. His plan also would require annual testing through 11th grade in high schools.

The president is unlikely to get what he wants. Republicans and Democrats weary from the near-constant bickering since the 2001 law was enacted are reluctant to engage in another grinding debate over the state of schools.

That is leaving an opening for the governors. Education experts say states such as Virginia and North Carolina have, within the past three years, taken the lead in developing policies to improve academic achievement in the nation's high schools, though there is little consensus on which policies are the most effective.

"The notion of state control of education is alive and kicking," said Jeffrey Henig, professor of political science and education at Teachers College at Columbia University, who believes the federal government will play a supple-

HIGH STANDARDS: Ohio Gov. Taft, center, and Virginia's Warner, right, promote school initiatives with Prudential Financial CEO Arthur Ryan Feb. 10, before a Washington summit co-hosted by the National Governors Association.

mental role, pressing states to raise standards further and to identify groups of students whose test scores continue to lag. "I think we are seeing the normal pull-and-tug, and we'll end up with a serious and long-term involvement of the feds, particularly in terms of pushing for testing and publishing of data."

"The initiative, I believe, for school reform in this country has always come from the governors," added Ohio Republican Gov. Bob Taft.

The focus on education was evident during a National Governors Association meeting in Washington the week of Feb. 21. The organization released a report concluding high school graduation requirements are lax, and that four in 10 graduates are not adequately prepared for college or the job market. The report added it would require billions of dollars in remedial schooling to address the situation.

Most educators believe an emphasis on high schools is overdue — especially efforts to combat a high dropout rate. The national high school graduation rate in 2002 was 71 percent, according to most recent statistics compiled by the conservative-leaning Manhattan Institute for Policy Research. Graduation rates for minorities are much lower, with 52 percent of all Hispanics and 56 percent of all blacks graduating on time.

Colleges and employers report that many of the students that graduate lack basic reading and math skills. The Manhattan Institute study, which is widely cited in education circles, found that the percentage of high school students who graduated with the skills and qualifications necessary to attend college increased from 25 percent in 1991 to 34 percent in 2002.

"These graduation rates are abysmal," said

CQ PHOTO / SCOTT J. FERRELL

James B. Hunt Jr., a former four-term governor of North Carolina (1977-1985, 1993-2001), who is chairman of an education think tank that bears his name at the University of North Carolina. "The high school graduation rates have really shocked us, and we want to do something about it."

Some governors are acting because they believe that student achievement is directly linked to economic growth.

Virginia Gov. Mark Warner, a Democrat, has implemented summer academies and online tutorials for 3,000 students to help them pass required tests in reading, writing and other subjects and get a high school diploma. Warner noted that the class of 2004 was the first to take such tests and that its graduation rate was "virtually identical" to past years. Many expected a drop in graduation rates due to tougher testing standards.

North Carolina Gov. Michael F. Easley, a Democrat, has proposed a plan that would allow high school students to take a five-year program to receive a high school diploma and a community college associate's degree. Students at 15 pilot schools involved in the project would save a year's worth of time and tuition costs on their way to gaining the associate's degree.

In Arkansas, Gov. Mike Huckabee, a Republican, helped revise a high school curriculum to put more emphasis on English, social studies and science. The new program also required students to take math in their junior or senior year. Parents have to sign a waiver for a student to transfer to a less-rigorous academic schedule, but even that curriculum requires more math courses.

The activity is reminiscent of efforts launched two decades ago by governors such as Bill Clinton in Arkansas, Richard W. Riley in South Carolina, Lamar Alexander in Tennessee and North Carolina's Hunt, to toughen education standards. The governors believed that raising student achievement in early grades and raising teacher qualifications were the best ways ultimately to create jobs and recruit business.

The philosophy crossed party lines. Bush as governor of Texas established statewide reading and math scores in his home state, which was in essence a precursor to No Child Left Behind.

SHRINKING SCHOOLS

State and local efforts have been bolstered by donations from the business community and philanthropies. The Bill and Melinda Gates Foundation has donated more than $113 million to create a partnership with New York City community groups aimed at shrinking the size of the city's high schools and limiting enrollment at each campus to no more than 500 to 600 students. Concurrently, Mayor Michael R. Bloomberg, a Republican, is attempting to overhaul the city's school system with an eye toward improving test scores. Advocates believe that smaller schools can offer a better, individualized education to students at risk of failing. The San Francisco-based research group WestEd found promising initial results; 92 percent of ninth-graders

> ## "The timing is right for governors to step forward as never before on education policy."
> — Gov. **Mark Warner**, D-Va., chairman, National Governors Association

in small high schools were promoted to 10th grade, compared with a citywide average of 68 percent.

Virginia's Warner, chairman of the National Governors Association, wants to develop a national standard for measuring the percentage of students who drop out and those who graduate in order to more easily compare rates between states. He also is advocating that states strike agreements with local colleges and universities so that high school courses in math, English and history are more closely aligned with college courses in those subjects. Warner also wants states to establish intervention programs to help students pass high school exit exams that are becoming more commonplace.

"The timing is right for governors to step forward as never before on education policy," Warner said. "We have a chance to forge a stronger and more productive partnership with Congress and the administration."

CONGRESS ON THE SIDELINES

The governors' initiatives have gained momentum partly because Congress is divided over how far it should go in influencing school policy.

Democrats believe the bipartisan collaboration seen during negotiations on the 2001 education law has evaporated. In both the House and Senate, they have complained that the Bush administration has shortchanged funding in the law by $27 billion and has not provided enough flexibility for school districts to make the law work. For that reason, they are reluctant to cut any new deals with the administration.

At the same time, conservatives want to limit further federal involvement in education policy, recalling the Republican revolution of the mid-1990s that preached the virtues of smaller government and advocated abolishing the Department of Education.

Andrew Rotherham, director of education policy at the Progressive Policy Institute and former Clinton administration domestic policy adviser, said members of Congress are most concerned about ensuring that the 2001 law is implemented properly and less inclined to expand its reach. Rotherham adds that lawmakers believe that high schools "are a different animal" than elementary and middle schools.

"There is a general consensus on how to improve education on the K-8 level," Rotherham said. "We don't have that consensus on high schools."

Hunt, the former North Carolina governor, said many in Congress are fatigued from the skirmishing over education funding. Those from states that had established their own accountability systems prior to enactment of the 2001 law are especially disinclined to expand federal testing mandates.

But Hunt remains hopeful that Bush's high school plan can prompt change at the state level and encourage innovation.

"The irony now is that conservatives are showing their true colors, complaining about the intrusion of states' rights. . . . For the Democrats, the trust is gone," said Rotherham. "Many figure that this work is happening in the states anyway, so why should the federal government get involved?" ∎

States Ready to Fill Gap In Stem Cell Research

Severe federal funding limits leave states to weigh the benefits and risks of the controversial science

SINCE PRESIDENT BUSH placed strict limits on federal government funding for embryonic stem cell research almost four years ago, state governments have started to come down on opposite sides of what is a divisive ethical debate, seeing an opportunity to benefit both medical science and their home-grown biotechnology industries.

California and New Jersey were the first to decide to help finance investigations that many hope will one day yield cures for Parkinson's disease, diabetes and other maladies. Other states may soon follow suit.

State and private money alone can be used by scientists in the United States to work with stem cells harvested since Bush's executive order of Aug. 9, 2001, which limited such research to the 78 lines of cells that existed at the time.

But researchers say they need new lines of cells to do their work, and that the federal prohibition limits the fast-growing field. Some research institutions have gone to great lengths to avoid running afoul of federal rules, such as constructing separate buildings to ensure that no federal money finances facilities where new cell lines are studied. Others keep meticulous records and purchase duplicate equipment to avoid using any government-funded resources.

"They are being scrupulously careful," said Debora Spar, a professor at the Harvard Business School. "It's at the level of separate buildings, separate doors, separate pencils."

The sharp philosophical divide on the issue of stem cell research in the nation's capital is unlikely to be bridged soon, however. So scientists and the biotech industry must decide how best to position themselves in an uncertain, and sometimes hostile, environment.

Scientists welcomed the decision by California voters last fall to fund new research, but

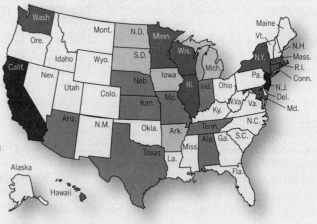

Taking a Stand on Research

California and New Jersey already finance stem cell research. Other states are considering similar proposals. Meanwhile, five states ban therapeutic cloning, a process used to create new stem cell strains. Other states are considering similar bans.

- ■ States that finance stem cell research
- ■ States with legislative proposals to promote stem cell research
- ■ States with legislative proposals to ban therapeutic cloning
- ■ States with bans on therapeutic cloning

NOTE: Nebraska law prohibits state funds from being used to finance embryonic stem cell research.

SOURCE: National Conference of State Legislatures

they say support and guidance from Washington would help eliminate such administrative headaches. A nod from the federal government also would create an environment in which scientists and biotech companies would not be burdened by the complexities inherent in working under a patchwork of state laws.

Congress may weigh in later this year, but if it does, it will probably move slowly because the issue raises moral questions posed by the destruction of human embryos and cloning — and evokes the intractable debate on abortion.

"What's really difficult in this issue is, first, foes of the research in Congress keep trying to pass laws to criminalize what we're doing; and second, this restriction on where federal funds can be used has created a nightmare accounting problem," said Larry Goldstein, a professor

at the University of California at San Diego's School of Medicine. "What we need is a reasonable national policy."

Stem cell researchers say Bush's 2001 executive order has paralyzed efforts to move toward eventual medical applications. The National Institutes of Health has said only 15 to 19 of the 78 cell lines that Bush approved are viable for research, and even those are of dubious quality. The existing lines are contaminated with mouse cells and represent a narrow segment of the population's racial diversity.

Scientists have used government-sanctioned lines to conduct basic research into how stem cells work. In tailoring treatments, however, scientists say they need new lines to represent a variety of genetic diseases and to avoid using contaminated cell lines on patients.

CQ GRAPHIC / YOLIE DAWSON

It is the nature of stem cells — primordial cells taken from days-old human embryos that are capable of developing into virtually any type of body tissue — that led to the ethical and religious conflict at the heart of this debate.

Harvesting stem cells for research destroys the embryos, which generally are taken from surpluses at in-vitro fertilization clinics. When Bush decided to limit such research, he was responding to social conservatives who contend that embryos should be protected and who have likened the work to taking a life.

Rep. Michael N. Castle, R-Del., and the House GOP leadership said they reached an agreement this month to debate and vote on the stem cell issue, but they have not worked out details on a timeline or the language of legislation that would be considered.

The bill most likely to come to a vote would allow funding for new stem cell lines derived from unused embryos held by fertilization clinics, where the donors grant permission. It would be an incremental step, and the president and some conservatives would probably fight any effort to relax current limits.

Meantime, Sen. Sam Brownback, R-Kan., and Rep. Dave Weldon, R-Fla., have proposed legislation to criminalize the cloning of human embryos for research, and similar bills passed the House in the last two Congresses. Advocates of so-called therapeutic cloning, which would not create embryos that could grow into humans, say that procedure would yield even more stem cells and allow scientists to aim their work at specific diseases.

PRESSURE TO FUND RESEARCH

As Congress debates this issue, states are feeling the pressure to act, particularly those that are home to biotechnology companies — and state legislatures are mirroring the divide that has split Congress.

"This is a whole fundamental issue of what states do with a federal government that puts ideology in front of biological research," said Irving L. Weissman, director of the Institute for Cancer/Stem Cell Biology and Medicine at Stanford University.

The most prominent state initiative on stem cell research has been California's Proposition 71, which voters approved in November. It authorized a $3 billion bond sale to finance research and facilities over the next 10 years.

New Jersey's legislature passed a measure in 2004 that established a Stem Cell Institute, and the governor has asked for $380 million to build the center and finance research.

Legislatures and governors in several other states are debating proposals to fund stem cell research. Connecticut, Illinois, Maryland, Massachusetts, New York and Wisconsin are among those that have legislation pending.

At the same time, Missouri, Arkansas and Kansas are among those that have banned or are working to ban procedures related to stem cell research, particularly the cloning of embryos to create new cell lines.

Pressure on states to find room to operate within the federal government's restrictions comes as they face rising budget deficits. Investing in stem cell research entails up-front costs, but it also presents the promise of attracting a lucrative industry. And states that ignore the

"You're going to have a regulatory patchwork, a crazy quilt, which is certainly not the most conducive environment in which to jump-start an industry."

— Professor **Debora Spar**, Harvard University

opportunity or that act to limit research might lose investments in other biotech fields if they are deemed inhospitable to scientific pursuits.

The issue has divided some legislatures and pitted legislators against governors. In Massachusetts, which has the second-highest concentration of biotech companies in the country, Republican Gov. Mitt Romney is expected to veto legislation that would condone stem cell research and finance facilities and research.

As ideological opponents dig in, some researchers and business groups have cast state efforts to sidestep the federal rules in economic terms, complaining that myriad state regulations create an uneven environment that may hamper research and lead to disparities in economic growth across regions.

Chief among those concerns is the specter of a "brain drain" as researchers and biotech companies relocate to states that encourage and finance stem cell investigations.

"California said very clearly that its money is to be spent only in California," said Weiss-

man. "So if any entity wants to do it, they'll have to relocate to California. . . . There will be a mass relocation of the best and brightest."

Defections of researchers and post-doctoral students, who would bring with them significant amounts of federal grants, could affect broader research in state institutions because any grant money they had that was unrelated to stem cells would leave the state.

And businesses would follow. "If you look at biotech and any high-tech industry in general, they're part of a pipeline that starts in universities," said Goldstein, the California professor.

Already, one biotech company in Worcester, Mass., that works with stem cells, Advanced Cell Technologies, has announced plans to open a research center in California.

"That's a situation that a state doesn't want to see," said Patrick Kelly, vice president for state government relations at the Biotechnology Industry Organization, a trade group. "States are in this because high-wage jobs lead to an increased tax base," he said.

Aside from economic losses in states that are left behind, variable state rules might have a dulling effect on the industry as a whole. "You're going to have a regulatory patchwork, a crazy quilt," said Harvard's Spar, "which is certainly not the most conducive environment in which to jump-start an industry."

OVERSEAS COMPETITION

The regulatory atmosphere will probably become more tangled, given the depth of opposition to expanded stem cell research. So, help from Washington is likely to come in small steps. "A pro-stem cell initiative coming out of this Congress is unlikely," said Kelly.

But lawmakers may have to revisit the issue as the research advances. "The first lab that comes up with an actual treatment for diabetes is going to turn the pressure on hugely to make more money available," Spar said.

Meanwhile, states are not alone in competing for top scientists. Great Britain, Singapore and China are all actively recruiting researchers, with their governments backing work on embryonic stem cells. Singapore has spent billions of dollars to set up a "biopolis" science park for stem cell research. Britain has created a Stem Cell Institute. China is trying to lure ethnic Chinese to return to the mainland to conduct research. And Australia and Israel also support research.

The pressure of international competition may nudge Washington to take another look. "If one of these cures or treatments were discovered in a non-U.S. facility," said Spar, "you'd have the scientific equivalent of Sputnik." ∎

Political Participation

After the 2004 elections, the United States experienced a simultaneous and seemingly incongruous rise in partisanship and in the number of moderate voters. With 2006 midterm elections on the horizon, politicians, voters and analysts predict even further change in the political landscape. This section examines current issues in electoral and party politics, voting behavior and public opinion.

The first article looks at how the Democrats and Republicans are reacting to the growing number of moderate voters. States that appear solidly "red" or "blue" based on their votes in the presidential election may actually be violet when taking into account their congressional and gubernatorial election statistics. Yet both parties hesitate to accommodate the center for fear of alienating their core supporters. Moderate politicians are becoming vulnerable as they attempt to balance their obligations to their parties and to their constituents.

The next two articles explore the influential role of religion in politics. Exit polls during the 2004 elections demonstrate that regular churchgoers, no matter their denomination, were more likely than ever to vote Republican. Religious conservatives are now pressing the Bush administration to pursue policies they favor on key issues, such as judicial nominees, abortion and same-sex marriage. Some conservative religious groups claim that public opinion is on their side; however, political analysts question whether the religious right has the power to push its agenda through Congress given the fragmented state of the movement, which makes it difficult for the religious conservatives to present a cohesive message to party leaders. Meanwhile, Democrats are pondering how they can reverse their image as the irreligious party that is out of touch with religious voters and their values. Some religious leaders advise the Democrats to capitalize on such policies as environmental regulation and anti-poverty programs to reshape the party's relationship with religious voters.

The last two articles examine how trends in congressional districts translate into partisan advantage on the national level and also present predictions for the 2006 midterm elections. The first article explores the demographic and political obstacles that stand in the Democrats' way of regaining control of the Republican-dominated House. Few districts split their votes by voting for one political party in the congressional elections and the other in the presidential election. Is it possible for the Democrats to win enough votes in these areas to take control of the House? The last article discusses the recent increase in redistricting, a process that formerly occurred once a decade. The stakes are so high for majority and minority parties that in California, Governor Arnold Schwarzenegger is contemplating turning the job over to a nonpartisan panel, instead of the state legislature.

Red States, Blue States — Or Shades of Violet?

Moderates increasingly seen by parties as a political appendix, 'not a necessary organ'

Colorado voters this year elected Democrat Ken Salazar to the Senate and his brother, John Salazar, to the House from what is usually a Republican-leaning district. In addition, state Democrats won narrow majorities in both chambers of the state legislature, wresting control from the GOP.

But in the red state-blue state construct that has become so much a part of the political discourse these days, Colorado is painted Republican red. The state favored President Bush by 5 percentage points, giving the GOP its ninth win in the past 10 races for the White House. Democrat John Kerry, who was born in Colorado, had targeted the state but scaled back his campaign effort to focus on contesting more competitive states. Kerry did only marginally better in the Colorado balloting than 2000 Democratic nominee Al Gore.

Maine, on the other hand, appears a dark "Democratic blue" based on Kerry's 8 percentage-point win over Bush, marking the fourth consecutive time the one-time "Yankee Republican" bastion went Democratic for president. Yet both of Maine's senators, Olympia J. Snowe and Susan Collins, are Republican moderates. The legislature, though controlled by Democrats, is closely divided.

These are among the many trend-defying figures that could stand out as evidence that certain states are not as red and blue as much of the political establishment would have you believe. Reach down-ballot in states such as Colorado, Maine, South Dakota, Rhode Island and Georgia, and the colors start to blur.

The question going forward is whether either the Democrats or Republicans can broaden their support and stake a claim as America's indisputably dominant party by seeing past the red and blue veneers.

CQ Weekly Nov. 27, 2004

> **❝Absent a wave generated by upset about the continuation of the Iraq war, or a major economic dislocation, it's difficult to see how either party will gain or lose many seats. ❞**
>
> —University of Virginia political scientist Larry Sabato

Political experts are not so sure. They say the goal of becoming a true national majority has been subsumed, in both parties' camps, by strategies aimed at magnifying support among "the base" — voters on the right for the Republicans and the left for the Democrats. Overall, party leaders have shown little inclination to reach out, either in their campaigns or in their policy agendas, to the center, and they instead end up eking out slim majorities that are just enough for victory.

The result is that highly regionalized partisan divisions in national politics may prevail for some time, barring a change in approach by one or both parties — or a sea change, brought on by either very good or very bad times, that carries the nation's voters definitively to one side or the other.

"Absent a wave generated by upset about the continuation of the Iraq war, or a major economic dislocation, it's difficult to see how either party will gain or lose many seats," said University of Virginia political scientist Larry Sabato.

Each election year, the parties pay tribute to centrist "swing" voters, and the parties' moderates are given enough slack to fashion campaigns to their constituencies. Democratic officials this year strongly backed "red state" Democrats such as South Dakota's Stephanie

Herseth and Georgia's Jim Marshall in their House re-election bids, even though both ran to the right of party orthodoxy. On the Republican side, Rep. Rob Simmons frequently brandished his independent voting record as he sought re-election in an eastern Connecticut district that voted strongly for Kerry.

But rather than viewing these independent thinkers as a path to broaden their support, both parties maintain the philosophy that moving too far to the center risks antagonizing core party activists and watering down their message.

TOLERATING, BARELY, THE INDEPENDENTS

Even winners are not made to feel rewarded for bringing moderate voters to the Republican tally. This was seen most vividly in the case of veteran Pennsylvania Republican Sen. Arlen Specter this year.

A leading moderate on social and organized labor issues, Specter emphasized his support for the more conservative Bush in order to narrowly survive a primary challenge from the right. Though Specter quickly shifted back to the middle for the general election campaign, Republican factions united and helped him win an easy victory for a fifth term.

But the same conservative forces that

An Electorate That Favors a Variety of Hues

The color scheme for the nation's political landscape is in bright primary colors: red for Republican victories and blue for Democratic wins. However, that is based exclusively on presidential politics. When all elections are taken into account, most states exhibit pastel hues. In nearly all states, the minority party holds one or more of the major levers of power. Below are four states that exemplify the tie-dyed realities under the red and blue veneers: Arkansas, a strongly Democratic state that votes Republican for president; North Dakota, which normally is strongly Republican but sends only Democrats to Congress; California, where a popular GOP governor has not made a dent in the Democrats' overall edge; and Wisconsin, a true toss-up state.

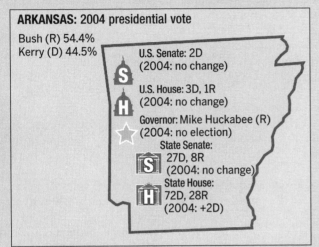

ARKANSAS: 2004 presidential vote

Bush (R) 54.4%
Kerry (D) 44.5%

U.S. Senate: 2D
(2004: no change)

U.S. House: 3D, 1R
(2004: no change)

Governor: Mike Huckabee (R)
(2004: no election)

State Senate:
27D, 8R
(2004: no change)

State House:
72D, 28R
(2004: +2D)

CALIFORNIA: 2004 presidential vote

Kerry (D) 54.7%,
Bush (R) 44.2%

U.S. Senate: 2D
(2004: no change)

U.S. House: 33D, 20R
(2004: no change)

Governor: Arnold
Schwarzenegger (R)
(2004: no election)

State Senate: 25D, 15R
(2004: no change)
State House: 48D, 32R
(2004: no change)

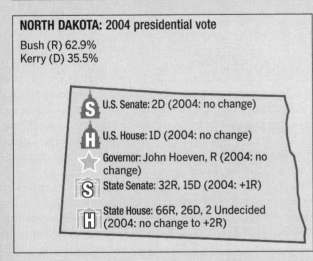

NORTH DAKOTA: 2004 presidential vote

Bush (R) 62.9%
Kerry (D) 35.5%

U.S. Senate: 2D (2004: no change)

U.S. House: 1D (2004: no change)

Governor: John Hoeven, R (2004: no change)

State Senate: 32R, 15D (2004: +1R)

State House: 66R, 26D, 2 Undecided (2004: no change to +2R)

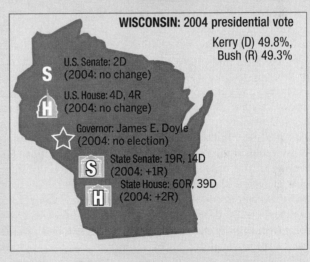

WISCONSIN: 2004 presidential vote

Kerry (D) 49.8%,
Bush (R) 49.3%

U.S. Senate: 2D
(2004: no change)

U.S. House: 4D, 4R
(2004: no change)

Governor: James E. Doyle
(2004: no election)

State Senate: 19R, 14D
(2004: +1R)
State House: 60R, 39D
(2004: +2R)

opposed Specter in the primary broke with him again after the election and tried to block him from the Judiciary Committee chairmanship that seniority had earned him. In order to survive that challenge, Specter had to justify himself to fellow Republicans and promise to support Bush's nominees to the federal judiciary. *(2004 CQ Weekly, p. 2731)*

"In both parties, those individuals who would have a more moderate stance have been punished by the party for doing it," said Charles S. Bullock, a political scientist at the University of Georgia. "Yet, if they try to stand in the good graces of their party, then their constituents may punish them."

Those moderates may exhibit the political dexterity necessary to win in places that nor-mally do not favor their party. But they often get pigeonholed as eccentrics rather than role models. That has become especially true in the House, as a long-standing stability in the nation's political maps has strongly favored conservative Republicans and liberal Democrats.

Congressional redistricting after the 2000 census exacerbated the skew of districts, creating safe constituencies for most House members. On Nov. 2, just nine of 433 House contests were decided by fewer than 5 percentage points.

The Republicans scored a net gain of between two and four seats, depending on the outcomes of two Dec. 4 runoffs in Louisiana. They were able to achieve that only because the redistricting in Texas strengthened the hand of Republican conservatives and weakened the dwindling ranks of Democratic moderates. The unprecedented mid-decade redistricting plan — engineered by Majority Leader Tom DeLay of Texas — resulted in the removal of five center-right Democratic incumbents and their replacement by five Republican loyalists.

Just as moderate Democrats are being winnowed in the South and West, moderate Republicans are tapering off in parts of the Midwest and Northeast where they once had major influence. For six terms, New York Republican Rep. Jack Quinn dominated a strongly Democratic Buffalo-area district with a centrist record that earned him support from organized labor. But Quinn did not seek re-election this year and was replaced by a Democrat, state Rep. Brian Higgins.

Analysts say the increasing homogeneity in the parties renders centrists far less influential than before.

"The difference is back then, party leaders had to account for these factions. They aren't factions anymore," said the University of Virginia's Sabato, comparing party moderates to a human appendix: "not a necessary organ."

"So naturally, they're disrespected and they're ignored and they get pressured to conform and they tend to get disgruntled, and the leadership gets disgruntled with them," he said.

Another reason party officials pursue campaign strategies aimed at turning out huge numbers of the ideologically attuned faithful is that it works. Republicans' mining the base appears to have played an important role in their four-seat gain this year in the Senate, which will boost the party from its minimal 51-seat majority to a solid 55 seats when the 109th Congress convenes in January 2005.

Senate Democratic Leader Tom Daschle was defeated for re-election in South Dakota by Republican John Thune, 51 percent to 49 percent — an outcome undoubtedly aided by Bush's 60 percent to 38 percent win over Kerry in the state.

Daschle was long known for working on home-state interests that transcended his constituents' partisan leanings. But his exposure as a "Washington Democrat" increased, especially after Bush's 2000 victory captured the White House for the Republicans following the two-term presidency of Democrat Bill Clinton. Thrust into the role of leading national spokesman for his party's interests, Daschle fell vulnerable to the GOP's efforts to cast him as a symbol of Democratic liberalism.

"The national party can push a candidate into an untenable position, as I think happened to Tom Daschle in South Dakota," said Ross K. Baker, a political scientist at Rutgers University. "Tom Daschle, as good as he was, as attentive as he was to South Dakota . . . he still had to contend with the fact that the party he represented, and was the voice and face for, was very much out of favor with South Dakotans."

The Republicans' big push to turn out conservative voters also gave them election-defining gains in the GOP-trending South, where Democrats were forced to defend five seats left open by retiring incumbents.

The Democrats kept themselves in the running in four of them — North Carolina, South Carolina, Florida and Louisiana — by fielding centrist candidates who could plausibly evade Republican efforts to label them as liberals. But their efforts were unavailing: A massive coordinated Republican voter turnout effort, aimed primarily at re-electing President Bush, helped solidly conservative Republicans win closely contested races in each of those states.

The Republicans' dominance in the South has severely thinned the ranks of conservative Democrats in that region. Republicans will hold 22 of the 26 Southern Senate seats in the 109th Congress next January; Democrats held 17 of the 26 Southern seats as recently as after the 1988 elections.

But the Democrats, despite their travails, managed a reverse spin in a Northern state where they have grown increasingly dominant. Illinois Republican Sen. Peter G. Fitzgerald is retiring and giving way to much-heralded Democrat Barack Obama, a state senator whose mostly liberal views are a closer match with that state's orientation.

CAMPAIGNING VS. GOVERNING

Analysts and some moderates themselves say the parties perpetuate the image that independent voices are unwelcome by their treatment of those centrists once they are in office.

Although some politicians may be given license to portray themselves as independent during their election campaigns, they face pressures to conform legislatively that ultimately may put them at electoral risk.

Rep. Christopher Shays, a Republican whose Connecticut district near New York City voted narrowly Democratic for president this year, was criticized for voting too frequently with GOP leaders. Democratic challenger Diane Farrell held Shays to a 52 percent to 48 percent win, the closest race of his career.

Yet Shays actually has a rather contrarian voting record, which includes the second-lowest party unity score among House Republicans. And he has paid a price for that among his GOP House colleagues.

Two years ago, Shays was passed over for the chairmanship of the Government Reform Committee in favor of Virginia Rep. Thomas M. Davis III — largely because Shays had bucked party leaders by cosponsoring an overhaul of campaign finance laws that they had opposed. Davis, though not much more conservative than Shays, earned the leadership's good will by chairing the party's House campaign unit, the National Republican Congressional Committee.

Republican leaders, in fact, laid down their marker following the 1994 elections that gave them control of the House, which they have maintained ever since.

Similarly, former California Rep. Carlos J. Moorhead, having won a 12th House term, had requisite seniority to chair either the Commerce or Judiciary committees. He wound up chairing neither: Moorhead had an accommodating style that served him well in his politically competitive district, but not with his more combatively conservative Republican colleagues. Moorhead did not seek re-election in 1996.

"What message does that send you? It sends the message that, on the Republican side, if you want to get ahead within the conference, you'd better toe the line, and that's a conservative line," said the University of Georgia's Bullock.

As a result, the Republicans, despite their good fortunes recently, could risk making their moderate members politically vulnerable — or compel them to leave the party altogether, as Vermont Sen. James M. Jeffords did when he left the GOP to become a Democratic-affiliated independent in 2001.

"In a relatively liberal state like Maine, if the Republican Party gets too far to the right nationally, some Democrat in Maine is going to say, 'How can Susan Collins, how can Olympia Snowe even explain the fact that they are Republicans?' " Baker said. "I think that's something that the Republicans have to be careful of, that they don't cause [Rhode Island Republican Sen. Lincoln] Chafee, Snowe and Collins to go the way of Jim Jeffords."

Democrats, too, cannot afford to forsake their own dissenting voices, especially if they want to regain a foothold in the increasingly Republican South. The risks of throwing in the towel have become glaringly evident in states such as Georgia, where old-time Democratic traditions remained strong until about a decade ago: As a result of the Nov. 2 elections — in which Bush carried the state by a 17 percentage-point margin — Republicans will hold the governor's office, both Senate seats, a majority in the House delegation, and solid control of both state legislative chambers.

Despite these realities, both parties nonetheless appear stuck in the mentality of a regionally bifurcated America.

"I would call it the endgame of the realignment that has been going on in this country since the early 1990s," said Keith Gaddie, a University of Oklahoma political scientist. "This is sort of the final reconciliation of geographic re-sorting of our politics." ■

Religious Right Lays Claim To Big Role in GOP Agenda

Lacking a clear leader, the movement may find itself struggling to be heard

Just elected to a fifth term, Arlen Specter is Pennsylvania's senior senator and one of the Senate's most senior Republicans. He is also now the No. 1 enemy of religious conservatives nationwide, and it may yet cost him something that otherwise would be his by right: chairmanship of the Judiciary Committee.

Never trusted by the religious right — he is one of the Senate's few Republicans in favor of abortion rights — Specter called down the full wrath of the movement this month by suggesting that the Senate probably would not confirm an anti-abortion nominee to the Supreme Court and that the 1973 ruling legalizing abortion is "inviolate."

"He either gets with the program or we shove him aside," thundered Richard Land, a leader in the Southern Baptist Convention, the nation's largest Protestant denomination.

Other religious conservatives were equally confrontational, and it was a measure of just how powerful and energized they are feeling these days.

More closely aligned with the Republican Party than ever, religious conservatives were a big factor — they argue the decisive factor — in President Bush's re-election Nov. 2 and the wider majorities the GOP now holds in the House and Senate. Even though some pollsters caution that the pivotal role of the movement has been overstated, religious conservatives now expect to play a dominant part in shaping the agenda in Washington. (Polling, p. 29)

They want Bush and congressional Republicans to put anti-abortion nominees on the federal bench, to quickly pass new restrictions on abortion and to push hard for a constitutional amendment to ban gay marriage.

But the religious right's increasingly tight alliance with the GOP, and the great breadth and apparent spontaneity of its turnout for Bush, are as problematic as they are empowering for a movement that has fought for nearly three decades to get to the center of the nation's public life.

This was the first election in recent memory in which large numbers of religious conservative voters turned up at the polls without a national organization, such as the Christian Coalition, mobilizing them. The coalition, which replaced the earlier Moral Majority as the leading national voice for the religious right in the 1990s, is no longer as influential as it once was, leaving the movement's leadership divided among dozens of groups, large and small.

The Bush campaign and the GOP filled some of that void, reaching out to individual church congregations and local leaders. But the network was loose, with many thousands of organizers. And the more diffuse and fragmented the movement, the more difficult it is for religious conservatives to address party leaders and the public with a unified voice — and to press their case clearly and effectively on the issues that matter most to them. Without a central organization, it is also more difficult for lawmakers to know with whom they should negotiate. Conversely, it is easier for them to play one group against the other.

"One of the interesting questions moving forward is will one person step up to fill that void," said John Green, a political scientist at the University of Akron and an expert on the religious right. "They're not going to get everything they want; no one does. But if they do not have a national spokesperson or a national organization, it will be difficult to have the kind of influence they hope to have."

They have spoken with one, loud voice on Specter. He may or may not survive the challenge from the right, and was expected to fight for his chairmanship during the lame-duck session that begins Nov. 16. (Specter, p. 27)

But on the broader agenda, religious conservatives face disagreements among some of the hundreds of organizations, denominations and congregations over issues and strategy. And they must decide how to balance their movement's goals with the needs of the Republican Party itself, which now has their nearly undivided loyalty.

Christian conservatives — generally described as white evangelicals or born-again Protestants — are more likely to describe themselves as Republicans today than in 1994, when they played a big part in handing the GOP control of the House for the first time in four decades. Conservative Catholics also have moved to the party.

At the same time, leading activists from the movement have crossed into politics and now work within the GOP establishment, in elected and unelected positions. Among the most prominent is Ralph Reed, former leader of the Christian Coalition, who was a top operative for the Bush re-election campaign. (2004 CQ Weekly, p. 2032)

Organizations such as Focus on the Family, the Family Research Council and Concerned Women for America also now have close ties to the GOP leadership in Congress and meet with them weekly as a group.

There is great value in that access, but as leaders of the civil rights and labor movements discovered before them, the more closely they align with one party, the more pressure they feel from party leaders to subsume their goals to the greater good of that party, said Amy Black, a political scientist at Wheaton College, an evangelical school in Illinois.

CQ Weekly Nov. 13, 2004

Crossing their party allies too often could sow ill will and undercut their influence. But the rank and file of the religious right expects its leaders to speak with an independent, "prophetic voice" about the need to reform what they see as a nation in moral decline, said Black.

"You can speak with a prophetic voice when you are outside the institutions," Black said. "To the extent that religious leaders are seen as partisans, it becomes harder for them to be seen as speaking with moral authority."

Analysts say the Christian Coalition faded in part because its membership believed it had lost its independent voice — had become, as Green puts it, "a mechanism for harnessing Christian conservatives for the Republican Party."

NOT GOING 'OVER THE MOON'

The movement's immediate next steps are, for the most part, clear. Religious conservatives say their movement has matured and grown more pragmatic, savvier about working the process. "We're going to continue to fight for a pro-life, pro-family agenda," said Janice Shaw Crouse of the Christian advocacy group Concerned Women. "But that does not mean we're going to go over the moon. We're going to be very targeted, very strategic."

First and foremost, they want Bush to have free rein to put conservative, anti-abortion judges on the federal bench, from the Supreme Court down. They view a conservative judiciary as key to the ultimate success on many other issues they care about, particularly abortion.

Next, they plan to continue a step-by-step restriction of abortion — leaving it to "die a death of a thousand cuts," as Land puts it. They will do so by focusing on legislation they hope will resonate broadly with the public.

"The things we can win at this point have to be things that can be supported by people who call themselves 'pro-choice,' " said Mike Schwartz, a lobbyist with Concerned Women.

In the 109th Congress, they will target two bills in particular: one that would prohibit anyone from taking a minor over state lines to avoid parental consent laws and another requiring abortion providers to notify a woman seeking an abortion 20 weeks or more into her pregnancy that her unborn child feels pain during the procedure.

Other priorities include language in a spending bill (HR 5006) that would deny

Key Conservative Groups

Social conservatives and the "moral values" movement that played a crucial role in President Bush's re-election are rooted in religious faiths, primarily Protestant evangelical and fundamentalist denominations and conservative Catholic groups, but are otherwise diverse. Following are some of the leading organizations:

Focus on the Family. Started in 1977, this group has a global reach through the syndicated radio program of its founder, James C. Dobson. During the 2004 campaign, Focus on the Family formed a group called Focus on the Family Action, which organized rallies to get Christians in battleground states to the polls.

Family Research Council. One of the main groups trying to ban same-sex marriage, the council says it wants public policy "that values human life and upholds the institutions of marriage and the family." It claims about 100,000 subscribers to e-mail alerts. Gary Bauer, a former domestic policy adviser in the Reagan administration, led the council for 12 years before resigning in 2000 to run for president. The current leader is Tony Perkins, a former Louisiana state legislator and "pro-family" activist.

The National Right to Life Committee. Founded in 1973 in response to the Supreme Court decision legalizing abortion, this group lobbies for restrictions on abortion, euthanasia and human cloning. It wields tremendous clout on those issues in Congress. It has 50 state affiliates, and its newspaper, the National Right to Life News, has a circulation of 400,000. Its stated goal is "to restore legal protection to innocent human life."

Concerned Women for America. This Christian advocacy group, founded in 1979, bills itself as the nation's "largest public policy women's organization," with about 600,000 members. The g roup says its mission is to "protect and promote Biblical values among all citizens — first through prayer, then education and finally by influencing our society — thereby reversing the decline in moral values in our nation."

Christian Coalition of America. Founded by the Rev. Pat Robertson after his failed presidential bid in 1988, this group replaced the original voice of the Religious Right, the Moral Majority. Its influence has waned since Robertson left in 2001, but it distributed 30 million voter guides in the 2004 elections and many more through its Web site.

Southern Baptist Convention. Founded in 1845, this largest Protestant denomination claims 16.3 million members worshipping in more than 42,000 churches. The "convention" refers both to the denomination and its annual meeting. It works through 1,200 local associations and 41 state conventions and fellowships. Its headquarters are in Nashville.

money to states and localities if they compel health providers or insurance companies to provide or pay for abortions or refer women to abortion providers.

On gay marriage, their hope is to build support in Congress and the public with multiple votes, perhaps on related bills that would, for example, forbid federal courts from hearing legal challenges to a 1996 law (PL 104-199) that defines marriage as the union of a man and a woman. Rep. Joe Pitts, R-Pa., a point man for religious conservatives in the House, calls it a "multivote strategy to grow the vote."

Beyond that, the groups want additional efforts to keep online pornography from children and legislation that would allow religious leaders to endorse political candidates and speak out on partisan matters without endangering their churches' tax-exempt status.

They acknowledge that the fights are going to be long and hard, but say the elec-

tion shows that public opinion is clearly on their side. In part they cite strong votes for 11 separate state constitutional amendments banning gay marriage.

Land and others say they trust Bush, who openly expresses his Christian beliefs, to fight for their agenda. "It's not because of power or politics," said Land. "It's because the most important evangelical lives at 1600 Pennsylvania Avenue, and he is looking to spend his political capital."

But at the same time, religious conservatives worry that the president or party leaders might back away from their agenda to mollify moderates.

Though Bush has made it clear he shares most goals of religious conservatives, the White House also takes care to set the religious right within the broader party coalition.

Presidents must always think of the broader good of their party — and that means balancing the demands of religious conserva-

Senate Seniority System Helps Specter Stay the Course

Arlen Specter believes in saying what he thinks, so long as it doesn't cost him his job.

One of the Senate's beleaguered band of moderate Republicans — there are five if the definition is stretched to include Arizona's John McCain — Specter walks a fine line between the conservative majority of his party, his own more moderate beliefs and the variegated ideology of his home state of Pennsylvania.

The result has been a somewhat contradictory career in which Specter veers from conservative to almost liberal positions, makes blunt statements and then retreats.

This has left religious conservatives, who like most ideological purists demand consistency from their politicians, flatly distrustful of him. And they are left cold by the idea of such an unpredictable moderate as the new chairman of the Senate Judiciary Committee, which would consider President Bush's judicial nominees, including possible successors to ailing Chief Justice William H. Rehnquist.

Specter seemed to confirm their worst suspicions the morning after the election, when he appeared to warn the newly re-elected president against nominating judicial nominees too conservative for Democrats to accept. (2004 CQ Weekly, p. 2598)

As quickly as conservative religious groups mobilized to deny Specter the chairmanship — normally a pro-forma decision by the committee based on seniority — the veteran lawyer defended himself, denying that he had warned Bush about anything, denying that he would apply his own litmus test to nominees, and pledging fealty to administration and party.

Specter stressed that he respected Bush's constitutional right to select conservative nominees, adding that he would fight to get them confirmed even if he disagreed with some of their views. Senate Republican leaders were conspicuously silent, seemingly content to let Specter censure himself.

"He has two conflicting motivations: staying true to his ideological beliefs and maintaining a position of power," said Nathaniel Persily, a professor of law at the University of Pennsylvania. "We're no longer in an era where chairmen can assume they run their own fiefdoms. More often than in the past, chairmen need to please the party leaders."

By week's end, Specter appeared to have survived at least the first round. Judiciary Committee Republicans are reluctant to veer too far from their seniority system, though allowing Specter to have his gavel may require an assurance, perhaps even written, that he will not block Bush's nominees.

Religious conservatives, however, were not letting up. Specter enraged them at the very moment they were feeling most influential, having helped re-elect Bush and four new Republican senators.

By week's end, the anti-tax group National Taxpayers Union had called for Republicans to block his ascension to the Judiciary chair, saying he could derail efforts to limit liability lawsuits. The group said Specter received the fifth-highest total of campaign contributions from lawyers and law firms during the 2003-04 election cycle: more than $1.8 million.

WILLING TO COMPROMISE

Specter is most notable for an agile mind, a tart, sometimes abrasive manner, and an ideological flexibility that he has shown time and time again during his 24 years in the Senate.

He is fond of asserting his independent streak. During President Bill Clinton's Senate impeachment trial in 1999, for instance, Specter cited Scottish legal precedent in saying he planned to vote "not proven" instead of "guilty" or "not guilty," partly to register his opinion that the trial had been too superficial. He ended up voting "not proven, therefore not guilty." (1999 Almanac, p. 13-3)

But Specter is capable of putting his moderate Republican beliefs aside when the GOP hierarchy wants to assert a more con-

(continued, p. 28)

tives against other parts of the coalition that have different priorities or oppose the religious right on abortion or other issues. That was why Bush backed Specter in a GOP primary early this year against an anti-abortion challenger, Rep. Patrick J. Toomey. The White House calculated that Specter had the best chance of holding Pennsylvania's Senate seat for the GOP.

In a news conference just after the Nov. 2 elections, Bush, to whom GOP leaders in Congress are looking to now set the agenda for the 109th Congress, did not mention religious conservatives' top issues.

His senior adviser and the man widely credited with engineering Bush's rise and re-election, Karl Rove, speaks of the big role "people of faith" played in the election. But he also emphasizes that the coalition that re-elected Bush was broad: "I think this was a broad grass-roots-oriented victory in which the president made a compelling case to the American people, and they've responded."

Crouse, for one, acknowledged the pressure to think of the good of the party. But she and other leaders say that the movement's goals, not the party's, come first. "We worked not for the party, not for the president, but for the issues," she said.

Conservative religious leaders downplay or dismiss concerns about the lack of a national organization, saying that a grass roots committed to the conservative agenda, rather than any one organization, is a much more potent political force. They also point out that the groups do coordinate closely among themselves and their allies on Capitol Hill.

DIVERSITY OF VOICES

Approximately 30 groups interested primarily in marriage and "life" issues, such as abortion, gather weekly in the Capitol to plot strategy with the GOP Values Action Teams, led in the House by Pitts and in the Senate by servative position.

In 2001, he voted for the repeal of regulations on repetitive-motion injuries (PL 107-5) that were issued in the final days of the Clinton administration even though he had often sided with organized labor on protecting office workers from such injuries. *(2001 Almanac, p. 13-3)*

As an Appropriations subcommittee chairman, he has demanded that the Bush administration spend more money to meet the goals of the 2001 No Child Left Behind education law (PL 107-110). But he later yielded to White House demands for tight limits on discretionary domestic spending. *(2003 Almanac, p. 2-18; 2001 Almanac, p. 8-3)*

Specter also has shown two sides of his personality on his party's Supreme Court nominations. After opposing Robert Bork's nomination in 1987 — which outraged conservatives — Specter took a leading role in the battle to confirm Clarence Thomas four years later. He aggressively grilled Anita Hill during Thomas' fiery confirmation hearing, accusing her of "flat-out perjury" in her sexual harassment claims against Thomas. Specter now points to his advocacy of Thomas as evidence that he can work for jurists with whom he personally disagrees. *(1987 Almanac, p. 271; 1991 Almanac, p, 274)*

If Specter gets the chairmanship, many observers believe, he will go to great lengths to accommodate Bush administration nominees and try to win swift confirmation votes for such candidates as Attorney General-designate Alberto Gonzales. *(2004 CQ Weekly, p. 2693)*

But Specter still is likely to confront the administration if he thinks the White House has not adequately consulted him on judicial matters.

Specter may survive the attack from conservatives, partly because the Senate rarely breaks from its seniority system.

appearances in the Keystone State. Specter used the appearances to make the case that his Washington connections would continue to bring home funding for local projects. He also got help from his Pennsylvania colleague, Republican Sen. Rick Santorum, a leading spokesman for social conservative causes, who has served as an intermediary during the current dispute.

"Many in the conservative movement view Specter as equally bad or worse than some Democrats," said Mark J. Rozell, a professor of public policy at George Mason University and an authority on the Christian right. "They're gunning for him."

"Social conservatives view this past election as the culmination of years of activism and believe it's time for some payback," Rozell said. "To have their agenda influenced or blocked by one moderate Republican senator is probably hugely frustrating to them."

But Senate GOP leaders remain leery of bowing to outside pressure, even from a politically influential constituency.

"The Senate," noted one senior Republican aide, "tends to err on the side of the institution over and against external forces."

INDEPENDENT OR DISLOYAL?

Another potential flash point with the administration might come when Judiciary holds hearings in 2005 on reauthorizing portions of the 2001 anti-terrorism law (PL 107-56) known as the Patriot Act. The White House wants more leeway in tracking suspects; Specter would limit the use of surveillance and search warrants.

Conservatives view friction between Specter and the administration as a sign of party disloyalty.

Bush helped Specter fend off a tough primary challenge from conservative Rep. Patrick J. Toomey this year by making campaign

---

Sam Brownback of Kansas. They range from the Family Research Council to the conservative Catholic group Tradition, Family, Property.

But those groups do differ on some issues. On the marriage amendment, there is disagreement over both substance and strategy. Concerned Women, for example, opposes the leading proposal, which other groups support, because it would allow states to recognize civil unions of gay couples.

On school vouchers, Southern Baptists, who include many public school teachers, are conflicted on the idea of allowing parents to use public money to send their children to

private and religious schools — an idea that some others back.

Richard Cizik, lobbyist with the National Association of Evangelicals, says some within the movement are too focused on a few "litmus test" issues. They need to work across ideological lines on a broad agenda, including care for the poor, racial justice and environmental protection, he said.

"Part of the problem these organizations find is that there is much disagreement within the community about what issues are the correct ones to focus on and what is the right position to take," said Black. "I teach at an evangelical college, and my students have a

wide range of positions."

One of the grandfathers of the religious right, Jerry Falwell, the founder of the Moral Majority, is already repositioning himself as the kind of spokesman that Green and others say the movement needs. Falwell says he is not looking to replace other leaders. But a week after the election he announced the formation of the Faith and Values Coalition to help lead an "evangelical revolution" and named himself chairman for a four-year term. "I will not be the czar by any means," he said, "but I will be the messenger."

Among other potential national leaders is James C. Dobson, founder of Focus on the

DENNIS BRACK / BLOOMBERG NEWS / LANDOV

Effect of 'Moral Values' Voters Exaggerated, Say Analysts

In an exit poll during the national election, 23 percent of voters identified themselves as white evangelical or born-again Christians; 22 percent said the most important issue in the country was "moral values," higher than terrorism, the Iraq war or the economy. In the 11 states where a ban on same-sex marriage was on the ballot, it was approved overwhelmingly.

These results made a clear case that conservative religious groups made the difference for President Bush on Election Day.

Or did they?

Some political analysts and pollsters say the exit poll is misleading and that religious conservative voters — and the social issues important to them — may not have been as dominant in the election as has been perceived. One reason they are skeptical is that "moral issues" were not a big factor in pre-election polling.

These detractors have problems with the survey itself, beginning with the term "moral values," which they say is ambiguous. Some exit poll respondents may have considered abortion or same-sex marriage to be a moral value; others may have thought it meant health care for the indigent or installing a democratic government in Iraq.

Moreover, "moral values" was one of several choices from which exit poll voters chose — and not a response to an open-ended question. And because "moral values" was not included in the 2000 exit poll, no comparison can be made.

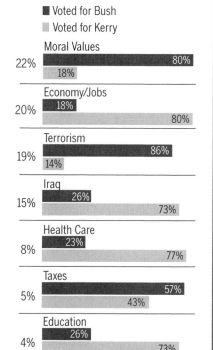

Top Issues for Voters

Below are the issues cited by voters in exit polls as the most important in the presidential campaign, the percentage who identified each issue and how those people voted for president.

■ Voted for Bush
■ Voted for Kerry

Moral Values
22% 80% / 18%

Economy/Jobs
20% 18% / 80%

Terrorism
19% 86% / 14%

Iraq
15% 26% / 73%

Health Care
8% 23% / 77%

Taxes
5% 57% / 43%

Education
4% 26% / 73%

SOURCE: CNN report of exit polling data collected by Edison Media Research and Mitofsky International

Analysts say that while religious conservative voters supported Bush and had little enthusiasm for Democrat John Kerry, the impact of hot-button social issues on this election has been overstated.

"It is certainly not the case that the primary engine driving voter decision-making across the board in this election was moral values such as abortion or gay marriage," said Paul Freedman, a political scientist at the University of Virginia.

Freedman said the survey data argues more persuasively that terrorism, not social policy, was the main issue that propelled Bush to re-election.

RISING TIDE OF VOTES

Scott Keeter, director of survey research for the Pew Research Center for People and the Press, said that although self-described evangelical voters may have given Bush a greater share of their votes than in 2000, they were roughly the same proportion of the electorate as four years ago.

"Our best estimates, based on polling that we did in 2000 compared with both what we did this time and what the exit polls did, is that there probably was only a small increase in the overall representation of evangelicals, not because there weren't more evangelicals voting — there certainly were — but because all of the other groups were also activated as well," Keeter said.

A survey by Democratic pollster Celinda Lake found that voters placed greater importance on economic and security considerations than moral values, which just 10 percent of voters said was the most important issue — a distant fourth, behind jobs and the economy, homeland security and terrorism, and Iraq.

"To call this the 'moral values' election, I believe, is greatly exaggerated," Lake said.

Some analysts say other data in the national exit poll does not point to an outsized influence by religious conservative voters. A large majority of voters said they back some legal protections for same-sex couples: 60 percent favored either marriage rights or civil unions, compared with 37 percent who favored no legal recognition.

And the proportion of voters who said they regularly attended church or thought abortion should be mostly or always illegal was about the same as in 2000. "It is certainly not the case that these regular churchgoers were coming out in droves at rates much greater than everybody else," Freedman said.

The state constitutional amendments banning same-sex marriage had an unclear effect on the presidential race, analysts said.

The perception has been that the amendments helped Bush in critical states. While he increased his overall vote share by 3.1 percentage points from 2000, to 51.0 percent from 47.9 percent, he improved upon his showing in Michigan by just 1.8 percentage points and in Ohio by just 1 point. In Oregon, Bush improved by less than 1 percentage point and actually lost the state by a wider margin than four years ago.

Crouse, left, says religious conservatives will be 'very targeted, very strategic.' Falwell, at right above, who founded the Moral Majority 25 years ago, has started a new group to mobilize evangelicals.

Family. He commands a huge audience through his syndicated radio program and played an active role in rallying Christians to the polls this year.

There is no doubt that this is the religious right's best opportunity yet to pursue its agenda, said Mark Rozell, a political scientist at George Mason University who studies the religious right. And much depends now on how Bush and religious conservatives manage their relationship with each other — and with other parts of the GOP coalition.

So far, the religious right has gotten modest returns on three decades of activism. It has made a difference at the margins — pulling back on the expansion of abortion rights, for example — but it cannot compare to the civil rights movement, the feminist revolution or the union movement, which fundamentally changed American society, Rozell said.

"I don't see the religious right movement ever getting that far," he said. "But if they are going to have a major impact on the fabric of society, now is the time." ∎

LEFT, CQ PHOTO / SCOTT J. FERRELL; RIGHT, AP PHOTO

Finding Faith In the Center

Democrats say it's time to challenge the GOP's hold on religious voters. Experts say they'll first need to shed the perception that their party is for the liberal, secular elite.

RONNIE SHOWS WAS fighting for political survival in the fall of 2002, after two terms in Congress, when he drove out to a family diner near Philadelphia, Miss., to meet 10 local ministers and try to win their support.

As Shows tells it, everything was going his way at first. The ministers liked his views on trade, on Medicare and other issues that have traditionally been a strong suit for Democrats. In a part of the nation hard hit by plant closings and job losses, the Democratic Party's populist message on economics seemed a surefire winner. The ministers also liked his opposition to abortion. He's a "pro-life" Democrat.

But when Shows finally asked for their endorsement, the answer was a flat no. Whatever his own position, the ministers said, his party leaders supported abortion on demand, and that was not acceptable.

Shows had been one of the most conservative Democrats in the House, and he often voted with Republicans. But he lost in an incumbent-to-incumbent matchup against Charles W. "Chip" Pickering Jr., a well-connected Republican first elected in 1996.

"In my part of the country," he says now with a trace of bitterness, "all you have to say is you're a Democrat, and they tune you out."

It was plain to Shows how much ground his party has lost in the culture wars of the

past decade and how estranged it has become from religious voters. In a nation of believers, Democrats have allowed the GOP to use religious and moral issues to portray them as a liberal secular elite out of touch with mainstream values — even hostile to traditional views of faith, family and morality.

As a result, in last year's elections President Bush won not only the vast majority of evangelical Christians, a deeply Republican constituency: He also took the Roman Catholic vote, which traditionally favors Democrats. Across denominations, regular churchgoers were more likely than ever to vote Republican.

Using abortion and same-sex marriage as wedge issues, Bush even made headway among black Protestant voters, who although still a strong Democratic constituency often hold conservative views on cultural issues.

Making the Democrats' predicament all the more confounding, many religious voters are sympathetic to the Democratic party's core agenda on economic and social issues, and there even appears to be room for discussion on abortion. Surveys by the Pew Forum on Religion & Public Life found wide support cutting across faiths and denominations for environmental regulation, expanded anti-poverty programs and aid for the disadvantaged — positions the party has championed for half a century.

But Democrats have failed to connect with religious voters or even to convey a sense of

moral conviction behind their policies in the way Bush has. His victory last year and popularity among the faithful has now forced them to look for ways to recapture the values debate by reframing it in their own terms and strengths. What they've found, significantly, is a number of religious leaders who have been thinking along similar lines.

Perhaps the most prominent among them is Jim Wallis, a left-leaning evangelical activist who 35 years ago founded the organization Sojourners and who has recently gained prominence through his best-selling book, "God's Politics: Why the Right Gets It Wrong and the Left Doesn't Get It." Wallis has long argued for a broader "faith-based" agenda focused on ending poverty and promoting social justice. In the process, he has challenged both the religious right and the secular left. And suddenly, he's a star in Democratic circles.

Many Democrats on Capitol Hill are avidly reading his book. He has met with lawmakers and their aides to discuss the faith dimensions of the federal budget and other issues that he believes could be taken out of the abstract and given a moral context. The Sojourners Web site declares that "Budgets are Moral Documents!" and urges people to write a form letter to members of Congress telling them to consider the impact of budget decisions on poor people.

That is not to say that Wallis is a political strategist or wants to be — his goal is to change

31

the public discourse on economic and social issues. If what Democrats want is "some Bible verses and a short course in God talk," he says, he's not interested. They need to be unafraid to show the religious or moral underpinnings of their policy positions, he says. "If you're motivated by moral values, let those shine through," he says he tells Democrats. "If you are a person of faith, don't be apologetic about that."

Democrats might not have to move far to gain the kind of support they need from middle-of-the-road churchgoers. The country remains almost evenly divided between the parties, so it would not take much to nudge the balance toward Democrats. At the same time, many congregations already are debating among themselves the relationship between their faith and politics on a broad range of issues: war and peace, the environment, poverty. That suggests they would be open to hearing what Democrats have to say.

First, Democrats will have to shed their image as an irreligious party, and in a way that does not alienate their secular supporters.

Democrats have believed that just speaking about policies and programs, particularly on economic issues, was enough to settle questions about their values, says John White, a political scientist at The Catholic University of America. But over the past generation, voters have come to think about the question of values separately from economic policies and their own economic well-being, he says.

The key is speaking clearly about one's own values and demonstrating respect for the values of others, he says. "A lot of people just want to know that you believe in something," White says. "And that you respect their own values position."

"When you make the values connection," he says, "you get a hearing on everything else. And I think it's that simple."

PAINFUL EDUCATION

In one sense, it's easy to overstate the Democrats' problem. Polling by the Pew Forum, a nonpartisan research center, found that for most Americans, religion is not the dominant factor in their political thinking, just one of many. Both parties receive most of their support from people who say they believe in God and consider themselves religious. And Bush's victory last year was no landslide.

At the same time, most Americans want religious faith to have a strong presence in public life, according to the Pew Forum, even though they support a clear separation between church and state. In polls last year, nearly seven of 10 respondents said the president should have strong religious beliefs. Only a quarter of respondents told Pew there is too much discussion of prayer or faith in politics.

Republicans and some other religious leaders say that the Democratic Party doesn't have a corner on compassion. To imply that Democratic policies are somehow truer to Biblical precepts is wrong and even offensive, they say.

Republicans and their supporters on the religious right have fed and nurtured the Democratic Party's image problems. They have been remarkably adept at defining both the terms of the values agenda and the party's own positions.

That's particularly true on abortion, where the GOP has managed to maneuver Democrats into debates over politically explosive issues, such as legislation in 2003 to ban a late-term procedure that opponents call "partial birth" abortion.

Republicans also have stoked the debate over same-sex marriage to put Democrats on the defensive and portray them as a threat to traditional families.

But Democrats have at times walked right into those traps by, for example, engaging on issues such as partial-birth abortion that seemed designed solely to make them appear out of the mainstream.

"When Democrats let others define us on social issues, such as abortion, and we can't pivot to bread-and-butter issues, we lose campaigns," says former Rep. Tim Roemer of Indiana, who recently lost a bid to become the new party chairman to former Vermont Gov. Howard Dean.

Democrats have been painfully slow to realize the importance of speaking about values, says White, who has written a book about the debate called "The Values Divide: American Politics and Culture in Transition." Now that the truth is starting to hit home, they have too often been skittish about the subject.

"We live in an uncertain age, where people long for certainty," White says. "I think that was one of the things that appealed to people about Bush."

On same-sex marriage, for example, Democrats seemed to be avoiding the subject rather

Faith and the Issues

Eight of 10 Americans claim some religious affiliation, the largest portion of them evangelical Protestants. This look at the landscape of faith is based on polling last year.

RELIGIOUS AFFILIATION

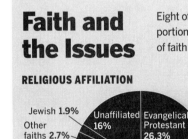

Jewish 1.9%
Other faiths 2.7%
Other Christian 2.7%
Hispanic Catholic 4.5%
Unaffiliated 16%
Evangelical Protestant 26.3%
Non-Hispanic Catholic 17.5%
Mainline Protestant 16.0%
Black Protestant 9.6%
Hispanic Protestant 2.8%

SOURCE: Pew Forum on Religion & Public Life survey of 4,000 U.S. adults in March-May 2004 (margin of error +/– 2 percentage points). Bush-Kerry data based on a follow-up poll of 2,730 in November and December 2004 (margin of error: 2.5 points).

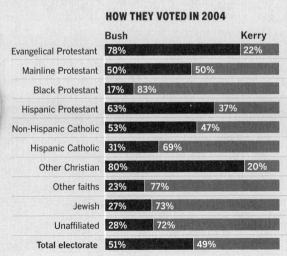

HOW THEY VOTED IN 2004

	Bush	Kerry
Evangelical Protestant	78%	22%
Mainline Protestant	50%	50%
Black Protestant	17%	83%
Hispanic Protestant	63%	37%
Non-Hispanic Catholic	53%	47%
Hispanic Catholic	31%	69%
Other Christian	80%	20%
Other faiths	23%	77%
Jewish	27%	73%
Unaffiliated	28%	72%
Total electorate	51%	49%

THEIR VIEWS ON ...

ABORTION SHOULD BE:

	Always illegal	Legal in a few circumstances	Legal in many circumstances	Legal and up to woman to decide
Evangelical Protestant	24%	45%	12%	19%
Mainline Protestant	6%	29%	21%	44%
Black Protestant	21%	33%	14%	32%
Hispanic Protestant	22%	40%	15%	23%
Non-Hispanic Catholic	13%	35%	17%	35%
Hispanic Catholic	18%	39%	17%	26%
Other Christian	35%	38%	10%	17%
Other faiths	3%	18%	21%	58%
Jewish	(Always illegal: none) 16%	24%	60%	
Unaffiliated	7%	20%	20%	53%
Total electorate	15%	33%	17%	35%

CQ GRAPHIC / JAMIE BAYLIS

than facing the issue head-on. Or they have framed cultural issues clumsily, White says. In the debate over federal funding for embryonic stem cell research, the party presented the choice as an either-or, between progress or no progress, he says. In supporting funding, Democrats seemed to brush past the ethical concerns of many religious voters who might have supported the party's positions if they were assured that Democrats would respect their views and take them into account as research proceeded.

The party has had leaders — most recently President Bill Clinton — who knew how to speak to religious people. But too often, Democrats have a tin ear for the language of faith, which Bush speaks so naturally. Dean, the party's new chairman, is the man who once named the Old Testament Book of Job as his favorite New Testament book.

Democratic presidential nominee John Kerry, who seemed uncomfortable last year talking about his faith or speaking out on moral issues, embodied the problems of the larger party.

At a party fundraiser during the campaign, Kerry kept quiet when comedian Whoopi Goldberg let loose with a profanity-laced diatribe against Bush. His silence was a stark contrast to Clinton's denunciation of rap singer Sister Souljah during the 1992 campaign, after an incendiary comment she made following the Los Angeles riots that seemed to condone the killing of whites. Clinton showed his willingness to anger an important party constituency on a matter of principle. By not

denouncing Goldberg's comments, Kerry only reinforced the view of religious voters that Democrats do not share their values, says political strategist Dan Gerstein, who is the former spokesman for Sen. Joseph I. Lieberman of Connecticut, a Democrat who does have a good reputation in many religious circles.

Religious voters "are not going to listen to us if they think we don't share their values," Gerstein says, "or at a bare minimum, respect their values."

Roemer says his party also has hurt its case by being intolerant of those, like him, who oppose abortion or hold other more conservative views on cultural issues. Roemer's race for chairman of the Democratic National Committee became at least in part a very public debate about the party's position on abortion, with abortion rights groups campaigning for Dean, who supports abortion rights.

The party, Roemer says, has let interest groups in its left wing define it and prevent it from reaching a middle ground.

What Shows found campaigning in Mississippi was that voters see "liberal Democrats for abortion, for gay rights and for taking your guns away."

Liberals and secular voters are an indispensable element of the Democratic party, of course, and leaders cannot afford to alienate them as they reach out to more conservative voters, says political scientist John C. Green of the University of Akron, a leading expert on the relationship between religion and politics.

And there are already voices criticizing Democrats for injecting more religion into the

public discourse. Barry W. Lynn, executive director of Americans United for Separation of Church and State, says that in a pluralistic, secular democracy both parties are on dangerous ground when they start trying to, as he sees it, out-religion each other.

"If your reason for supporting a particular policy is based on a Bible verse, you ought to be a minister rather than a politician," he says.

By the same token, Green says, party leaders cannot let liberals and secular voters hold them back from connecting with a religious constituency. "The Democrats have a classic coalition problem," Green says. "How do you keep your secular base happy while also reaching out to religious voters?"

FERMENT IN THE CHURCHES

The party may not need to make big changes in its core agenda to attract religious centrists, Green says. Polling that he and others did last year for the Pew Forum found broad sympathy, cutting across faiths and denominations, with a number of traditional Democratic positions. Pew found strong backing for environmental regulation and considerable support for expanded anti-poverty programs and aid for the disadvantaged. It also found widespread skepticism about free trade — a core Republican position.

What Democrats must do, Green says, is ease the minds of religious centrists on culturally divisive issues, particularly abortion, that have driven them toward the GOP.

"Whether it's modifying the way the Democrats discuss the issues or moderating

THE ENVIRONMENT:

Strict rules to protect the environment are necessary even if they cost jobs or result in higher prices:

	Agree	Disagree	No opinion
Evangelical Protestant	52%	31%	17%
Mainline Protestant	61%	20%	19%
Black Protestant	39%	39%	22%
Hispanic Protestant	43%	33%	24%
Non-Hispanic Catholic	60%	22%	18%
Hispanic Catholic	47%	36%	17%
Other Christian	58%	21%	21%
Other faiths	62%	20%	18%
Jewish	67%	20%	13%
Unaffiliated	56%	24%	20%
Total electorate	55%	27%	18%

ANTI-POVERTY PROGRAMS:

The government should spend more to fight hunger and poverty even if it means higher taxes on . . .

	. . . the middle class			. . . the wealthy		
	Agree	Disagree	No opinion	Agree	Disagree	No opinion
Evangelical Protestant	43%	40%	17%	55%	25%	20%
Mainline Protestant	52%	31%	17%	59%	24%	17%
Black Protestant	53%	31%	16%	68%	14%	18%
Hispanic Protestant	43%	37%	20%	57%	24%	19%
Non-Hispanic Catholic	51%	34%	15%	63%	19%	18%
Hispanic Catholic	50%	36%	14%	64%	20%	16%
Other Christian	41%	32%	27%	56%	21%	23%
Other faiths	58%	37%	5%	73%	17%	10%
Jewish	65%	27%	8%	80%	9%	11%
Unaffiliated	57%	32%	11%	67%	18%	15%
Total electorate	50%	35%	15%	62%	20%	18%

their issue positions, there are a lot of votes to be gained among centrist Christians," he says.

There's also a great deal of energy and ideas flowing through religious circles, if Democrats can tap into it. Wallis' book, for one thing, was well timed, although he has been shaping and honing its ideas for years. Sojourners, a network of liberal or "progressive" Christians working for social causes, grew out of the anti-Vietnam War movement of the 1970s. Wallis' message now: Many liberals misunderstand and dismiss religious faith as irrelevant to public life, while the right ignores the Biblical call to promote peace and justice, particularly for the poor.

"We contend today with both religious and secular fundamentalists, neither of whom must have their way," Wallis writes. "One group would impose the doctrines of political theocracy on their fellow citizens, while the other would deprive the public square of needed moral and spiritual values often shaped by faith."

He calls for believers to engage on a wider agenda than the issues traditionally associated with the religious right. And in that, he is echoed by other religious leaders.

Mainline Protestant churches, which have struggled for years to mount an effective response to the religious right, have been particularly vocal on this score. "Social justice and poverty are issues that have vanished from the public conversation," said the Rev. John M. Buchanan, pastor of Fourth Presbyterian Church in Chicago and a past leader of the Presbyterian Church (U.S.A.), the largest of several branches of Presbyterianism in the United States.

Bob Edgar, a United Methodist minister and former Democratic congressman who now is a leader of the National Council of Churches, says the religious left was particularly galvanized by the war in Iraq, which Edgar and other religious leaders have strongly opposed.

And like Democrats, mainline Protestant leaders have been wrestling with how to reach to the center. Many of their churches have been riven by the same cultural issues that divide the rest of America. Same-sex marriage and abortion are important issues, says Edgar, but "the key moral values we talk about are peace, poverty and the planet Earth."

Rather than just dismissing the right out of hand, as they have in the past, mainline leaders have begun to fight on the right's terms, making a Biblical case for their own social and economic agenda, says Green. He's been struck by the "sheer volume of chatter" on the religious left.

CHALLENGING THE PARTIES: Wallis, right, at a Feb. 23 writers symposium at Point Loma Nazarene University in San Diego, says both parties need a 'faith-based' agenda focused on ending poverty and promoting social justice.

"They're talking up a storm," he says. "And they're making a real effort to reach out to Democratic leaders."

Some are dubious of talk about a revival among liberal or progressive Christians. Too often mainline ministers prove to be generals with no troops, says James. L. Guth, a political scientist at Furman University who worked with Green on the Pew Forum polling. Every so often, there's been talk of a new revival, he says, but it invariably sputters out.

"If I had a dime for every time I've seen that story in The New York Times over the past 20 years, I'd be rich," Guth says.

Green takes a different view. Post-election polling showed that liberals — or as he calls them, "modernists" — across faiths and denominations turned out in large numbers for Kerry.

"It may come to nothing in the end, but it does suggest that there's something out there for progressives to take advantage of," he says.

In evangelical circles also, "there is an increasingly sophisticated wrestling with what is a faith-filled political life," says Ron Sider, a longtime evangelical activist and leader.

Last fall, just before the election, the National Association of Evangelicals approved a "call to civic responsibility" urging evangelicals to use their growing influence to fight for environmental quality and the poor, as well as the sanctity of life and traditional families. The group said the document, "For the Health of the Nation," was a milestone in the emergence of evangelicals as a force in public life.

There's still a great deal of debate inside the organization, even among the drafters themselves, about how that document ought to be

applied and what role government should play in addressing the issues that concern evangelicals. Members of the association will hold meetings in Washington this week to discuss the document's political implications, including one session on Capitol Hill with Democratic and Republican lawmakers and aides.

But they've already begun to act: In January, 77 leaders of evangelical ministries, churches, seminaries and colleges signed a letter demanding that Bush put more emphasis on fighting hunger and poverty. They wrote, they said, out of their "commitment to moral values," including the sanctity of human life.

Catholics, meanwhile, are struggling to define their own political positions at a time when the agendas of both major parties conflict with some church teachings. In the run-up to last fall's elections, Catholic thinkers and even some bishops clashed publicly over abortion and other issues — and which party a faithful Catholic should support.

"There is enormous ferment going on," says Sider, one of the drafters of the evangelical statement of principles. "And it offers opportunity and risk for both parties."

Another evangelical, Randy Brinson, has been encouraging Democrats to reach out to religious groups. Brinson, a Southern Baptist from Montgomery, Ala., is the founder of "Redeem the Vote," a Christian rock road show that crisscrossed electoral swing states last year urging young believers to register and vote.

Brinson's group claims to have registered nearly 78,000 voters, and it is safe to assume that most went for Bush and other Republican candidates. But since the election, he has been

BARBARA MARTIN FOR CQ

For 'Values' War, Some Advice From the Front

Democrats are talking to a number of religious leaders for advice on how the party can better communicate with people of faith and gain more control of the debate on social issues, which they concede now occurs on the GOP's terms. Many are liberal-leaning clerics who share views with Democrats; others want both parties to spend more time on the concerns of religious constituents. Three with a message:

❝It's in the best interest of evangelicals to reach out to both parties.❞

RANDY BRINSON
Religion: Southern Baptist
Ministry: Redeem the Vote

A physician who describes himself as an evangelical activist, Brinson says he is trying to persuade both Democrats and Republicans to respond to the concerns of religious voters. He worries that some leaders of the religious right have tied themselves too closely to the GOP — the agenda of which, he says, may not always line up with those of the people in the pews.

Last year, he founded Redeem the Vote, which he describes as a nonpartisan effort to reach "young people of faith" and engage them in the political process. He worked with Christian musical acts like Anointed and Jonah33 to stage concerts and voter rallies. Brinson says he got his start in politics in the 1974 gubernatorial campaign of Republican James B. Edwards of South Carolina. Later, he was a health care adviser to another Republican governor, Fob James of Alabama. In 2000, he campaigned for George W. Bush.

❝Our message draws inspiration from a set of values rooted in sacred scriptures and reflected in the spirit of America's founding documents.❞

JAMES A. FORBES JR.
Religion: Interdenominational Christian
Ministry: Riverside Church, New York City

One of the nation's best-known preachers, Forbes has been trying for some time to organize liberal or "progressive" religious leaders and engage them in the major issues of the day. The church he leads is a large liberal, interdenominational congregation on Manhattan's Upper West Side, just north of Columbia University.

Forbes spoke up prominently last year for Democratic presidential candidate John Kerry, whose positions on the environment, Social Security and other issues he says best embodied Christian imperatives to stand up for the vulnerable and guard God's creation.

He also addressed the 2004 Democratic National Convention in Boston, saying that he represented "an emerging movement of progressive and interfaith religious leaders who are joining voices to call America back to her true self."

❝We were frustrated with both parties. Both sides were talking only about the middle class.❞

BOB EDGAR
Religion: Methodist
Ministry: General secretary, National Council of Churches

Edgar, a Democratic House member from Pennsylvania from 1975 through 1986, has lately been speaking out against the war in Iraq — opposition to which he says woke up religious progressives from a slumber that had lasted more than a generation. But their concerns are even broader, including poverty and protection of the environment. Their focus is on the people Edgar calls "middle church" — centrists who he says have felt left out of the cultural battles between the left and the right.

In his 12 years in Congress, Edgar represented a suburban Philadelphia district that Republicans had controlled for decades before he came along. He is also a Methodist minister, and since 2000 has led the National Council of Churches, an ecumenical organization of Protestant, Anglican and Orthodox churches that together claim a membership of about 50 million.

telling Democrats in the House and elsewhere that they can speak both to the faith of religious voters and their healthy self-interest on issues that have always been a strong suit for Democrats: Social Security and Medicare, the environment, health care, the poor.

Democrats have to get past powerful wedge issues first, particularly abortion and same-sex marriage. But even there, Brinson and others see room for dialogue if the party is prepared for a real exchange of ideas.

"The door is open," he says.

Searching for Opportunity

Democratic leaders aren't trying to convert the religious right. Most of the religious leaders they are consulting, like Wallis, lean left.

Wallis is also a minority voice among evangelicals, who are one of the most conservative of constituencies. Nearly eight out of 10 voted for Bush last year. The fact that evangelicals are focusing on issues the Democratic Party has owned in the past does not mean they are necessarily looking for new alliances with Democrats. One of the leading advocates of a new evangelical environmentalism talks about co-opting the traditional environmental movement, not joining it.

At the other end of the political-religious spectrum are Jewish voters, most of whom vote Democratic.

But other religious groups, particularly Catholics and mainline Protestants, are split between the parties, with substantial numbers of centrists who could go either way. With the electorate as a whole still closely divided, there are enough votes in the center to tip the balance the Democrats' way.

That's the party's aim now: to widen its base of support as far as it can toward the center of the religious spectrum.

The staff at the Democratic National Committee has been talking about how to connect with religious congregations, and they are now looking for a director of religious outreach.

In the House, Democratic leader Nancy Pelosi of California has formed a "faith-based working group," chaired by Rep. James E. Clyburn, a minister's son from South Carolina, to reach out to religious leaders and help the party better speak the language of faith.

Besides Wallis and Brinson, the religious leaders that Democrats are consulting with include Edgar of the National Council of Churches and James A. Forbes Jr., senior minister of the historic Riverside Church in New York City.

Where these discussions will lead is not clear.

Wooing the Religious Voter

Democrats are trying to connect with more religious voters on several domestic issues, including:

- **Social Security.** Democrats say President Bush is trying to undermine the program and they cast their position in terms of the Biblical admonitions to care for parents, widows and the oppressed. The party so far has not offered a plan of its own, arguing in part that Bush has falsely stirred up fears of an immediate crisis.

- **Budget.** Democrats deride Bush's budget as "immoral" because they say it provides too little for housing, education and the poor — both at home and abroad. They say deficit spending is immoral, since it passes on debt to future generations. And they say that morality and the nation's own self-interest argue for giving more aid to the needy and vulnerable. For example, they say more money for international development will both help the poor and reduce anti-American ferment overseas.

- **Taxes.** Bush skews tax cuts to the wealthy, Democrats contend, which they call an injustice to the poor. They say rolling back the tax cuts Bush has promoted for the wealthiest Americans would bring in badly needed money for such other priorities as providing health care to the uninsured.

- **Environment.** Evangelicals speak of "creation care" rather than environmentalism, and this is the basic argument adopted by Democrats: God expects people to take care of His creation, to be good stewards.

One member of Pelosi's working group, Rep. David E. Price of North Carolina, says that all concerned ought to be open to rethinking the substance of issues.

"I think our democratic dialogue – small 'd' democratic – can only be enriched by our faith," says Price, who holds graduate degrees in theology and political science from Yale University. "All I'm saying is, we shouldn't expect to remain unchanged in the process."

Democratic Sen. Hillary Rodham Clinton, in a January speech in New York, agitated abortion rights groups when she called abortion a tragedy and urged all concerned to work together to reduce its rate. In other recent speeches, she has talked about the nexus between religion and public life, and said people ought to "live out their faith in the public square."

Democratic leaders, in fact, have not called for any fundamental changes in the party's platform. They speak of their problem mostly in terms of communication and outreach. Pelosi says Democrats have failed in the past because they have let Republicans define them, rather than defining themselves.

"I know you won't see any change in our platform or the views that many of us hold," Pelosi says.

On Social Security and the budget, the main issues now consuming Congress, Democrats have begun to express their opposition to Republican proposals in Biblical terms, for instance calling Bush's budget "immoral" because, they contend, it shortchanges the needy, the disadvantaged and children.

Mike McCurry, a former press secretary for President Clinton who is now advising Pelosi and others on this issue, says Democrats need to do more than add a few scriptural quotes to their speeches. The party will be mistaken, he says, if it thinks of this problem as special-interest politics, where a slice of the electorate can be addressed separately. "The reality is it's everybody," he says. "The vast majority of people who vote claim to be believers."

Democratic positions on help for the poor and other issues have a religious dimension, he says, and the party needs to find people who can speak authentically and clearly to it.

"Above all, we shouldn't cede the moral high ground to Republicans because they think they have a corner on the faith market," he says.

This is how Clyburn puts it: "Democrats gave the country Social Security, Medicare. That was our way of taking care of the widows and orphans, taking care of the 'least of these.' We've walked the walk."

Mountains to Cross

Some religious leaders say that in any religious-political alliance they would want a chance to help shape the party's agenda.

"We've certainly seen that on the right," says O. Wesley Allen Jr., a Methodist minister who teaches preaching at a seminary in Lexington, Ky., affiliated with the Christian Church (Disciples of Christ). "Look at the way the religious right has reshaped the Republican Party."

Richard Cizik, lobbyist for the National Association of Evangelicals and another of

REDEEMING THE VOTE: Brinson, shown with his wife, Pam, at church in Montgomery, Ala., on Feb. 27, used a traveling rock show to register thousands of young voters for the GOP, but he also tells Democrats, 'The door is open.'

the drafters of "For the Health of the Nation," is skeptical that Democratic leaders really want a dialogue with religious groups. They "just seem to want to finesse the problem" he says, by talking differently about the same old programs and positions.

Moreover, just because evangelicals and other religious groups want to help the poor, the sick and the environment does not mean they will support Democratic policies. Many evangelical Christians believe that changes in society begin with personal salvation, with an emphasis on taking personal responsibility for sin. Democrats often see the world the other way around, with an emphasis on governmental solutions, not individual responsibility, Cizik and others say.

"Unless you acknowledge as Democrats that individual responsibility is first, evangelicals aren't going to hearken to governmental action," Cizik says.

Cizik hopes to get evangelicals involved in environmental causes. He marched in a recent anti-abortion rally in Washington carrying a sign that read, "Stop mercury poisoning of the unborn." But he wants evangelicals to co-opt the traditional environmental movement, which he says has gone wrong by putting too much emphasis on big-government solutions and embracing the "population control movement."

Conservative Christian leader Gary L. Bauer says that liberals do not own the moral high ground on poverty, the environment and the needs of the less fortunate. "Those of us who support free markets, economic stimulus and faith-based problems are helping the poor in a way that will be a more effective way," he says.

Bauer and others also are dubious that Democrats can get past cultural issues, particularly abortion, without fundamentally rethinking their positions. One conservative Catholic bishop last year called abortion a "foundational" issue — meaning that no good Catholic can vote for any candidate who supports abortion rights, no matter what the other issues in a campaign.

But Brinson, who says he personally favors a ban on abortion, says it is possible for Democrats to get past the cultural issues to speak to those other concerns. So do others who oppose abortion. Sen. Clinton, they say, took a big step toward doing that with her speech in New York in January urging that both sides focus on preventing abortions. Some Democrats quote former President Clinton's dictum that abortion should be "safe, legal and rare."

The party also would help its case, Brinson says, by accepting restrictions on the procedure, such as parental notification for minors who want an abortion.

In fact, the Pew Center's polling suggests there may be middle ground to be had on abortion. There was not a plurality in any religious group for either banning abortion outright or leaving it entirely up to women to decide. Most respondents — 50 percent — chose one of two middle options, saying that abortion should be "legal in few circumstances" or "legal in many circumstances."

There's middle ground to be had on same-sex marriage, too, says White. The right approach is for Democrats to stress clearly that they respect the sanctity of traditional marriage but also want to be sure everyone is treated fairly, he says. The key to that issue and many more is speaking clearly about values — your own and those of others.

Allen, who leans left, says he also is convinced that many people in church pews every Sunday would rally around a broader message of social and economic justice, focused on the poor and the dispossessed.

He says he sometimes wonders what motivates the centrists in his own congregation. But he says Democrats have a chance to move them. "I don't know that the people in the pews are clamoring for that, but they need to hear it," he says. "And I do think, if approached correctly, they will listen. I do have faith in that." ■

JAY SAILORS FOR CQ

Odds Still Heavily Against Midterm House Takeover

CQ's study of the 2004 presidential vote by district shows Democrats' prospect of a decade in minority

GEORGE W. BUSH'S popular vote percentage margin last year was the smallest ever for a president who won re-election, and his margin in the Electoral College was the narrowest for a victorious incumbent in nine decades. Had the race been decided by how many congressional districts each candidate carried, however, Bush would have won his second term in a relative landslide.

The president won the most votes in 255 House districts, or 59 percent of the national total, according to a Congressional Quarterly calculation of the 2004 presidential vote by congressional district — a significantly better showing than either Bush's share of the popular vote (51 percent) or his majority in the Electoral College (286 votes, or 53 percent).

The presidency, of course, is not determined by the outcomes in the 435 districts. But Bush's significant edge in that tally has serious implications for the 2006 midterm election and House contests into the next decade. The statistic underscores, in a new and important way, the high demographic and political obstacles that Democrats must clear in order to win control of the House, which has been in Republican hands for a decade.

Next year, Democrats will need to make themselves competitive in considerably more of the districts that Bush carried in 2004 to have hope of scoring the 15-seat net gain they need for a majority. (Republicans currently hold 232 seats, or 53 percent of the total.) And their targets of opportunity appear limited: There were just 18 districts last year where a Republican won election to the House even though the majority of the presidential vote went to Democratic nominee John Kerry.

But in more than twice as many districts, 41, it is the Democrats who would appear to be on

defense. Those are the districts where their candidates won for Congress but Bush won the presidential vote.

Gary C. Jacobson, an expert on congressional elections at the University of California at San Diego, said the underlying GOP lean of the congressional map is so substantial that a Democratic resurgence depends on events that the party cannot engineer. Only something such as a recession or a foreign policy crisis, he said, could compel a sufficient number of voters in a sufficient number of districts to vote against Republican House candidates.

For the Democrats, the Republicans' "structural advantage is such that they can't win without having a pro-Democratic wind at their back, no matter what they do," Jacobson said. "And so, from their perspective, they're looking at a tough future for the next decade or so."

DEMOCRATIC DEMOGRAPHICS

Why Bush won a disproportionate number of House districts has a lot to do with demographics. Many Democrats represent geographically compact, urban and overwhelmingly liberal-voting districts in which they, and Kerry, racked up giant majorities. Republican voters are more evenly dispersed, resulting in somewhat lower victory margins — but more victories — for GOP candidates.

"Republican voters are distributed more efficiently," Jacobson said.

Kerry's best district was New York's 15th, which takes in Harlem and the rest of northern Manhattan and is four-fifths black or Hispanic; he won 90 percent of the vote there.

Bush's best district was Texas' 11th, which includes his boyhood home of Midland but sprawls over 35,000 square miles. He took 78 percent of the vote there — a strong showing, but a threshold that Kerry topped in two dozen districts, many of them with demo-

graphics similar to New York's 15th.

Redistricting after the 2000 census exacerbated the imbalances. Republicans were in charge of redrawing the congressional boundaries in the four most hotly contested presidential battlegrounds: Florida, Ohio, Pennsylvania and Michigan. Bush and Kerry each won two, and the president had a narrow edge in the aggregate popular vote of the four states — but Republicans won 51 of those states' 77 House districts, in large part because the maps packed Democratic voters into overwhelmingly liberal enclaves and thereby created opportunities for Republicans elsewhere.

That was occurring simultaneously with a rise in "straight ticket" voting: backing one party's candidates for all offices. The 59 districts last year where voters wanted a president of one party but a House member from the other was the lowest number of "split" districts (14 percent) since at least 1952, the first election with complete presidential-vote-by-district data. In the legendarily close election of 2000, by contrast, there were 86 split districts (20 percent). The high point was 192 districts (44 percent) in 1972, when President Richard Nixon won a landslide re-election with a heavily Democratic House; the decline has been relatively steady ever since.

Perhaps the biggest reason for the drop-off in split-ticket voting is the partisan realignment of the South. In 1972, most conservative white Southerners shifted their presidential allegiance to the Republicans but still voted their Democratic traditions, dating to before the Civil War, in contests for other offices. Over the past three decades, though, that shift has moved way down the ballot, with many voters going Republican for president, Congress and many other offices.

The Democratic road back might conceivably begin in the 18 districts with Kerry majorities and GOP House members. But the party was not even competitive last year in most of those districts: Only five of the Republicans won by fewer than 10 percentage points.

One of those landslide winners was Jim Leach, who now represents the most heavily pro-Kerry district in the nation that is held by a Republican. After Leach fought off the toughest re-election challenge of his career in 2002, in a radically redrawn Iowa district, Democrats declined to seriously test him in 2004, and he won by 20 points in a district Kerry carried by 12 points.

DEVISING A STRATEGY

Two years ago, Democratic strategists spoke of fielding vigorous challengers to longtime Republican incumbents in districts that were competitive in the presidential race, but that strategy — to the extent that it materialized at all — bore minimal fruit. Of the 27 districts that Democratic nominee Al Gore carried in 2000 that also had GOP House members in the 108th Congress, the Democrats took back only two of them in 2004: the seat in Buffalo, N.Y., vacated by Jack Quinn and the eastern Georgia seat that freshman Max Burns had won in 2002 in something of a fluke.

One Republican in a Kerry district even ran unopposed in 2004: James T. Walsh, who represents a Syracuse-centered New York district and was held to less than 60 percent in three consecutive elections in the 1990s.

Democrats insist that they already have positioned themselves for greater success in some of the 18 Kerry-Republican districts. They appear to have already lined up credible challengers to E. Clay Shaw Jr. in southeast Florida and to Nancy L. Johnson and Christopher Shays in Connecticut. They also have their eyes on the suburban Denver seat of Bob Beauprez and the Iowa seat of Jim Nussle, both of whom are expected to run for governor.

But even if Democrats manage to wrest away most of the Kerry-Republican districts, that will not be enough to win the House.

"Just by the numbers, in order to broaden the playing field, we're going to have to expand our sights into places where Bush won in 2004, and we feel like there are some places where we have some good chances," said Bill Burton, communications director for the Democratic Congressional Campaign Committee.

More than half the Bush-Democratic districts, 22, are in the South. The most lopsided among them was the Texas 17th, centered on Waco, where Chet Edwards survived the mid-decade redistricting designed to defeat him and won with 51 percent — even though Bush

Shrinking Roster of Split Districts

Last year, voters in only 59 congressional districts (14 percent of the national total) backed the presidential nominee of one party but a House nominee of the other major party — the lowest number of "split districts" since at least 1952.

Split districts

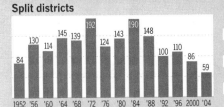

1952	'56	'60	'64	'68	'72	'76	'80	'84	'88	'92	'96	2000	'04
84	130	114	145	139	192	124	143	190	148	100	110	86	59

Republican winners in Kerry districts (18)

	Kerry's margin	House member	Member's margin
Iowa 2	11.5%	Leach	20%
Conn. 2	9.7%	Simmons	8%
Del. at-large	7.6%	Castle	39%
Iowa 1	6.5%	Nussle	12%
Pa. 7	6.3%	Weldon	18%
Conn. 4	6.1%	Shays	5%
Ill. 10	5.5%	Kirk	28%
N.H. 2	5.1%	Bass	20%
Pa. 8	3.4%	Fitzpatrick	12%
Pa. 6	3.3%	Gerlach	2%
N.M. 1	3.3%	Wilson	9%
Colo. 7	3.2%	Beauprez	12%
Wash. 8	2.6%	Reichert	5%
N.Y. 25	2.5%	Walsh	90%
Ky. 3	2.0%	Northup	22%
Fla. 22	1.8%	Shaw	27%
Conn. 5	0.4%	Johnson	22%
Pa. 15	0.2%	Dent	19%

Democratic winners in Bush districts (41)

	Bush's margin	House member	Member's margin
Texas 17	39.5%	Edwards	4%
Miss. 4	36.9%	Taylor	30%
Utah 2	34.6%	Matheson	12%
Mo. 4	28.9%	Skelton	34%
N.D. at-large	27.4%	Pomeroy	19%
S.D. at-large	21.5%	Herseth	7%
Ala. 5	20.5%	Cramer	46%
Va. 9	20.2%	Boucher	20%
Tenn. 6	19.7%	Gordon	31%
Okla. 2	18.7%	Boren	32%
Ky. 6	17.1%	Chandler	19%
La. 3	16.8%	Melancon	0.5%
Tenn. 4	16.4%	Davis	11%
W. Va. 1	16.2%	Mollohan	36%
Pa. 17	16.2%	Holden	20%
S.C. 5	15.6%	Spratt	26%
Minn. 7	12.4%	Peterson	32%
N.C. 7	12.0%	McIntyre	46%
Ga. 3	11.9%	Marshall	26%
Ill. 8	11.5%	Bean	3%
Colo. 3	11.4%	Salazar	4%
N.C. 2	10.7%	Etheridge	25%
Kan. 3	10.6%	Moore	11%
Texas 27	9.9%	Ortiz	28%
Texas 15	9.8%	Hinojosa	17%
Fla. 2	8.8%	Boyd	23%
Mich. 1	7.8%	Stupak	33%
W. Va. 3	7.2%	Rahall	30%
Ga. 2	7.1%	Bishop	34%
Tenn. 8	6.4%	Tanner	49%
Texas 28	5.0%	Cuellar	20%
Ark. 1	4.5%	Berry	33%
Ark. 2	3.9%	Snyder	16%
Ark. 4	3.9%	Ross	100%
Wash. 3	1.9%	Baird	24%
Calif. 47	1.4%	Loretta Sanchez	21%
Ohio 6	1.3%	Strickland	100%
Ore. 5	1.2%	Hooley	9%
N.Y. 1	0.7%	Bishop	12%
Calif. 18	0.2%	Cardoza	35%
Iowa 3	0.1%	Boswell	10%

took 69 percent of the district's vote.

Edwards, though, brought the benefits of 14 years of incumbency to the campaign. The more pressing challenge for Democrats is fielding strong candidates in open districts and against Republican incumbents in pro-Bush terrain.

Many of these districts appear, at least on paper, to be out of reach — including the next seat to come open: that of Ohio's 2nd, stretching east from the Cincinnati suburbs, which Republican Rob Portman will vacate after he is confirmed as U.S. trade representative. Bush took 64 percent of its vote last year.

Yet to build a majority, Democrats will have to contest some strong Bush districts, their best options being places where the Republicans were re-elected last year by margins narrower than Bush's. Most House members out-

poll their presidential nominee, mainly because of the institutional and fundraising advantages they can bring to bear against weaker challengers. Those who are unable to meet this political expectation are viewed as vulnerable.

The most prominent case in point is Majority Leader Tom DeLay, who won his 11th term with a career-low 55 percent last year even as Bush swept his suburban Houston district with 64 percent. A liberal advocacy group has already aired television advertising in Texas criticizing DeLay, who has faced a stream of ethics questions. But DeLay and his allies scoff at the idea that these attacks put him at serious electoral risk, calling them part of a smear campaign. And the Democrats would have to field an unusually formidable candidate to contend on this Republican turf. ∎

CQ GRAPHIC / YOLIE DAWSON

New Redistricting Plans Could Open Floodgates

Redrawing of House lines in Georgia has Democrats eyeing Illinois; Schwarzenegger has a less partisan idea

FOR FOUR DECADES, congressional redistricting followed a predictable script: A state legislature would draw new lines, or a court would take on the task to break a deadlock. Either way, the boundaries were fixed for five elections, until the next census and reapportionment of the House.

That tradition was famously set aside in Texas two years ago, when newly empowered Republicans asserted that it was their duty to legislate a replacement for a map drawn by judges. But this winter the custom is being brushed aside in two more places, and for two new reasons.

The rationale is purely partisan in Georgia, where the new GOP majority at the statehouse says it simply wants to get rid of the contorted boundaries that the Democrats made when they ran the process four years ago. But the reasoning is the opposite in California, where one of the nation's most prominent GOP governors wants to burnish his good-government image by creating a nonpartisan panel to draw a new and more politically competitive map.

This surge in redistricting activity signals that the once-a-decade truism is no more — and that skirmishes over congressional boundaries from coast to coast could be a defining characteristic of American politics almost every year for the foreseeable future.

The Georgia effort has raised the still-vague prospect that Democrats might soon seek to retaliate in the three states — Illinois, New Mexico and Louisiana — where they have taken control of state government since the last remap.

"The thing we're waiting to see is whether a Democratic state will have the guts to do the same thing Tom DeLay did" in Texas, says Nathaniel Persily, a law professor at the University of Pennsylvania.

CQ Weekly Feb. 28, 2005

Who Draws the Lines?

The 2003 congressional redistricting by the Republican-run Texas Legislature has prompted similar mid-decade mapmaking efforts in several other states. But not all lines are drawn in state capitals. How the lines used in the 2004 election were drawn:

- State legislature (28)
- State and federal courts (8)
- Independent commission (5)
- Iowa map by state agency; Indiana map dictated by governor after General Assembly deadlocked.
- Single House member (7)

Current House delegations in states where one party controls state lawmaking now — but didn't when current lines were drawn:

Now in Democratic control:
Illinois (9 R, 10 D)
Louisiana (5 R, 2 D)
New Mexico (2 R, 1 D)

Now in Republican control:
Georgia (7 R, 6 D)
Indiana (7 R, 2 D)
Missouri (5 R, 4 D)
South Carolina (4 R, 2 D)

This churning, analysts and political operatives say, is the result of the closeness of the numbers that each party has in the House. The Republicans began the 109th Congress holding 232 seats, or 53 percent of the total — a solid margin of control but hardly an insurmountable one for the Democrats.

"Given the relative partisan parity in the House, interim redistricting now offers a much greater potential payoff," University of Chicago law professor Adam Cox wrote in the June 2004 New York University Law Review. And that holds true both for the party trying to pad its majority and for the party trying to erode it.

The potential for a substantial gain was recognized and exploited effectively by DeLay, the House majority leader and the driving force behind the redistricting of his home state in 2003. The number of Republican House members from Texas surged to 21 after last fall's election, from 15 two years earlier, cushioning the GOP's margin in the House and making it all the more unlikely that Democrats can win control anytime soon.

Georgia Republicans are confident that they can approve a map by next month that in 2006 will add one or two more GOP seats to the half-dozen DeLay delivered.

Then there are those who think partisanship and the drawing of overwhelmingly "safe" seats is so rampant that legislatures should be put out of the redistricting business. That school of thought is espoused most prominently by Gov. Arnold Schwarzenegger of California, even though his fellow Republicans could suffer more if he succeeds in having an independent commission redraw his state's lines for the midterm election.

CQ GRAPHIC / YOLIE DAWSON

Despite the current maneuvering, some analysts doubt that frequent redistricting will become routine. Tim Storey, a redistricting expert at the National Conference of State Legislatures, says that the opportunities for Democrats are too meager to make it worth their while to retaliate with partisan remaps of their own.

Mark Braden, a Republican election lawyer at Baker & Hostetler, says there is significant "inertia behind existing plans" because incumbents are loath to tinker with lines that have enabled them to win. He said Texas was an anomaly because Republicans had a rare chance to replace a map favorable to Democrats with one that netted such a significant GOP gain. "I'd be surprised if this became a regular pattern," Braden says.

SEEMS LIKE OLD TIMES

Until a half-century ago, it was not uncommon for legislatures to redistrict every few years for entirely political purposes. But that changed with a series of Supreme Court rulings in the 1960s that established the "one man, one vote" principle and, seemingly, a precedent of once-per-decade redistricting. The main exception came when states drew maps that disenfranchised blacks or Hispanics — and were ordered back to the drawing board by judges citing the Voting Rights Act.

That has not happened in this decade. But judges drew the initial maps in nine states after legislatures deadlocked in their initial efforts. Texas has reduced that number to eight; the GOP majority in the Colorado General Assembly tried to do away with court-drawn lines in 2003, but the state courts blocked them.

No such rationale exists in Georgia, where new GOP majorities in the state House and Senate settled on a map last week that they hope will yield for them 9 of the state's 13 House seats. (Under the current Democratic map, the GOP holds a 7-6 edge.) For the map to be used in 2006, it will need to win GOP Gov. Sonny Perdue's signature before the legislative session concludes at the end of March, and then be blessed by either the Justice Department or a federal court in Washington as complying with the Voting Rights Act. If that happens, Democrats can be counted on to challenge the new boundaries in court.

The map targets Jim Marshall and John Barrow, the only white Democrats in the delegation; strengthens the political hand of Republican Phil Gingrey, whose district, at least on paper, is competitive; and ensures safe seats for the other six Republican incumbents.

"I think anytime there is a wrong out there, and you have the ability to correct it, then

Remap Role Model

IT'S NOT KNOWN whether House Majority Leader Tom DeLay sought any historical role models in 2003 when he pressed his fellow Republicans in Texas to conduct an unusual mid-decade overhaul of the state's congressional district map — with the goal of bolstering his party's congressional majority.

SPEAKER RANDALL: A Tom DeLay for the 19th century.

DeLay would have had to go back a far piece for a precedent, but he would have found him in Speaker Samuel J. Randall, a Pennsylvania Democrat who in 1878 implored his Ohio Democratic cohorts to redraw their state's congressional map in time for that year's highly competitive House elections.

With "re-redistricting" suddenly making a comeback after a long hiatus — spurred first by those Texas Republicans, and now by Georgia Republicans looking for partisan gain and by California's governor looking for more competition — University of North Carolina political scientist Erik J. Engstrom notes that redrawing congressional lines in the middle of a decade was commonplace in the late 19th century.

Randall's 1878 gambit was the first of six congressional redistrictings in seven election cycles that were undertaken in Ohio. The parties frequently swapped control of the state legislature — and power to handle line-drawing duties.

"When they came into power after the

new election in the state legislature, they would make the first order of business redrawing the congressional districts," Engstrom says.

"It was clearly just pure partisan gerrymandering, and they flipped a lot of seats that way," he adds, noting, "Both parties were doing it."

According to The New York Times of April 23, 1878, Randall told Ohio Democrats that revising their congressional map was of "the utmost importance" to the party. "Mr. Randall," the paper reported, "gives as a reason that the indications point to Republican success in carrying the next House unless some effort of this kind is made by Democrats where they have power."

The gambit worked: Democrats won 11 of 20 Ohio House seats — after winning eight two years earlier — and held on to their House majority. Incidentally, two Ohio Republicans who avoided Randall's wrath that year were future presidents James A. Garfield and William McKinley.

And as for the Texas Democratic state legislators who thought they made political history in 2003 by slipping out to Oklahoma and New Mexico in a failed effort to block consideration of redistricting legislation: Engstrom notes that Indiana legislators fled the state one time in the late 19th century to thwart a congressional remap.

that's what you need to do," says freshman Rep. Lynn Westmoreland, a former Georgia state House GOP leader and a driving force behind the redistricting.

For their part, Democrats have opportunities for a similarly partisan gambit in only three states, and in none does reopening the redistricting process seem imminent.

In Illinois, a remapping by the newly in-control Democrats could help the cause of Rep. Rahm Emanuel of Chicago, the chairman of the House Democrats' campaign arm. But it would incur the wrath of Speaker J. Dennis Hastert, who personally controlled the process for the GOP in his home state four years ago. In New Mexico, Democratic Gov. Bill Richardson has shown no zeal for using his

state to launch a new front for partisan warfare. And in Louisiana, party aides said reopening the map is not on their radar screen.

As an alternative, Democrats could seek to undermine the GOP's edge by joining "good government" groups in pushing to shift control of redistricting in most states from overtly partisan legislatures to commissions with mandates to keep partisanship out of the process.

"Democrats should not only threaten vengeance, but embrace reform," the Democratic Leadership Council, a group of centrists, wrote in an e-mail commentary Feb. 24.

The most prominent figure in that effort is Schwarzenegger, who wants the lines defining his state's 53 House seats — by far the biggest delegation — to be redrawn immedi-

LIBRARY OF CONGRESS

ately by a panel of retired judges. Schwarzenegger laments the lack of competition under a "sweetheart" deal that incumbents of both parties cut in 2001: Not only were all the House races in the state won last year by the incumbent party — 33 Democrats, 20 Republicans — but none were even close. In fact, none of the 153 congressional or state legislative seats contested in California last fall changed hands.

"We have to stop this, because this is not true democracy," the governor said at a Feb. 17 news conference in Washington with the government watchdog group Common Cause.

Common Cause generally opposes mid-decade redistricting. But its president, Chellie Pingree, says the group backs Schwarzenegger's plan in hopes that its enactment would start a national wave.

California trends Democratic, and most of the party's members of the legislature are cool to the proposal. Republicans in the U.S. House delegation are nervous that a new map would jeopardize some of their safe seats. Conservatives say the plan also would weaken their influence and strengthen the hand of GOP moderates, since competitive districts tend to produce more centrist candidates.

Still, analysts question whether a new map could be drawn to yield a proliferation of competitive races. Most of the Democratic-held districts are urban and compact — and difficult to radically reconfigure — or are fortified by the Voting Rights Act because they have large black

"The thing we're waiting to see is whether a Democratic state will have the guts to do the same thing Tom DeLay did. "

— Nathaniel Persily,
University of Pennsylvania law professor

and Hispanic populations.

Also, the advantage of incumbency can trump the partisan edge that the other party might have because of registration, says Bruce Cain, a political scientist at the University of California at Berkeley, "so it's not obvious to me that you're going to have truly competitive seats."

In addition, Democrats who are adopting the "redistricting reform" mantle are not necessarily surrendering their partisan prerogatives. Some who say the party should promote commissions also advocate concentrating their efforts in Ohio, Michigan and Florida — three politically divided and populous states where Republicans succeeded at drawing partisan maps for this decade.

In Florida, Democrats are working to put on the 2006 ballot the question of whether a commission should redraw congressional and legislative lines in time for 2008. The current map has produced a delegation of 18 Republicans and seven Democrats.

The courts also have a role to play. The Supreme Court last year issued a fractured and inconclusive ruling, in *Vieth v. Jubelirer*, about how extensively political considerations could be taken into account in redistricting. It then ordered new federal court consideration of the redrawn Texas map, suggesting that it may use the motives for that document to decide the constitutional boundaries of political gerrymandering sometime in the future. ∎

Government Institutions

The articles in this section provide insight into the workings of the major institutions of the U.S. government. The constitutional doctrine of separation of powers fractures the power of the national government, checking any one branch's attempts to implement its will unilaterally. Other factors, including political parties, elections and coalitions of interest, help to reintegrate the power that the Constitution separates. Nonetheless, officials in each branch of the government must deal with different institutional rules and norms, as well as different political considerations, strategies and tactics.

The first three articles set the stage for the 109th Congress. Following the 2004 elections, the Republican leadership of the House and Senate now has a comfortable majority. The first selection profiles the membership characteristics of the new Congress and explores the political implications of these demographic factors, highlighting age, race, gender and military service among the membership. The next article illuminates the process of selecting members to serve on standing committees, highlighting the nuances involved in picking committee chairs and in preserving some measure of seniority and committee power. The third selection digs more deeply, into the politics behind the reorganization of the important "money" committees—the House Appropriations Committee and the Senate Appropriations Committee—and considers what this reorganization may mean for the budget process. The last article in the Congress section offers an example of how parties and coalitions of interest can reintegrate divided power to achieve shared political objectives. Federal rules are drafted and implemented by federal agencies, which are part of the executive branch, under authorizing statutes passed by Congress. Republicans in Congress, Bush administration officials and business lobbyists are currently working together to overhaul the federal rule-making process to change the way agencies issue rules. Among their priorities is making it easier to sunset regulations and allow business interests to challenge the risk studies, economic analyses and data on which federal agencies base their policies.

The two articles in the presidency section analyze the challenges of President George W. Bush in his second term. The president's goals are ambitious, yet his ability to influence other political actors is diminished because their electoral fortunes are no longer tied to his. Bush has set an agenda for entitlement and tax policy that is, as characterized by the first article, "about nothing less than turning the social contracts of the New Deal and Great Society on their heads." How he will fare is a matter of his political skill, the acumen of his advisors, his ability to maintain the support of Republicans in Congress and his success in sustaining some sense of a public mandate for action. The second article in this section demonstrates the obstacles the president faces in convincing citizens and lawmakers that the Social Security system is in crisis and that his initiative to create private retirement accounts is key to a viable solution.

The last article examines the politics of judicial appointments, especially the prospects for bitter partisan warfare over any upcoming Supreme Court nominations. Chief Justice William H. Rehnquist's expected retirement will raise the stakes in an already-heated conflict between Senate Democrats and Republicans over the president's conservative judicial nominees. This analysis profiles potential nominees and the specter of the "nuclear option" for prohibiting potential Democratic filibusters of floor confirmation votes. A bipartisan compromise was ultimately reached on such use of the filibuster on May 23, 2005.

A Touch of Gray on Capitol Hill

Lawmakers are older and more politically savvy, but fewer have military backgrounds: What are the cumulative effects?

THE 109TH CONGRESS has its notable demographics. The average age of senators is the highest ever, and the average House member is older than at any time in at least a century. The rise of the "citizen politician," heralded by the newly installed Republican majority a decade ago, appears no more: New House members have tended to arrive with years of officeholding on their résumés — and a majority of senators have used the House as a steppingstone. Gains in the congressional rosters of women and ethnic minorities are incremental since last year, but the totals have set records nonetheless.

But it is the accelerating decline in military service among members that may be the most eye-catching statistic, given the prominent issues of war and security that this Congress faces.

In 1969, as Richard M. Nixon took office at the height of the Vietnam War, three of four members of Congress had been in the military. In 1991, when Congress authorized President George Bush to wage war to end Iraq's occupation of Kuwait, just more than half the members — 52 percent — were veterans.

But the 109th Congress, which will legislate on the nation's current military campaigns in Iraq, Afghanistan and elsewhere in the war on terrorism, includes just 140 veterans — 109 in the House and 31 in the Senate — barely one-quarter of the membership. That is a 9 percent decline just since the 108th Congress and a 49 percent drop since the Persian Gulf War 14 years ago.

The dwindling number of veterans in Congress is largely the result of the institution of an all-volunteer army in 1973 and the aging of the World War II generation. This is a concern for the most ardent defense hawks in Congress and of organizations that advocate for veterans. Their apprehensions are acute in this time of armed conflict and budgetary constraints that could pinch funding for veterans' health care.

"I think a veteran has a better understanding of what this country has to really deal with, what a soldier has to deal with, when we declare war on someone or we have to go to war," said Rep. John Salazar, a Democratic freshman from Colorado who served in the Army and has a son in the military.

CQ Weekly Jan. 31, 2005

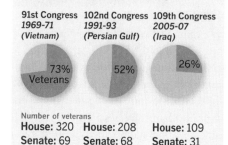

Uniform Decline

Military veterans dominated Congress through the 1960s, but their numbers have declined rapidly in recent years.

91st Congress 1969-71 (Vietnam)	102nd Congress 1991-93 (Persian Gulf)	109th Congress 2005-07 (Iraq)
73% Veterans	52%	26%

Number of veterans

House: 320	House: 208	House: 109
Senate: 69	Senate: 68	Senate: 31

Kentucky Republican Geoff Davis, another newly elected House member with an Army background, said military service "helps to bring into perspective the translation from theory to reality, which I think is often lost in legislation or policy that affects the military."

Some suggest that lawmakers might have demanded more oversight and answers about the Bush administration's Iraq policy if more of them had served in the armed forces. "There may have been some second-guessing as to whether going to war was the right thing to do, had we had more former service members," said Steve Robertson, the legislative director for the American Legion. "Because the last guy who wants to go to war is a veteran."

Yet, even some who lament the decline of veterans on the congressional rolls emphasize that military service is not a prerequisite to understanding defense policy or supporting veterans.

For example, veterans' groups were incensed this month when House Republican leaders replaced New Jersey Rep. Christopher H. Smith — a fervent supporter of increased federal spending on veterans' priorities — with Indiana Republican Steve Buyer, a conservative stalwart who favors the Bush administration's more frugal approach. Smith has no military experience, while Buyer did active duty in the Army during the 1980s and still is in the reserves. *(2005 CQ Weekly, p. 72)*

"You don't have to be a veteran to love a vet," said Joe Davis, director of public affairs for

the Veterans of Foreign Wars, although he added: "It does help to know what it is like to walk in a veteran's shoes."

AGE AND THE SOCIAL SECURITY DEBATE

Passing up military service was a decision made years ago for most lawmakers, given the increased "graying" of their ranks.

Many will be able to bring personal insight to the debate over another item on the legislative agenda: ensuring the solvency of Social Security. Its trustees have said the program's trust funds will be drained in 2042 if no changes are made to current policies for generating revenue and apportioning benefits. By that year, not one member of the 109th Congress will be below the retirement age; the youngest, 29-year-old Republican freshman Rep. Patrick T. McHenry of North Carolina, will turn 67 that fall. And, if the actuarial tables are correct, the vast majority of current members will be dead.

The average age of a senator in the 109th Congress is 60.4, a record. The oldest is 87-year-old West Virginia Democrat Robert C. Byrd — who also is the most senior lawmaker in either chamber, having entered his 47th year as senator and 53rd as a member of Congress. Byrd will pass the late South Carolina Republican Strom Thurmond as the longest-serving senator in June 2006, seven months before his current and eighth term expires.

Massachusetts Democrat John Kerry, still in the Senate after his unsuccessful challenge to President Bush last year, is 61, making him the 50th oldest senator. The youngest is 40-year-old New Hampshire Republican John E. Sununu.

The average age in the House is 55 — the highest since at least 1907, the earliest date for which the Congressional Research Service has data. The oldest member is 81-year-old Texas Republican Ralph M. Hall. McHenry is the only lawmaker in his 20s, though nine are younger than 35.

Of the 40 freshmen, eight Republicans and four Democrats are at least 55 years old. The oldest is 67-year-old Republican Joe Schwarz of Michigan. And with their years come sprinklings of added political seasoning. Twenty members of the Class of 2004 — fully half — arrived with at least a decade in elected office.

CQ GRAPHIC / JAMEY FRY

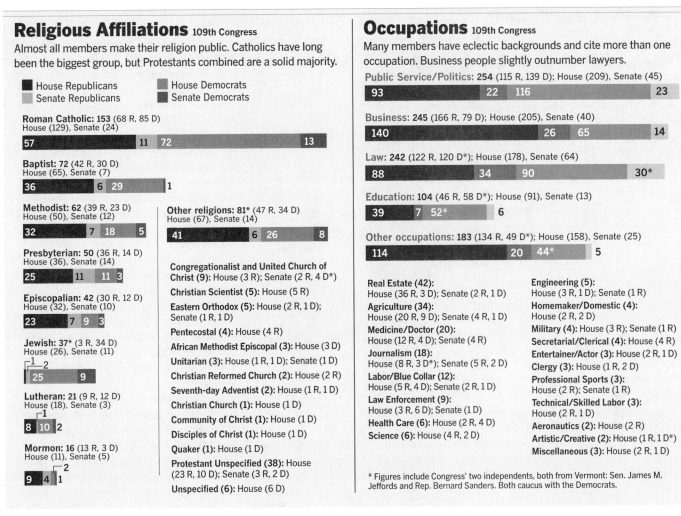

Religious Affiliations 109th Congress

Almost all members make their religion public. Catholics have long been the biggest group, but Protestants combined are a solid majority.

■ House Republicans   ▨ House Democrats
▨ Senate Republicans   ■ Senate Democrats

Roman Catholic: 153 (68 R, 85 D)
House (129), Senate (24)
57 | 11 | 72 | 13

Baptist: 72 (42 R, 30 D)
House (65), Senate (7)
36 | 6 | 29 | 1

Methodist: 62 (39 R, 23 D)
House (50), Senate (12)
32 | 7 | 18 | 5

Presbyterian: 50 (36 R, 14 D)
House (36), Senate (14)
25 | 11 | 11 | 3

Episcopalian: 42 (30 R, 12 D)
House (32), Senate (10)
23 | 7 | 9 | 3

Jewish: 37* (3 R, 34 D)
House (26), Senate (11)
1 | 2
25 | 9

Lutheran: 21 (9 R, 12 D)
House (18), Senate (3)
1
8 | 10 | 2

Mormon: 16 (13 R, 3 D)
House (11), Senate (5)
2
9 | 4 | 1

Other religions: 81* (47 R, 34 D)
House (67), Senate (14)
41 | 6 | 26 | 8

Congregationalist and United Church of Christ (9): House (3 R); Senate (2 R, 4 D*)
Christian Scientist (5): House (5 R)
Eastern Orthodox (5): House (2 R, 1 D); Senate (1 R, 1 D)
Pentecostal (4): House (4 R)
African Methodist Episcopal (3): House (3 D)
Unitarian (3): House (1 R, 1 D); Senate (1 D)
Christian Reformed Church (2): House (2 R)
Seventh-day Adventist (2): House (1 R, 1 D)
Christian Church (1): House (1 D)
Community of Christ (1): House (1 D)
Disciples of Christ (1): House (1 D)
Quaker (1): House (1 D)
Protestant Unspecified (38): House (23 R, 10 D); Senate (3 R, 2 D)
Unspecified (6): House (6 D)

Occupations 109th Congress

Many members have eclectic backgrounds and cite more than one occupation. Business people slightly outnumber lawyers.

Public Service/Politics: 254 (115 R, 139 D); House (209), Senate (45)
93 | 22 | 116 | 23

Business: 245 (166 R, 79 D); House (205), Senate (40)
140 | 26 | 65 | 14

Law: 242 (122 R, 120 D*); House (178), Senate (64)
88 | 34 | 90 | 30*

Education: 104 (46 R, 58 D*); House (91), Senate (13)
39 | 7 | 52* | 6

Other occupations: 183 (134 R, 49 D*); House (158), Senate (25)
114 | 20 | 44* | 5

Real Estate (42): House (36 R, 3 D); Senate (2 R, 1 D)
Agriculture (34): House (20 R, 9 D); Senate (4 R, 1 D)
Medicine/Doctor (20): House (12 R, 4 D); Senate (4 R)
Journalism (18): House (8 R, 3 D*); Senate (5 R, 2 D)
Labor/Blue Collar (12): House (5 R, 4 D); Senate (2 R, 1 D)
Law Enforcement (9): House (3 R, 6 D); Senate (1 D)
Health Care (6): House (2 R, 4 D)
Science (6): House (4 R, 2 D)

Engineering (5): House (3 R, 1 D); Senate (1 R)
Homemaker/Domestic (4): House (2 R, 2 D)
Military (4): House (3 R); Senate (1 R)
Secretarial/Clerical (4): House (4 R)
Entertainer/Actor (3): House (2 R, 1 D)
Clergy (3): House (1 R, 2 D)
Professional Sports (3): House (2 R); Senate (1 R)
Technical/Skilled Labor (3): House (2 R, 1 D)
Aeronautics (2): House (2 R)
Artistic/Creative (2): House (1 R, 1 D*)
Miscellaneous (3): House (2 R, 1 D)

* Figures include Congress' two independents, both from Vermont: Sen. James M. Jeffords and Rep. Bernard Sanders. Both caucus with the Democrats.

Republican John R. "Randy" Kuhl Jr. of New York and California Democrat Jim Costa each served 24 years in the state legislature. Schwarz spent 15 years in the Michigan Senate.

This contrasts sharply with Class of 1994, the Republican-dominated group that swept into office on the "Contract With America" and heralded a GOP takeover after four decades in the House minority. Fewer than one in five of those freshmen had served at least 10 years in an elected office; many of them arrived declaring, prematurely, that political careerism was waning.

Political analysts say older candidates might fare better than younger ones because they have had more time to build a base of contacts and financial contributors — or possess personal wealth that can finance a campaign.

"The increasing costs of campaigns in open seats and competitive incumbent-held seats puts a premium on candidates who have money or access to money as a consequence of their earlier careers," said Thomas E. Mann, a congressional scholar at the Brookings Institution.

The average age of Congress also has increased slightly because there was relatively low turnover in the 2004 election. Medical advances also have allowed people to live longer

and maintain active lifestyles in their later years.

Moreover, several of those who departed last fall — either to pursue other office or seek careers in the private sector — were on the young end of the congressional spectrum. Among the prominent mid-career "retirees" were Illinois Republican Peter G. Fitzgerald, just 44 when he retired from the Senate after one term; Louisiana Democrat John B. Breaux, who ended a 32-year congressional career at age 60; Oklahoma Republican Don Nickles, who left after four Senate terms and is only 56; and California Democrat Cal Dooley, 50, who left the House after 14 years to head the National Food Processors Association. Colorado Republican Scott McInnis, 51, retired from the House after a dozen years to become a land use lobbyist; and Pennsylvania Republican James C. Greenwood, 53, also left the House after 12 years to head the Biotechnology Industry Organization.

Not all outgoing House members are taking their credentials to the private sector: Increasing numbers are making the short move to the other side of the Capitol.

For the first time in at least half a century, most senators previously served in the House.

The number of senators with House experience has risen in each of the past six elections, from 40 a decade ago to 52 today.

TRANSITIONAL POLITICS

This group includes six of the nine senators first elected last year: Republicans Richard M. Burr of North Carolina, Jim DeMint of South Carolina, David Vitter of Louisiana, Johnny Isakson of Georgia, John Thune of South Dakota and Tom Coburn of Oklahoma. The first four segued directly from the House; Thune had left the House in 2002 to make his first Senate bid, while Coburn did not seek a fourth House term in 2000 to uphold a term limit pledge.

The attractions of serving in the Senate are obvious to many ambitious House members. One senator among 100 draws greater individual attention, serves a longer term and routinely wields more influence over the legislative process than one of 435 House members.

That is especially true for the more-junior House members, who have not accumulated seniority and who are more likely to run for the Senate than senior members in established positions of legislative power.

"Generally speaking, the House is not a very

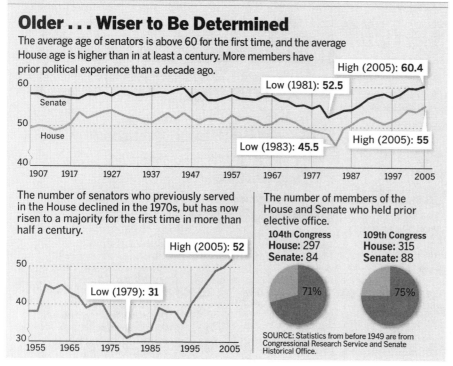

Older . . . Wiser to Be Determined

The average age of senators is above 60 for the first time, and the average House age is higher than in at least a century. More members have prior political experience than a decade ago.

High (2005): **60.4**

Low (1981): **52.5**

Senate

House

Low (1983): **45.5**

High (2005): **55**

1907 1917 1927 1937 1947 1957 1967 1977 1987 1997 2005

The number of senators who previously served in the House declined in the 1970s, but has now risen to a majority for the first time in more than half a century.

High (2005): **52**

Low (1979): **31**

1955 1965 1975 1985 1995 2005

The number of members of the House and Senate who held prior elective office.

104th Congress	109th Congress
House: 297	House: 315
Senate: 84	Senate: 88
71%	75%

SOURCE: Statistics from before 1949 are from Congressional Research Service and Senate Historical Office.

attractive place for a rank-and-file legislator," said Steven Smith, the director of the Weidenbaum Center on the Economy, Government, and Public Policy at Washington University in St. Louis. "You need substantial seniority to get up in the committee system and up in the party leadership to have much influence on matters in the House."

House rule changes instituted by the Republican majority, which have tempered the benefits of seniority, may also be dampening members' desire to stay there.

"At one time, long-term House membership was a very attractive political career, and that may not satisfy people as much, especially when you have limited terms of committee chairs and where power no longer rests with committees the way it once did," said Bruce Oppenheimer, a political scientist at Vanderbilt University.

Gary C. Jacobson, a political scientist at the University of California at San Diego, attributed the escalation more to newfound opportunities for some House members to run for Senate — not to a magnified interest in serving on the Capitol's north side.

The political realignment of the South from a Democratic bastion to a Republican-leaning region has provided ample opportunities for House Republicans. Last year, the GOP won all six Southern Senate seats that incumbents were not defending; five were won by candidates with House experience.

Smith said that more muscular recruitment efforts by the Senate campaign committees also could explain why there are more senators with House experience.

Campaign committees used to raise money for incumbents and do little else; now they are sophisticated political organizations that make recruitment a top priority. And House members have already proven proficient at winning elections and raising the millions of dollars needed in today's high-priced campaigns.

"It may be that House members are already well positioned, with the relationships they have with PACs doing business in Washington," Oppenheimer said. "Maybe they have an edge over people who are in other offices who might think about running for the Senate."

RACE AND GENDER DYNAMICS

There are a couple of ways of looking at the overall gender and racial demographics of Congress. On the one hand, they have changed only marginally: The congressional membership still has a disproportionate number of wealthy, well-educated, upper-middle-aged white men who come from backgrounds in law or business, with blacks, Hispanics and especially women represented in numbers lower than their percentages of the national population.

On the other hand, gains — steady, if slow — continue to be made in virtually every successive election cycle. There are more women in Congress than ever: 65 House members this year, plus the delegates from the District of Columbia, Guam and the Virgin Islands. That is an increase of five over the past Congress.

Doris Matsui, a Democratic lobbyist, is virtually certain to fill the vacant seat created by the

death of her husband, Robert, and become the 66th woman in the House. She is overwhelmingly favored to win the seat outright by garnering a majority in a March 8 special election primary in California's Sacramento-based 5th District. (*2005 CQ Weekly, p. 80*)

Prospects for increased representation of women in Congress appear to be tied to their growing presence in state legislatures: Of the eight women freshmen in the House, all but one previously served as state lawmakers. Some see an omen for the future in the fact that women now hold 23 percent of all state legislative seats — a higher share than in the House (15 percent) or the Senate (14 percent). Women make up a greater share of the membership in 43 state legislatures than in Congress. Still, 51 percent of the U.S. population is female.

And progress was unavailing for women in the Senate last year. While all five women senators on the ballots won new terms, the five other women who were major party nominees were defeated.

Yet a woman's narrow loss was offset by a big advance for another group — Hispanics — in Florida, where Republican Mel Martinez edged Democrat Betty Castor by 1 percentage point. The elections of Martinez and Colorado Democrat Ken Salazar gave Hispanics their first Senate presence since Democrat Joseph M. Montoya of New Mexico left in 1977. This also is the first time there have been two Hispanic senators at the same time.

Adding to the Senate's diversity was the election of Barack Obama, the first black senator since another Illinois Democrat, Carol Moseley Braun, was defeated after one term in 1998 — and only the third ever popularly elected.

Although Hispanics are slightly more numerous than blacks in the general population, they lag in congressional representation: there are 40 blacks in the House (9 percent, as compared with 12.3 percent of the population) and 23 Hispanics (5 percent, vs. 12.5 percent of the population). Gains have been slower for Hispanics largely because they are younger per capita and have lower levels of citizenship, voter registration and turnout than either blacks or non-Hispanic whites.

The number of black House members increased sharply in the early 1990s, when federal courts decreed that the Voting Rights Act required the drawing of heavily black House districts to remedy the effects of racial discrimination. But their numbers have increased only marginally in the past decade.

Success for African-American candidates is still typically found in districts where they can tap a sizable black voter base. Black House

CQ GRAPHIC / JAMEY FRY

Women and Minorities in the 109th Congress

Just 40 years ago, women held a tiny share of the seats in Congress, and minorities had even fewer. The upward trend in their congressional ranks has reflected tectonic shifts in American society in years since. Yet after a big spike in the early 1990s, gains for these groups have been gradual, and their representation in Congress remains below their proportions in the population at large. The most notable advances in the 2004 elections were in the Senate, which gained its first black member since 1999 and its first Hispanics since 1977.

Blacks

Senate (1 D)
Illinois: Barack Obama, D

House (40 D)
Alabama: Artur Davis, D
California: Barbara Lee, D; Juanita Millender-McDonald, D; Maxine Waters, D; Diane Watson, D
Florida: Corinne Brown, D; Alcee L. Hastings, D; Kendrick B. Meek, D
Georgia: Sanford D. Bishop Jr., D; John Lewis, D; Cynthia A. McKinney, D; David Scott, D
Illinois: Danny K. Davis, D; Jesse L. Jackson Jr., D; Bobby L. Rush, D
Indiana: Julia Carson, D
Louisiana: William J. Jefferson, D
Maryland: Elijah E. Cummings, D; Albert R. Wynn, D
Michigan: John Conyers Jr., D; Carolyn Cheeks Kilpatrick, D
Mississippi: Bennie Thompson, D
Missouri: William Lacy Clay, D; Emanuel Cleaver II, D
New Jersey: Donald M. Payne, D
New York: Gregory W. Meeks, D; Major R. Owens, D; Charles B. Rangel, D; Edolphus Towns, D
North Carolina: G. K. Butterfield, D; Melvin Watt, D
Ohio: Stephanie Tubbs Jones, D
Pennsylvania: Chaka Fattah, D
South Carolina: James E. Clyburn, D
Tennessee: Harold E. Ford Jr., D
Texas: Al Green, D; Sheila Jackson-Lee, D; Eddie Bernice Johnson, D
Virginia: Robert C. Scott, D
Wisconsin: Gwen Moore, D

Hispanics

Senate (2; 1 R, 1 D)
Colorado: Ken Salazar, D
Florida: Mel Martinez, R

House (23; 19 D, 4 R)
Arizona: Raúl M. Grijalva, D; Ed Pastor, D
California: Joe Baca, D; Xavier Becerra, D; Grace F. Napolitano, D; Lucille Roybal-Allard, D; Linda T. Sánchez, D; Loretta Sanchez, D; Hilda L. Solis, D
Colorado: John Salazar, D
Florida: Lincoln Diaz-Balart, R; Mario Diaz-Balart, R; Ileana Ros-Lehtinen, R
Illinois: Luis V. Gutierrez, D
New Jersey: Robert Menendez, D
New York: José E. Serrano, D; Nydia M. Velázquez, D
Texas: Henry Bonilla, R; Henry Cuellar, D; Charlie Gonzalez, D; Ruben Hinojosa, D; Solomon P. Ortiz, D; Silvestre Reyes, D

Steady Gains, Seeking More

Women and minority members of the House and Senate, combined

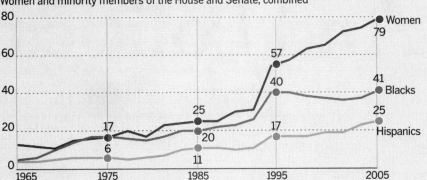

Asians and Pacific Islanders

Senate (2 D)
Hawaii: Daniel K. Akaka, D; Daniel K. Inouye, D

House (2 D)
California: Michael M. Honda, D
Oregon: David Wu, D

American Indians

House (1 R)
Oklahoma: Tom Cole, R

Asian Indians

House (1 R)
Louisiana: Bobby Jindal, R

Women

Senate (14; 5 R, 9 D)
Alaska: Lisa Murkowski, R
Arkansas: Blanche Lincoln, D
California: Barbara Boxer, D; Dianne Feinstein, D
Louisiana: Mary L. Landrieu, D
Maine: Susan Collins, R; Olympia J. Snowe, R
Maryland: Barbara A. Mikulski, D
Michigan: Debbie Stabenow, D
New York: Hillary Rodham Clinton, D
North Carolina: Elizabeth Dole, R
Texas: Kay Bailey Hutchison, R
Washington: Maria Cantwell, D; Patty Murray, D

House (65; 23 R, 42 D)
California: Mary Bono, R; Lois Capps, D; Susan A. Davis, D; Anna G. Eshoo, D; Jane Harman, D; Barbara Lee, D; Zoe Lofgren, D; Juanita Millender-McDonald, D; Grace F. Napolitano, D; Nancy Pelosi, D; Lucille Roybal-Allard, D; Linda T. Sánchez, D; Loretta Sanchez, D; Hilda L. Solis, D; Ellen O. Tauscher, D; Maxine Waters, D; Diane Watson, D; Lynn Woolsey, D
Colorado: Diana DeGette, D; Marilyn Musgrave, R
Connecticut: Rosa DeLauro, D; Nancy L. Johnson, R
Florida: Corinne Brown, D; Ginny Brown-Waite, R; Katherine Harris, R; Ileana Ros-Lehtinen, R; Debbie Wasserman-Schultz, D
Georgia: Cynthia A. McKinney, D
Illinois: Melissa Bean, D; Judy Biggert, R; Jan Schakowsky, D
Indiana: Julia Carson, D
Kentucky: Anne M. Northup, R
Michigan: Carolyn Cheeks Kilpatrick, D; Candice S. Miller, R
Minnesota: Betty McCollum, D
Missouri: Jo Ann Emerson, R
Nevada: Shelley Berkley, D
New Mexico: Heather A. Wilson, R
New York: Sue W. Kelly, R; Nita M. Lowey, D; Carolyn B. Maloney, D; Carolyn McCarthy, D; Louise M. Slaughter, D; Nydia M. Velázquez, D
North Carolina: Virginia Foxx, R; Sue Myrick, R
Ohio: Stephanie Tubbs Jones, D; Marcy Kaptur, D; Deborah Pryce, R
Oregon: Darlene Hooley, D
Pennsylvania: Melissa A. Hart, R; Allyson Y. Schwartz, D
South Dakota: Stephanie Herseth, D
Tennessee: Marsha Blackburn, R
Texas: Kay Granger, R; Sheila Jackson-Lee, D; Eddie Bernice Johnson, D
Virginia: Jo Ann Davis, R; Thelma Drake, R
Washington: Cathy McMorris, R
West Virginia: Shelley Moore Capito, R
Wisconsin: Tammy Baldwin, D; Gwen Moore, D
Wyoming: Barbara Cubin, R

CQ GRAPHIC / JAMEY FRY

members hold all but four of the 37 House districts in which blacks make up at least one-third of the population — but just seven of the 398 other House seats across the nation.

Nonetheless, the 2004 election produced victories for a pair of big-city black Democrats whose districts did not have overwhelmingly minority populations. Democrat Emanuel Cleaver II, a former mayor of Kansas City, won in Missouri's 5th District, where the population is 24 percent black. There is precedent here: Black Democrat Alan Wheat held the Kansas City-based seat from 1983 to 1995.

Democrat Gwen Moore's victory in Wisconsin's 4th District was more of a breakthrough. She became Milwaukee's first black representative by winning in the open 4th District, where 33 percent of the residents are black. ■

Seniority, Loyalty And Political Need

INTRAPARTY PRIORITIES SHAPE THE MAKEUP OF COMMITTEES, WHICH HAVE SHED SOME INFLUENCE

JERRY LEWIS OF CALIFORNIA spent more than a year courting the Republican leadership in his successful bid to win the chairmanship of the prized and powerful House Appropriations Committee. He contributed more than $1 million to Republican candidates in 2004 and vowed to push for fiscal restraint if he got the job. Undoubtedly, his track record as chairman of two of the most important Appropriations subcommittees during the previous decade worked in his favor, as did lobbying by the powerful California delegation, the second-largest state contingent in the House GOP.

The protracted campaign among Lewis, Harold Rogers of Kentucky and Ralph Regula of Ohio was just one of a multitude of committee-related battles, high-profile and not so, that marked the beginning of the 109th Congress — and so many before it. And, as soon as Lewis won the job in January, he made even more news by proposing the most sweeping reconfiguration in three decades of Appropriations subcommittees and their jurisdiction. The ensuing turf battles, within the House and between the House and Senate, were the No. 1 topic of water cooler conversations in congressional offices for weeks this winter — the most recent reminder that committees and subcommittees, although no longer the concentrated power centers of years past, retain an integral role in the legislative and political life of Congress.

With its roots in the British Parliament, the committee system incubates almost every bill that eventually becomes law. But of the thousands of bills referred to committees for consideration each session, only a fraction ever pass through the crucible of a committee markup — and few bills of importance find their way to the House or Senate floor without taking that initial step. The House has 21 standing committees and the Senate has 20; there are four joint committees.

In an institution where prestige and power go hand in hand, com-

AT THE PINNACLE: Lewis, left, bested Rogers, right, and Ralph Regula for the House Appropriations gavel.

mittee assignments are among the most telling status symbols. That is because it is in the committees where a lawmaker can most readily develop and demonstrate policy expertise, apply a personal stamp to legislation and thereby establish power bases — not only on Capitol Hill but in the legislative, regulatory, lobbying and political fundraising nexus of whatever industries fall under the purviews of his or her committees. That is why bidding for committee assignments is one of the most important endeavors for a congressional freshman. A newcomer's assignments will go a long way to determining her legislative niche, ability to persuade her constituency of the parochial benefits of her legislative endeavors — and, in many cases, her ease at raising money for the next election.

All this is especially true in the House, where the committees generally afford a greater opportunity than do Senate committees for shaping legislation. In addition, the sheer size of the House, combined with party rules, means the power is more diffuse and the areas of policy expertise are more specialized than across the Capitol, where just 100 senators vie for all the power. (In the House, each member is effectively restricted to chairing or serving as the top minority party member on just one panel; in the Senate, there are enough such jobs that eight subcommittee gavels were awarded to GOP freshman as soon as they arrived this winter.)

"It's the most important decision you can make," New York Democrat Charles E. Schumer, then a House member, told the freshman class elected in 1986. "If you're on a good committee, you'll enjoy legislating and accomplish something. If you're on a bad committee, you won't enjoy it here."

THE ASSIGNING PROCESS

In the House, the leadership has increasingly driven committee assignments during the last decade; both parties have special panels that fill vacancies — with close oversight and direction from the top — after

CQ PHOTO / SCOTT J. FERRELL

weighing the ideologies, demographics, partisan loyalty and political needs of each applicant. In her two-plus years as Democratic leader, Nancy Pelosi of California has made it a priority to boost the representation on many of the most sought-after panels of junior members and conservatives, in particular, but also Hispanics and blacks. (On both sides of the Capitol, the Democrats have had to make do with fewer seats and smaller committee budgets than ever this year, because the gain of GOP seats in both the House and Senate in the last election have translated to more advantageous panel membership ratios and spending levels for the Republicans.)

Fealty to the leadership has been the driving criterion for the House Republican Steering Committee, which also takes the lead in filling full committee chairmanships. Lewis did nothing to compromise himself on this score in securing the Appropriations gavel this year. And the loyalty of Californian David Dreier was sufficient that the caucus' six-year term limit for chairman was waived so he could continue running the Rules Committee.

But in January, the Veterans' Affairs Committee chairmanship was taken away from New Jersey's Christopher H. Smith, who repeatedly butted heads with GOP leaders over funding levels for veterans' programs during his four years at the helm; he was the first committee chairman to be deposed since Republicans took control of the House in 1995. Steve Buyer of Indiana, who's a reliable voter for the leadership, got the job instead.

In the Senate, seniority remains of paramount importance, although for the first time last year Republicans gave their floor leader the authority to ignore tenure in making some committee assignments for the 109th Congress — power that the Senate's Democratic leader and, of course, the two House leaders have long held. Majority Leader Bill Frist of Tennessee was authorized to fill half of all open seats on the most prestigious dozen panels, known as the "A" committees. (The other seats continue to be filled based on seniority.) The change caused frustration among moderates, swing-state senators and the longest-serving senators; they argued that by emphasizing the importance of loyalty, Frist would have too many weapons for thwarting, or punishing, too much independent behavior by his colleagues in the GOP caucus.

CHAIRMANSHIP CHANGES

The 109th Congress is the first in which Senate committees felt the impact of GOP-imposed term limits for committee chairmen. The cap affected four senators — Alaska's Ted Stevens on Appropriations, Arizona's John McCain on Commerce, Utah's Orrin G. Hatch on Judiciary and Pennsylvania's Arlen Specter on Veterans' Affairs — who had chaired those committees since 1995, their tenures interrupted only for the final 18 months of the 107th Congress, after Vermont's James M. Jeffords quit the GOP and tipped Senate control to the Democrats. As a result, GOP senators voted in 2002 to delay the impact of the term limits until January 2005.

The musical chairs resulting from those term limits, and the retirements of two GOP veterans last fall, resulted in nine full committee chairmanships changing hands. Seniority and comity resulted in

> **"It's the most important decision you can make. If you're on a good committee, you'll enjoy legislating and accomplish something. If you're on a bad committee, you won't enjoy it here."**
> — Charles E. Schumer, D-N.Y., then a House member, advising the House freshman class of 1986

smooth transitions on all but two of the committees.

Specter, the most senior and perhaps the most outspoken member in the dwindling cluster of Senate GOP moderates, had to fight an intense and unusually public two-week battle to secure the chairmanship of Judiciary. Intense opposition was mounted by religious and conservative activists; they have long distrusted the Pennsylvanian, in part because he is the only Judiciary Republican who supports abortion rights, and they derided him as a poor choice to lead the committee as the vanguard of President Bush's efforts to put a more conservative cast on the federal courts. Specter was saved by appealing to his colleagues about the virtues of sticking by the seniority system — and by promising not to make his own views a "litmus test" that could stop the confirmation of judges opposed to abortion rights.

The other contretemps continues at the Senate Commerce, Science and Transportation Committee — the only legislative panel in Congress that did not finish the normally routine business of organizing itself for the next two years before the spring recess. Although compelled to step aside as chairman, McCain had expected to claim the chairmanship of its subcommittee on telecommunications — a topic of particular interest to him. But Stevens, the new chairman, has different ideas than McCain about telecom matters — and so he took the unusual step of creating 10 subcommittees, none of them with telecom as its jurisdiction (Stevens put it under his own purview as full committee chairman) and none of them with McCain at the helm. The delays in making these moves, however — and the fact that the jurisdiction of the subcommittees have not been settled — means that senators are still deciding which panels they want to be on.

In the House, the Committee on Standards of Official Conduct also has not organized — the consequence of a Democratic protest against some changes in House ethics rules instituted by the Republicans.

HOPING FOR THE BEST

All members want to win assignments and accrue seniority on the "best" committees, although the meaning of that term varies from lawmaker to lawmaker. A seat on the Agriculture Committee is a must have for a lawmaker from the Grain Belt, for example, but generally of little use to a House member from suburbia.

Still, four House committees are so widely prized that members serving on them must step down from all other committees: Appropriations, which allocates all discretionary spending; Ways and Means, which writes tax, trade, health care and welfare bills; Energy and Commerce, which has unusually wide-ranging jurisdiction, from air quality to Internet access; and Rules, which is the gatekeeper for all bills and amendments pushing for time on the House floor. (There are no such "exclusive" committees in the Senate, though the parties have rules limiting the number of assignments to the most powerful panels. For example, no senator may sit on both Appropriations and Finance, which has jurisdiction similar to House Ways and Means.

Of course, a committee's status and power is not set in stone. In the 1950s and 1960s, for example, the chairman of House Rules, Virginia's

Howard W. Smith, was capable of going against the wishes of the Democratic leadership and singlehandedly blocking civil rights legislation; now, the same panel almost always acts as an agent of the GOP leadership. Although it remains prestigious, it is not an ideal place for members intent on building their careers as legislators in their own right. As a result, four of its nine Republicans members — Thomas M. Reynolds of New York, Sue Myrick of North Carolina, Deborah Pryce of Ohio and John Linder of Georgia — transferred to top-tier legislative committees this year.

"When you have a very assertive leadership, as you do now, you're taking orders" on Rules, not setting policy, said Scott Adler, a political science professor at the University of Colorado at Boulder.

Congressional scholars agree that the power of the committee chairmen, especially in the House, continues to be on a decline that began when the Republicans took over a decade ago. No chairmen have anything close to the power wielded by Smith — or even the most recent roster of Democratic chairmen.

"Twenty years ago, you'd look at the Appropriations Committee" to find the most powerful institution in the House, said David W. Brady, deputy director of Stanford University's Hoover Institution. Under the Republicans, "Now it's the caucus."

Former Rep. Bill Frenzel of Minnesota (1971-91) — who rose to be the senior Republican on both the Budget and House Administration committees and is now a guest scholar at the Brookings Institution — described committee power as cyclical. "There's always going to be an ebb and flow between the caucus, the leadership and committee chairs," he said.

At the moment, Frenzel said, the chairmen with the most power and autonomy are those who acknowledge at the outset that the leadership will demand a strong hand in the decision-making process — and who factor a degree of leadership insistence into their own decision-making. Frenzel cited Chairman Bill Thomas, R-Calif., of House Ways and Means as particularly adept at protecting his committee's autonomy.

THIS YEAR'S CHANGES

A handful of important changes in the committee structures have been instituted this year. Perhaps the most important has been the overhaul of the two Appropriations panels, which had worked with the same, carefully matched 13 subcommittees since 1971. But, in a process driven by Lewis, the House has pared its spending subcommittees to 10; the Senate followed suit by reducing their roster to 12. On both sides of the Capitol, a subcommittee that had allocated money to a sprawling and disconnected set of agencies — among them NASA, EPA and the departments of Veterans Affairs and Housing and Urban Development — was eliminated and the agencies parceled out to other panels. The House abolished its distinct District of Columbia and Legislative Branch panels and moved some Defense Department programs to a renamed Military Construction panel; the Senate did not. And House and Senate appropriators picked different subcommittees to have jurisdiction over State Department funding.

The reorganization faced substantial resistance in the Senate and lingering skepticism since it was finished. Opponents of the reshuffling fear that it could further bog down the appropriations process — which has slowed considerably in recent years as Congress has struggled with holding the line on discretionary domestic spending increases.

For the first time since the Sept. 11 terrorist attacks, Congress has a permanent Homeland Security Committee. The House panel's status upgrade was sparked by recommendations of the independent Sept. 11 commission. Headed by Rep. Christopher Cox, R-Calif., the committee now holds jurisdiction over the Transportation Security Administration, as well as border and port security, some Customs functions and the organization and administration of the Department of Homeland Security.

Its approximate counterpart in the Senate, headed by Susan Collins, R-Maine, is the renamed Homeland Security and Governmental Affairs Committee. Both committees share departmental oversight with a handful of others. In addition, Cox's committee has oversight of some major department components that Collins' panel does not. In the Senate, for example, transportation security falls under the purview of the Commerce Committee.

Critics, such as John C. Fortier of the American Enterprise Institute, contend that the reorganization falls short of the commission's recommendations and predict that the jurisdictional limitations will prove a significant legislative and oversight hindrance to both panels.

Also in response to a Sept. 11 commission recommendation, the Senate repealed the Intelligence Committee's term limits, allowing panelists to stay on after the completion of an eight-year term. Senators also gave Frist authority to appoint the committee's chairman; as expected, he picked Pat Roberts of Kansas, enabling that eight-year veteran to remain as the committee's top Republican. ∎

A Nip and Tuck Revives Spending Process
Cochran's deft strategy brings Senate more in line with House

APPROPRIATORS HAVE A TALL order this year in trying to attain the sharp spending cuts called for in the president's budget while avoiding a year-end omnibus spending package that has become standard practice of late.

But some deft maneuvering March 2 by the new chairman of the Senate Appropriations Committee may allow the regular appropriations process to at least get started this year.

Sen. Thad Cochran, a Mississippi Republican with 32 years on Capitol Hill, managed to persuade his colleagues to eliminate a subcommittee and reshuffle the jurisdictions of several others to bring the panel's structure more in line with that of its recently reconfigured House counterpart.

House Appropriations Chairman Jerry Lewis, R-Calif., pared his panel to 10 subcommittees in early February. Without a reorganization on the Senate side, the House and Senate subcommittees would have had conflicting jurisdictions, making it virtually impossible to produce stand-alone spending bills. (Chart, p. 52; 2005 CQ Weekly, pp. 307, 408)

There still will undoubtedly be logistical complications as appropriators work toward conference agreements on spending bills with subcommittee structures that remain asymmetrical. And, despite Republican leaders' predictions that the omnibus is a thing of the past, there is no guarantee that the two chambers can navigate the "road map" the Budget committees will draft without combining bills.

Yet Republicans on both sides of the Capitol said Cochran's gambit would smooth relations between the chambers and increase the chances of enacting most, if not all, of the regular spending laws separately this year.

"I think we can work with them based on this," said Sen. Richard C. Shelby, R-Ala., who will take the gavel of a reconstituted subcommittee overseeing spending for the Commerce and Justice departments, as well as NASA.

"That's a huge step for the Senate," said House Majority Leader Tom DeLay, R-Texas, who laid out the first proposal for reorganizing his chamber's spending panel.

The unanimous vote in favor of Cochran's

plan, as reported by GOP appropriators who attended the closed-door committee meeting, was a far cry from two previous gatherings at which panel members vociferously opposed restructuring proposals.

By the time he recommended his plan, Cochran had marshaled support by offering up his own subcommittee chairmanship and alleviating the concerns of other senior appropriators. "He led. He got it done," said Mike DeWine, R-Ohio, who will remain chairman of

the Senate District of Columbia Appropriations Subcommittee.

Cochran appeared to mollify Defense Subcommittee Chairman Ted Stevens, R-Alaska, by keeping Stevens' turf intact and giving the Senate an apparent advantage in talks with the House. Lewis moved defense health and environment accounts into a renamed Military Quality of Life and Veterans' Affairs Subcommittee, which has jurisdiction over military construction and veterans' programs.

"I think that Cochran was brilliant in not bifurcating defense," said one former senior Senate aide.

"Ted Stevens," the aide added, "will be able to work both subcommittee chairmen on the House side and play them off each other, because he'll have the whole budget."

Aides seemed confident that the remaining House-Senate mismatches — mainly over Defense and State Department funding — can be overcome. "The two significant misalignments are Defense and State/Foreign Ops. Who better to have trying to resolve those than Ted Stevens and the majority whip?" said a Senate GOP Appropriations aide. The whip in question is Mitch McConnell, R-Ky., who will head an expanded State and Foreign Operations Subcommittee. "If you're going to have a misalignment, put capable folks in charge."

But the linchpin of the plan may well have been Cochran's decision to draw his own blood first, offering to give up the Homeland Security panel to ensure a softer landing for the

other chairmen.

Through a series of gavel exchanges, VA-HUD Chairman Christopher S. Bond, R-Mo., will chair the subcommittee on the departments of Transportation, Treasury, and Housing and Urban Development, allowing him to keep oversight of housing programs. That paved the way for Shelby's move to the Commerce-Justice-Science panel, which won by gaining NASA but lost oversight of State to the Foreign Operations Subcommittee.

> It's very workable. . . . You might have a few additional conferees on bills.
>
> — John M. Scofield, House Appropriations spokesman

Shelby's move pushed Judd Gregg, R-N.H., out of the C-J-S chairmanship and into Cochran's spot at Homeland Security — a shift that did not appear to sit well with Gregg. "I don't have much choice," said Gregg.

Like her fellow "cardinal" McConnell, Kay Bailey Hutchison, R-Texas, will chair her former panel, but with significant additions. Hutchison's Military Construction Subcommittee will also fund Veterans' Affairs.

Sam Brownback, R-Kan., is the only new cardinal, taking over the Legislative Branch Subcommittee chairmanship left open by former Sen. Ben Nighthorse Campbell, R-Colo., who retired at the end of the 108th Congress.

SEEKING SYMMETRY

Although Senate appropriators said they had made their last changes, Lewis left open the possibility March 3 that the House and Senate panels could make further attempts to synchronize their structures. "There could be some adjustments one way or the other," Lewis said. "I don't want my feet set in concrete."

Lawmakers and aides say the complications of an asymmetrical structure are nothing compared with the mess that awaited them had the Senate Appropriations panel decided not to reorganize at all, keeping its 13 subcommittees including VA-HUD.

"It's very workable" said House Appropriations spokesman John Scofield. "You might have a few additional conferees on bills." ∎

Changes to Appropriations Subcommittees

The Senate Appropriations Committee has decided to follow the House's lead and realign the jurisdictions of several of its subcommittees. However, the new setup does not completely mimic the House's reorganization.

The Senate committee now has 12 subcommittees, while the House Appropriations Committee has 10. Both committees eliminated the VA-HUD panel and distributed the pieces in

largely the same manner to other subcommittees.

But House appropriators also agreed to dissolve the subcommittees for the District of Columbia and Legislative Branch. They moved some Defense Department programs to a renamed military construction panel; the Senate did not. And House and Senate appropriators will be funding the State Department through different subcommittees.

HOUSE: Chairman Jerry Lewis, R-Calif.   **SENATE: Chairman Thad Cochran, R-Miss.**

CHAIRMAN	SUBCOMMITTEE AND JURISDICTION	SUBCOMMITTEE AND JURISDICTION	CHAIRMAN
Henry Bonilla R-Texas	**Agriculture** * Department of Agriculture and related agencies; Food and Drug Administration	**Agriculture** * Department of Agriculture and related agencies; Food and Drug Administration	Robert F. Bennett R-Utah
C.W. Bill Young R-Fla.	**Defense** Military spending and intelligence programs	**Defense** * Military spending and intelligence programs; defense health and environment programs	Ted Stevens R-Alaska
David L. Hobson R-Ohio	**Energy and Water Development** Department of Energy and related agencies; Army Corps of Engineers	**Energy and Water Development** Department of Energy and related agencies; Army Corps of Engineers	Pete V. Domenici R-N.M.
Jim Kolbe R-Ariz.	**Foreign Operations** * U.S. foreign assistance programs	**State , Foreign Operations and Related Programs** Department of State; U.S. foreign assistance programs	Mitch McConnell R-Ky.
Harold Rogers R-Ky.	**Homeland Security** * Department of Homeland Security	**Homeland Security** * Department of Homeland Security	Judd Gregg R-N.H.
Charles H. Taylor R-N.C.	**Interior and Environment** Department of the Interior and related agencies; EPA and environmental programs	**Interior and Related Agencies** Department of the Interior and related agencies, EPA	Conrad Burns R-Mont.
Ralph Regula R-Ohio	**Labor, Health and Human Services and Education** Departments of Labor, Health and Human Services, Education and other agencies	**Labor, Health and Human Services and Education** Departments of Labor, Health and Human Services, Education and related agencies	Arlen Specter R-Pa.
James T. Walsh R-N.Y.	**Military Quality of Life and Veterans Affairs** Military construction and family housing, Department of Veterans Affairs; defense health and environment programs	**Military Construction and Veterans Affairs** Military construction and family housing; Department of Veterans Affairs	Kay Bailey Hutchison R-Texas
Frank R. Wolf R-Va.	**Science, State, Justice and Commerce** Departments of State, Justice and Commerce; NASA; NSF; Office of Science and Technology Policy	**Commerce, Justice and Science** Departments of Commerce and Justice; NASA; NSF; Office of Science and Technology Policy	Richard C. Shelby R-Ala.
Joe Knollenberg R-Mich.	**Transportation, Treasury, HUD, the Judiciary and the District of Columbia** Departments of Transportation, Treasury and Housing and Urban Development; federal judiciary; District of Columbia	**Transportation, Treasury, the Judiciary and HUD** Departments of Transportation, Treasury and Housing and Urban Development; federal judiciary	Christopher S. Bond R-Mo.
		District of Columbia * Federal assistance to the District of Columbia; approval of D.C. budget	Mike DeWine R-Ohio
	* No change in jurisdiction	**Legislative Branch** * Operations of the House and Senate	Sam Brownback R-Kan.

GOP Adds New Tactics To War on Regulations

Republicans and their business backers hope to nip unwanted rules in the bud by changing the process

THE BUSH ADMINISTRATION and congressional Republicans devoted considerable effort in the past four years to scaling back government regulation. And the effort is nowhere near over. As the president starts his new term and the GOP starts another year in control of the legislative process, the White House and Congress are embarking on a bolder strategy to change the way regulations are made — and eliminated.

Soon after Election Day, industry groups began consulting with House Republican aides and officials in the White House's influential Office of Information and Regulatory Affairs (OIRA) about overhauling regulatory procedures that could result in more business-friendly environmental, health and safety rules. Republicans are writing legislation that would make it easier to sunset regulations and to allow critics to challenge the risk studies, economic analyses and other data on which federal agencies base their policies. And the administration plans to use its fiscal 2006 budget, which will be unveiled next week, to propose a mechanism for deleting or restructuring government programs.

Groups including the U.S. Chamber of Commerce, the National Federation of Independent Business and the National Association of Manufacturers, as well as trade associations such as the American Chemistry Council, are urging Republicans to use a bill on its agenda this year — reauthorizing a decade-old law written to limit government paperwork — as a vehicle for significantly changing the process that agencies use to issue rules.

The business groups say changes are needed to shield them from unnecessarily expensive regulations. Many of the examples they cite are environmental rules, including a soon-to-be-finalized EPA regulation on allowable levels of mercury emissions from power plants, separate clean air rules on particulate matter and policies defining solid waste.

NEW URGENCY

The matter has gained urgency in the business community since Nov. 15, when a federal judge in Alexandria, Va., Gerald Bruce Lee,

> **"There is no shortage of ideas on how the regulatory and paperwork burden could be reduced through legislative action."**
>
> — **John D. Graham**, director of the White House Office of Information and Regulatory Affairs

found that he lacked the authority to review the way federal agencies use data to justify new regulations. Lee's ruling came in a lawsuit by salt producers and the U.S. Chamber, which alleged that the government's National Heart, Lung and Blood Institute inappropriately asserted that lower levels of sodium intake can reduce blood pressure in all individuals.

"We're not going to let this drop," says William Kovacs, a vice president of the U.S. Chamber, predicting a "huge battle shaping up between Congress and the agencies" over how

to assess what rules are effective and necessary.

The efforts are spurring intense resistance from congressional Democrats, who generally do not want federal agencies' regulatory reach curtailed — especially if that means that power over government rule-making, or lack of rule-making, is concentrated at a conservative White House. Public interest groups say the actions are likely to divert agency resources and stall important rules from taking effect or remaining in place.

"We have the evidence that the White House is serious about regulatory reforms, one way or another," says Robert Shull, an analyst at OMB Watch, a Washington public policy group. He argues that the policies, coupled with changes the administration already is pursuing administratively, would give the business community de facto veto power over rules it found objectionable.

The Republican strategy is focused in the House Government Reform Committee, where GOP lawmakers are preparing to move legislation this spring to update the Paperwork Reduction Act. The law, written in 1980 and renewed when Republicans took control of Congress in 1995, is designed to reduce the burden of federal rules on individuals, educational institutions, and state and local governments.

"Instead of a mere reauthorization, we'd like to put some teeth into it," said the panel's chairman, GOP Rep. Thomas M. Davis III of Virginia.

Republicans want to revise the language to, among other things, automatically sunset, or at least review, major regulations after 10 years.

Included in any such legislation will be an attempt to amend a separate law known as the Data Quality Act. That is but a 221-word slip of a provision, added to the fiscal 2001 omnibus appropriations law, that allows groups to challenge the data on which agencies base their policies.

Another effort to rein in agencies comes from the chairman of the House Energy and Commerce Committee, Republican Joe L. Barton of Texas, who is launching an investigation of whether agencies are ignoring a requirement in the Data Quality Act that federal agencies issue only information of the highest "quality, objectivity, utility and integrity."

The proposals, combined with more changes that OIRA is putting in place administratively, would cumulatively shift power from the individual agencies to the White House — a development that, Democrats and other critics maintain, could inject more politics into the already contentious rule-making process.

Encouraging Sunsets

The most contentious proposals that Republicans are considering, in many observers' view, would terminate major regulations after a decade on the books.

"The default now is that if you don't review something, it stays in place," says Susan Dudley, director of regulatory studies at the Mercatus Center, a market-oriented think tank at George Mason University. "But if the default changes, so that after five to 10 years we're going to assume that something's no longer necessary, then that changes the incentives. If something is working, then you certainly don't want it to stop . . . but if it's not, then you want it to be easy to eliminate."

But even some industry lobbyists acknowledge that Congress is not likely to automatically delete laws it has enacted.

If Congress does not enact a blanket sunset, industry groups will press for more frequent reviews of regulations. The oversight actions — known as "Section 610 reviews," for the relevant section in the Regulatory Flexibility Act authorizing them — are supposed to be conducted for significant rules within 10 years of their creation. But agencies do not continually review rules, and industry groups want to strengthen the requirements.

Business groups hope Republicans also will codify an executive order on rule-making — used by Presidents Bill Clinton and George Bush — that says agencies should issue regulations only when benefits justify the costs. Since 1993, all major rules with an annual economic impact of $100 million or more have had to be approved by OIRA before taking effect.

Supporters of OIRA, which is a branch of the Office of Management and Budget, want to give the office more funding and expanded oversight over independent agencies, such as the Internal Revenue Service, which are now largely exempt from OIRA review. Supporters of stricter regulatory controls also are reviving proposals to create a spending limit that would restrict the cumulative regulatory costs that could be mandated on the public.

Adding to the deregulatory momentum, another office within OMB is promoting a different set of legislative proposals to streamline government. The agency's deputy director for management, Clay Johnson III, promised last week that Bush's Feb. 7 budget proposal will ask Congress to create a pair of new panels that would have the power to eliminate or reconfigure government programs.

Under the expected proposal, federal programs would end automatically after 10 years unless one of the panels, dubbed a "sunset commission," intervened and deemed the programs effective enough to survive. The other sort of panel, labeled a "results commission," could be created at any time to propose — subject to congressional rejection — that a collection of federal projects be consolidated into other programs that serve essentially the same purpose. The model is the Base Realignment and Closure Commission process designed to mothball military installations. Although it was never adopted, the final version of the fiscal 2005 congressional budget resolution called for similar legislation.

A Senate Stall?

House Government Reform's deliberations will address fundamental questions about government regulation: How should agencies balance the need to protect the public against the costs of adding more rules for industry to follow? Are any obsolete regulations in place? Should agencies be required to prove in court that the studies and information on which they are basing their decisions are objective, high-quality data?

But the legislative effort may go no further than the House. In the Senate, any similar initiative will face committed opposition not only from Democrats but probably some moderate Republicans as well. Susan Collins of Maine, who chairs the Homeland Security and Governmental Affairs Committee, which has jurisdiction over federal regulatory policy, voices skepticism about making sweeping changes to regulatory procedures. Still, GOP leaders could bypass critics by attaching the regulatory changes to some must-pass measure, where plucking them out could prove procedurally, if not politically, problematic.

If Republican leaders prevail, it will continue a pattern seen throughout Bush's first term. His administration has sought opportunities to restrain agencies from issuing rules that business groups consider a burden. And it has slowly gained additional authority over agencies through OIRA.

Since its creation almost a quarter-century ago, the office has attracted criticism from environmental activists, public interest groups and others, who say it places too many barriers in front of agencies with technical expertise that OIRA lacks.

Critics say OIRA's current director, John D. Graham, is stalling, changing or derailing important regulations through the use of scientific tools. For example, critics cite efforts to

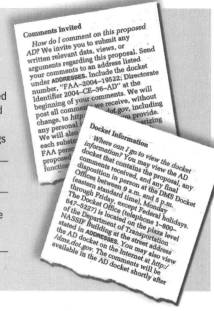

Making It a Rule

The Administrative Procedures Act of 1946 set these steps for adding to the federal rule book:

- An agency must publish a notice of proposed rule-making in the Federal Register. It should include information about the time, place, and nature of public rule-making proceedings and a description of the proposal.

- Interested parties must have a chance to submit written comments on the proposal.

- After the public comment period, a final rule may be issued. It must contain a concise general statement of the basis and purpose of the rule.

- An effective date is set. It must be at least 30 days after the final rule is published.

CQ GRAPHIC / YOLIE DAWSON

challenge agencies to use more in-depth cost-benefit analyses, revise their methods for risk assessments, or respond in writing to critics of a regulation. Graham wants government to be accountable for the decisions it imposes on the public. He is proud that in some cases, proposals that he considers inefficient and costly have been halted.

"Even by conservative estimates, this administration has slowed the growth of burdensome new rules by at least 75 percent when compared to the previous administration, while still moving forward with crucial safeguards," Graham told the Senate Small Business and Entrepreneurship Committee last spring.

Asked about this year's deregulatory drive, he said last week: "There is no shortage of ideas on how the regulatory and paperwork burden could be reduced through legislative action." He added that OIRA is "also moving forward on administrative actions to reduce unnecessary regulatory burden, particularly in the manufacturing sector of the economy."

MAKING HIS INFLUENCE FELT

One way that Graham is making a mark is by targeting specific rules for changes. In February, he will issue his third inventory since 2001 of regulations that the government will try to revise. This year's list will be culled from 189 rules nominated by the public — mostly industry groups or conservative think tanks with which the White House collaborates on regulatory policy, among them the Mercatus Center, the Heritage Foundation and the Competitive Enterprise Institute. Some of the regulations that business groups say are burdensome are the Federal Communications Commission's "Do Not Fax" rule; a rule that reduced the threshold for reporting releases of lead; groundwater cleanup rules; and the process for listing threatened and endangered species.

About one-fourth of the rules that groups have nominated for changes in the past four years have actually been revised in proposals or in final rules that have the effect of law.

Graham also has been calling on agencies to consult with his office before they formally submit rules to him so that he can influence the policies early in the rule-making process.

Another example of Graham's influence can be seen in guidelines on peer review procedures that his office issued in December. Many federal agencies have long subjected their studies and data to the review of outside experts, but there have been no centralized standards instructing agencies how and when to conduct such reviews. Graham is changing that and establishing uniform standards for any regulation with a projected economic impact of $500 million or more.

Public interest groups, such as Public Citizen and OMB Watch, say that they are pleased that the final peer review guidelines affect a smaller number of rules than originally considered. But they object to Graham's guidelines, describing them as an unnecessary, back-door way to subject proposed regulations to review by industry-aligned analysts.

Though many in Congress have not been paying attention to the emerging regulatory issues, industry groups and their public interest lobbyist opponents say the changes could result in major long-term revisions in the way rules are made.

Says Jim Tozzi, a lobbyist who was the deputy OIRA administrator in the Reagan administration and is credited by GOP lawmakers with writing the Data Quality Act: "It's a big deal." ∎

> ❝Instead of a mere reauthorization, we'd like to put some teeth into [the 1980 Paperwork Reduction Act.]❞
>
> — Rep. **Thomas M. Davis III**, R-Va.,

Reinventing Bush Country

The president transformed U.S. foreign policy in his first term, and now hopes to do the same domestically. Possible obstacles: ambitious goals and a hazy mandate.

IT WASN'T SO LONG AGO that presidents with big ideas couldn't get them past Congress and the bureaucracy. Ronald Reagan tried to simplify the tax code, and even got an overhaul in 1986, but no one would call it simple today. Bill Clinton tried to reshape the entire health care system and fell on his face. He spent most of the rest of his term using the power of the presidency to promote causes such as school uniforms and stopping children from smoking.

George W. Bush has changed the rules of the game. His foreign policies during his first term — pre-emptive strikes against nations to prevent terrorist attacks and acting without the approval of the United Nations — were radical departures that did not seem to be on the horizon when he took office. Presidents usually have a stronger hand in foreign policy than they do in domestic affairs, and Bush had more power than most after the Sept. 11 terrorist attacks. But by reshaping foreign policy so completely, he may have set the stage for big changes at home too.

Bush did have some big successes on the domestic front in his first term — two substantial tax cuts, the "No Child Left Behind" education law and a new prescription drug benefit for Medicare — but Sept. 11 put the rest of his plans on hold. The first term was about terrorism and foreign policy because it had to be. Now, as he starts his second term, Bush isn't facing that same kind of crisis. But he's proposing a domestic agenda that,

in its own way, is as bold as the changes he made to the nation's approach to foreign policy in his first term. This time, his agenda is about nothing less than turning the social contracts of the New Deal and Great Society on their heads.

If Bush gets his way, he will recast the role of government to "help people improve their lives, not try to run their lives." That's a big difference from the New Deal goal of using government to protect people from the failures of the free market, or the Great Society goal of using government programs to make people's lives better. If Bush manages to defy the odds and get what he wants, "it would probably rank as the greatest change in domestic policy since the '60s," said Alan Brinkley, a Columbia University historian who has written two books on the New Deal.

In practice, Bush envisions a government that worries less about setting rules to protect people and more about encouraging them to make their own choices about saving and spending. It would be a government that sees itself less as a regulator of the business world than a partner that does what is needed to help business flourish. A major theme of his second term will be to recognize that "America must be the best place in the world to do business," as he told The Wall Street Journal. All of these goals reflect the guiding philosophy of the people Bush has surrounded himself with — the domestic policy architects who will be feeding him ideas and helping him to achieve his ambitious goals over the next four years.

Bush is betting that most Americans have become affluent enough that a government safety net is less urgent to them. "The New Deal was aimed at a society full of have-nots. Now, we're a society full of haves," said John Kenneth White, a political scientist at The Catholic University of America who is at work on a book to be called "The New Century: Social Change and Political Response." That's a big gamble, since it assumes most people are ready to entrust their futures to the ups and downs of the economy. But others say it's long past time for an upgrade. In a society of job-hopping workers and revolutionary advances in information technology, "the Great Society model is proving to be a little long in the tooth," said Michael Franc, vice president of government relations at the Heritage Foundation, a Washington think tank that produces reams of policy advice for conservatives.

SETTING THE AGENDA

Bush's wish list is unusually long for a second-term president: Private savings accounts for Social Security. A top-to-bottom overhaul of the tax code. Laws to limit lawsuits. Tax credits and expanded tax-free savings accounts to help Americans pay for their own health coverage. A more business-friendly environment, with less regulation and looser overtime laws. And tying it all together, the promise of an "ownership society" in which more individuals would have a chance to own homes, businesses, health care plans and retirement benefits.

HIS VIEW: At the inaugural, Bush promised to address 'essential work at home: the unfinished work of American freedom.'

CQ PHOTO / SCOTT J. FERRELL

RISE OF THE 'VULCANS'

Wolfowitz was hardly the only influence on Bush. In "Rise of the Vulcans: The History of Bush's War Cabinet," James Mann of the Center for Strategic and International Studies traces years of relationships between Cheney and Wolfowitz and other Bush advisers, including Defense Secretary Donald H. Rumsfeld and incoming Secretary of State Condoleezza Rice. Mann finds that the "Vulcans," which they nicknamed themselves after the Roman god of fire, largely determined the policy choices that led Bush to declare war on Iraq.

"There was no question that the Vulcans' venture into Iraq grew out of their previous 35 years of thinking about America's role in the world," Mann wrote. "It represented a final step in the transfer of ideas that the Vulcans had formed during the Cold War into a post-Cold War world — the ideas that the United States should emphasize military strength, should spread its ideals and should not accommodate other centers of power."

These foreign policy architects are prominent, well-known members of the Bush administration. And there are clearly well-known administration officials who will have a major hand in shaping the president's domestic policies, such as senior adviser Karl Rove, Bush's political mastermind. But some of the most important players in the upcoming debates will be the domestic policy experts who aren't household names, or anything close to it.

Unless you've been following the Social Security debate closely, for example, you may not have heard of Charles P. Blahous III, Bush's point man on Social Security policy. But he's been around for years, toiling away as a staff aide to senators and commissions that have examined the future of the program. The last one was Bush's Social Security commission, which laid out three ways of carving private savings accounts from the program — one of which is getting a serious look from the White House. And he wrote a lengthy book about how to overhaul the program, laying out his own views in detail just a year before Bush hired him.

Dr. Mark B. McClellan, administrator of the Centers for Medicare and Medicaid Services, isn't particularly well-known outside the health care field, but his views on health

If Bush succeeds, the role of government will change to give a freer hand to businesses and put individuals in control of their benefits, reflecting the fact that lifetime employment with one company is largely a relic of the past. Depending on one's point of view, that is either a long-overdue update of the nation's social contract or the unraveling of it.

That social contract was built at a time when Americans felt the role of government was to take care of the casualties of free-market competition. But Bush and his allies "no longer feel that's the major need in social policy," said Edward D. Berkowitz, a professor of history at The George Washington University and author of "America's Welfare State: From Roosevelt to Reagan." In Bush's view, what is more important now is a public policy that understands that people who move from job to job, and have access to a wealth of information on the best health care services and retirement investments, do not expect their employers — or the government — to provide all of their benefits anymore.

It has been said, and not just by the president, that Bush doesn't need people to tell him what to think. But no president designs all of his policies down to the last detail himself, and Bush is no exception. To get the best sense of how his plans are likely to come

together, one has to look at their roots. That's why it is worth keeping an eye on the domestic policy experts who have put in years of work on the ideas behind Bush's agenda. These advisers will determine the first cut of policy options — and, in some cases, the broader ideas — that Bush will look at when he decides how to carry out his agenda.

Even the most surprising developments in a presidency shouldn't necessarily be surprises. Nothing in Bush's 2000 campaign hinted that he would launch a pre-emptive war against Saddam Hussein, or that he had thought much about the subject at all. But Paul D. Wolfowitz, Bush's deputy Defense secretary, clearly had. In 1992, as an undersecretary for policy when Dick Cheney was running the Defense Department, Wolfowitz supervised the drafting of a policy statement that endorsed using military force to prevent weapons of mass destruction from spreading to other nations, including Iraq and North Korea.

And in 1997, Wolfowitz co-wrote an article for The Weekly Standard that called for the use of force to remove Saddam from power. The title: "Overthrow Him." Wolfowitz has Cheney's ear. And Cheney, now the most powerful vice president in modern times, has Bush's ear.

care policy have an influence on the White House and congressional Republicans that goes well beyond his assigned duties.

The influential but low-key force behind Bush's environmental policies is James L. Connaughton, chairman of the White House Council on Environmental Quality. He's the designer of Bush's air pollution legislation — the White House calls it "Clear Skies" — and the 2003 forest policy law, called "Healthy Forests," that allows more logging on federal lands as a way to reduce the risk of wildfires. And many of Bush's key social policies, such as promoting marriage and encouraging sexual abstinence, will be spearheaded by Wade F. Horn, an assistant secretary at the Department of Health and Human Services who helped found a national group that encourages fathers to get more involved in raising their children.

These networks of advisers inside and outside of the administration will be crucial to the success of a domestic agenda that is full of lightning rods. Just as the foreign policy gurus set a series of options in front of Bush that ultimately drew Iraq into the war on terrorism, the work of these domestic policy thinkers gives a fairly good sense of the direction Bush is likely to take over the next four years.

UNFINISHED BUSINESS

The ideas themselves are not necessarily new. Instead, they represent the unfinished business Republicans have been trying to accomplish not just since Bush's first term, but for decades.

The notion of private savings accounts for Social Security, for example, has been discussed by conservative economists since the 1950s, and the libertarian Cato Institute put out a proposal as early as 1980. It has taken off since centrist Democrats began endorsing the approach in the 1990s — a far cry from the days of the 1964 presidential campaign, when Democratic President Lyndon B. Johnson bludgeoned Republican Barry Goldwater for suggesting that the entire Social Security program should become voluntary.

Simplifying the tax code, meanwhile, has been a Republican goal since the 1980s and resurfaced in the 1990s, when then-House Majority Leader Dick Armey, R-Texas, and others proposed taxing most people at the same rate regardless of their income. Limits on lawsuits and damage awards, a goal business groups have been pushing at the federal and state levels since the 1980s, have been on Bush's radar screen since his first term as

Texas governor, when a "tort reform" package was one of his signature accomplishments.

"What President Bush is trying to do is correct some of the major impediments to economic growth that face this country," said Edwin Meese III, a fellow at the Heritage Foundation who served as attorney general and domestic policy adviser under Ronald Reagan. The 1986 tax overhaul "has had a lot of barnacles added onto it since then," and Social Security's long-term problems create economic insecurity as well, he said.

No one should underestimate the intensity of the debate that lies ahead — especially since Bush has chosen to lead off by transforming Social Security, the most enduring legacy of the New Deal and the program that largely wiped out poverty among the elderly. If that program gets siphoned into private savings accounts, there will be smart investors who do well and inexperienced ones who do badly; there will be people who retire at just the right time to enjoy big gains on their investments, and there will be people who retire at exactly the wrong time. But "that's not what Social Security was supposed to be," Brinkley said. "It was supposed to be a universal benefit that everyone could count on."

There's certainly no guarantee Bush will be successful. So far, he's not having much luck rallying centrist Democrats to support his Social Security overhaul plans. Meanwhile, the early talk of Bush's "mandate" is fading as his 51 percent to 48 percent victory over Sen. John Kerry, D-Mass., begins to look less impressive. "You don't have a mandate every time you have a winner," said George C. Edwards III, director of the Center for Presidential Studies at Texas A&M University.

And some analysts predict that even if Bush is successful, the actual scope of the changes will fall short of their billing. Jack Pitney, a former House Republican staff aide and now professor of government at Claremont McKenna College in Southern California, noted that the enactment of private savings accounts would still leave the Social Security program in place.

And the last time Congress overhauled the tax code, under Reagan in 1986, the goal of a radically simplified system slipped away as tax breaks began to creep back in over the years. "The New Deal and the Great Society will be with us for some time to come," Pitney said.

ADVICE, NOT DIRECTION

Whatever success Bush does have, however, will depend in part on the team he has around him. It's easy to exaggerate the influence that any adviser can have on a president. Bush relied heavily on his foreign policy advisers because he had little experience with the subject before becoming president, but his views on domestic policy were fairly well defined, at least in broad terms.

"Bush never said, 'Tell me what I should do,' " recalls Martin Anderson, one of a group of academics at the conservative Hoover Institution at Stanford University that conducted policy seminars with then-Gov. Bush in Austin in 1998. "He'd always say, 'I'm running for president. If I win, here's what I want to do. What's the best way to do that?' " Even so, Anderson said, Bush does pay close attention to his advisers when they suggest how to accomplish his goals — as the Hoover fellows did when they put together his first tax cut package — and what the consequences of different options would be.

That means no one should be shocked if, for example, Bush embraces a Social Security plan that cuts benefits to future retirees. Blahous was the executive director of a commission that recommended tying benefits to prices rather than wages, which generally increase faster — the same idea that caused a firestorm when it was touted earlier this month in a leaked e-mail by another Bush adviser. And Blahous in his book recommended raising the retirement age and revising the Consumer Price Index — used to determine annual cost-of-living increases — on the grounds that it overstates inflation.

These are the kinds of painful details that matter, especially since Bush didn't discuss them during the campaign. He carefully stayed away from sore subjects such as how to restrain future Social Security spending, since private accounts by themselves wouldn't do that, or what kind of tax overhaul he had in mind. By the end of the campaign, in fact, he rarely mentioned the tax code in his stump speeches at all. "You can't claim a mandate when you haven't made your case to the people," Edwards said.

Bush's domestic agenda would be ambitious for any president. It also goes against the grain of what most recent second-term presidents have been able to accomplish. President Franklin D. Roosevelt launched the New Deal in his first term, and Johnson's Great Society came together after his election as president in his own right. Both men also won by wider margins than Bush and had larger majorities in Congress. "It's really quite unusual for presidents to get big things through in a second term," said Brinkley. And Bush's domestic agenda could still be overwhelmed by the consequences of the Iraq war he launched in his first term, depending on how stable that country is after the scheduled Jan. 30 election.

Even if Bush gets what he wants, most analysts don't see an outright end to the New Deal and Great Society eras of government activism, which are deeply ingrained in such areas as welfare and agriculture. "It may be enough to open the wedge for future Republican presidents," said Paul C. Light, a professor of public service at New York University and a senior fellow at the Brookings Institution.

"The New Deal was aimed at a society full of have-nots. Now we're a society full of haves."

— John Kenneth White, Catholic University

But it could be quite a wedge. If Bush's domestic successes come close to matching his rhetoric, the second term could end with federal taxes based more on consumption than on income, lower spending on non-defense domestic programs in order to reduce the deficit, and a new direction for Social Security to make room for private savings accounts.

For most Americans, the government would be less willing to save them from the consequences of their choices, including their mistakes. That's the basic idea of the ownership society — that people will take more responsibility for what they own — and it will be sorely tested if Bush succeeds. "The notion here is that there's no fallback if you fail," said Light. "If you happen to pick Enron rather than ExxonMobil . . . you're responsible for your mistakes. The question is whether Americans are ready for that." ■

No Market for Next New Deal

Selling Bush's overhaul of Social Security proves nearly impossible as those with the most at stake tune out and older generations remain deeply opposed to change

EVEN AT 92, Robert J. Myers still has the sharp eye and stubborn nature of a government statistician. As one of the architects of Social Security and later its chief actuary, he is quick to invoke the program's egalitarian roots when sizing up current efforts to reshape the pension program.

"Everyone knows they will get a benefit," said Myers, who, during parts of four decades in government, testified 175 times on the program or related matters. "If it's less than what they paid in, they should take some satisfaction that they are helping their neighbors."

Myers' generation felt the effects of the Depression and embraced the notion that a responsible government gets involved enough in people's lives to ensure that retirees have economic security after a lifetime of work. He worked in the administration of Franklin D. Roosevelt, calculating how to keep the program solvent through 1980; he later served as executive director of the commission headed by current Federal Reserve Chairman Alan Greenspan that made the last major changes to the program, in 1983.

Now he watches from his suburban Maryland home as a president 34 years his junior attempts to advance a plan that would reconceive the core of that program by making individuals take personal responsibility for managing their retirement income through individual investment accounts. *(2005 CQ Weekly, p. 838)*

President Bush, in turn, is trying to sell the

SOCIAL CONTRACT: Myers says Bush's plan undermines the core premise of Social Security.

plan to yet another generation of even younger workers who have a hard time even envisioning themselves as retired. Polls show that people age 18-29 are receptive to Bush's idea, though it is unclear whether they are paying very close attention to the details. Support falls among those age 30-64 and even further for individuals age 65 and above.

Therein lies the problem for Bush in attempting to sell his plan to the public. The youngest people, who have the greatest financial stake in the future of the program, are less engaged in the debate, in part because they won't be drawing Social Security benefits for decades. The people who are most tuned in to the issue — retirees and those near retirement — are those who have the greatest emotional stake in the social contract envisioned by Myers and other architects of the program.

"The White House is in a bit of a conundrum," said Carroll Doherty, editor of the Pew Research Center for People and the Press. "For a younger worker, it's hard to get excited about something that will affect their financial wellbeing 30 years from now."

The result is that three months into his second term, Bush's main domestic initiative is in deep trouble. Congressional Republicans, who were expected to move legislation to implement the plan, have been rattled by the angry public response voiced at town hall meetings and are urging the administration to back off or provide them with some kind of political cover.

In fact, the more Bush promotes his proposal, the more unpopular it seems to become. Halfway through his 60-day, 60-city campaign-style tour to sell the initiative, nearly seven in 10 Americans disapprove of his handling of Social Security, according to one recent Washington Post-ABC News survey.

A Pew center poll of 1,505 adults taken March 17-21 found that support for the president's plan has weakened significantly among younger people since February, with 49 percent of those age 18-29 favoring private accounts, compared with 66 percent the previous month.

Even some conservatives, who by and large

CQ PHOTO / SCOTT J. FERRELL

SELLING CHANGE: Bush, stumping in Iowa on March 30, is pressing on with his pitch for personal accounts.

AP PHOTO / J. SCOTT APPLEWHITE

support personal accounts, complain that Bush's plan would go beyond the government's baseline obligation and prompt an unnecessary expansion of the Social Security system.

Many top congressional Republicans are not feeling any pressure to act other than from the White House. Senate Finance Chairman Charles E. Grassley of Iowa, who stumped with Bush in his home state last week, has said he plans to hold a markup of bipartisan Social Security legislation this summer.

A DIFFERENT CHALLENGE

It is not as if recent Congresses have been afraid to embrace ambitious proposals to reshape entitlement programs. Congress and President Bill Clinton in 1996 dismantled the

❝People, whether they're sitting on a tractor or anywhere else in society, are beginning to hear a message: We have a problem.❞

— **President Bush** in Cedar Rapids, Iowa, on March 30.

welfare system, replacing open-ended assistance with block grants to states and new work requirements. In 2003, Bush and congressional Republicans overhauled Medicare, giving private insurers a much greater role in administering benefits and providing new prescription drug coverage.

And in some ways, the time is right for Bush to try to remake Social Security. Because the pension program operates as a "pay as you go" system by relying on taxes paid by current workers to fund the benefits of today's retirees, it is financially unprepared to deal with the 78 million baby boomers who will begin retiring later in the decade. In 2050, there will be approximately two workers paying taxes for each retiree, compared with about three now. *(2005 CQ Weekly, p. 835)*

The complicated nature of Social Security also makes it a tempting target for change. The program is bigger than its founders ever envisioned, with more than 2,500 separate rules for paying taxes and receiving benefits. Within a decade of its inception, Congress added benefits for dependents of retired work-

A Hydra-Headed Retirement Crisis

BABY BOOMERS WILL PUT A STRAIN on more than the Social Security system when they begin retiring in another decade. Their demands for government-subsidized health care, corporate-paid pensions and a variety of other services will multiply the economic costs of their golden years and the challenges for lawmakers.

In fact, the gradual retirement of nearly 78 million Americans born between 1946 and 1964 — a cohort that has radically changed the nation's culture as it has aged — will put unprecedented pressure on the social safety net. The long-term liabilities of the Medicare and Medicaid health care entitlement programs threaten to crowd out other domestic priorities. The government may be called on to bail out private pension funds if companies cannot meet their obligations to retiring boomers. All of this requires advanced planning.

"Continuing on our current unsustainable fiscal path will gradually erode, if not suddenly damage, our economy, our standard of living, and ultimately our national security," said David M. Walker, comptroller general of the nonpartisan General Accountability Office, an investigative arm of Congress.

Walker and others are concerned about the expanding share of the federal budget consumed by mandatory entitlement spending for such programs as Social Security, Medicare, Medicaid, unemployment insurance and agricultural crop subsidies. In such programs, people receive federal payments as long as they meet eligibility standards written into law; Congress does not control the spending through annual appropriations. Mandatory spending now accounts for about 64 percent of the federal budget.

The government might be able to respond to the baby boom pressure on federal programs with tactical adjustments, such as increasing the retirement age. If Americans choose to work longer or if more immigrants enter the country and contribute to taxes, the nation's cash flow could improve.

But the long-term economic strength of the government will be greatly affected by retirement-related issues. The nation has never grappled with a confluence of retirement-related pressures so intense.

"This huge change in the structure of our population will expose all of our financial retirement systems to severe stress and will require adjustments for which there are no historic precedents," Federal Reserve Chairman Alan Greenspan testified in March. "The important economic implication ... is that, with fewer workers rel-

> ## "Social Security's in trouble. The private pension system is in trouble. Personal savings, as we measure it . . . is, I believe, the lowest in the world."
>
> — **Bruce Josten**, U.S. Chamber of Commerce

ative to dependents, each worker's output will have to support a greater number of people."

Some say that a more holistic approach is needed, with Congress attacking the universe of problems associated with baby boomer retirement, and not just Social Security, as the Bush administration has proposed. Medicare, for instance, is considered to be in a more precarious financial position now anyway.

But some scholars and experts doubt that Congress will even make progress in addressing Social Security, much less find the will to debate other complex fiscal issues. The serious nature of the other problems could even be complicating the administration's ability to win passage of a Social Security overhaul.

"Social Security is already a very tough sell," said Thomas Mann, a presidential scholar at the left-leaning Brookings Institution. "One of the arguments that people use against the president is he's overlooking much more serious problems: the public finance problems in Medicare and Medicaid and difficulties in the private pension system, and the public responsibilities for some of that."

A CONVERGENCE OF CRISES

The demographics are daunting. In 25 years, one-fourth of the adult population of the United States will be over age 65, compared with about 17 percent today. Even without the Social Security issue, the country faces serious problems with private retirement plans. In fact, more big companies may well default on their promised pensions — a fact that some consider an argument for keeping Social Security solvent.

Americans are living longer, but many are not saving enough to support themselves in retirement. Nest eggs often are little larger than the value of the family house. Some are depending heavily on employer-sponsored pensions that are expensive for companies to maintain and on a Social Security system that carries a $4 trillion deficit over the next 75 years.

"For years this country's had a three-legged stool, if you will, for retirement: Social Security, private pensions and personal savings," said Bruce Josten, executive vice president of government affairs for the U.S. Chamber of Commerce, at a conference earlier this year. "Social Security's in trouble. The private pension system is in big trouble. Personal savings, as we measure it, absent home ownership, is, I believe, the lowest in the world."

The pension system's troubles have become evident as a number of companies either have gone bankrupt or have tried to get out from under their plans, forcing the federal government to pick up the costs of payments to retirees. Companies in weakened industries such as airlines are seeking to shed expensive liabilities such as pensions that they promised workers when revenues and profits were high.

During the recent economic downturn, a number of companies declared bankruptcy and left their pension systems to the Pension Benefit Guaranty Corporation, a government agency that assures payments to retirees when U.S. businesses default on their employees' retirement plans. The program last enjoyed a surplus in fiscal 2001. Last year, it suffered a $23.5 billion deficit.

The pension corporation was created by Congress in 1974 to

ensure that workers who had been expecting pensions from their employees would not be abandoned if companies went bankrupt or otherwise defaulted because of economic setbacks. Although the federal program pays benefits to retirees, they are not as generous as the ones that companies promised.

Currently, the agency is funding benefits to more than 500,000 retirees covered by about 3,500 plans. About 31,200 private pension plans are regulated by it, with the companies paying premiums to the government.

By about 2020, experts estimate, the pension corporation's trust fund will be facing depletion and will no longer be able to fund more bailouts.

President Bush announced earlier this year that he wants to revamp the program. The administration wants to require businesses to increase their contributions to existing pension plan programs so that the plans will have more resources to cover retirement payments.

Bush also wants companies that are not adequately funding their retirement plans or that have poor credit ratings to pay higher premiums to the government in order to ensure the pension board's solvency.

According to Robert Reischauer, the president of the Urban Institute and a former director of the Congressional Budget Office, anything the government does to address problems with the pension corporation "is going to lead companies to drop defined-benefit plans." That is because most solutions would require companies to back up their plans with more resources or would impose more limits on what companies could do when a plan was underfunded. Reischauer noted that most companies are already moving away from traditional, defined-benefit plans and toward defined-contribution plans such as 401(k) funds.

CARING FOR BOOMERS

Added to those problems are rapidly rising and unpredictable medical costs that taxpayers fund through Medicare, the federal health care program for the elderly, and Medicaid, the federal-state health program for the poor.

Long-term nursing home care, which is covered by Medicaid, is a particularly vexing problem. State officials complain that the federal government should pick up more of the costs, because the states can't afford to pay their part of the bill. Federal lawmakers shrug and say they can't afford it either.

Medicare expenses are estimated to climb from 2.6 percent of the nation's gross domestic product (GDP) to 13.6 percent by 2079, according to the intermediate assumptions in the 2005 report by the trustees of the Social Security and Medicare programs. The report was released March 23. In comparison, Social Security benefits represent 4.3 percent of GDP today and are projected to rise to 6.4 percent of GDP in 2079, according to the trustees.

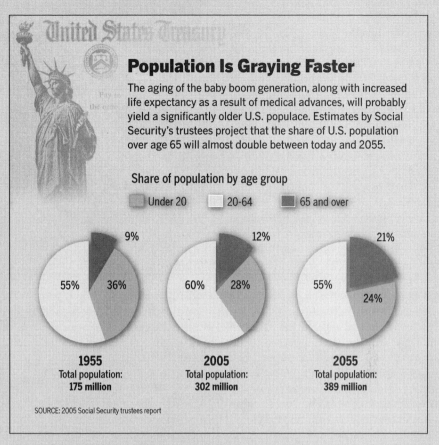

Population Is Graying Faster

The aging of the baby boom generation, along with increased life expectancy as a result of medical advances, will probably yield a significantly older U.S. populace. Estimates by Social Security's trustees project that the share of U.S. population over age 65 will almost double between today and 2055.

Share of population by age group

Under 20   20-64   65 and over

1955
Total population:
175 million
9% · 55% · 36%

2005
Total population:
302 million
12% · 60% · 28%

2055
Total population:
389 million
21% · 55% · 24%

SOURCE: 2005 Social Security trustees report

Medicare's fund for hospital care is expected to run out in 2020, the trustees said. Social Security's account is estimated to be exhausted in 2041.

The cost of caring for low-income Americans through Medicaid is also skyrocketing. Medicaid now is the second-largest expense in most states, after education. In some states, it consumes one-fifth of the budget.

Much of that is due to the cost of long-term care, which will probably spike as the baby boomers age. Medicaid paid for half of all nursing home care in 2002, according to a report by the Kaiser Commission on Medicaid and the Uninsured.

Tackling Medicare and Medicaid costs is more difficult for Congress and the administration than trying to revamp Social Security, however. To make Medicare financially viable for the long term, lawmakers might have to curtail some kinds of care, and they don't have any sweeteners, such as the attraction of personal accounts in Social Security, that might appeal to younger people. The last time Congress addressed Medicare, in 2003, it actually added billions of dollars in new spending and trillions of dollars in long-term liabilities.

Despite the notion that lawmakers could mull over the cluster of retirement challenges as a whole as well as separate spheres, most experts say that they doubt that Congress will take a broader view.

Reischauer says that if Congress cannot deal with one facet of the problem, such as Social Security, it is difficult to envision how it might address larger issues. "We can't agree to eat the chips," he says, "How are we going to agree on the whole enchilada?"

CQ GRAPHIC / YOLIE DAWSON

ers and survivors of deceased ones.

Later, coverage was extended to farm workers and the disabled. In the 1970s, Congress authorized the indexing of benefits to the rate of inflation, making the program financially vulnerable in times when prices grow faster than wages. The expansions have made Social Security the government's biggest and, in some ways, most mystifying program. Few workers, for example, are aware of the arcane formula used to calculate benefits, based on their 35 highest earning years.

Social Security has been buffeted by financial difficulties over the years. The worst came in the early 1980s, when low wage growth and consumer price index increases of more than 10 percent left the pension system close to insolvency.

When Social Security's primary trust fund had only enough reserves to pay about one-and-a-half months of benefits, in 1981, President Ronald Reagan appointed the commission, on which Myers worked, that recommended a series of remedies, including raising Social Security tax rates, delaying cost-of-living adjustments and gradually raising the retirement age from 65 to 67 by 2027. Congress adopted the recommendations in 1983.

In contrast, the notion of creating private accounts for retirement savings is not an especially radical concept for some Americans. Many middle-class and wealthy Americans already save for retirement by investing in securities. Younger workers are skeptical that Social Security will be around long enough to help them in retirement. Bush, fortified by a conservative Congress, has little to lose by tailoring his message to groups such as those.

Increasing the level of private savings could ease Social Security's long-term financing problem by reducing retirees' dependence on guaranteed government benefits. But Bush's advocacy of the accounts goes beyond simple math.

They are emblematic of his concept of an "ownership society," in which individuals have more direct control over their health care spending and retirement savings. He would accomplish that by giving owners of personal accounts the option of selecting from the same type of investment options now available to federal workers under their Thrift Savings Plan: perhaps a half-dozen funds tied to blue-chip stocks, government bonds or international equities. A "default" option would shift a worker's assets from stocks to more conservative bonds over the course of his career.

Personal accounts "provide individual control, ownership and offer individuals the opportuni-

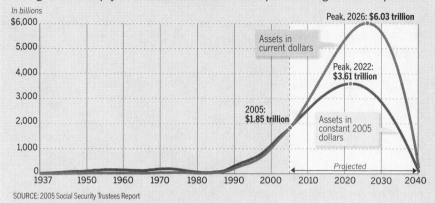

Trust Funds Increase in Value

Social Security's trust funds, which trustees currently project will be exhausted in 2041, have grown since a payroll tax increase enacted in 1983 produced large annual surpluses.

SOURCE: 2005 Social Security Trustees Report

ty to partake in the benefits of investing in private-sector markets," said Mark J. Warshawsky, assistant secretary for economic policy at the Treasury Department. "The only way to truly save for our retirement and give our children and grandchildren a fair deal is with personal accounts."

INTENSE RESISTANCE

One of Bush's arguments to demonstrate the program's long-term troubles is that people should not assume that what they pay in will be there when they retire. The Social Security trust fund, he points out, does not mean the government has collected payroll taxes and let them build up in order to pay benefits when people retire.

"A lot of people think, well, we're collecting your money and we're holding it for you, and then when you retire, we're going to give it back to you," Bush said at a stop in Tucson last month. "That's not the way it works. We're collecting your money, and . . . if there's more money than the benefits promised to be paid in our hands, we're spending it and leaving behind an IOU. That's how it works. It's called a pay-as-you-go system. You pay, we go ahead and spend it."

But program loyalists argue that IOU is at the heart of the Social Security program built in Myers' time. The roots of social insurance extend back to Germany's "Iron Chancellor," Otto von Bismarck, who established the first social security system in 1889 to contend with unemployment in his rapidly industrializing nation and the growth of socialism in Europe at that time. Britain, France, Russia and Japan soon established similar old-age pension programs. But the idea was slow to catch on in the United States, where it seemed at odds with the prevailing ethos of self-reliance during a time of prosperity.

The Depression changed everything. Bank failures wiped out personal savings, and the broader crash of financial markets devastated many industrial and trade union pension plans, leaving workers without accumulated savings. The fallout triggered cross-generational support for a national pension plan.

Myers says the program's designers knew that Congress would periodically have to tweak the system to adjust for changes in wage growth, life expectancy and other variables. He is among those arguing that the system could be fixed with some relatively easy adjustments, short of introducing private accounts. *(System changes, p. 111)*

Resistance to Bush's plan for big changes is intense — and not just from Democrats concerned that the president is intent on dismantling a central pillar of the New Deal. Some moderate Republicans, such as Sen. Olympia J. Snowe of Maine, object to diverting payroll taxes, while Sen. Mike DeWine of Ohio does not support the added government borrowing necessary to pay for Bush's plan.

Such concerns are hardly unexpected, considering the nature of the president's initiative. Bush is proposing to revamp a venerable program that has essentially delivered on all of its promises and kept a great number of senior citizens out of poverty. The Government Accountability Office has calculated that in 2000, 48 percent of Social Security recipients would have lived in poverty had it not been for their benefit checks. Many in Congress believe it is risky to tinker with the government's biggest safety net and that they can afford to wait to make changes.

The unease also stems from the fact that Bush's plan would take effect at a time when globalization, soft wage growth and technological changes are weighing hard on lower-skilled workers, whose jobs are vulnerable to

CQ GRAPHIC / JAMEY FRY

corporate downsizing and U.S. companies' contracting work overseas. Social Security's benefit formula is weighted to pay those individuals more, relative to what they have paid into the system, than wealthier workers. Bush's plan also comes as health care costs are skyrocketing, employers are cutting back on their employees' retirement plans and Medicare is in worse fiscal shape long-term than Social Security. *(Retirement squeeze, p. 62)*

"This administration thinks that you can save for heart surgery and for living to 100," said Laurence J. Kotlikoff, chairman of the economics department at Boston University and author of "The Coming Generational Storm: What You Need to Know About America's Economic Future."

"They're confusing the role of savings and the role of insurance. The government has a role protecting people from adverse outcomes that are not their making," he said, adding that the financial markets can never guarantee that every retiree walks away with a certain benefit the way the government can.

That is because not everybody can win playing the financial markets. Bush's plan puts the onus on individuals to make assumptions about what investments will appreciate over time. And though millions of Americans own IRAs, 401(k)s and other investments tied to stocks and bonds, middle-age and older workers are uneasy about making their retirement savings vulnerable to investment cycles. The establishment of private accounts will erase the progressive nature of the system and, in the view of many, foster a kind of "winner take all" retirement culture built around wealth accumulation.

A CRISIS OR NOT?

Despite the opposition, Bush, guided by his chief political adviser, Karl Rove, is continuing to press the issue. During the nationwide tour, the president and his top aides have avoided characterizing personal accounts as a panacea, saying they will not solve Social Security's financial problems and, at best, will complement, not replace, the traditional government benefit. But he says workers will benefit from taking direct control of their retirement savings.

While Bush talks about his program in the context of fixing Social Security's long-term problems, he acknowledges that individual investment accounts alone won't shore up the program's finances.

To pay for the establishment of the individual accounts and bring the program's books into balance, any overhaul plan that conforms to Bush's principles also will have to include some

AP PHOTO

Status Quo Through the Ages

In its 70 years, Social Security has gained special status with Americans over most government programs — to the point where politicians have often been afraid to tinker with it.

1935: President Franklin D. Roosevelt, above, signs the Social Security Act, placing millions of workers under a federal pension system.

1937: The Federal Insurance Contribution Act requires workers to pay taxes to support the Social Security system.

1939: Congress adds benefits for dependents of retired workers and surviving dependents of deceased workers.

1940: The first monthly Social Security benefit check is paid to Ida Mae Fuller, a retired law clerk in Ludlow, Vt.

1956: Congress adds disabled workers over age 50 to the system. Women become eligible for benefits at age 62 instead of 65.

1961: Men become eligible for early retirement benefits at age 62.

1965: Concern about the health care needs of the elderly prompts creation of the Medicare and Medicaid programs.

1975: Annual cost-of-living adjustments passed by Congress take effect, indexing benefits to the inflation rate. The formula overstates inflation by 25 percent, prompting unnecessarily large payments.

1977: Congress corrects the formula and increases the payroll tax rate.

1982: Inflation rises faster than wages, contrary to projections. Social Security is forced to pay far more in benefits than it takes in through tax collections.

1983: Acting on the recommendations of a bipartisan commission to keep the system solvent, Congress cuts benefits, delays cost-of-living adjustments and

gradually raises the retirement age to 67.

1985: Social Security's trust funds are moved "off budget" so that funds intended for the pension system can be tracked separately from the rest of federal taxes and spending.

1994: Social Security's trustees predict the trust funds will be depleted by 2029, seven years earlier than they had projected in 1993.

1996: The trustees report the system will begin running deficits in 2012.

2005: The trustees project the surge of retiring baby boomers will cause the system in 2017 to begin paying more in benefits than it collects in taxes, absent any changes in current law. Trustees predict the trust funds will be depleted in 2041, absent any changes in current law.

combination of higher taxes, benefit reductions and increased government borrowing.

So far, Congress has avoided deciding what to do about private accounts, preferring to discuss ways to fortify the system's finances. But the Social Security debate ultimately will have to circle back to Bush's personal accounts and address the central question of how much the government should continue to guarantee retirement security.

The White House assumes that personal accounts will generate annual returns in line with the historic return from broad stock market indices, or about 4.6 percent above inflation. But with the economy projected to grow much more slowly in the next half-century, it is unclear whether stocks and bonds will be able to meet those expectations.

Robert Shiller, an economist at Yale University, recently calculated that the median return on Bush's "default" option consisting of stocks and bonds would be 3.4 percent, based on market trends extending back to 1871. That would be barely higher than the return posted by Treasury securities in the existing system. The reason is historically low returns on bonds, the investments Bush would make workers rely on more as they got older.

"The private plan is not a good deal — it's a loser most of the time," said Shiller, who likens Bush's proposal to borrowing money to trade in stocks.

There are other unanswered questions about Bush's plan. One is whether there would be periodic cash drains on Social Security if most account holders were allowed to withdraw their money in lump sums. Another uncertainty is what kind of new administrative burdens the accounts would place on the government and employers. Bush's plan would require more meticulous record keeping because workers' payouts would be directly linked to how much they

sequestered from their payroll taxes.

One compromise under discussion would establish private accounts outside Social Security, using additional government borrowing or some other financing mechanism. The accounts would become an optional savings tool for workers, who could still expect to receive regular Social Security benefit checks.

These "add-on" accounts appeal to many involved in the debate because they would not divert any tax collections from Social Security and would keep the existing system intact. Should Bush decide to compromise and accept the add-ons, he could take political credit for overhauling the pension system.

Administration officials, such as White House chief economic adviser Al Hubbard, have dismissed this option, saying add-on accounts are an easy way out that would not address Social Security's long-term solvency. They continue to press for the inclusion of private accounts within Social Security, saying such a move would reduce dependency on the guaranteed government benefit.

"Add-on accounts would just create a new entitlement program," said Warshawsky, the assistant Treasury secretary, because they would create a new government-subsidized investment option without addressing Social Security's long-term problems.

Participants on both sides of the debate say they believe passage of a Social Security overhaul this year could lead to subsequent rounds of legislation that would further transform the program. Defenders of the traditional system worry that if Bush can push his program through Congress, the focus on accumulating wealth through private accounts will lessen reliance on the guaranteed benefit and weaken political support for the traditional program among middle-class voters.

"If people get, say, $800 a month from the

private account and $200 from the defined benefit, they and their bosses will start questioning why they are paying all this money in payroll taxes and getting so little in return," said Dean Baker, co-director of the liberal-leaning Center for Economic and Policy Research. "You wonder whether they will take another pass at the program and scale back the guaranteed benefit."

Skeptics also question whether Bush eventually would have to cut Social Security disability benefits to pay for the cost of establishing personal accounts. Bush has vowed not to touch those benefits.

House and Senate Democrats for now appear to be embracing the strategy congressional Republicans used in 1993 to oppose Clinton's health care plan. They are simply refusing to negotiate a compromise or offer an alternative plan. But pressure to offer an alternative could intensify if Bush's plan continues to founder and Democrats feel compelled to demonstrate that they want to make Social Security sustainable.

Bush is continuing to urge quick action, saying it is irresponsible of Congress not to shore up the system before the first baby boomers retire.

"This issue is beginning to permeate. People, whether they're sitting on a tractor or anywhere else in society, are beginning to hear the message: We have a problem," Bush told an audience at a community college in Cedar Rapids, Iowa, on March 30.

Myers, who has the perspective of a veteran of past Social Security debates, believes both sides should move cautiously.

"The existing system generally runs well. People get paid a reasonable amount in benefits, and they get paid on time," Myers said. "The problem really is long-term. People shouldn't be pushing the panic button." ∎

Fiercest Fight in Partisan War May Be Over Supreme Court

Democrats hope any nominee will be a moderate, but Bush's actions signal otherwise

Just two hours after Vice President Dick Cheney gaveled the Senate to order for the start of the 109th Congress, Majority Leader Bill Frist stood at his desk and delivered a blunt warning to the chamber's Democrats.

Frist, R-Tenn., all but promised to execute an esoteric parliamentary maneuver known as the "nuclear option" that would change the rules and short-circuit the minority's ability to block floor votes on nominees to the federal bench if Democrats engage in even one filibuster. (*Going nuclear, p. 69*)

"If my Democratic colleagues exercise restraint and don't filibuster judicial nominees, Senate traditions will be restored," Frist said.

The tough talk may have been at odds with the bonhomie that typically prevails on the opening day of a session. But it was symptomatic of the tense partisan acrimony that has developed over the ideological makeup of the federal courts, and over the Senate's constitutional prerogative to offer the president advice and consent on his nominees.

The atmosphere is likely to become even more strained this year as the Senate braces for the first Supreme Court vacancy in more than a decade. Chief Justice William H. Rehnquist, a conservative who is 80 years old and battling thyroid cancer, is widely expected to announce his retirement before the court's current term ends in June. Two other justices — 74-year-old Sandra Day O'Connor, who is often the deciding vote in 5-4 cases, and 84-year-old John Paul Stevens, who has sat on the court for almost 30 years and currently leads its liberal wing — have been the subjects of similar speculation.

Any retirement will set off a series of delicate

Rehnquist, seen in 2003, has been the focus of talk of a court vacancy since his diagnosis of thyroid cancer.

political calculations within the White House and Congress that will dramatically influence what else gets done in the 109th Congress, as well as offer clues about how both parties will deal with future judicial nominations.

"My hope is, with the Supreme Court nomination, the White House understands the dual role" played by the president and the Senate in the confirmation process, said Byron L. Dorgan of North Dakota, Senate Democratic Policy Committee chairman. "If they send us someone who is completely objectionable, we are going to have a big fight."

When a retirement occurs, Bush is expected to fill the vacancy from a short list of about

eight conservative jurists, most of who now sit on federal appellate courts. If Rehnquist retires first, Bush may elevate one of the current justices — the most likely candidates are Antonin Scalia and Clarence Thomas — to chief justice. Democrats would have to decide whether to use the filibuster to block a nominee and test Frist's resolve. (*Possible nominees, p. 71*)

Legal scholars expect that the stakes will be raised when a justice such as O'Connor or Stevens retires first, because that would give Bush an opportunity to change the ideological composition of the court. Replacing Rehnquist with another conservative would not change the court's split on such divisive issues as abortion rights, though it would give opponents of Bush's conservative picks a high-profile forum to air their views.

"If it's Rehnquist, this would be in some measure a dress rehearsal as people get their arguments perfected," said Neal Devins, a professor of government at the College of William and Mary.

TIMING A RETIREMENT

The opening salvo in any Supreme Court battle will be carefully choreographed. Although the high court has studiously avoided giving any hint that the seriously ill Rehnquist will retire, the White House probably already knows the chief justice's intentions. In the past, justices have privately informed the president in advance that they intended to retire.

"Justices typically do that," said Michael Comiskey, a political science professor at Pennsylvania State University. "They often tip the White House."

If Rehnquist does leave, he probably will make an announcement well before June, to

BLOOMBERG NEWS PHOTO / CHRIS KLEPONIS / LANDOV

give Bush time to name a replacement who can be confirmed before the next court term begins in October.

Rehnquist's retirement announcement would be swiftly followed by Bush's nomination to fill his seat. The administration will want to avoid a replay of 1987, when Justice Lewis F. Powell Jr. announced his retirement in late June. President Ronald Reagan quickly tapped Robert H. Bork, an ultra-conservative appellate court judge, to replace Powell, a leading centrist on the court.

But the Democratic-controlled Senate took no action on Bork's nomination until the fall, after the annual August recess. The interval gave liberal activists opposed to Bork enough time to stoke the opposition that ultimately scuttled his nomination in the Senate. *(1987 Almanac, p. 271)*

Beginnings of Confrontation

The next confirmation fight will take place against a political backdrop that has changed substantially in the decade since President Bill Clinton tapped attorney Ruth Bader Ginsburg in 1993 to succeed conservative Justice Byron R. White and appeals court judge Stephen G. Breyer the next year to replace liberal Harry A. Blackmun. *(1994 Almanac, p. 303; 1993 Almanac, p. 318)*

Clinton consulted with Senate Republicans, who were then in the minority, on both of his selections. He was rewarded with smooth confirmations of his nominees, who were seen as ideological moderates.

But after Republicans gained control of the Senate in 1995, they bottled up dozens of Clinton's lower court picks in the Judiciary Committee, in most cases without even giving them a hearing.

Democrats retaliated in the last Congress by taking the unusual step of filibustering 10 of Bush's nominees to federal appeals courts, arguing that they held views that were out of the mainstream or were simply unqualified. Frustrated Republicans made judicial filibusters a prominent campaign issue in several key Senate races in 2002 and 2004, and Bush decried Democratic tactics on the stump during his re-election campaign in 2004. The highest-profile Democratic casualty was former Minority Leader Tom Daschle of South Dakota, who lost his bid for a fourth term in November. *(2004 CQ Weekly, p. 2598)*

Bush will have to weigh competing concerns in deciding who to nominate to the high court. He may be inclined to tap a conservative

in the mold of several of the lower court nominees blocked by the Democrats. That would satisfy the president's socially conservative base, which is credited with helping re-elect him and deliver Republican electoral gains in Congress. In picking a conservative, Bush would also force Democrats to make political calculations about whether and how much to oppose the nomination.

Democrats may view some conservative jurists as more palatable than others. If Rehnquist retires and Bush nominates a middle-of-the-road conservative, such as 4th Circuit appeals court Judge J. Harvie Wilkinson, the confirmation process will probably be relatively easy. Wilkinson, a former law clerk of Justice Powell, is widely respected in legal circles and best known as an energetic opponent of race-based preferences.

"That's the real choice the White House faces here," said David J. Garrow, a constitutional law scholar at Emory University. The Bush administration can put forward a controversial nominee, such as 5th Circuit Appeals Court Judge Emilio Garza, according to Garrow, or the administration can "divide and conquer the Democrats by choosing a reasonable, well-qualified conservative like Wilkinson or [D.C. Circuit Appeals Court Judge John] Roberts."

Added political scientist Comiskey, "People are too quick to assume there will be a major conflict."

A consensus nominee would go a long way toward building the sort of bipartisan comity in the Senate that Bush will need if he wants Congress to enact the major items on his agenda this year, such as an overhaul of Social Security.

So far, though, the president appears to be bracing for a showdown. On Dec. 23, the White House announced that Bush intended to renominate seven of his 10 filibustered appellate court nominees.

That group includes William H. Pryor Jr., whom Bush temporarily installed on the 11th Circuit appeals court in 2004 by using his constitutional authority to appoint judges during Senate recesses. Democrats had opposed Pryor because of his stands on environmental, reproductive and gay rights issues.

Bush's decision to renominate the group angered Democrats, who are likely to block floor votes again on all seven candidates.

"It was a mistake for the president to appoint people who have been duly considered by the Senate and rejected," said Russell D. Feingold, D-Wis., a member of the Judiciary

Committee. "It's not his way or the highway, and that's how the president is treating it."

But Bush may be calculating that the GOP will reap electoral dividends in 2006 when several Democratic senators from states that Bush carried in one or both of his campaigns will be up for re-election. Those lawmakers include Jeff Bingaman of New Mexico, Ben Nelson of Nebraska and Bill Nelson of Florida. The latter two voted at least once in the 108th Congress to invoke cloture and end the filibuster of a lower court nominee.

"A president who looks at the big picture and would like to leave a major legacy is someone who would try to be more conciliatory and would be more likely to compromise," said Sheldon Goldman, a political science professor at the University of Massachusetts at Amherst. "But President George W. Bush seems to be a really high stakes poker player. He's a man who takes risks, and he believes the pay-off will be worth it."

Democrats' Options

Senate Democrats will probably not settle on a Supreme Court strategy before a justice retires. And their appetite for confrontation is not that great. Although the Democrats filibustered 10 of Bush's lower court nominees in the 108th Congress, they voted to confirm 203 district and appellate court judges, or 24 percent of the total, to lifetime terms. *(2004 CQ Weekly, p. 2867)*

Republicans, who say the 10 filibusters were a major reason the GOP increased its Senate majority, are confident that Democrats will forswear judicial filibusters altogether. But so far, Democrats have shown no signs of yielding.

"We will object when on substance we should object," said Sen. Debbie Stabenow of Michigan.

Democrats are insisting that Bush consult with them on any high court picks. In a Dec. 3 letter to the president, Senate Minority Leader Harry Reid of Nevada said the two men should "resolve to be partners in the solemn responsibility of filling vacancies on the Supreme Court."

However, Bush's intention to renominate his filibustered lower court nominees amounted to an implicit rebuff of Reid's overture.

Regardless of the Democrats' resolve to block a few lower court nominees, senators from solidly conservative Southern states would find it politically difficult to oppose — let alone filibuster — Bush's pick to replace the conservative Rehnquist, unless the nom-

Parliamentary Toolbox Full of Options To Renovate Filibuster Rules

There are many parliamentary tactics that Senate Republican leaders might use to thwart the chamber's Democrats from filibustering President Bush's judicial nominees. But they would need an almost unified GOP caucus to pull off any of a series of maneuvers that collectively have come to be known as the "nuclear option."

Majority Leader Bill Frist, R-Tenn., said Jan. 4 that he would resort to such a gambit to force a change in Senate rules if Democrats block a floor vote on any judicial pick. The threat is serious: Such an action would overturn generations of precedent and further polarize the already fractious chamber, hence the apocalyptic moniker.

> *[The president]* shall nominate, and by and with the Advice and Consent of the Senate, shall appoint Ambassadors, other public Ministers and Consuls, Judges of the Supreme Court, and all other Officers of the United States.
>
> — *Article II, Section 2, Clause 2*

Any scenario for thwarting filibusters would hinge on a ruling from the presiding officer — probably Vice President Dick Cheney, who under the Constitution also serves as president of the Senate — that only a simple majority vote is needed either to shut off debate on a judicial nomination or to change Senate rules on such votes. As currently applied, Senate rules require 60 votes to break filibusters against judges — a supermajority that Republicans were unable to muster on a score of occasions in the 108th Congress.

The presiding officer's ruling would then need the backing of at least 50 senators during one or more subsequent procedural votes, assuming all 100 senators were present and voting, and Cheney was on hand to break any ties.

But it is not clear that Frist has the votes. Some veteran Republican senators view such a rules change as a destructive break with the chamber's traditions of decorum. Others believe it might bite the GOP when it next finds itself in the minority.

"We cannot operate like the House," said Sen. John McCain, R-Ariz. "We were meant by the framers of the Constitution to have the minority have influence."

INSPIRED BY HISTORY

Frist and other Republicans complain that Democratic filibusters of 10 of Bush's choices for federal appellate courts in the 108th Congress amounted to an unconstitutional obstruction of the Senate's role to give "advice and consent" on nominees.

"Right now, we cannot be certain judicial filibusters will cease," Frist said on Jan. 4. "So I reserve the right to propose changes . . . and do not acquiesce to carrying over all the rules from the last Congress."

Frist's reference to Senate rules was a signal that he may employ a strategy used in 1975 to change the rules on invoking cloture and ending filibusters generally in the chamber.

But the tactic would run counter to the Senate's tradition as a continuing legislative body. Although elections are held for the entire House every two years, only one-third of the Senate's seats are on the ballot at any one time. And the Senate does not formally adopt its rules anew at the beginning of each Congress.

"Having watched it in practice, I frankly think it's a terrible idea — it is not based on the Senate rules and precedents, it is based on an exercise of raw power," said Robert Dove, an assistant Senate parliamentarian in 1975, who served as parliamentarian from 1981 through 1986 and again from 1995 through 2000.

Under one scenario, if Democrats filibuster one of Bush's nominees, Frist may offer a motion to adopt a new rule — or change existing rules — regarding filibusters of judicial nominees.

The presiding officer in the Republican-controlled chamber would announce that existing Senate rules do not govern such a motion at the beginning of a Congress, and decide that debate on Frist's motion may be ended by a simple majority vote.

Democrats would probably appeal, but Frist could counter by moving to table their appeal, which requires only a simple majority to succeed.

Such a strategy was tested in 1975, when Sen. James B. Pearson, R-Kan. (1962-78), pushed to reduce the Senate's threshold for shutting off general debate from two-thirds of those present and voting to three-fifths of the membership.

Pearson claimed that a simple majority was enough to end discussion on the issue and force a vote on the resolution proposing the rules change. He cited the Senate's constitutional authority to determine its own rules — the same argument that Frist may use.

Pearson ultimately prevailed during a debate that turned angry. But lawmakers who were uneasy about setting a precedent did not vote on the rules change right away and instead negotiated a compromise behind closed doors. The deal dictated that cloture may be invoked to shut off general debate with a three-fifths majority. But the two-thirds threshold was preserved when it comes to ending debate on rules changes. Those rules remain on the books. *(1975 Almanac, p. 35)* inee was deemed substantially more conservative.

Democrats also would be hard-pressed to try to block the prospective elevation of associate Justice Thomas, who would be the first African-American chief justice.

If Rehnquist is the first to retire, Democrats may decide that given all the inherent political risks, it would be better to hold their fire and wait for subsequent confirmation fights.

THE CONFIRMATION PROCESS

Democrats will have a chance to size up any nominee during what promises to be an extensive series of hearings in the fractious Judiciary Committee.

"To assume that some kind of effort like [a filibuster] has to be made is not fair to the president," said Feingold, who observed that his fellow Democrats would not march in "lockstep" at the beginning of the process. "But if there is a disregard for the minority, then discussions like that should be held."

The confirmation hearings will take place

Conservative Majority, Liberals in Dissent

The Supreme Court consists of a sometimes-fragile conservative majority and a fairly cohesive bloc of four liberal-leaning justices. There have been no changes in membership for more than 10 years, but with conservative Chief Justice William H. Rehnquist fighting thyroid cancer and liberal Associate Justice John Paul Stevens nearing 85, a shakeup is inevitable in the near future.
— *Kenneth Jost, The CQ Researcher*

The Conservatives

1: Clarence Thomas
Age: 56
Began Supreme Court service in 1991 (nominated by President George Bush):
Most willing to re-examine old decisions

2: Antonin Scalia
Age: 68
Began Supreme Court service in 1986 (nominated by President Ronald Reagan):
Strongest voice against pornography, gay rights

3: William H. Rehnquist
Age: 80
Began Supreme Court service in 1972 (nominated by President Richard M. Nixon): elevated to chief justice in 1986 (nominated by Reagan):
Crafted shift on states' rights, church-state issues

The Swing Votes

4: Anthony M. Kennedy
Age: 68
Began Supreme Court service in 1988 (nominated by Reagan):
His shift on abortion saved Roe v. Wade

5: Sandra Day O'Connor
Age: 74
Began Supreme Court service in 1981 (nominated by Reagan):
Pivotal vote to uphold racial preferences by colleges

The Liberals

6: Stephen G. Breyer
Age: 66
Began Supreme Court service in 1994 (nominated by President Bill Clinton): *Backs congressional, federal prerogatives*

7: David H. Souter
Age: 65
Began Supreme Court service in 1990 (nominated by Bush): *Strongest voice for church-state separation*

8: Ruth Bader Ginsburg
Age: 71
Began Supreme Court service in 1993 (nominated by Clinton): *Staunch liberal on civil rights, women's issues*

9: John Paul Stevens
Age: 84
Began Supreme Court service in 1975 (nominated by President Gerald R. Ford): *Most protective of rights of suspects, defendants*

Some Potential Supreme Court Nominees

	WHY PRESIDENT BUSH WOULD PICK	WHAT THE CONTROVERSY WOULD BE
SAMUEL ALITO JR. (Judge, 3rd Circuit Court of Appeals) **Age:** 54 **Education:** A.B., Princeton U.; J.D., Yale U. **Residence:** West Caldwell, N.J.	An assistant solicitor general in the Reagan administration, Alito has been nicknamed "Scalito" because of his ideological similarity to Justice Antonin Scalia. Bush has said that he would nominate Supreme Court candidates in Scalia's mold.	Dissenting from the 3rd Circuit's opinion in *Planned Parenthood of Southeastern Pennsylvania v. Casey,* Alito said a Pennsylvania law requiring women seeking abortions to notify their husbands should have been upheld.
JANICE ROGERS BROWN (Justice, California Supreme Court) **Age:** 55 **Education:** B.A., California State U., Sacramento; J.D., UCLA; L.L.M., U. of Virginia **Residence:** Sacramento	One of the most conservative jurists on California's high court, Brown would be the first African-American woman nominated to the Supreme Court.	Brown has drawn the ire of minorities for voting to uphold California's anti-affirmative action law. Senate Democrats filibustered her nomination to the D.C Circuit Court of Appeals in the 108th Congress.
MIGUEL A. ESTRADA (Partner, Gibson, Dunn & Crutcher) **Age:** 43 **Education:** A.B., Columbia College.; J.D., Harvard U. **Residence:** Alexandria, Va.	A former clerk to Justice Anthony M. Kennedy, Estrada's rags-to-riches story has been praised by Bush. Estrada took himself out of contention for a D.C. Circuit seat after Senate Republicans failed seven times in 2003 to shut off debate on his nomination.	Democrats, who have likened Estrada's ideology to that of Justice Clarence Thomas, would reprise their argument against Estrada that his public record is far too skimpy for the Senate to assess his fitness for the federal bench — at any level.
EMILIO GARZA (Judge, 5th Circuit Court of Appeals) **Age:** 57 **Education:** B.A., M.A., Notre Dame U.; J.D., U. of Texas **Residence:** San Antonio	Nominated by President Ronald Reagan to a federal district judgeship in 1988, Garza was later elevated to the 5th Circuit in 1991. If Bush wants to nominate a Hispanic to the first vacancy, Garza is the most likely candidate.	Garza has been openly critical of *Roe v. Wade,* calling it "inimical to the Constitution." He would also face criticism for his skepticism that the Constitution embodies a right to privacy.
EDITH JONES (Judge, 5th Circuit Court of Appeals) **Age:** 54 **Education:** B.A., Cornell U.; J.D. U. of Texas **Residence:** Houston	An avowed conservative, Jones was a finalist for the 1990 Supreme Court nomination that went to David H. Souter. She is an expert in bankruptcy law.	Jones has openly questioned the validity of *Roe,* writing in one opinion that "the facts no longer matter" because the Supreme Court determined the issue of abortion rights "through constitutional adjudication."
J. MICHAEL LUTTIG (Judge, 4th Circuit Court of Appeals) **Age:** 50 **Education:** B.A., Washington and Lee U.; J.D., U. of Virginia **Residence:** Vienna, Va.	A former Scalia clerk, Luttig helped shepherd the Thomas and Souter nominations through the Senate while serving as a Justice Department official in the first Bush administration.	Luttig has drawn fire from women's groups for a 4th Circuit opinion that struck down part of a domestic violence law (PL 103-322). The Supreme Court later affirmed the opinion.
THEODORE OLSON (Partner, Gibson, Dunn & Crutcher) **Age:** 64 **Education:** B.A., U. of the Pacific; J.D., U. of California, Berkeley **Residence:** Great Falls, Va.	As solicitor general during Bush's first term, Olson won most of the cases he argued before the Supreme Court that resulted in a decision. He resigned last year and returned to private law practice.	Olson was confirmed as solicitor general by a narrow 51-47 in 2001, after Democrats charged that he was evasive in describing his role in a private investigation of President Bill Clinton and first lady Hillary Rodham Clinton. Olson represented Bush during the 2000 presidential election dispute.
J. HARVIE WILKINSON III (Judge, 4th Circuit Court of Appeals) **Age:** 60 **Education:** B.A., Yale U.; J.D. U. of Virginia **Residence:** Charlottesville, Va.	A former clerk for Justice Lewis F. Powell Jr., Wilkinson is seen as a conservative pragmatist in the style of his former mentor.	Wilkinson is a staunch opponent of affirmative action. He wrote the 4th Circuit opinion holding that American citizen Yaser Esam Hamdi could be denied *habeas corpus.* The Supreme Court later vacated that decision.

against a background of increasing friction in recent years between the Republican-controlled Congress and the courts. (*2004 CQ Weekly, p. 2148*)

Even Rehnquist commented on those tensions in his 2004 year-end report on the federal judiciary, saying, "Let us hope that the Supreme Court and all of our courts will continue to command sufficient public respect to enable them to survive basic attacks on the judicial independence that has made our judicial system a model for much of the world."

No matter who the next Supreme Court nominee is, he or she is bound to face extensive questioning from the Judiciary Committee on abortion, particularly the high court's 1973 ruling in *Roe v. Wade*, which found that women have a constitutional right to obtain abortions. The two new Republican panel members, Sam Brownback of Kansas and freshman Tom Coburn of Oklahoma, are both staunchly anti-abortion. Chairman Arlen Specter of Pennsylvania is the only panel Republican who supports abortion rights.

A Bush nomination to the high court would be the first by an anti-abortion president since the court ruled 5-4 in a 1992 case, *Planned Parenthood of Southeastern Pennsylvania v. Casey*, to reaffirm the core components of Roe.

Both Ginsburg and Breyer, the only two high court nominees to come before the Senate since Casey, made it clear during their confirmation hearings that they backed the notion that there is a constitutional right to abortion.

The current court is seen as divided 6-3 on the merits of Roe, with Rehnquist, Scalia and Thomas in the minority. But it has been more evenly divided on narrower abortion issues. And in 2000 the court ruled 5-4 against a Nebraska law barring an abortion procedure that critics call "partial birth" abortion.

Despite the fact that Bush's first pick would probably be to replace Rehnquist, the nominee will have to be careful in answering queries about abortion, to avoid alienating senators from both parties who favor abortion rights.

During his 1991 confirmation hearings, Thomas shied from the subject by saying he had never thoroughly examined Roe and did not have an opinion on it.

CIRCUMSPECT RESPONSES

Whomever Bush might name to the high court is likely to be circumspect, perhaps making observations about the court's longstanding wariness toward overturning established legal precedents, particularly its own decisions. The

court hews to the doctrine, known as stare decisis (Latin for "to stand by that which is decided"), to foster stability in the American legal system.

"The nominee may deflect abortion and talk about stare decisis, and that might allow the nominee to walk through," Devins said.

Besides abortion, the members of the Judiciary Committee will probably ask the next nominee about varied contentious topics.

Rehnquist's most enduring legacy will be a series of decisions in recent years that have interpreted parts of the Constitution in ways that have curbed Congress' lawmaking authority in favor of states' rights.

For example, in 1995 the court ruled in *United States v. Lopez* that Congress exceeded its constitutional authority to regulate interstate commerce when it enacted a crime law (PL 101-647) that established gun-free zones within 1,000 feet of schools. In 1997, the court ruled in *City of Boerne v. Flores* that the 14th Amendment did not permit Congress to bar states from enacting laws that interfered with their citizens' First Amendment right of religious expression. (*1995 Almanac, p. 6-40*)

"Federalism and Congress' power under the interstate commerce clause will be bigger issues than they were 10 years ago," Comiskey said.

Social conservatives on the Judiciary Committee, such as Jeff Sessions, R-Ala., and John Cornyn, R-Texas, may probe the nominees' views on religious expression, and on the politically explosive subject of gay marriage.

Last June, the Supreme Court reversed an earlier decision by the U.S. Court of Appeals for the 9th Circuit that the phrase "under God" in the Pledge of Allegiance is an unconstitutional establishment of religion. But the justices reversed the 9th Circuit on technical rather than constitutional grounds. That spurred social conservatives in the House — which has no role in confirming Supreme Court justices — to pass a bill to deny jurisdiction by federal courts over constitutional challenges to the wording of the Pledge. The Senate did not act on the measure.

The court in 2003 ruled in *Lawrence v. Texas* — with Rehnquist in the minority — that homosexuals have a constitutional right to engage in consensual sex.

The broadly written opinion by Justice Anthony M. Kennedy left social conservatives convinced that the justices eventually will rule that a 1996 law (PL 104-199) barring same-sex marriage is unconstitutional as well.

Democrats on the committee are apt to question the nominee about how much legal

leeway Bush should have to imprison people suspected of terrorism indefinitely, without charging them with a crime.

In a series of 2004 decisions, the Supreme Court repudiated the administration's strategy of indefinitely imprisoning alleged "enemy combatants," including U.S. citizens, without allowing them to challenge their detention in court. (*2004 CQ Weekly, p. 1628*)

So far, the Republican-controlled Congress has not moved to exercise its constitutional authority to set "rules concerning captures on land and water," or to rewrite federal law on "habeas corpus" — the right to challenge imprisonment. Legal experts say that congressional action would improve the administration's chances of surviving further legal challenges to its detention policies.

Besides displaying a healthy respect for precedents, the nominee will have several other ways to avoid being pinned down under questioning.

The nominee might tell lawmakers that he wants to avoid pre-judging an issue before being asked to decide upon it as a justice. That tactic would be particularly successful if the nominee lacked a published record on the subject.

The nominee might also back away from a record as, for example, a state attorney general by arguing that he was acting according to the wishes of a superior, such as a state governor. Justice David H. Souter made that argument to deflect questions about his record as New Hampshire attorney general.

No matter how recalcitrant a nominee may be — and how frustrated lawmakers may become by responses to his questions — he probably would not be derailed for ducking questions. Ultimately, even the most chagrined senator will be forced to back down out of respect for the traditional view of judges as independent arbiters of the law.

SPECTER AND INTEREST GROUPS

The Judiciary Committee hearings will be gaveled open by Specter, the newly minted chairman of the panel.

Senate Democrats had hoped they would have a de facto ally in Specter, who possesses one of the most liberal voting records among Senate Republicans.

But those expectations changed Nov. 3, when Specter remarked at a post-election news conference that "when you talk about judges who would change the right of a woman to choose, overturn *Roe v. Wade*, I think that is unlikely."

At the Center of Any Supreme Court Fight

A handful of senators and White House officials will choreograph the nomination process for the next Supreme Court nominee. With relations in the Senate already frayed by battles over lower court nominees, Republicans and Democrats will vie for the rhetorical high ground and decide whether and when to use parliamentary maneuvers to their advantage.

Harry Reid: Liberal activists are confident that the Nevada Democrat, who succeeded Tom Daschle of South Dakota as minority leader, will not hesitate to lead his party's opposition — and perhaps even filibuster — of a Bush Supreme Court nominee. Reid has said he prefers to work with Republicans rather than fight them. But so far, the White House appears to be resisting his overtures to cooperate on judicial nominations. Reid has vowed to retaliate if Republicans move to short-circuit Senate rules on filibusters of judicial nominees.

Bill Frist: The Tennessee Republican and Senate majority leader has threatened to change the chamber's rules and lower the threshold for ending debate on a judicial nominee from three-fifths of all senators (60) to a simple majority. Frist almost certainly would attempt to make the change if Democrats block a Bush Supreme Court nominee, arguing that Senate rules do not automatically carry over to the 109th Congress. Democrats are likely to remind Frist that he supported a filibuster in 2000 against Richard A. Paez, President Bill Clinton's nominee to the 9th Circuit U.S. Court of Appeals.

Arlen Specter: The new Senate Judiciary chairman is a Republican moderate from Pennsylvania who favors abortion rights. Specter triggered fiery criticism from social conservatives for implying after the November elections that the Senate would not confirm a Supreme Court nominee who openly favors overturning *Roe v. Wade*. In order to claim the Judiciary Committee gavel following the criticism, Specter pledged to speed Bush's nominees through the committee, even if he did not agree with some of their views. And he hinted he may back Frist in a move to change Senate rules on filibusters. Specter voted against conservative Supreme Court nominee Robert Bork in 1987, but aggressively grilled Anita Hill during Clarence Thomas' 1991 Supreme Court confirmation hearing.

John Cornyn: Although he has only been in the Senate for two years, the Texas Republican and former state Supreme Court justice has become a leading conservative voice on judicial nominations. He is likely to be a prominent defender of a Bush Supreme Court nominee. Cornyn rose to political prominence in Texas a few years before President Bush, and the two became close political allies.

Richard J. Durbin: From his seat on Judiciary, the Illinois Democrat and new Senate minority whip was a leading critic of several of Bush's lower court nominees in the 108th Congress. Durbin would help lead his party's questioning during confirmation hearings on a Supreme Court nominee. And as Reid's successor as whip, Durbin will assume an even greater role devising strategy during floor debate.

Patrick J. Leahy: A liberal from Vermont, the ranking Democrat on Senate Judiciary has become a favorite target of criticism from GOP activists who are frustrated by Democratic filibusters of several of Bush's lower court nominees. Leahy will play a prominent role in confirmation hearings on a Bush Supreme Court nominee, and probably would press any nominee to reveal his or her position on several issues, including abortion. Leahy will continue to help lead opposition to seven Bush lower court nominees whom Democrats filibustered in the 108th Congress and whom Bush has said he will nominate again this year.

Harriet Miers: Tapped by Bush to succeed Alberto R. Gonzales, the White House counsel-designate is likely to help prepare any Bush Supreme Court nominee for the Senate confirmation process. She is called a "trusted adviser" by the president and currently serves as assistant to the president and deputy White House chief of staff. Miers has held prominent positions in several law firms.

His comments triggered intense criticism from anti-abortion social conservatives and ultimately forced Specter to make a public pledge to move Bush's judicial nominees through the committee quickly, regardless of his own position on the nominee. Specter also signaled that he is unlikely to oppose anyone Bush nominates to the Supreme Court.

The Pennsylvania Republican, who cherishes his reputation as one of the few mavericks in the Senate Republican Conference, has bristled at the suggestion that he sacrificed his independence to claim the Judiciary gavel. But although Specter has made it clear he wants to be consulted on Bush's selections, it remains to be seen whether he will play a major role in nominations, except to shepherd them through his committee. *(p. 27)*

Conservatives have distrusted Specter ever since he voted against confirming Bork in 1987. Their assessment did not change even after Specter aggressively questioned Anita Hill after she made allegations of sexual harassment against Thomas while the Senate was considering his nomination.

"His great apostasy is that he voted against Robert Bork, and for that the right wing will not forgive him," said political scientist Goldman.

Specter and the rest of the Senate will be buffeted by conservative and liberal activists alike, who will vociferously support or oppose any Bush nominee.

AFTER BORK

The modern era of activism around Supreme Court nominations began with the Bork fight in 1987, when liberals mobilized to defeat the nominee. The clamoring from activists on all sides will be even more intense for the next confirmation.

In December 2004, People for the American

> ❝ **If they send us someone who is completely objectionable, we are going to have a big fight.** ❞
>
> — Sen. **Byron L. Dorgan**, D-N.D.,

Way, a liberal lobbying group, launched a $2 million fundraising drive for a "Supreme Court Defense Fund." Ralph Neas, president of the group, sent an e-mail to supporters urging them to "help us prepare for a battle we know how to win."

Paul M. Weyrich, chairman of the conservative Free Congress Foundation, says his organization has a "judicial coalition" of hundreds of groups around the country that is ready to stoke public opinion and pressure wavering senators.

Religious conservatives, who claim a great deal of credit for Bush's re-election, are prepared to lobby for a Bush nominee who they hope will oppose abortion rights and gay marriage. "Believe me, it's going to crank up like never been seen before," said Weyrich, who also serves on the executive committee of the Arlington Group, an informal coalition of religious activist groups.

Nevertheless, lobbying by outside activists will probably have only a limited influence on senators as they decide how to vote on Bush's first nomination to the high court. Neither Bush nor Senate Democrats want to be seen as beholden to outside groups.

If the first fight is over Rehnquist's successor, it will be more difficult for liberal activists to persuade their Democratic allies to block the nomination. Bork's nomination was thwarted not only because of his conservative views, but because he was named to replace a centrist justice.

"Where the fight will come in is when a liberal dies or steps down and where the vote on abortion would change," Weyrich said. "I think that is when [both sides] go all out."

Liberal activists say the chief justice's seat is important because that person chairs the private conferences the nine justices hold to discuss cases. Depending on whether he is in the majority or the minority on a decision, the chief justice has the right to assign the relevant opinion. He also handles administrative duties for the court.

But in terms of confirming a replacement for a retiring justice, the more salient issue for the Senate will be whether the court's ideological lineup is shifting.

"My view is that the chief is just the first among equals," Comiskey said. "What really matters is whether the justice who is retiring is one of the swing voters.... The more important issue is how much the particular vacancy is likely to affect the composition of the court." ■

Politics and Public Policy

The articles in this section highlight key issues on the public agenda in early 2005 and the steps the government is taking to address them. These polarizing topics range from how to balance the ever-growing deficit to how to regulate steroid use among professional baseball players. Congress in particular has taken a greater interest in weighing in on new policy issues, especially ones that have historically been outside its domain.

The first selection focuses on the Pentagon's plan to reorganize and strengthen the U.S. Army. The war in Iraq has revealed the Army's need for more soldiers, better training and equipment that can withstand desert climates. Despite dropping retention rates, the Defense Department hopes to restructure the Army quickly to bolster its efforts in Iraq and the war on terrorism. However, the cost may mean cuts in funding for the Air Force and Navy.

The next three articles focus on current fiscal policy. Although budget experts have repeatedly warned that the government's spending is "unsustainable," Republican politicians continue to push for tax cuts, while those already implemented have left state and local governments without revenue to fulfill their spending obligations. Economists recommend economic neutrality to cure the current tax code of its complexities and the system's tendency to promote consumer spending and discourage investing.

The fifth article investigates how lawmakers are responding to recent claims that the FDA hastily approved certain drugs—namely, Vioxx and other popular painkillers—before considering the results of studies claiming that the medicines could potentially double patients' risks for heart attacks and strokes. Public health advocates want to know whether such lack of oversight indicates a broader problem in the agency's methods and mindset.

The next article examines illegal immigration and its financial impact on state and local governments. Illegal immigrants boost business by accepting low-wage jobs but simultaneously cause increases in public spending on education and health care—costs that cities are not prepared to meet. This dichotomy is forcing Congress and the Bush administration to look for ways to balance the benefits to business with the costs to taxpayers.

The seventh and eighth contributions explore new frontiers in law and justice. Congress recently launched unprecedented investigations into long-term health care (the Terri Schiavo case) and steroid use in major league baseball. Critics contend that lawmakers are exploiting news headlines to advance a predominantly conservative agenda and demand that Congress demonstrate appropriate jurisdiction. Meanwhile, the Supreme Court has agreed to hear cases about file-sharing and Internet piracy that pit the entertainment industry against the technology companies whose products enable users to exploit copyrighted material. A court decision is expected in summer 2005.

The final two articles focus on social welfare topics relating to older adults. The first evaluates the two major approaches to "fixing" Social Security: modest tweaks, such as increasing the retirement age, versus a complete overhaul. For the moment, Medicare, which some lawmakers argue is in even greater need of reform, has taken a backseat to the Social Security debate. The Medicare trust fund has already begun paying out more than it takes in, whereas Social Security is not projected to run out of money until sometime after 2019. The last article in this section tackles the looming Medicare problem, which according to critics, illustrates the U.S. government's inability to prioritize the nation's problems.

Shaping a Modern Fighting Force

Can Rumsfeld's transformation plan succeed without permanently increasing the number of troops — and is there time to do it before the next conflict erupts?

THE ARMY THAT DASHED UP the Euphrates Valley in 16 days to capture Baghdad in 2003 was invincible in its speed and overwhelming firepower. But when its mission slowed to one of occupation — patrolling city streets and plodding through crowded neighborhoods — the Army became vulnerable to insurgents.

Vehicles that had raced largely unscathed across the desert were later targeted by crude roadside bombs in Iraq's cities and towns, their crews hunted by snipers. Soldiers found themselves scavenging rusty steel plates from dumps to fortify their vehicles, calling it "hillbilly armor." And when the Pentagon sent

CQ Weekly Feb. 28, 2005

heavier trucks, the insurgents just planted bigger bombs.

Every war requires adjustments by those who fight it: new tactics, training and weapons. But the changing nature of the conflict in Iraq — from a Blitzkrieg invasion to a two-year insurgency — has caught the Army out of step and left the Defense Department scrambling to regain its balance.

It has become increasingly clear that the Army the United States went to war with is not the Army it needs to quell the rebellion in a country of 25 million people.

The danger is that the Iraq conflict will sap the Army's strength at the very time it is needed to wage a global war on terrorism that could drag on for decades. The Army has been worn thin across the globe, with the majority

of its brigades deployed overseas and more than half of them in Iraq.

Moreover, its equipment is wearing out under Iraq's harsh desert conditions. The Pentagon has run up billions of dollars in maintenance bills that it has put off for now but eventually will have to pay.

At the same time, recruiting and retention rates have Army officials nervous, as the casualty lists from Iraq have grown. Long months of active duty have made service less attractive in the reserves, which now provide 40 percent of U.S. forces in Iraq. The commander of the Army Reserve writes that they are "rapidly degenerating into a 'broken' force" that will be unable to fulfill its mission.

There is no question that the Army will have to change substantially to manage both its

WEAPONS HUNT: Members of the U.S. Marines search for arms caches and ammunition in Ramadi, an Iraqi insurgent stronghold.

ERIK DECASTRO / REUTERS / LANDOV

role in Iraq and the broader war on terrorism. But as Congress, the White House and the Pentagon confront these issues, they are finding that any changes in spending, organization and military doctrine will involve trade-offs and risks.

If the Pentagon puts more money into the Army, it will have to cut funding for the Navy and Air Force, weakening those services. Non-combat soldiers who retrain for jobs in the infantry may not be so effective in their new combat role. Under a new force structure, smaller combat teams risk losing the tactical expertise and leadership training that larger units have traditionally provided. And a new focus on fighting Iraq-style, low-intensity conflicts could jeopardize the Army's ability to wage higher-intensity wars.

Defense Secretary Donald H. Rumsfeld and Army Chief of Staff Gen. Peter J. Schoomaker have begun a major reorganization, emphasizing smaller units, more infantry and special-operations forces, and moving specialists from

the reserve into active duty — all without permanently increasing the size of the Army.

Their plan is to shift about 100,000 sol-

"We're doing exactly what we need to do. The only thing I want to do is do it faster."

— Gen. **Peter J. Schoomaker**, Army chief of staff

diers to new positions within the Army over the next few years. "This is monumental," said Gen. Richard A. Cody, the Army's vice chief of staff. "It's the largest change in the

Army since the 1930s."

To help pay for the changes, Rumsfeld wants to take money away from the Air Force and Navy, the glamour services of the past two decades with their aircraft carriers and fighter jets. The modest shift in funds, according to Army experts, reflects the reality that in the Iraq occupation and future guerrilla wars, boots on the ground matter more.

Many within and outside the military do not agree with Rumsfeld's plan. Some lawmakers and their states have a stake in the weapons systems he wants to scale back or change. Others think the United States should simply increase the size of its Army, not just reorganize it. Still others think it would be a mistake to revamp the entire service because of one war.

And as retired Maj. Gen. Robert Scales, a former commandant of the Army War College, says, Rumsfeld's plan might not go far enough.

"If you believe that Iraq and Afghanistan are harbingers of the future, that we're going to be fighting radical Islam for decades if not

Plan Calls for a Faster, More Flexible Army

Reorganization plans

MORE SOLDIERS . . .

Fiscal 2004:
482,400 soldiers required by law

By the end of fiscal 2006:
512,400 soldiers, under emergency authority

. . . AND MORE BRIGADES

2004:
Total brigades: **33**

2006:
Total brigades: **43**

KILL ZONE: U.S. snipers hone their shooting skills at a firing range outside of Baghdad.

SOURCE: Department of Defense; Congressional Research Service

Retraining plans

The Army plans to retrain more than 100,000 of its soldiers — or about 10 percent of its active duty, National Guard and reserve forces over the next few years. The idea is to take soldiers whose specialties are less in demand these days and teach them the kinds of skills they will need in Iraq, Afghanistan and possible future conflicts. In the past two years, 34,000 such moves have occurred.

PEOPLE TRAINED IN:	ARE BEING RETRAINED IN:
Field artillery	Infantry
Air defense	Military police
Engineering	Civil affairs
Armor	Intelligence
Logistics	Transportation
	Petroleum and water distribution
	Psychological operations
	Biological detection

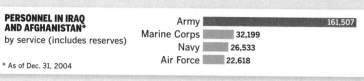

PERSONNEL IN IRAQ AND AFGHANISTAN*
by service (includes reserves)

* As of Dec. 31, 2004

Army	161,507
Marine Corps	32,199
Navy	26,533
Air Force	22,618

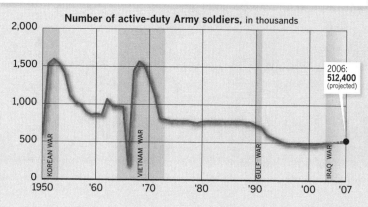

Number of active-duty Army soldiers, in thousands

2006: **512,400** (projected)

KOREAN WAR   VIETNAM WAR   GULF WAR   IRAQ WAR

1950   '60   '70   '80   '90   '00   '07

---

a century, then you cannot continue with the apportionment of the defense budget the way it is. As much as I love the Navy and the Air Force, they do not play in this style of war. They never have."

THE ARMY THEY HAVE

The Army was already playing catch-up to some extent when the war began. Troop levels and spending on future weapons systems were relatively low. After the 1991 Persian Gulf War, then-Defense Secretary Dick Cheney cut the active-duty force from 780,000 soldiers to 480,000 — a 38 percent drop in troop strength. With its soldiers preparing to invade Iraq in the spring of 2003, the Army had to find an extra $10 billion just to buy the necessary equipment.

Following the invasion, with Iraqi resistance to the U.S. occupation growing, the Army found it did not have enough foot soldiers to patrol restive cities and towns. Month after

month, the Pentagon shuffled troop rotations, called up more National Guard and reserve units, kept badly needed soldiers from leaving the service, and shifted some from South Korea, in the process reducing the number of ground forces in a potential trouble spot.

Many of the soldiers scheduled to return home from Iraq after a year or more of fighting were told to stay put, and deployments in some cases stretched as long as 15 months, taxing soldiers mentally and physically.

Conditions on the ground were not the lightning-fast war that troops had trained for, and the resistance to the occupation became steadily more determined.

"During one particular event, the terrorist detonated an [improvised explosive device], injuring a soldier," according to a May 2004 Army study. "Knowing his comrades would be quick to respond to the injured troop, he waited for additional soldiers to show up and

detonated a second explosion, which produced multiple injuries. These methods have a large psychological effect on troops."

The same study found that some soldiers were woefully unprepared to act as peacekeepers in a strange land, fighting insurgents while trying to win friends among the local population. Strong-arm tactics such as detaining family members of suspects, destroying their houses and firing on cars that tried to run checkpoints might be good military tactics, the study said, but they risked alienating the populace.

Some soldiers have adapted to their new role. When raiding a mosque, for example, some troops will cover their boots with plastic surgical booties to respect the Muslim practice of removing shoes before entering a place of worship. And if a cleric is arrested, soldiers are told to notify the Ministry of Religious Affairs so a replacement can be found quickly.

Equipment problems have been equally frus-

PHOTO COURTESY OF THE U.S. ARMY; GRAPHICS / JAMIE BAYLIS

trating. Most Army officials agree they were caught flat-footed on several items essential to fighting a counterinsurgency war. For example, in May 2003, when President Bush declared an end to major combat operations, the Army was producing only 15 Humvees a month fitted with extra heavily reinforced armor on the assumption that it would need only 235.

But ground commanders had gravely underestimated the threat of improvised explosive devices buried in roads. Before the invasion, rocket-propelled grenades were the most feared and presented a formidable threat to forces. But the roadside devices became the weapons of choice for most insurgents because of the anonymity they provide. The enemy can hide several yards away and quietly detonate the bomb using a garage door opener or other rudimentary trigger, before disappearing into a crowd. The blasts, which tear through the Army's thin-skinned Humvees and trucks, are responsible for the deaths of half the more than 1,400 U.S. soldiers killed in Iraq so far.

By October 2004, ground commanders called for about 8,100 of the more protected Humvees, and production soared. The Army expects to meet the requirement by April.

THE ARMY THEY WANT

Rumsfeld's hopes for remodeling the Army are in the hands of Schoomaker, a 59-year-old former Special Operations commander. Rumsfeld brought the four-star general out of retirement to replace Gen. Eric Shinseki, who reportedly fell out of favor with the Defense chief after telling Congress that the Army would need "several hundred thousand" troops to occupy Iraq.

Schoomaker and Rumsfeld oppose any permanent boost in overall troop strength, though they are enacting a temporary increase of 30,000 in order to give the Army maneuvering room necessary to carry out other personnel changes. Part of the increase would be accomplished by a practice called "stop loss," which keeps soldiers from leaving the service even if their commitments are finished.

Schoomaker has said that in the future the Army is more likely to be fighting "conflicts" than "wars," and his plan is to organize the force around smaller, more "modular" combat teams that would fight more efficiently and maneuver themselves on the battlefield with less reliance on divisional headquarters.

Because the Army must be able to battle a major force one day and scout out terrorists in a foreign city the next, Schoomaker says these combat teams would use a sophisticated network of sensors and radios to move quickly across the battlefield and to be plugged into any fight. Rather than lugging as much artillery as brigades have in the past, the teams would rely upon the Air Force and Navy for cover.

Meanwhile, Schoomaker has initiated an effort to retrain soldiers to fill empty slots needed in Iraq. To manage post-combat operations there, commanders on the ground wanted more military police officers, interrogators, linguists and civil affairs soldiers, and fewer artillerymen, air defense troops and ordnance soldiers. Many of those needed specialties could be found in the National Guard and reserve, but the units were under heavy strain from repeated deployments. So Schoomaker began what he called "rebalancing" the force.

Among his first moves was retraining a brigade of National Guard artillerymen into military police officers. Last year at Fort Leonard Wood, Mo., Tennessee National Guard artillerymen who had been trained in handling 155-mm howitzers were taught the art of managing large crowds and other police duties.

The Army also embarked on new training programs to teach soldiers how to fight counterinsurgency warfare. Every soldier will be trained for what the Army calls a "360-degree battle space," meaning a war with no front line. That includes learning how to survive ambushes and roadside bombs.

Schoomaker also has adjusted the Army's long-term procurement plans so that more money will be available for current equipment and supplies. Last year, Schoomaker restructured or adjusted 126 programs to "address immediate wartime needs," said an Army "posture" statement released in February.

One of those changes was to the Army's Future Combat System, which is envisioned as a massive "system of systems" involving 18 types of manned and unmanned vehicles and aircraft linked by a sophisticated communications network. The program, launched in 2000, was widely considered too complex and unrealistic, in part because of the more than 30 million lines of software code that experts say will be needed to link the systems together. Last July, Schoomaker announced that the service would not equip its first brigade with every component of the new system until fiscal year 2014 — two years later than previously planned.

At the same time, Schoomaker wants the Army to make use of some elements of the system as early as possible, and some of the advanced networking technology should be available by 2008.

Using a mix of diverted resources and emergency wartime supplemental dollars, the Army is also playing catch-up in equipping a force battling the insurgency in Iraq. That means paying for the heavily armored Humvees and more aerial reconnaissance drones, as well as replacing helicopters and vehicles destroyed in combat. Units have been established to cut through procurement bottlenecks to get new technology, such as robots that can explore caves or disable explosive devices, to soldiers in the field.

The Army's big challenge, Schoomaker says, is time. In recent congressional testimony, he compared his situation with that of Army Chief of Staff George C. Marshall early in World War II, when he said the war's urgency gave him the money he needed, but didn't give him the time. Before the war, there was little money but all the time in the world.

"The goodness here is that we're able to use the momentum of this great operational tempo . . . and leverage this additional money we're getting through supplemental dollars to get to do this change much more quickly," Schoomaker said in a recent interview.

"I'm very confident that between now and [2007], we'll have our head and shoulders through the portholes," he added.

OPPOSITION FROM WITHIN

All change comes slowly to the Army, the largest, oldest and most important military service because it is the only one that can occupy and hold territory for any length of time. Skeptics of the Rumsfeld-Schoomaker reorganization plan worry that changing the service by making its units lighter and more maneuverable risks its effectiveness in future conflicts. At the same time, the stresses that the Army is suffering in Iraq, left unrelieved, might also do serious harm to a military service the country relies on.

"We have an administration that believes that the old way of waging war is gone for good, that the future is about space, it's about unmanned vehicles and it's about the network," said Loren Thompson, chief operating officer of the Lexington Institute, a national security think tank, and a consultant to defense industries.

"[Administration officials] might be right," Thompson said. "But if they're wrong, the Army is not correctly postured."

Many officers and members of the broader defense community are reluctant to part with the Army's organization and its traditional role as an irresistible juggernaut based on infantry, artillery and 70-ton tanks. Some experts said they worry that the brigades will prove too light for conventional land warfare, or "high-intensity combat."

"If you ever actually got in a real war where you were taking casualties, you would grind through these things pretty quickly," said James Jay Carafano, a retired Army officer and defense analyst at the conservative Heritage Foundation. "They're not terribly robust."

Retired Col. Douglas A. Macgregor, whose 1997 book "Breaking the Phalanx" called for reorganizing the Army into smaller, more mobile combat groups, says he is not happy with Schoomaker's approach, which he calls too "light on armor, light on firepower and heavy on wishful thinking."

Macgregor, who was shunned by Army leaders during his tenure because of his blustery approach, said Schoomaker's twist on his proposal mistakenly assumes that better intelligence, high-tech communication systems and speed on the battlefield can replace in large measure the Army's offensive and defensive might.

"There is no evidence that information is a substitute for armor and firepower," he said. "They're cutting combat power and reducing capabilities to get more pieces to move around."

Other experts say an increase in the Army's size might be inevitable. The Pentagon's plan to boost the service's capability through design, not numbers, is too idealistic, they say, and can't immediately fix one of the toughest challenges for the Army: a lack of foot soldiers.

"The root problem in the Army is that it doesn't have enough infantry," said retired Lt. Gen. Jay Garner, former director of the Pentagon's Office of Reconstruction and Humanitarian Assistance in Iraq.

Though Schoomaker's retraining plan will increase the number of infantry soldiers, it is difficult to bring them up to speed on new skills, Garner said.

"It's taking a good carpenter and telling him to be a plumber," he said. "You just don't take people with years of experience in the Army and give them a whole new skill."

Max Boot, a senior fellow at the Council on Foreign Relations, estimates that infantry makes up only about 4.6 percent of the entire active-duty military, with about 51,000 infantry soldiers in the Army and 20,000 in the Marine Corps.

"I think we need more than 30,000 [additional] soldiers, even if [the Army] makes it permanent," said Boot. "I don't know of any defense expert who doesn't agree. Fundamentally, you need to increase the size of the Army."

The cost of the Pentagon's refusal to build a permanently bigger Army could be the loss of valuable soldiers, whose repeated deployments wear down families, said retired Gen. Dennis J. Reimer, the Army's chief of staff under President Bill Clinton. "You can't keep going back to the well three or four times. . . . You've got to take care of them," Reimer said. "Once you start to lose them, it happens quickly, and it's hard to reverse."

Some military experts also question the wisdom of Schoomaker's plan to shift the focus away from the Army's divisions, which act as incubators for future leaders. Unlike a brigade, which is typically focused on the day-to-day operations of a military campaign, divisions can plan three to 10 days in advance, which can prove invaluable in warfare. Further, divisions are known in the Army to grow senior-level officers who become skilled in the art of executing war.

"I'm not against having more brigades," said Garner, also an advocate of a bigger Army. "I'm against getting rid of the divisional force structure."

Army officials downplay these concerns. The retraining of soldiers to increase the size of the infantry, for example, is on track and has met with little resistance from soldiers who understand that the Army is changing and needs a new mix of skills, they said in recent interviews.

And Schoomaker's overall plan follows the direction in which the Army has been headed since the collapse of the Soviet Union: a leaner organization with better technology and lighter weapons and equipment to make it nimbler.

Schoomaker says his reorganization plan will still produce valuable leaders by retaining several division-based headquarters — smaller than today's divisions, but managed by general officers who will work alongside joint task forces to "leverage" the firepower of the other military services. That in turn will reduce some of the burden on Army troops, he said.

"We're doing exactly what we need to do," Schoomaker said. "The

only thing I want to do is do it faster."

The Pentagon's fast-moving plan comes with a price, of course, and restructuring the Army for the war on terrorism will be a budget battle as much as anything else.

A POCKETBOOK ISSUE

The Pentagon squeezed $38 billion — equal to about half the Army's annual budget — into its new six-year budget plan to pay for Army reorganization alone. The administration plans to fund another $10 billion through emergency supplemental bills. According to a senior Army official, Rumsfeld considered the fiscal 2006-11 budget only after ruling out cuts to Schoomaker's modularity plan. Accordingly, the Air Force and Navy bore the brunt of the $30 billion in net budget cuts that Rumsfeld wants to make, in part to pay for the Army plan.

Although substantial, the cuts reflect only 1 percent of the annual wartime defense budget, which now reaches a half a trillion dollars.

But even this modest redirection of funds has triggered criticism from the industries and lawmakers affected by them. Senators worried about their local shipbuilding industries, including Republican John W. Warner of Virginia, the chairman of the Armed Services Committee, inveighed against the plan at hearings this month. And House Republicans questioned the rationale for cutting the Air Force's F/A-22 Rap-

OCCUPATION DUTY: American soldiers race to the scene of a July 14 car bomb explosion in the Iraqi capital. Such bombs, along with improvised roadside charges, are responsible for half of the more than 1,400 U.S. military deaths in Iraq so far.

AP / KHALID MOHAMMED

Taking a Lesson From Wars

U.S. military doctrine has evolved significantly over the past century in response to the lessons learned from America's wars. Here is a breakdown of the major military conflicts, the lessons learned, and the new strategies and tactics they spawned:

In Iraq, the emphasis is now on lighter units and dismounted infantry to fight the insurgency.

World War I. Frontal infantry attacks against fixed positions defended by machine guns don't work. ● Submarines are effective weapons against enemy shipping. ● Chemical weapons are ineffective because shifting winds can result in friendly casualties.

World War II. Coordinated attacks by massed air forces and mechanized ground forces are effective. ● Fixed defenses don't work against mobile forces. ● Air power is paramount against military and economic targets. ● Possession of an atomic bomb is critical for superpower status.

Korean War. Only low-level, all-weather bombers can penetrate the enemy's radar defenses. ● Large numbers of trained and equipped military reserves are needed for sustained fighting. ● Military preparedness should not be allowed to slip in interwar years.

Vietnam War. The Powell doctrine is formulated during the first Bush administration by Joint Chiefs of Staff Chairman Gen. Colin L. Powell, who had been a young major in Vietnam. The doctrine states that the United States should use overwhelming military force only as a last resort; only where the national interest is clearly involved; only when there is strong public support; and only in the likelihood of a relatively quick, inexpensive victory. National will can be more decisive than military force.

Persian Gulf War. U.S. military power can defeat any conventional force. ● Better technology is needed to connect all units to an electronic virtual battlefield to improve coordination and avoid friendly fire casualties.

U.S. forces relied on heavy armor during Persian Gulf War.

Kosovo Campaign. In certain cases, air power alone can achieve battlefield goals. ● NATO must enhance all aspects of its defense capabilities.

Afghanistan. In some cases, U.S. Special Forces working with local anti-government forces can bring about regime change.

Iraq War. Rejection of Powell doctrine in favor of new doctrine of pre-emptive war. ● Combination of heavy armor and air power remain an effective war fighting strategy. But during an extended military occupation, emphasis should be on lighter and smaller counterinsurgency forces.

Sources: National Defense University

REUTERS / AKRAM SALEH / LANDOV, TOP: AP / SADAYUKI MIKAMI, BOTTOM

tor warplane program, which has already cost billions of dollars in research and development.

Further, lawmakers say, the $48 billion price tag for the Army's reorganization probably won't be the end of it. Ike Skelton of Missouri, the ranking Democrat on the House Armed Services Committee, who is considered one of the Army's staunchest allies on Capitol Hill, recently called the Army's reorganization project "audacious," and he added that "a syn-

onym for audacious is 'risky.'"

Meanwhile, not all lawmakers are buying Rumsfeld's contention that he can recast the Army to fight the wars of the 21st century without permanently increasing its size. Those members of Congress do not necessarily oppose the reorganization; they just don't think the plan will be enough to reduce the strain on the Army. Lawmakers worry that the stressful deployments will eventually break the force if

more troops aren't added to the payrolls.

Congress, in fact, wrote an increase of 20,000 troops into the defense authorization law enacted last year and added money to pay for it, but Schoomaker was already planning his temporary boost of 30,000. He and Rumsfeld have asked Congress not to make the increase permanent, explaining that only about 10 percent of the Army's 1.2 million soldiers in the active force, National Guard and reserve are

Urgency Driving Army Line Item

REORGANIZING THE ARMY around smaller combat units in order to fight the wars of the future is expected to take several years and cost at least $48 billion. Rather than risk a long congressional debate on the plan, however, the Pentagon is trying to pay for the first two years worth of transformation – $10 billion – through emergency supplemental appropriations for the war in Iraq.

Even those who don't agree with this budgetary end run admire the Pentagon's savvy in proposing it.

NEW ARMY FAN: Change is needed to fight 21st century wars, Cordesman says.

"I have to say in a way if I were the secretary of Defense I might be tempted to try this, too," says Gordon Adams, an associate director of the Office of Management and Budget during the Clinton administration, who nevertheless does not support funding long-term needs through supplementals.

The administration's decision to put $5 billion for the Army's reorganization into President Bush's $81.9 billion supplemental spending request underscores the view held by some military experts that transforming the Army is too urgent a task to risk the delays and pitfalls of the regular budget process.

Anthony H. Cordesman, a military expert at the Center for Strategic and International Studies, a nonpartisan defense and foreign policy think tank, argues that the Army – in part because of poor budget planning and a lack of forceful lobbying on Capitol Hill – is not the force it should be to fight 21st century wars. He maintains that this transformation is an urgent task that cannot wait for a contentious budget debate in Congress this year.

"You have immediate, real-time requirements that are being validated in the field in Iraq and in Afghanistan; you're not talking about long-term theory in force transformation or future combat systems," Cordesman says. "Essentially, what we're doing is playing catch-up with the fact that the Army's force structure did not change quickly after the Cold War."

Under the initiative, the Army has begun reorganizing its combat brigades into more numerous but smaller combat teams that will be less tied to a divisional headquarters than in the past. They will come in three standard variations based on the type of equipment they use.

The Pentagon phrase for this is "modularity." The White House is proposing to fund the program through emergency supplementals in fiscal 2005 and fiscal 2006, before incorporating it into the president's annual budget request in fiscal 2007.

Several Democrats and Republicans call the maneuver a budgetary subterfuge; by taking the reorganization funding out of the budget baseline, they say the White House can ensure quick passage while pretending to restrain defense spending. "The regular appropriations bill obviously also will be enacted," said Steven Kosiak, defense budget analyst with the Center for Strategic and Budgetary Assessments. "They want to present a defense budget top line that looks like it is showing some restraint."

At a Senate Armed Services Committee hearing Feb. 17, Defense Department comptroller Tina W. Jonas said the Army wants to reorganize the 4th Infantry Division (Mechanized) by September. "We could have waited and put them in the base line budget," Jonas said, but Army Chief of Staff Gen. Peter J. Schoomaker "suggested that it was urgent, and I think we agreed."

Defense analysts say the White House strategy should insulate the reorganization funding from the fiscal trade-offs of the regular budget process. "It's hard to raise money to do this kind of thing," said Adams, who is now a professor of international affairs at George Washington University. But everyone knows the supplemental "is going to go through, because nobody is going to say I didn't support America's men and women overseas." If lawmakers were to consider the funding during the fiscal 2006 budget process, it might well be put on the chopping block with other items in the Army's operations and maintenance account. "This is the Peter they rob to pay Paul," Adams says.

Air Force Gen. Richard Myers, chairman of the Joint Chiefs of Staff, acknowledged as much at the Feb. 17 hearing. The reorganization, he said, was still being refined. "To insert those large numbers in the '06 budget with the uncertainty surrounding them, would've perturbated a lot of the '06 budget," Myers said.

To Cordesman, delaying or cutting the reorganization program should not be an option. "I think the chief of staff of the Army would argue, and with great justice, that it was needed a decade ago and when you have men and women dying in the field the urgency, I think, is fairly obvious."

deployed in Iraq at any one time.

"The problem is less the number of soldiers in the Army and more that the Army was poorly organized and has been unable to draw on all the forces it has for missions abroad," Rumsfeld told lawmakers this month.

In addition to skeptical lawmakers, the Army's plan has other obstacles to face. Lifting the "stop loss" orders might unleash a mass exodus from the Army. And just as funding spiked in the past to fuel the nation's previous wars, budgets tend to dry up once war ends. Experts call it the "natural law" of defense spending.

"If we come out of Iraq and we say, 'We're

out of Iraq, let's cut back on defense spending because we have to balance the budget,' then we'll be back in the hollow force," said Carafano of the Heritage Foundation.

The potential decline in spending takes on new meaning in light of Iraq and the toll it takes on equipment. Vehicles and aircraft there are operating at a rate five times higher than those used in training, according to Army officials.

Until now, the Army has deferred maintenance on equipment still being used in Iraq. But at some point, officials say, the 8,100 heavily armored Humvees, trucks, tanks and aircraft that were sent to Iraq will have to be

repaired. Based on the service's experience in the 1991 Persian Gulf War, Schoomaker expects that the Army will need at least two years and billions of dollars to repair all the equipment. Some in Congress say the repair bill could run as high as $17 billion.

If Congress doesn't provide extra dollars through more supplemental bills, the Army might be forced to pay for the looming "bow wave" of maintenance costs on its own. In that case, it might have to draw funds from high-priority modernization programs such as the Future Combat System.

Schoomaker says he isn't concerned about

PHOTO COURTESY OF CENTER FOR STRATEGIC AND INTERNATIONAL STUDIES a lack of funds and has vowed support for the Future Combat System and other modernization programs, insisting that they are vitally important to the future Army.

"This business of how we resource our armed forces has got to be rethought," he told lawmakers, so that Army leaders are not "digging ourselves out of foxholes every time we've got a need for something."

In any event, "I don't lose any sleep over it," Schoomaker said in an interview. All he needs

> **"It's the largest change in the Army since the 1930s."**
>
> — Gen. **Richard A. Cody**,
> Army vice chief of staff

is some breathing room to get the job done. "Just hide in the bushes and watch," he said.

Despite his insouciance, Schoomaker's success in completing the Army's restructuring also depends on events that are out of his control, such as an unexpected flare-up in the Middle East or some other part of the world.

If the Army were to leave Iraq and go into Iran, "it would be a huge crisis" because the force would be too worn down, said Garner, who retired in 1997 as the Army's assistant vice chief of staff. "I don't think the Army could take it." ∎

Save a Skeptical Eye For Deficit Dance

Dire warnings about the nation's red ink aren't backed up by an appetite for action

IT'S BUDGET SEASON in Congress. And one might conclude from newspaper headlines, the odd business news release and testimony on Capitol Hill that there is growing sentiment for reining in the federal deficit and trying to achieve a balanced budget — or even a surplus. Consider:

• Federal Reserve Chairman Alan Greenspan won front-page attention earlier this month when he told the House Budget Committee that the federal budget is on an "unsustainable" course.

• The Business Roundtable, an association of about 150 chief executive officers of U.S. corporations, issued a policy statement in December saying the administration and Congress should "take a disciplined approach toward achieving a balanced budget."

• Comptroller General David M. Walker, who heads the Government Accountability Office, the closest thing the federal government has to an auditor, has repeatedly complained that the deficit, and entitlement programs in particular, must be addressed. "Absent meaningful changes to these programs, the nation will ultimately have to choose among persistent, escalating federal deficits, huge tax increases, and/or dramatic budget cuts," he told the House Ways and Means Committee last week.

But even with all that firepower behind the notion of fiscal responsibility, lawmakers are mostly engaged in an annual minuet where the dance steps make it seem they are moving in one direction, but in the end, the procession heads the opposite way.

For Republicans, this ritual involves casting themselves as the party of deficit hawks, but also making sure their tax-cut agenda isn't

derailed. Democrats who want to tar their opponents for profligacy have to endorse budget actions that in no way indicate a predilection for cutting programs that might actually offend a single registered voter.

The budget resolutions under consideration in the House and the Senate bow toward trimming the deficit — just as President Bush delivered on his promise of proposing a budget that reduces the deficit for fiscal 2009 to half what it is today. All accomplish their aims by refusing to account for certain costs or presuming that some tough choices aren't really so difficult.

In fact, there is precious little appetite in Washington for serious deficit reduction. And while public interest may be picking up, ordinary folks aren't ready to storm the Capitol. In fact, when pressed on specific needs, most Americans would have the government spend more, not less — and they don't want to pay higher taxes, either.

A January opinion poll by the Pew Research

CQ Weekly March 14, 2005

Center for People and the Press ranked the deficit as ninth out of 23 important national issues that ought to be addressed — lower than improving the nation's schools, fixing Social Security and Medicare, or solving the problems of the poor. So while politicians are apt to mention the deficit from time to time, there are reasons not to expect any significant movement this year. Here are the main ones:

TAX CUTS ARE THE PRIORITY

When Republicans took the reins on Capitol Hill in 1995, they hinged their party identity to the idea of balancing the budget. That meant a year of trench warfare with President Bill Clinton, who landed a triumphant re-election victory and a big share of the credit for bringing the budget into surplus in 1998.

When Bush took office in 2001, however, Republicans seized on that surplus to underwrite their true mission: cutting taxes. Conservative voters were enthralled and energized by a succession of tax cuts enacted in 2001, 2002, 2003 and 2004. Bush's re-election campaign was all about tending to the conservative base. And tax cuts remain on the agenda to keep that base happy for the 2006 congressional elections.

The recently enacted tax cuts all expire eventually, but few do so in the next year or two. Still, the budget resolutions will probably make possible later votes to extend several popular tax cuts beyond their scheduled expiration dates. As for the idea that Congress will make a few modest tweaks to tax law to generate deficit-reducing revenue, forget it.

THE DEFICIT ISN'T SO BIG

Democrats crow with every new budget estimate that the deficit has

DEFICIT WARNING: Current spending, Greenspan says, is unsustainable.

JAY MALLIN / BLOOMBERG NEWS / LANDOV

grown to an all-time high. That may be true in dollar terms, but it is a misleading complaint. In fact, economists would rather measure the deficit by the ability of the country to borrow enough to finance it. That means gauging it in relation to the size of the gross domestic product (GDP) — the sum of all goods and services produced by the economy, and a good proxy for national income.

Using that yardstick, the deficit is not expected to reach the levels experienced in the early 1990s, when economic worries and market pressures demanded action. In that period, the deficit ranged between 3.9 percent of GDP and 4.7 percent. But for fiscal 2004, the deficit — which was a record $412 billion in nominal terms, amounted to just 3.6 percent of GDP.

That's higher than most economists would say can be sustained without impairing growth. But both the White House Office of Management and Budget, and the Congressional Budget Office project that the deficit would fall below 2 percent of GDP by 2007 under Bush's budget.

Unless the deficit rises as a share of GDP — and with the economy expanding at or above its historical annual growth rate of 3.5 percent — nominal budget shortfalls won't force Congress to change course.

WALL STREET DOESN'T CARE

In 1993, when the economy was struggling to recover from the 1990 recession, Wall Street clamped a vise on Clinton and his congressional allies, pressuring them to work to control a deficit that appeared to be headed out of control. Things are different today.

"I don't ever hear about it any more, to tell you the truth," said Jim Glassman, senior U.S. economist for J.P. Morgan Chase. "Despite the long-term budget picture being the way it is, it's not an issue in the markets."

Interest rates are the principal reason: They are historically low. There is no easy way to correlate movements in interest rates with changes in the budget balance, but there are no signs that the deficit is pushing rates higher. Many things affect U.S. interest rates. Chief among them is economic growth, both nationally and globally, which alters demand for credit in much bigger ways than does a rise in borrowing by the federal government.

The yield on 10-year Treasury notes, the benchmark for everything from fixed-rate mortgages to long-term borrowing by corporations, is about 4.5 percent — below where it was in 2001, the year of the biggest federal

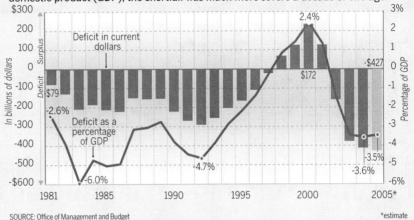

How Big Is the Deficit?

The U.S. government has run deficits for most of the past quarter-century, with the only exceptions being fiscal 1998-2001. Never has the deficit been as large in dollar terms as in the past several years. However, when measured against U.S. gross domestic product (GDP), the shortfall was much more severe a decade or two ago.

SOURCE: Office of Management and Budget

*estimate

budget surplus. The current yield is just a half percentage point above the 4.01 percent average for 2003, the lowest in 40 years.

Rates are low in part because foreign investors are buying Treasury securities faster than the government can sell them. International demand can cut two ways, but most bond market traders see little chance that overseas investors will dump their holdings or even slow their purchases much. If they do, domestic demand is expected to pick up the slack.

THERE'S NO POLITICAL COST

Politicians rarely lose their jobs because the deficit gets too big. Ross Perot contributed to the re-election defeat of President George Bush in 1992 by making the budget deficit a proxy for his competence — or lack thereof — in running the government. But Bush had also reneged in 1990 on his "read my lips" pledge not to raise taxes.

Clinton lost his congressional majorities after brokering a deficit-reduction deal in 1993 that was laden with tax increases.

But consider the Republican victories in the 2002 congressional elections and their impressive gains at the polls last November, which came after the administration replaced record budget surpluses with record deficits.

The bigger political cost often comes when members vote to impose sacrifices in the form of higher taxes or program cuts. Even the modest trims in farm subsidies, defense or Medicaid envisioned by Bush's budget are reminding lawmakers of the pain involved in trying to

reduce spending. Congress will try to force those or similar cuts into law using the budget reconciliation process, which protects program cuts and tax increases from a Senate filibuster. But altogether they might reduce the deficit by $40 billion over five years.

That's a lot of trouble for a comparatively small gain. And changes in economic performance can quickly change the revenue picture more than that amount. In fact, the fiscal 2005 deficit — which was supposed to exceed the record $412 billion shortfall in fiscal 2004 — may turn out to be smaller. The accumulated deficit for the first five months of the current fiscal year is $5 billion less than a year ago, Treasury Department figures showed last week.

WHAT AREN'T WE COUNTING?

There's one more reason not to expect big momentum for deficit reduction anytime soon. Congressional budget math is very fuzzy. The debate will be about a "baseline" and spending expectations, but it will fail to account for the cost of military actions in Iraq and Afghanistan. And it will ignore the future costs of overhauling the Social Security system or changing the so-called alternative minimum tax, a parallel tax structure that is beginning to bite the middle class, which it was never intended to affect.

All of those will add costs to the bottom line that won't show up until the books are tallied after the next fiscal year ends Sept. 30, 2006.

People who are really concerned about the deficit will be watching that space. ■

CQ GRAPHIC / YOLIE DAWSON

Code Words: Tax Neutrality

Building a fairer, more balanced tax system is a goal of many economists, but bringing the politicians aboard requires them to take away the candy dish

If you drive a car, I'll tax the street
If you try to sit, I'll tax your seat
If you get too cold, I'll tax the heat
If you take a walk, I'll tax your feet
— George Harrison

IN 1966, THE BEATLES sang a musical lament about the 95 percent top income tax rate levied at the time in Britain and the way the tax system seemed intended to thwart every incentive to work and enjoy life.

CQ Weekly Feb. 7, 2005

No disrespect to Harrison, but the song could have been written by an economist.

The lyric resonates still in 21st century America, where we pay almost 30 percent of national income in combined taxes to the federal government, to the 50 states, and to city, county and regional authorities. Although rates here are nowhere near as high as they were in Britain four decades ago, the tax system is nonetheless reviled for its complexity, its perceived inequities, and the way it distorts the economic choices.

Paying taxes has always been a

sore point here. Just ask King George III.

Or ask George W. Bush, who made cutting taxes a hallmark of his first term as president.

Now Congress and the country are girding for the next round in the national debate over taxes, and a central point of contention is not just whether the U.S. imposes too heavy a tax burden. That question has been front and center since Bush moved into the White House in

104 Years of Taxes

Federal and state taxes as a share of national income soared from about 6 percent in 1900 to about 30 percent for the period from 1969 through 2000. Total taxes have fallen since, to just under 28 percent of income in 2004.

SOURCE: Tax Foundation

INCOME TAX IS BORN:
In 1913, Congress enacted the first modern income tax law.

◄ **WAR COSTS:** Taxes rose after the United States entered World War I, and then declined. U.S. entry in World War II pushed taxes above 25 percent of income for the first time.

Effective state tax rate
Effective federal tax rate

Percentage of national income
35%
30
25
20
15
10
5

1900   1910   1920   1930   1940   1950

January 2001, and for now has been decided in favor of a deep reduction in the amount the American people hand over to the government to pay for all manner of services.

As Bush sets out to overhaul the federal tax code, many economists would like the debate to focus on how to structure the system so that it doesn't favor one activity over another.

That is a big idea that sometimes goes by the name economic neutrality. These days many of its adherents complain in particular that the tax code encourages consumption and discourages investment. They want to reverse that.

"It's a worthy goal to not have the tax system determining where investment flows or who spends how much for what," said Alice Rivlin, a senior fellow at the Brookings Institution in Washington. She served as director of the White House Office of Management and Budget under President Bill Clinton and later as vice chairman of the Federal Reserve.

Nowadays, Rivlin said, the tax code is riddled with special treatment of one sort or another. "It would be better from an efficiency point of view, from an economic growth point of view, to get rid of a lot of the provisions and lower the rates," she said.

But most economists caution that although economic neutrality is a nice goal in theory, achieving it will be difficult, if not impossible.

That's because politicians always want to give away "candy" to favored constituencies, in the words of Kevin A. Hassett, an economist at the American Enterprise Institute and an advocate of shifting the tax burden onto consumption and off investment.

"The whole idea of tax theory is that you try to design a tax program that has as little distortive effect as possible," Hassett said. "Since the code has never looked like that, there's lots of room for mischief."

For a brief moment almost two decades ago, the federal tax code resembled a more economically neutral document.

Politicians and economists alike pay homage to the 1986 Tax Reform Act, the only tax law anyone can recall being universally blessed with the sobriquet "reform." That law was touted mostly for its attempt to "simplify" the code, but it would just as well have met the test of making tax law more economically neutral.

It wiped scores of special tax breaks off the books to broaden the base of taxable income, and tax rates were cut dramatically. Reduced tax rates had the effect of lessening the value of the few remaining deductions, yet the tax system still raised as much revenue as before.

"Every once in a while we have a major reform like 1986, but those are rare," said William A. Niskanen, chairman of the libertarian Cato Institute in Washington.

EQUAL TAXES?

Limiting the ways the tax code distorts economic behavior is, of course, not the only issue that will affect the coming debate, particularly in the eyes of politicians.

Before Congress votes on any "reform" proposal — presuming the debate gets that far — the same fundamental issues that always arise in the political tug of war over taxes will also be aired: Is the proposal equitable to all, and does

it meet the longstanding goal of making the system "progressive," so that those of greater means bear a greater share of the cost? Will the tax code become less complex, or will "reform" add to its already complicated nature? Will it raise sufficient revenue, or is this a back-door move to trim the size of government by curtailing receipts?

On. Jan. 7, Bush signed an executive order creating a nine-member advisory committee to come up with ideas to rewrite federal tax laws. By July 31, the panel is supposed to give its "revenue neutral" options to the Treasury Department. The goal is for the Bush administration to embrace one of the options and forward it to Capitol Hill.

Bush's executive order bows to some political concerns by calling on the panel to find ways to simplify the law and to "share the burdens and the benefits of the federal tax structure in an appropriately progressive manner." But it also singles out home ownership and charitable giving as activities the tax code should reward — as it does now.

That opens the door to complexity and favors, and may limit the possibility for wholesale change.

From time to time, the tax code has become so overloaded and complex that Congress has

NEW DIRECTION: President Bill Clinton signed a deficit-reduction bill in 1993 that along with the booming economy sparked a steady rise in the national tax take. President George Bush reversed that course with a series of tax cuts in 2001, 2002, 2003, and 2004.

POLITICS: Taxes rose after President Lyndon B. Johnson signed the Medicare and Medicaid law in 1965, and fell slightly with President Ronald Reagan's tax cut in 1981.

Effective state tax rate

Effective federal tax rate

1960　1970　1980　1990　2000　2004

had to strip it down and start over, Hassett said, endorsing the notion of a 1986-style overhaul. "It could be about time for that 20 years later."

So far, though, the history of tax cuts in the administration does not bode well, Niskanen said.

"In 2001, Bush went in with a proposal to reduce the number of tax brackets from five to four. He ended up with six, and more complications in the code," Niskanen said. Then, in 2004, Congress enacted a corporate tax cut bill, only a small part of which was necessary, he said. "The rest of it was all candy for different parties."

Niskanen, who was acting chairman of President Ronald Reagan's Council of Economic Advisers just before enactment of the 1986 law, recalled two years of effort to sell politicians on that comprehensive overhaul of the code.

Noting that the effort was headed for the trash heap after tax writers in both chambers had larded the bill with special-interest provisions, and that it took a pitcher of beer at the Irish Times pub in Washington to give Senate Finance Chairman Bob Packwood, R-Ore., the courage to scrap the existing code and take away the candy dish, Niskanen said he doubts there will be real reform this time.

"We won't rewrite the code," he said. "We'll have another incremental step."

TAXING CONSUMPTION

Those who began the current debate — chiefly residing in the right wing of the political spectrum — say the tax code favors consumption over savings and needlessly stifles economic growth to no good purpose.

Most want to eliminate, or at least severely limit, tax on investments and instead tax consumers for the money they spend. At their most optimistic, some analysts say shifting to such a consumption tax might add a trillion dollars a year to the $12 trillion U.S. economy by stimulating new investment.

"You can really do miraculous things with tax reform," Hassett said.

Most economists agree that if such a change could be made in a way that was perceived to be equitable and progressive, it would bring economic benefits. But politically, it is tough.

While some have called for eliminating all taxes on stock dividends and capital gains from the sale of assets, many, particularly those on the political left, say such a plan is decidedly unegalitarian: The burden would be placed entirely on workers, and wealth alone would be rewarded.

"These are theological questions," said Clint Stretch, director of national tax policy in Washington for the accounting firm of Deloitte &

Ten Most Expensive Federal Tax Breaks

In billions of dollars for fiscal 2005-2009

Tax Break	Amount
Exclusion of employer pension contributions and earnings	$567.8
Exclusion of employer contributions for employee medical care	493.7
Mortgage interest deduction on owner-occupied residences	434.2
Reduced rates of tax on dividends and long-term capital gains	356.8
Tax credit for children younger than 17	231.7
Exclusion of capital gains at death	215.6
Earned-income tax credit	195.0
Deduction for state and local taxes	185.8
Deduction for charitable contributions	169.3
Exclusion of income on life insurance and annuities	145.0

SOURCE: Joint Committee on Taxation

Touche. "Economic equality and efficiency are often arguments advanced to support the conclusion you have already reached," he said.

There are many ways to tax consumption, including scrapping the income tax system and imposing a national retail sales tax, or a so-called value-added tax, such as those in Europe, where a tax is imposed at every stage of production. Such direct taxes on consumption have some fans. But they are inherently "regressive" and impose a disproportionate burden on poor people, unless the system is further complicated by a system of rebates.

But there are ways to unencumber investment that may have appeal across the aisle.

Hassett, for instance, argues that job losses and trade concerns are easy levers to promote reduced taxes on investment. "If multinationals want to locate plants in low-tax jurisdictions abroad, you can't stop it without lowering the cost of investment here," he said.

Rivlin and Niskanen served presidents of different parties and very different political philosophies, yet each sees merit in a so-called "progressive consumed income tax," one that gives taxpayers incentives to set aside a portion of income as savings.

"If we had a tax code that taxed consumption progressively, it would be a better tax code," Rivlin said. "Liberals or people who care about fairness to low-income people are concerned about consumption taxes. A consumed income tax is a different matter," she said.

The math for such a tax is relatively simple: Subtract from current income any amount added to savings and pay tax on the rest.

"You don't want to cut taxes on savings from prior income — the Democrats have a legitimate beef on that," Niskanen said. "You've got to be careful in the design of the proposal and the rhetoric used to describe it."

In the last several decades, the tax code has already moved in this direction with the creation of individual retirement accounts and company-sponsored 401(k) plans.

But retired people or those close to retirement would not benefit from such a wholesale shift in tax policy. Rivlin suggests phasing in the change to address the generational disparity. Taxpayers would be allowed to calculate what they owed using both the old system and the new system, and pay whichever total was less. "But that would complicate the tax code for a couple decades," she said.

THE TAX BURDEN TODAY

If Congress does start to take seriously the idea of taxing consumption and encouraging investment, the subject of the tax debate will shift abruptly for the public.

For most Americans, the attention is on how much we pay, and little else. Congress has enacted a score of major tax laws in the past three decades. With the one exception of 1986, the debate was always over how much to cut taxes or how much to raise them.

Collectively, we Americans work until mid-April every year to pay all the taxes we owe to all levels of government — before we start earning a dime for ourselves, according to the Tax Foundation, a nonpartisan group that has been studying the U.S. tax system since 1937.

Perhaps the remarkable thing is that in the United States the tax burden remained relatively flat at about 30 percent of national income for generations, essentially capped by the shared political judgment that enough is enough. Most tax cuts and increases had a relatively small effect on overall collections, although the consequences for individual taxpayers were often quite large.

Then came 2001, and the burden started falling. Over the past four years, Congress has enacted tax cuts worth about $2 trillion over the next decade. Those cuts have already pushed down the tax burden to a point not seen in generations.

The first time total U.S. taxes crested over 30 percent of national income, in 1969, was — perhaps coincidentally — the first federal budget surplus year in a decade. The Tax Foundation's analysis shows that, for the next three decades, the tax burden stayed very close to 30 percent, falling as low as 28.6 percent in 1971 and rising as high as 33.6 percent in 2000. That year was not-so-coincidentally the third of four successive federal budget surpluses, the biggest on record and the longest string since Herbert Hoover was president.

In fact, the share of national income collected in taxes rose each year of the Clinton administration, and has fallen every year Bush has been in office. For 2004, the Tax Foundation estimates, the tax burden declined to 27.8 percent, the lowest in 37 years. That was also the year of a record budget deficit of $412.3 billion. The group will report its estimate for 2005 in early April.

State taxes are also falling as a share of income, though it is the federal government's share that has shown the most marked decline: down to 17.9 percent of income in 2004, the lowest since 1949.

State and local governments collected 10 percent of income in taxes last year, the smallest amount since 1986, in part because most state income tax systems are closely linked to the federal code.

That may pose a long-range problem for states that are also increasingly picking up costs from the federal government. "The base has been eroded in the federal code, and that erodes their base," Niskanen said. "They'll need to find new sources of revenue."

LARDING THE TAX CODE

Economic neutrality is an esoteric concept and a subject rarely raised during political discussions of tax policy. That's in part because politicians and economists tend to view the world in different ways.

"There is tension between economic discussion and one of moral values," said Deloitte's Stretch. "On the individual side of the tax code, efforts to strengthen the country socially outweigh economic neutrality and economic efficiency."

> ❝It's a worthy goal to not have the tax system determining where investment flows or who spends how much for what.❞
>
> — Alice Rivlin,
> senior fellow, Brookings Institution

Economists are quick to find fault with even the most politically popular provisions of tax law. Take the deduction for interest paid on home mortgages. It is the third most expensive tax break in federal law, costing $434.2 billion in forgone revenue over five years, according to the Joint Tax Committee of Congress. Home ownership has soared to where less than a third of all U.S. households are renters.

"We made a national decision to foster home ownership and made mortgage interest deductible," Rivlin said. But, she added, "there are reasons why the current way of doing that isn't very fair. It's of greater advantage to high-income taxpayers, and I don't think people intended that."

Rivlin favors capping the amount of interest that can be deducted and not indexing that amount for inflation. Eventually, "it would just go away," she said.

Hassett, who called the mortgage interest deduction "the most growth-defeating distortion" in the code, offers the same prescription for change as Rivlin. "To eliminate it would have a negative effect on home building, but probably not prices," Hassett said. "It's possible that's politically feasible."

The second most expensive so-called tax expenditure is for health insurance bought by companies for their workers. Companies deduct what they pay, and employees don't have to count it as income. The provision will cost $493.7 billion over five years and is the "most egregious" in Niskanen's book. Not only is it seen as a distortion because it penalizes people who don't have company-paid coverage, but health policies are favored because other insurance isn't marketed through the workplace.

Hassett singles out the $1,000 child tax credit, enacted in 1997 and expanded in 2001, as a subsidy with no clear economic purpose. It may serve to satisfy a political or social justice motivation, he said, but it doesn't provide an economic incentive or improve efficiency. "Maybe social justice can be served a better way," he said.

POLITICAL IMPERATIVE

It is not clear when, if ever, Congress might take a crack at wholesale changes in tax law. Two other initiatives are ahead of it: overhauling Social Security and making permanent the temporary tax cuts of the past four years.

Both will be hugely expensive, in political and financial terms. And Bush made clear in his State of the Union address Feb. 2 that those are his priorities — not reforming the tax code from top to bottom.

If Bush's advisory committee does produce a plan for streamlining and retooling tax laws, what its recommendations will look like and whether there will be a political constituency for them are likewise difficult to predict.

Proponents of a major change, such as Hassett, hope for a serious menu of options, but panel members already have indicated they will limit their proposals to two or three.

Niskanen laments that the nine-member committee is heavily weighted with politicians, led by two former senators, chairman Connie Mack, a Florida Republican, and vice chairman John B. Breaux, a Louisiana Democrat. It contains only one economist who is an expert in tax policy: James Poterba, of the Massachusetts Institute of Technology.

"A move toward a consumption-based tax is desirable and largely acceptable to Congress, even Democrats," Niskanen said, ever hopeful.

But he's also realistic that the timing is not good. "We'll get a political judgment from the commission," he said. "It will be nothing as comprehensive as the '86 reform."

For Rivlin, the role Bush plays will tell the tale. "There's always a chance," she said. "But tax reform is complicated, and it would be hard to pull off, even if you had a president who wanted to take a thorough tax reform and push it forward." ■

Revenue Down

Tax cuts have put states and the feds in a tighter box

JUST FOUR YEARS AGO, federal and state tax revenues were surging. Those fat coffers fueled a budget windfall that — combined with lawmakers' budget-balancing efforts — resulted in four consecutive years of federal surpluses and plenty of black ink at the state level.

That now seems a rather distant memory. After the demise of the Internet boom and four consecutive years of tax cuts, federal and state tax collections have dropped to the lowest levels in decades, when measured as a share of total national income.

Before the decline, the combined state-federal tax burden on Americans had held for three decades at about 30 percent of income. At the moment, that figure stands at 27.8 percent, according to the Tax Foundation — the lowest in 37 years.

While the economy will boom again, few analysts expect a re-emergence of the heady days of the late 1990s. And that raises serious questions about whether the tax system can provide the money needed to finance national, state and local government commitments into the future.

"There are not enough revenues out into the future to pay for what are the best estimates of spending," says Eric M. Engen, a resident scholar at the conservative American Enterprise Institute. "This isn't a budget problem that's going to go away."

Some conservatives do not view this as a "revenue problem" — instead, they see a need to cut spending and dramatically reduce the size of government.

But many politicians on both sides of the aisle say that given what voters expect of the state and federal government in terms of services, the fiscal situation is unsustainable.

According to the nonpartisan Congressional Budget Office (CBO), sharply rising health care costs, combined with the coming retirement of the baby boom generation, means that Social Security, Medicare and Medicaid will soon rise significantly as a share of total federal spending, and will outpace revenues.

In short, Congress and the White House

CQ Weekly Feb. 7, 2005

soon will be compelled to decide between "reducing the growth of federal spending, increasing taxation, boosting federal borrowing, or some combination of those approaches," CBO states in its January 2005 budget and economic update.

NOT SUFFICIENT

Maya MacGuineas, director of the New America Foundation's fiscal policy program and co-founder of Centrists.org, a think tank and Internet site that advocates "bipartisan policy making," argues that neither the federal nor state tax systems are sufficient to provide the revenue called for by voters, and that both are badly in need of review.

"What's truly troubling is that both in the short term and in the long term, the relationship between what we want to spend and what we want to pay for government is completely broken down," MacGuineas says.

Some conservatives and centrists suggest that the shortfalls expected in the not-too-distant future are too large to be fixed by tax increases — that there is, in fact, a limit to the tax burden that state and federal lawmakers can place on Americans.

Tax revenue projections are a tricky game; they have undergone a roller coaster ride in the past several years. In January 2001, at the height of the Internet boom, the CBO predicted that the federal government would take in $2.57 trillion in tax receipts in 2005.

But four years later, the CBO is projecting receipts of $2.06 trillion — a $510 billion decline.

Congress and the president are responsible for about 41 percent of the difference, according to CBO figures. Since 2001, there have been four rounds of GOP tax cuts that reduced expected tax collections by about $2 trillion over 10 years. About 59 percent of the change stems from economic and so-called technical factors. The recession that took hold in 2001 stunted economic growth and the incomes of dot.com millionaires that had kept the Treasury flush with cash in the late 1990s. In addition, the inability to forecast a falloff in revenue associated with the stock market further led to

a lower revenue projection.

By the end of 2004, federal tax receipts as a percentage of net national income had plummeted to 17.9 percent, according to the Tax Foundation — the lowest level since 1949, when it was 15.7 percent.

State and local revenues as a percentage of net national income have likewise dropped to 10 percent, the lowest level since 1986.

In 2003, according to CBO's latest budget and economic outlook, tax receipts as a percentage of gross domestic product (GDP) rose for the first time since 2000. Robust profit growth in 2004 caused corporate tax receipts to increase by 44 percent over 2003, to a total of $189 billion.

However, that figure is almost 9 percent lower than the amount of corporate income taxes collected in 2000.

In the late 1990s, corporate tax receipts, as a percentage of GDP, reached a peak of 2.2 percent before dropping — as a result of both the economic slump and the enactment of business tax cuts — to 1.2 percent of GDP in 2002.

Profits have increased since, but as a percentage of GDP, corporate taxes aren't expected to return to the levels of the late 1990s. Rather, they are projected to rise in 2005 and 2006 before beginning another slide. This stems in part from enactment of additional business-oriented tax cuts during the past two years.

OPTIMISTIC ASSUMPTIONS

While CBO projects overall tax receipts to begin rising as a percentage of the economy until they are equal to 19.6 percent of GDP in 2015, a level "matched or exceeded only a half dozen times since 1945," this projected growth is based on assumptions that may prove to be incorrect.

One reason receipts are expected to grow is the forecast that incomes will outpace inflation and taxpayers will find themselves in higher tax brackets — a phenomenon often referred to as "real bracket creep."

CBO has also assumed — as the law requires it to — that taxes will increase over the next 10 years as tax cuts enacted during President Bush's first term expire. But that is far from a

State Tax Burdens: All Over the Map

Total Tax Levied, State by State *Percentage of income, 2004*

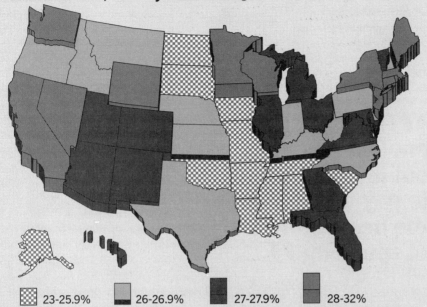

Legend: 23-25.9% | 26-26.9% | 27-27.9% | 28-32%

The above map shows the effective tax rate for each state, combining levies at the federal, state and local level. State and local taxes vary considerably and are assessed in many ways — including taxes on individual and corporate income, retail sales, cigarettes, gasoline and alcohol. The tables on the right show the states with the largest and smallest tax levies. Unlike the map, the tables do not account for the way states shift their tax burden onto non-residents. The tables below show some of the differences in how states raise revenue.

States That Tax Gasoline the Most

Cents per gallon, as of December 2003

New York	32.7
Illinois	30.0
Rhode Island	30.0
Wisconsin	28.5
Washington	28.0
Montana	27.0
Connecticut	25.0
Idaho	25.0
Nebraska	24.6
Maine	24.6

States With No Sales Tax

Alaska	New Hampshire
Delaware	Oregon
Montana	

States With No Individual Income Tax

Alaska	Tennessee*
Florida	Texas
Nevada	Washington
New Hampshire*	Wyoming
South Dakota	

*These states tax interest and dividends

States That Tax Cigarettes the Most

Per carton, as of December 2003

New Jersey	$2.05
Rhode Island	1.71
Connecticut	1.51
Massachusetts	1.51
New York	1.50
Hawaii	1.30
Oregon	1.28
Michigan	1.25
Vermont	1.19
Arizona	1.18

States That Tax the Most

Amount taxed per capita

Hawaii	$2,768
Delaware	2,710
Connecticut	2,620
Minnesota	2,586
Vermont	2,494
Massachusetts	2,310
New York	2,263
California	2,231
Wyoming	2,204
Michigan	2,180

Amount taxed per $1,000 of income

Hawaii	$91.85
Vermont	83.92
West Virginia	83.32
Delaware	82.38
New Mexico	82.27
Arkansas	79.21
Kentucky	75.92
Minnesota	75.66
Mississippi	73.71
Maine	73.08

States That Tax the Least

Amount taxed per capita

South Dakota	$1,286
Texas	1,328
Tennessee	1,351
South Carolina	1,407
Oregon	1,469
New Hampshire	1,487
Florida	1,500
Missouri	1,535
Alabama	1,536
Colorado	1,549

Amount taxed per $1,000 of income

New Hampshire	$42.75
Colorado	45.64
Texas	45.98
South Dakota	47.16
Tennessee	49.03
Florida	49.91
Oregon	50.68
Missouri	52.73
Illinois	52.83
Virginia	53.26

Note: State data above for 2002

SOURCE: Tax Foundation

CQ GRAPHIC / MARILYN GATES-DAVIS AND JAMEY FRY

sure thing. It's actually quite unlikely, historically speaking. And Bush has said one of his second term priorities is to make those tax cuts permanent.

Some economists argue that economic growth, fueled by tax cuts, will serve as an engine to erase much of the fiscal gap.

Stephen Moore, president of the Free Enterprise Fund, a conservative lobbying group, argues that if the economy were to grow at a 3.5 percent to 4 percent clip for 5 to 10 years, the federal debt, measured against GDP, would be pared back to a post-World war II low, erasing a major fiscal liability.

"If the economy picks up . . . the debt problem will largely go away," Moore says.

But few analysts expect the growth-driven revenue boom of the late 1990s to repeat itself, much less provide enough money to erase the budget deficit as it did once before.

"I think it's important to recognize that we are unlikely to grow our way out of this problem," CBO director J. Douglas Holtz-Eakin told the Senate Budget Committee on Feb. 1.

Federal mandatory spending, meanwhile, is rising quickly and set to accelerate when the baby boom generation starts collecting Social Security and Medicare.

Medicaid and Medicare alone are projected to increase from 4.2 percent of GDP to 11.5 percent in 2030; Social Security outlays are expected to rise to about 6 percent of GDP in the next three decades, under current law, while Social Security taxes will remain at about 5 percent of GDP.

"Revenues, relative to GDP, will creep up slowly because of the structure of the tax system," Engen said. "Spending is just going to ramp up at a much faster rate."

"We're raising about 16 percent of GDP in revenues and spending about 20 percent, and that's going to go up over time," said Alan Auerbach, a tax policy and public finance economist at the University of California at Berkeley. "There is no way, under the current configuration of taxes, that revenues will be sufficient to pay for a higher and rising level of spending."

NOT A REVENUE PROBLEM

To some tax cut advocates, an expected dearth of revenues is no problem at all. Rather, government has promised too much, as in many European nations, they say.

Indeed, Democrats have long maintained that the GOP's tolerance of cutting taxes amid deficits is in part a strategy to "starve the beast" and accomplish their goal of forcing reduc-

tions in spending.

To Chris Edwards, director of tax policy at the libertarian Cato Institute, spending is the issue. "I don't think there's a revenue shortfall — the problem is that the entitlement programs are scheduled to rise so quickly," he says.

The fundamental question for voters and policy makers, Edwards argues, is: "Do they

> ## "There are not enough revenues out into the future to pay for what are the best estimates of spending."
>
> — **Eric M. Engen**, resident scholar at the American Enterprise Institute

want the federal government to become substantially larger than the postwar average size?"

State governments will inevitably play a role in these decisions. The rising health care costs that threaten the long-term federal budget outlook also have significant implications for the states, as does the growth in spending at the state level for education and prisons.

"It's the exact same challenge we face at the federal level," says MacGuineas, who served as an advisor to Arizona Republican Sen. John McCain during his 2000 presidential primary bid. "States should also be rethinking their taxes," MacGuineas said.

In part, this stems from the fact that some states tie their income taxes to federal law — so that when Congress acts to cut taxes, state

treasuries often shrink as well.

Iris J. Lav, deputy director of the Center on Budget and Policy Priorities, a liberal-leaning think tank, argues that some states may need to roll back recent tax cuts, as some already have, to address what she maintains are structural deficits — deficits that will persist unless revenue increases or spending cuts are enacted.

But she contends that a more fundamental state revenue problem lies with the structure of many state tax systems.

Most states rely heavily on sales taxes for revenue, but tend to exempt many services from the tax — despite the fact that the economic bases of most states continue to shift from goods to services.

The growth in tax revenue, Lav says, "is not sufficient to fund the normal growth of expenditures. That's true in most states."

If Congress decides to push additional spending obligations onto the states, the revenue squeeze may be exacerbated.

This already is being felt at the state level when it comes to Medicaid, the joint federal-state health program for the poor. Indeed, the National Governors Association is lobbying hard against possible GOP plans to cut the amount of money the federal government contributes to Medicaid.

States do not have the option of running red ink interminably, and as a result will more quickly feel pressure to raise taxes. "States don't have the same flexibility" as the federal government, Auerbach says.

But state lawmakers also may have more difficulty raising revenue. Lav argues that the federal tax code can often be more "elastic" than state tax codes — essentially, a change in the economy does not raise the same proportion of revenue on the state level.

And state lawmakers are closer to their constituents, and perhaps more vulnerable to anti-tax revolts.

Tax Brackets for 2005

Every year, the IRS adjusts the income levels for each of the six tax brackets to account for inflation. The brackets create progessivity in the system; income earned above a certain threshold is taxed at a higher rate. For a single taxpayer:

With taxable income as much as:	Taxed owed is as much as:
$7,300	$730
$29,700	$4,090
$71,950	$14,652.50
$150,150	$36,548.50
$326,450	$94,727.50 plus 35% of the amount over $326,450

Testing the Limit

The question of sustainability — whether the government is getting the revenue it needs to fulfill its spending obligations — may ultimately lead to a test of the question of whether lawmakers impose a tax burden higher than the post-1970 historical norm.

"I don't think there's much of a willingness at all to go above that," MacGuineas says. "It's hard to envision taxpayers tolerating tax levels that would fund the current promises."

Cato's Edwards argues that Americans will not, for instance, accept lawmakers voting to raise the payroll tax by the amount needed to cover the $3.7 trillion shortfall that Social Security faces over 75 years. "I couldn't imagine the government putting that kind of burden on young workers in the future," Edwards says.

And Americans will not accept the comparably large tax burdens that Europeans rely on to finance larger governments, he maintains. "I think Americans are fundamentally different than Europeans," he says.

If that assessment is true, it is going to make things enormously difficult for politicians in coming decades.

"I wouldn't want to be a member of Congress in years down the road," Edwards said. ■

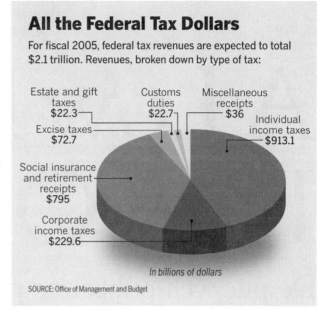

All the Federal Tax Dollars

For fiscal 2005, federal tax revenues are expected to total $2.1 trillion. Revenues, broken down by type of tax:

Estate and gift taxes $22.3
Customs duties $22.7
Miscellaneous receipts $36
Individual income taxes $913.1
Excise taxes $72.7
Social insurance and retirement receipts $795
Corporate income taxes $229.6

In billions of dollars

SOURCE: Office of Management and Budget

A Low Dose of FDA Oversight

Despite well-publicized problems with approved drugs and charges that the agency is too cozy with industry, lawmakers are loath to prescribe heavier regulation

WHEN FOOD AND DRUG ADMINISTRATION officials were summoned to Capitol Hill last month to explain why they reacted slowly to warnings that the blockbuster drug Vioxx increased risk of heart attacks and stroke, there were no angry chairmen or anxious witnesses. The mood was, in fact, rather calm and conciliatory.

Sen. Michael B. Enzi, chairman of the Health, Education, Labor and Pensions Committee, sought to put FDA officials at ease as they settled into their seats for the March 1 hearing on Vioxx, saying health risks associated with the drug were serious, but not alarming. "Every time we take a drug, we take a risk," the Wyoming Republican said. "Part of our job is to make sure that we don't over-react, but that we appropriately react."

Enzi went further at another hearing on the topic two days later, saying the purpose of the gathering was to reassure the public that the FDA was on the job. "I kind of refer to this hearing room as the 'reassurance room,' " he said, explaining that the Banking Committee used the chamber to reassure the public after Sept. 11 that the stock market was still working. "Part of what we're doing with these hearings is giv-

CALM REASSURANCE: Enzi, left, used a hearing with Crawford, right, last month to reassure the public, an attitude that reflected his party's hands-off approach to the agency.

ing some reassurance on the condition of FDA."

Across the Capitol, the Republican who chairs the House panel with jurisdiction over the agency questioned whether there even was a need for hearings. Safety concerns surrounding Vioxx and other arthritis painkillers were "being blown out of proportion," Energy and Commerce Chairman Joe L. Barton said in an interview. He said he might hold a hearing on the issue but did not think that more legislation was needed to fix any problems at the agency. "There's nothing significantly wrong in the approval process in the FDA," the Texas Republican said.

Thirteen years ago, at a time when AIDS patients were clamoring for faster approval of potentially life-saving drugs, Congress reacted decisively, setting the FDA on a very specific path with a clear direction. It would move faster to get drugs to the market with the help of "user fees" from the industry as a way to get the agency the resources it would need to speed up things.

Following of the Vioxx episode, experts, members of Congress and former agency officials have questioned the FDA's regulatory processes and suggested that they be adjusted, if not overhauled. The biggest concern is the way the agency monitors drugs' performance after they have been approved.

CQ PHOTO / SCOTT J. FERRELL

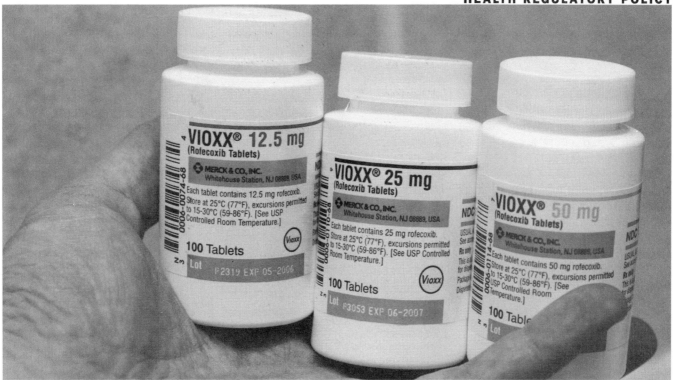

FOCUS ON SAFETY: Disclosures of health risks associated with Vioxx and other popular pain medicines have raised questions about whether FDA is emphasizing speed over safety.

"You cannot come away with any other impression than that throughout the last decade, the agency was pushed to be more open with industry," said former FDA Commissioner David Kessler. "And in some ways, that is fine. But it can't come at the sacrifice of the public health."

Congress, which provides the FDA with its legal authority, funding and direction through oversight, appears to have little interest in veering from the direction it set the agency on back in 1992. Even at a time when several popular prescription drugs on the market have been shown to pose serious risks, lawmakers are demonstrating little inclination to weigh in with aggressive oversight. That is particularly remarkable considering that during much of the past two decades, Congress has exercised tight control over the FDA.

Part of this is the Republican philosophy of less government regulation of business. Nowhere is there a better example of today's regulatory environment than in the congressional relationship with the FDA.

But there are other reasons for the ambivalence on Capitol Hill specific to the FDA. Many in Congress, including Democrats, are politically invested in the 1992 law, known as the Prescription Drug User Fee Act (PDUFA). The Republicans who lead Congress are loath to conduct intensive oversight into whether the government is capable of assuring prescription drug safety. The FDA is not asking for expanded regulatory powers. And finally, the implications of giving the agency more authority, and the money required to go with it, are problematic at a time of budget deficits.

The FDA has one of the most diverse portfolios of any regulatory body in the government, overseeing almost one-fourth of the dollars that consumers spend. Beyond prescription drugs, it is involved in regulating medical devices, human tissues for transplantation, vaccines and biological materials used to fight diseases. The agency also plans defenses against bioterrorism, inspects pharmaceutical plants and, through old laws still on the books, even regulates such matters as the sale of pet turtles.

The case involving Vioxx has raised questions about the FDA's capabilities, however. Top agency officials responded slowly to studies — as well as warnings from some of their own scientists — that the pain medicine, which the FDA approved in six months after an expedited review in 1999, could potentially double patients' risks of heart attack or stroke. The concerns extended to other chemically similar and popular pain medicines, including Pfizer Inc.'s Celebrex and Bextra.

Vioxx manufacturer Merck & Co. decided to pull the drug from the market last September after evidence surfaced that the product could be linked to as many as 55,000 patient deaths. On April 7 Pfizer, at the urging of the FDA, withdrew Bextra because of safety concerns and added a strongly worded safety warning to the package insert for Celebrex.

The FDA has formed an internal review board to evaluate health risks posed by approved drugs. Though Senate panels held three hearings into the Vioxx matter over the last half year,

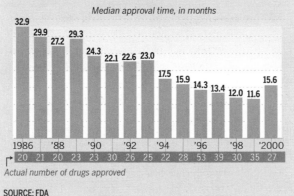

Faster Drug Approvals

The median time that the FDA took before approving new drug applications declined immediately after Congress overhauled the review process in 1992 but leveled off through 2000, the last year for which complete data is available.

Median approval time, in months

1986		'88		'90		'92		'94		'96		'98		'2000
32.9	29.9	27.2	29.3	24.3	22.1	22.6	23.0	17.5	15.9	14.3	13.4	12.0	11.6	15.6

Actual number of drugs approved

| 20 | 21 | 20 | 23 | 23 | 30 | 26 | 25 | 22 | 28 | 53 | 39 | 30 | 35 | 27 |

SOURCE: FDA

MIKE SEGAR / REUTERS / LANDOV

Tracking Drug Recalls

A total of 24 FDA-approved prescription drugs have been recalled since 1977. Half were approved after a 1992 law sped up agency reviews.

YEAR WITHDRAWN	DRUG TRADE NAME (CHEMICAL NAME)	PURPOSE	YEAR APPROVED	TOTAL APPROVAL TIME (IN MONTHS)	HEALTH RISKS THAT LED TO WITHDRAWAL
1977	Triazure (azaribine)	Psoriasis treatment	1975	*	Stroke
1980	Selecryn (ticrynafen)	Blood pressure reduction	1979	*	Liver toxicity
1982	Oraflex (benoxaprofen)	Pain relief	1982	*	Liver toxicity
1983	Zomax (zomepirac sodium)	Pain relief	1980	*	Fatal allergic reaction
1986	Suprol (suprofen)	Pain relief	1985	*	Flank pain syndrome
1986	Merital (nomifenside maleate)	Antidepressant	1984	*	Hemolytic anemia
1991	Enkaid (encainide hcl)	Correct irregular heart beat	1986	*	Fatal arrhythmias
1992	Omniflox (temafloxin)	Antibiotic	1992	26	Hypoglycemia and kidney failure
1993	Manoplax (flosequinan)	Congestive heart failure treatment	1992	27	Increased mortality
1997	Pondimin (fenfluramine)	Appetite suppressant	1973	76	Heart valve disease
1997	Redux (dexfenfluramine)	Appetite suppressant	1996	35	Heart valve disease
1998	Seldane (terfenadine)	Antihistamine	1985	26	Fatal arrhythmias
1998	Posicor (mibefradil)	Blood pressure reduction (calcium-channel blocker)	1997	15	Fatal arrhythmias
1998	Duract (bromfenac sodium)	Pain relief	1997	28	Liver toxicity
1999	Hismanal (astemizole)	Antihistamine	1988	46	Fatal arrhythmias
1999	Raxar (grepafloxacin hcl)	Antibiotic	1997	12	Fatal arrhythmias
2000	Rezulin (troglitazone)	Type 2 diabetes treatment	1997	6	Liver toxicity
2000	Propulsid (cisapride)	Acid & peptic disorder relief	1993	23	Fatal arrhythmias
2000	Lotronex (alosetron)	Irritable bowel syndrome relief	2000	7	Ischemic colitis and severe constipation
2001	Raplon (rapacuronium bromide)	Anesthetic	1999	14	Severe breathing difficulty
2001	Baycol (cerivastatin)	Cholesterol reduction	1997	12	Severe muscle damage leading to kidney failure
2004	Vioxx (rofexocib)	Pain relief	1999	6	Heart attack and stroke
2005	Tysabri (natalizumab)	Multiple sclerosis treatment	2004	6	Fatal neurologic disease
2005	Bextra (valdecoxib)	Pain relief	2001	10	Severe skin and cardiovascular problems

* Data not routinely disclosed by the FDA

SOURCES: American Medical Association, Government Accountability Office, FDA

most members of Congress are deferring to the agency after concluding that the FDA is adequately equipped to deal with such crises.

Agency critics, such as Rep. John D. Dingell, D-Mich., say the FDA has gone beyond its traditional role as regulator and has closely collaborated with the drug industry.

For example, the number of FDA warning letters to drug companies about inappropriate advertising has fallen from a peak of 157 letters in 1998 to 23 last year, according to FDA documents. And in the past five years, the agency has intervened in a handful of product liability cases, arguing that drug companies shouldn't be held accountable if patients are not aware of negative side effects that are not mentioned in drug labels.

Dingell, the ranking Democrat on the House Energy and Commerce Committee and a former chairman who was known for rigorous investigations that put regulators and regulated companies alike on the spot, says oversight of the agency would be different if he were still in charge. "But the Republicans do not believe in oversight," he said, "particularly when it comes to the drug industry. They want the FDA to be even more cozy with the drug companies."

He and others point to the close relationship between the committees of jurisdiction and the drug and biotechnology industries. Republican Billy Tauzin of Louisiana, a former House Energy and Commerce chairman, is now president of the Pharmaceutical Manufacturers Association (PhRMA), the drug industry's chief lobbying group; and James C. Greenwood, R-Pa., a former chairman of the Energy and Commerce Oversight and Investi-

gations Subcommittee, heads the Biotechnology Industry Association. Both men retired from Congress last year.

The hands-off approach is rooted in the belief that virtually every drug is capable of posing some risk within the broad population, and that it would be prohibitively expensive and time-consuming to design trials to identify every potential adverse reaction. This line of thought holds that patients and doctors should bear more responsibility for assessing health risks.

That approach has resulted in some unqualified successes, particularly in the quick approval of some promising cancer drugs and medicines capable of combating the AIDS virus. Also, even though the FDA has streamlined its regulatory reviews, its drug evalua-

CQ GRAPHIC / MARILYN GATES-DAVIS

tion process still is widely regarded as the most stringent in the world. It can take a drug company eight years to push a promising medicine through the agency's rigorous series of trials.

And Congress has encouraged regulators to expedite approvals based on fewer trials, and to work harder to help drugmakers navigate the regulatory process.

Some former Bush administration FDA officials say the attention generated by the recent recalls obscures the fact that the drug supply chain is safe, and that Congress need not wade into the fray. They point to the FDA's assertive stance in the Bextra and Celebrex cases as evidence the agency is attuned to public safety.

Scott Gottlieb, a health policy scholar at the conservative American Enterprise Institute and a top aide to former FDA Commissioner Mark McClellan, said drug safety problems are not more prevalent than in the past, but that scientists have gotten better at detecting them.

"It's only because we're looking more," he said. "Drugs are actually safer, and we know more about them at approval than ever before."

Lawmakers, such as Enzi and Barton, say the current attention to the risks of drugs ignores the benefits. Forgetting about the benefits, said former FDA general counsel Daniel Troy, is "dangerous."

"We really risk going back to the days of [having] drug lags, when many more drugs were available in Europe than here," he said. "The current focus runs some grave risks right now of inducing inappropriately risk-averse behavior at the agency."

Troy and others argue that drug manufacturers have strong financial incentives to sell only safe drugs. If they ignore health risks, they will surely face litigation, such as the Vioxx-related lawsuits now being brought against Merck.

FASTER APPROVALS

The point at which Congress set the FDA on the path of faster approvals came with the user fee act in 1992. Republicans and Democrats since the AIDS crisis in the 1980s had pres-

sured the agency to streamline the approval process for new drugs. The 1992 law was modeled on a proposal by Vice President Dan Quayle that for the first time imposed user fees on drug companies for the purpose of hiring more drug reviewers and upgrading the FDA's computer systems.

Democrats were eager to mollify AIDS activists, one of their important political constituencies. The Clinton administration later embraced the law because officials were convinced that Congress would not appropriate enough money to hire the number of drug reviewers needed to modernize the FDA's systems. Republicans at the time charged that the FDA was squelching innovation with cumbersome and unnecessary rules, and were calling for some of the agency's review functions to be privatized.

The original PDUFA law and two reauthorizations, in 1997 and 2002, were passed by wide margins in a bipartisan fashion.

The 1997 law went further than its predecessor by mandating faster reviews of clinical trials and expanding the fast-track process for approving new drugs to include vaccines and biological products designed to fight diseases. It also required the creation of advisory panels consisting of outside experts to review drugs within 60 days of the submission of an application, and required the FDA to report panel recommendations within 90 days of receiving them.

Today, reopening the law would amount to

an acknowledgement that it — or the underlying notion that an industry would pay user fees to the regulator that approves its products — had failed, or at least was flawed. Some top senators and congressmen who helped negotiate PDUFA in the early 1990s appear reluctant to consider any sweeping measure.

Democrats are particularly in a bind, having thrown their support behind PDUFA in 1992. They are reluctant to pass any sweeping measure that would unravel the compromises of the past or undermine the user fee system, which pours hundreds of millions of dollars each year into FDA's budget.

However, in the wake of the Vioxx withdrawal, Sen. Edward M. Kennedy of Massachusetts is calling for measures to toughen the FDA's oversight of drug companies, such as giving the agency more authority to approve drug advertising or allowing the Office of Drug Safety, which monitors drugs, to report directly to the FDA commissioner. As the top Democrat on Enzi's panel, Kennedy is hoping to find some path to a compromise with committee Republicans despite sharp disagreements over the issues.

But Kennedy is not employing all of the tools at his disposal to force the committee to act. He is not, for instance, demanding more public hearings to build momentum for a bill or threatening to delay the confirmation of Crawford over drug safety issues.

Some members continue to press for more oversight. Senate Finance Chairman Charles E. Grassley, R-Iowa, the FDA's most prominent critic in the Senate, wants to allow the Office of Drug Safety to report directly to the FDA commissioner rather than to the FDA drug center director, who also oversees the approval of drugs. Grassley, whose committee has limited jurisdiction over the agency, also would require drug companies to make all clinical trial results public, even if they were not favorable to the companies' products.

"The culture of FDA has tilted too far in favor of the interests of pharmaceutical companies, in some cases at the expense of public

INFLUENTIAL LOBBYISTS: Former Energy and Commerce Chairman Tauzin, left, and Investigations Subcommittee Chairman Greenwood, seen during a 2002 hearing on the insider trading case surrounding Martha Stewart, now head the drug and biotechnology industry trade groups.

AP PHOTO / DENNIS COOK

health," Grassley wrote to Crawford on March 16.

But Grassley, who also has Social Security and various tax issues on his plate, is waging a lonely battle. Since the Vioxx hearings, few in the chamber have indicated a willingness to restructure the FDA's functions. The next opportunity might come in 2007, when PDUFA is again up for reauthorization.

FDA's Mindset

FDA officials say they are even-handed in their decisions and contend that PDUFA has not fundamentally changed the agency's mind-set. "Our position is we're really agnostic about where the resources come from," Steven Galson, acting director of the FDA's Center for Drug Evaluation and Research, which oversees drug approval, said in an interview. "We reject the notion we're biased because of user fees. We've hired more people, and . . . it's worked quite well."

Another reason Congress is unlikely to move quickly is that House and Senate members alike are aware that any intensive examination of drug safety would probably set off debate on a host of marginally related but politically incendiary issues.

Most Democrats and a growing number of Republicans would almost certainly try to use FDA hearings or any proposed legislation to make it easier for consumers to import medicines from countries where they typically sell for less than in the United States.

Social conservatives could be expected to use the debate to press for more curbs on abortion, possibly including a ban on the emergency contraceptive known as the morning-after pill that is now under FDA review. Abortion politics already has factored into the confirmation process for Crawford, who was nominated in February to head the agency. Democratic Sens. Patty Murray of Washington and Hillary Rodham Clinton of New York announced April 6 that they would place a hold on Crawford's nomination until the FDA makes a decision on over-the-counter sales of the morning-after pill.

Among the biggest concerns is the agency's monitoring of drugs on the market after they are approved. The FDA relies on doctors and drug companies to report adverse reactions, a process critics contend leaves much to chance. The MedWatch system the agency installed

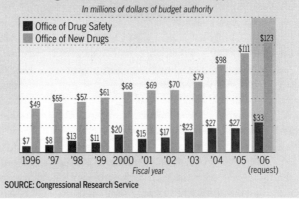

Priority On Drug Reviews

Funding for the FDA Office of Drug Safety over the past decade has been dwarfed by spending on the agency's Office of New Drugs, which reviews manufacturers' applications.

In millions of dollars of budget authority

■ Office of Drug Safety
▨ Office of New Drugs

Fiscal year	Office of Drug Safety	Office of New Drugs
1996	$7	$49
'97	$8	$55
'98	$13	$57
'99	$11	$61
2000	$20	$68
'01	$15	$69
'02	$17	$70
'03	$23	$79
'04	$27	$98
'05	$27	$111
'06 (request)	$33	$123

SOURCE: Congressional Research Service

for doctors and consumers to report problems collects only about 10 percent of serious adverse drug reactions, according to the agency's own estimates.

Over the past decade, Congress has generally directed more money in the appropriations process toward speeding up the review process than toward safety reviews of approved medicines.

Within the FDA's Center for Drug Evaluation and Research, more than four-fifths of the budget is directed to the Office of New Drugs, a division of more than 1,000 people that reviews applications for drug approvals. The Office of Drug Safety is far smaller, with a staff of about 109 individuals.

Former officials say the FDA is short on essential resources. "The agency was out there with its hand out on these [drug safety] matters," said Jane E. Henney, who served as FDA commission from 1999 to 2001. "You can't look at the agency and say, 'You didn't try to tell us.'"

The agency has become increasingly reliant on user fees derived from the 1992 law. The FDA has collected more than $1.4 billion in fees since PDUFA was enacted, and fees now constitute nearly half of its resources for drug regulation. In fiscal 2005, Congress appropriated $71.3 million for the FDA's Office of Drug Safety and Office of New Drugs; the offices received $66.2 million that year from fee collections.

Quirks in the Organization

One reason for the funding woes is that the congressional committees that control the FDA's budget are agriculture appropriations panels that are not oriented to health care issues.

The organizational quirk is due to the fact that the FDA's origins were in the Agriculture Department. The practical effect is that spending on the agency must compete with crop insurance, food and nutrition programs, and commodity price supports for a limited pool of funds. The fiscal 2005 agriculture appropriations bill contained $17 billion in discretionary spending. Some of the biggest increases for the FDA were in the areas of food safety — a reflection of appropriators' orientation toward agriculture.

President Bush's 2006 budget calls for spending $33.4 million on the FDA's Office of Drug Safety, a $5 million increase over 2005 levels. Many in Congress believe the user fees levied on drug companies through PDUFA give the FDA a dedicated stream of money that can address the most pressing drug safety concerns, and that Congress need not substantially increase spending on the agency. But some Republicans say increases such as what the administration is proposing aren't enough to compensate for years of underfunding.

"I know they don't get enough resources," says Sen. Orrin G. Hatch, R-Utah. "I think we've taken [the FDA] for granted."

In such an environment, Congress seems inclined to continue allowing the agency to sort out its challenges and establish priorities within the framework of existing laws. Absent a major public health threat, lawmakers are likely to give Crawford, a career FDA employee, time to set an agenda once he is confirmed.

"It's very difficult to get legislation through, period," said PhRMA's Tauzin. "If you can cure a problem within an agency through its administrative powers, you ought to do that first. Now the question is, are they doing a good enough job?"

While some observers think the answer is no, and question whether the agency can achieve the proper balance between speed and safety on its own, they doubt that Congress will use the current concerns over Vioxx and other pain drugs as justification to act.

"The right balance is when we can speed up drug development without worrying about safety," said Ray Woosley, vice president for health sciences at the University of Arizona, who was considered for the post of FDA commissioner during Bush's first term. "I talk to a lot of medical reviewers, and a lot of people think we're not there yet." ■

CQ GRAPHIC / YOLIE DAWSON

An Uneasy Deal With Illegal Workforce

States and cities are hit with the bill as costs for education and medical care mount, but the nation seems in no hurry to end its reliance on undocumented laborers

SILER CITY, N.C.

WHEN A WOMAN named Marta arrived in this rural town from Mexico three years ago via California, she paid $1,000 for a counterfeit Social Security card that ensured her a job at one of the two local poultry processing plants that have been a magnet for undocumented Latino immigrants. "None of the factories will let you work without papers," she says.

The poultry plant where she worked could have checked her documents with the Department of Homeland Security, but it did not. The law requires only that the documents appear authentic, and they did. The company is hungry for workers willing to cut up chicken carcasses for $8 an hour. Illegal immigrants are drawn to the relatively high wages — about $16,000 a year — compared with what they might earn at home.

With the money she has been able to save, Marta — she declines to give her last name — paid smugglers, or "coyotes," $2,000 apiece, plus expenses, to have her five children transported one at a time from Mexico to her door at a Siler City trailer park.

The result of this system is that here in Chatham County, a primarily rural area 50 miles west of the state capital of Raleigh, the Latino population has increased tenfold in the past decade. The state's estimated population of illegal immigrants grew by 700 percent between 1990 and 2000 and now ranks among the top 10 states in illegal immigrant popula-

tions. The immigration has been a boon to North Carolina business, filling thousands of low-wage jobs in poultry processing, service industries such as hotels and restaurants, home construction and agriculture.

The benefits to business, in fact, are the main reason Congress is stalemated on immigration policy, unable to pass legislation that might more strictly control illegal immigration or to establish a guest worker program, as President Bush has proposed, that might allow millions of immigrants to settle here legally.

Meanwhile, the expanding population of more than 10 million undocumented immigrants, living and working in the shadow of American society and not even accurately counted, is racking up considerable costs. While the factories may benefit, the cost to society is high.

"Cheap labor is cheap to the employer, not to the taxpayer," says Colorado Republican Tom Tancredo, the most vocal advocate in Congress for tougher immigration policies and enforcement.

Two of Marta's children attend schools in Siler City that are struggling with classrooms where as many as 70 percent of the students speak Spanish at home. Illegal immigrants are unlikely to have health insurance; when Marta gets sick, she must go to a county-run health clinic or the emergency room of the local hospital. If she is disabled or reaches retirement age, she cannot collect money from the Social Security system, even though she may contribute to it for years. As far as the system goes, she does not exist. If she requires care, the taxpayers will have to pay for it.

CQ Weekly March 14, 2005

CHRIS HILDRETH FOR CQ

LIVING IN THE SHADOWS: A trailer park in Siler City, N.C., is home to dozens of Latin American immigrants, many of them illegal, who work at nearby poultry processing plants. The scene is becoming common in the Southeast and other areas of the country where low-skill jobs attract low-wage workers who used to congregate near the border. Fake Social Security and identification cards satisfy employers and help illegal immigrants get driver's licenses in some states.

The key to survival for illegal immigrants is remaining anonymous. They are reluctant to complain about substandard housing or to report stolen property, an assault or an abusive spouse. But the costs of law enforcement, of hiring bilingual police officers and caring for immigrants who are jailed are borne by the public.

The tide of illegal immigration has washed over nearly every domestic government program, from Social Security to Medicaid, from home health to homeland security, from education to environmental protection. But Congress has done little to defray the costs, which are borne mostly by local governments.

As a report published in January by the investment banking and securities firm Bear, Stearns & Co. Inc. concluded, "The United States is simply hooked on cheap, illegal workers and deferring the costs of providing public services to these quasi-Americans."

A WINK AND A NOD

Illegal immigration was supposed to at least slow down after Congress passed the Immi-gration Reform and Control Act in 1986. The law granted amnesty to 2.7 million people living in the country illegally but imposed tough sanctions on employers who hired undocumented workers. The law, however, has never been strictly enforced.

Immigration experts say the United States can have all the walls it wants in the Southwest, but the only thing that will halt illegal immigration is drying up the supply of jobs — what is called interior enforcement. By the late 1990s, the Immigration and Naturalization Service, at the urging of Congress, had all but given up on interior enforcement and the accompanying workplace raids, shifting its emphasis to catching smugglers and reinforcing the border.

The Border Patrol nearly tripled its force of

"Cheap labor is cheap to the employer, not to the taxpayer. "

— Rep. Tom Tancredo, R-Colo.

agents and built new barriers along the most heavily traveled urban stretches of the border in Arizona, California and Texas. Those high-profile moves were popular with politicians and the public. But instead of stopping the flow, it simply pushed it out of public view toward isolated sections of Arizona. Entry became more expensive as fees to smugglers went up — and more deadly for immigrants who could not survive the heat of the Sonoran Desert.

Clamping down on the border may have reduced the number of crossings, but it increased the number of undocumented immigrants who stay in the United States instead of going back and forth to their home countries. And tougher border enforcement did nothing about the estimated 40 percent of those who enter the country legally and then overstay their visas. In most cases, they simply disappear.

Once they pass through checkpoints on the roads leading out of the border region, illegal immigrants have little fear of getting caught — and numerous job opportunities awaiting them. Though the 1986 law outlawed hiring illegal immigrants, employers satisfy their legal obligation as long as they see identification that looks real. In fact, employers have a real incentive not to ask too many questions: Denying someone a job can prompt a discrimination lawsuit. What developed was a burgeoning industry in fake documents that could satisfy the government requirements.

The result is a national population of illegal immigrants larger than that of New York City and about equal to the entire state of Michigan and growing by an estimated 500,000 every year.

Bush's solution is a guest worker program that might ease the flood of illegal immigrants by allowing foreigners to work in the United States for at least three years. Mexican President Vicente Fox, who meets with Bush and Canadian Prime Minister Paul Martin in two weeks, wants the president to use his political capital to get the guest worker program passed.

But many Republicans adamantly oppose any such program that might benefit those who have entered the country illegally.

BUSINESS DECISIONS

The unspoken truth that perpetuates this stalemate is that there are plenty of beneficiaries of the status quo, including businesses and families that employ illegal labor and the immigrants themselves, who want jobs — any jobs.

Those beneficiaries are easy to find in Siler City, where the two poultry plants sit like bookends on opposite sides of a town of 7,500 people. Humming refrigerator trucks share the loading docks with trailers full of hundreds of caged chickens. Inside, 1,200 workers make the plants the area's largest private employers.

Poultry processors have automated tasks such as plucking feathers and slaughtering

CHRIS HILDRETH FOR CQ

The Opposite Of Outsourcing

THINK OF ILLEGAL IMMIGRATION as the flip side of U.S. companies contracting to get their work done overseas. The easy availability of illegal immigrants permits American employers to use inexpensive foreign labor for the kinds of jobs that cannot be relocated to other countries: processing meat and harvesting perishable fruits, landscaping and construction, cooking food or cleaning offices and hotel rooms.

The Pew Hispanic Center, a nonpartisan research organization, estimates that 10 percent of the workforce in U.S. restaurants, 25 percent of those employed as domestic help in private households and almost 60 percent of crop workers are here illegally.

"Illegal immigration has been America's way of competing with low-wage forces of Asia and Latin America," concluded the investment banking and security firm Bear Stearns and Co. Inc. in a January report on illegal immigration.

Most Americans have jobs that require them to be close to their customers or clients — even when they are highly skilled people such as heart surgeons or physics professors. But James P. Smith, a labor economist for the Rand Corporation a nonprofit research firm, argues that some domestic industries — including the growing and harvesting of perishable food, tobacco and textile materials — simply may be unable to continue operating without illegal immigrant labor.

For many employers, hiring immigrant workers is not quite as cheap as sending jobs overseas, where the wages paid are usually far lower than what illegal immigrants earn in the United States. More

> **"Illegal immigration has been America's way of competing with the low-wage forces of Asia and Latin America."**

than half of undocumented workers in the United States are paid "on the books," which means they are earning at least the minimum wage. But illegal labor is cheaper than the alternative: raising wages sufficiently to attract people who are in this country legally to jobs they often are dirty, difficult and dull. "This is work that is quite unpleasant and that most Americans have grown out of," Smith says. Raising wages in these low-skill jobs could wind up fueling inflation and stalling economic growth, says University of Chicago political scientist Daniel W. Drezner.

Some experts contend that the United States should stop treating illegal immigration as just a law enforcement and border control issue and think about it instead as a consequence of global economic integration. Princeton sociologist Douglas S. Massey argues that the United States should view illegal immigration as a natural outgrowth of the integration of the North American economy.

"We should view it as inevitable and work to minimize the costs, including increasing the quota for legal immigration instead of wasting $3 billion on useless border enforcement and undermining our own wages and working conditions," Massey says.

Taken to the extreme, integrating the economies of Mexico and the United States would mean allowing workers to flow freely back and forth across the border. In theory, both economies would benefit, says Ronald D. Lee, an economist at the University of California at Berkeley.

But there also could be severe problems, particularly as wages for U.S. and Mexican workers in low-skill jobs equalized, Lee says. And tens of thousands more Latin Americans might be drawn north. "Not everyone would profit," says Lee. "You would expect in theory that native domestic workers in the United States would be hurt and those in Mexico would benefit."

the birds, leaving the monotonous and often dangerous work of cutting up the chickens and removing bones to low-skill, low-wage workers. The Labor Department says they have some of the highest rates of repetitive-stress injuries of any industry.

Nonetheless, Marta has no regrets about moving to the United States. "I didn't have anything in my country," she says. "My children didn't have a future; there is no employment for people like me."

On the surface, Siler City too has benefited from the influx of illegal immigrants, helping reverse the economic decline of a town best known as the fictional shopping destination on the "Andy Griffith Show." Ever since the 1970s, local plants that made everything from neckties to tread rubber have been closing or moving overseas.

The Latino immigrants, 70 percent of whom are here illegally, officials estimate, have increased the town's population by more than half since they began arriving in the mid-1990s. At first, it was just men who were recruited to work at the poultry plants or who heard about jobs there and at local textile mills by word of mouth. By 2000, it was whole families arriving from places like Veracruz and Oaxaca, Mexico, or from Tucson, Ariz., or San Diego, their first stops across the border.

"The Latinos here are doing the heavy lifting," says Vince Sanabria, executive director of the Hispanic Liaison, a nonprofit social services agency based in Siler City. "They put their hard-earned dollars back into the local economy and are doing the work no one else wants to do."

They spend their money at the local Wal-Mart and half a dozen mom and pop "tiendas" scattered through the half-empty down-

town. Shoppers there can buy almost any grocery item found back home in Mexico, plus piñatas hanging from the ceiling, whole pigs being butchered behind the meat counter or bus tickets to somewhere else. They can also wire money to Mexico, part of an estimated $30 billion annual flow of remittances to Latin America and the Caribbean that benefits U.S. banks.

And when the growing Catholic parish outgrew its modest red brick church in Siler City, immigrant contributions helped build a mission style, cream-colored replacement that is hard to miss amid cow pastures on the highway into town. Says Jane Wrenn, director of the local Chamber of Commerce, "We all reap the benefits."

Nationally, consumers benefit from illegal immigrants, and not just the middle-class and high-income families who employ them to

ECONOMIC BOOST: Several small, family-run stores, or 'tiendas,' have opened along Siler City's main shopping strip to serve the growing Latino population.

clean their homes, care for their children or mow their lawns.

Everyone gains from the lower-priced goods and services, such as the chicken breasts produced at Siler City's plants.

"We all participate in that cycle of illegality," says John Herrera, vice president of the Durham, N.C.-based Center for Community Self-Help, a community development financial institution that serves the local Latino population. "Employers and consumers create the demand to purchase those products, and anyone who benefits from that illegal activity is a participant."

UNEQUAL DISTRIBUTION

Though immigration advocates argue that new arrivals fill the sorts of jobs Americans don't want or won't be able to fill as the workforce ages, some studies suggest that illegal immigration suppresses the wages of the least skilled Americans.

Calculating the impact on government budgets is trickier. But it is clear that there is a mismatch between where the revenue flows and who pays most of the costs. "This is an old problem that has spread from gateway states to the rest of the country," says Princeton sociologist Douglas S. Massey. "The federal government sets immigration policy and reaps the benefits, but all the costs are paid at the state and local level."

The federal government collects income and payroll taxes from the 50 percent to 60 percent of illegal immigrants whose work is reported by businesses and individuals. And since illegal immigrants rely on fake Social Security numbers, their payroll taxes pile up in a fund for mismatched and invalid Social Security numbers that contained $463 billion as of 2002, according to the latest Economic Report of the President. The money offsets other federal spending.

Meanwhile, states and local governments wind up footing most of the bills. States and localities are getting the worst of both worlds: The federal government neither reduces the flow of illegal immigration nor helps defray the costs.

Border communities still bear the brunt of the costs of caring for illegal immigrants and their children. But the impact has spread to parts of the Midwest and South, some of which have had no significant immigration for 100 years and lack the infrastructure or experience to deal with newcomers, says Pew Hispanic Center demographer Jeffrey S. Passel. A decade after the influx began, local governments around Siler City are still struggling to catch up.

PAYING THE HOSPITAL BILL

Siler City's growing Latino population first caught the attention of local officials in 1996 when an outbreak of rubella, or German measles, was traced to poultry plant workers.

The disease quickly spread among immigrants who lacked vaccinations or booster shots, creating one of the largest incidents of the disease since vaccines became widely available in the 1960s.

Chatham County's health department scrambled to vaccinate the Latino community, visiting churches, trailer parks, supermarkets and the city's annual chicken festival. They had to overcome illegal immigrants' fear of authorities, which was not helped by the deployment of uniformed medics from the North Carolina National Guard.

These days, health officials are focused on the more basic needs of the undocumented population. The county Health Department moved its clinics from the county seat in Pittsboro to Siler City so patients can go there rather than the emergency room, which costs more.

Hospitals must treat anyone who arrives in need of emergency care, regardless of their immigration status. In the past 16 months, that requirement has meant the county has had to pay part of the bill for 445 undocumented residents who needed emergency care. With so many immigrants of childbearing age, the vast majority of those cases are births. Since the hospital in Siler City is so small, it does not deliver babies, and the immigrants go to a hospital in another county, but Chatham must still cover the cost. The births also mean

CHRIS HILDRETH FOR CQ

Immigrant Nation

Of the estimated 35 million foreign-born people living in the United States, nearly 30 percent are here illegally. They account for just 3 percent of the nation's population, but their number is growing rapidly and spreading far beyond the border states. Estimates vary, but some of the biggest increases are in the Southeast and West. The breakdown in 2003:

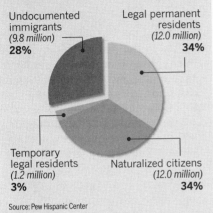

Undocumented immigrants (9.8 million) **28%**

Legal permanent residents (12.0 million) **34%**

Temporary legal residents (1.2 million) **3%**

Naturalized citizens (12.0 million) **34%**

Source: Pew Hispanic Center

States with the fastest growth in illegal immigrants in the 1990s

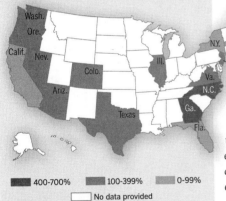

- ■ 400-700%
- ■ 100-399%
- ■ 0-99%
- □ No data provided

Estimated undocumented population in 2000

California	2.2 million
Texas	1 million
New York	489,000
Illinois	432,000
Florida	337,000
Arizona	283,000
Georgia	228,000
New Jersey	221,000
North Carolina	206,000
Colorado	144,000
Washington	136,000
Virginia	103,000
Nevada	101,000
Oregon	90,000
Massachusetts	87,000

Source: Department of Homeland Security

CQ GRAPHIC / MARILYN GATES-DAVIS

significant business for Siler City's only pediatrician, Dr. Jim Schwankl.

The poultry plants offer health insurance at an affordable rate, though health officials say relatively few employees take advantage of it because they are not used to thinking about preventative care as a worthwhile investment. So the medical bills — more than 80 percent at Schwankl's office — are paid by Medicaid, the federal-state health program for the poor and disabled. The county and state of North Carolina pay a third of the Medicaid expenses, while the federal government picks up the remaining two-thirds.

Marta's health problems began long before she arrived in Siler City, but she underwent surgery again in 2003 to remove eight kidney stones. The impact of caring for such patients on Siler City's hospital is less severe than in border states. Arizona hospitals say the cost of providing emergency care for illegal immigrants has pushed them to the brink of bankruptcy.

A 2002 study commissioned by the United States/Mexico Border Counties Coalition found that hospitals in 24 counties in four states that share a border with Mexico incur nearly $190 million in uncompensated costs for treating illegal immigrants.

States have long sought relief from the federal government, but that assistance has been slow in coming. The 1996 Immigration Reform Act, which reduced government benefits for non-citizens, authorized reimbursements to hospitals for emergency care and ambulance services provided to illegals injured during border crossings, but neither program has been funded.

The 2003 Medicare drug law included $250 million in annual payments to local hospitals for such expenses. Three border senators, Republicans Kay Bailey Hutchison of Texas and Jon Kyl of Arizona and Democrat Dianne Feinstein of California, complained in February that the money had not been paid out.

LEARNING LESSONS

You can chart the growth of Siler City's Latino population by looking at its exploding school enrollment. The number of Latino students in Chatham County schools went from 4 in 1986 to 300 in the mid 1990s and close to 1,400 today. Sixty-eight percent of students in Siler City's elementary school are now Latino. An average of one new arrival each day signs up for classes at the school's intake center for Spanish speakers.

Contrary to public perception, it has always been education, rather than any form of welfare, that is the biggest social cost of illegal immigration. The vast majority of illegal immigrants are under the age of 40, and they tend to have children at a higher rate than the native-born population. Handling the load required the Siler City schools to hire 18 teachers of English as a second language. The schools' calendars and notes to parents are printed in both English and Spanish. Some school staffers work full time seeking out new arrivals to make sure their children enroll in school, and a summer program for the children of migrant workers helps them catch up.

Hispanic students drop out of school at a higher rate than white and African-American students. Marta says she's proud that one of her children will graduate from high school this year; another, who works as a handyman, earned his general equivalence diploma, and a third is in middle school. "They didn't smoke, they didn't drink, they really treated me well," she says.

For those who do graduate, actually affording college is a challenge. El Pueblo, a Raleigh-based advocacy group, estimates that as many as 1,450 illegal immigrants graduate from North Carolina high schools each year. The Urban Institute, a nonpartisan social and economic policy research organization, figures the number nationally is 65,000.

Under the 1996 immigration act, states that provide in-state tuition or other higher-education benefits to undocumented immigrants are required to provide the same tuition break to out-of-state residents. The result is that few states offer such benefits. A bill to reverse that decision has languished in Congress for more than three years.

LIVING ON THE EDGE

Just off Siler City's main shopping strip is a trailer park where many illegal immigrants live. Spanish music blares from cars parked on muddy lots where garbage piles up outside rusting mobile homes. A dozen or more immigrants from more than one family might live inside. Yet until recently this was not the worst housing in town: At a trailer park that is now closed, raw sewage flowed in the open.

Those are some of the challenges faced by social workers from Chatham County's child protective service, who have a rapidly growing caseload of neglect and abuse cases. The county has scrambled to find the money anywhere it can for nine additional social workers.

"It's definitely made an impact on our budget," says John Tanner, head of the county social

Immigration Opinions, Options Vary Widely

Divisions within the Republican Party over immigration policy make it unlikely that Congress will pass any comprehensive legislation to curb illegal immigration this year. What follows are some of the elements already proposed in Congress or by outside experts:

GUEST WORKERS

Business and labor both like the idea of a new guest worker program, which could help legalize millions of undocumented immigrants already in the country, and the approach has the support of President Bush and some leading Democrats, including Edward M. Kennedy of Massachusetts. Bush wants a guest worker program that would match foreign workers with employers who can't find U.S. labor to fill their jobs. The guest workers would be given three-year visas. The details of Bush's plan remain sketchy — particularly how many times workers could renew their visas.

A more complete guest worker plan was introduced in the last Congress by a trio of Arizona Republicans: House members Jeff Flake and Jim Kolbe and Sen. John McCain. Their plan would create a category of visas for foreign workers to fill full-time jobs in the United States for three years, plus a single extension of three years. The jobs would first have to be advertised to U.S. workers for two weeks through an electronic registry. To ease concerns that immigrants would benefit from breaking the law, the bill would require applicants to pay a fee. Holders of the new visas would be able to seek work in any field, not just agriculture — as was the case with guest worker programs in the past.

Texas Republican Sen. John Cornyn advocates a more limited guest worker program that would require the Labor secretary to adjust the number of immigrant workers according to U.S. economic conditions. Foreign workers would be able to apply for one-year visas for a total stay of up to three years.

Critics say that by allowing guest workers to enter industries besides agriculture, the government would be opening nearly every job in America to competition from foreigners willing to work for lower wages. They also question whether employers would go through the extra expense of using guest workers and whether the workers would leave when their visas expired.

BORDER ENFORCEMENT

Stricter control of the borders, particularly the 1,933-mile boundary with Mexico, has long been the most popular approach to curbing illegal immigration. National security has been added to the reasons since the Sept. 11 terrorist attacks, and immigration is now in the hands of the Department of Homeland Security.

The intelligence overhaul law signed by Bush in 2004 authorized hiring an additional 10,000 Border Patrol agents over the next five years, which would almost double the force. But Bush's fiscal 2006 budget calls for adding only 210 more agents this year, far short of the 2,000 envisioned by Congress, prompting criticism from border-state representatives.

LEGALIZATION

Among the many sensitive issues is what to do about the estimated 10 million illegal immigrants already in the United States.

Many House Republicans oppose any measure that would reward them for breaking the law. That is why supporters of giving them a path to legal status avoid using the term "amnesty."

In a mass amnesty in 1986, close to 2.7 million illegal immigrants who could prove they had resided continuously in the United States since before 1982 were allowed to remain.

Last year in the Senate, then-Democratic Minority Leader Tom Daschle of South Dakota and Republican Chuck Hagel of Nebraska introduced legislation that would have allowed some undocumented workers and their families to adjust their immigration status to legal permanent residency and eventual citizenship if they met a string of requirements. The immigrants would have to pass national security and criminal background checks, reside in the United States for at least five years, work a minimum of four years in the country, and pay all federal taxes and a $1,000 fine in addition to required application fees.

EMPLOYER SANCTIONS

Experts say aggressive enforcement of immigration laws beyond the border, including penalizing employers who hire illegal immigrants, is a vital part of stemming the flow. Republican David Dreier of California introduced a bill (HR 98) in January that would require employers to check the legality of new hires. Counterfeit-proof, machine-readable Social Security cards would be matched against an employment eligibility database at the Homeland Security Department.

Employers now may verify documents with Homeland Security, but attempts to make the program mandatory have met fierce resistance from business and civil libertarians. Detractors point to the failings of the employer sanction system established in the 1986 Immigration Reform and Control Act. Employers were prohibited from knowingly hiring undocumented workers, but they had no easy way of verifying the immigration status of job applicants, and counterfeiters readily supplied authentic-looking documents. Labor unions complained that employers used the requirement as a weapon against workers attempting to organize.

DEPORTATION ORDERS

Even without better workplace enforcement, more-modest measures are being considered. For instance, to make sure those already ordered out of the country actually leave, David Martin, former Immigration and Naturalization Service chief lawyer, advocates better use of a tool already on the books. Since 1996, Congress has provided for civil fines of $500 a day against people who fail to appear after being issued final orders of deportation. Though the fines have never been implemented, Martin, who is now a law professor at the University of Virginia, says they could motivate deportees who have some money to show up on time or face big penalties.

AN ILLEGAL PATH: Mexicans picking raspberries in New Mexico last summer, left; the customs line before crossing the U.S.-Mexico border, right.

AP PHOTO / TOBY JORRIN, LEFT; JACK SMITH / EPA / LANDOV

services department. Social worker Millie Enas says her staff does all it can, and she keeps a wish list of all the new services she'd like to offer — if only she had the money.

Siler City's police force of 18 officers, meanwhile, has seen a modest increase in crime because of illegal immigrants. But Police Chief Lewis S. Phillips Jr. says the biggest problem illegals pose is on the road. "Their driving habits, with no licenses and no insurance, is a big issue," he says.

Driver's licenses have become a focal point for rising frustration about illegal immigration in North Carolina and elsewhere. Licenses became an issue in last year's North Carolina governor's race, and two bills in the state legislature would bar illegal immigrants from getting licenses. The bills are similar to Proposition 200, a ballot initiative in Arizona requiring anyone registering to vote or applying for state services to show proof of eligibility. The initiative passed in November over the objections of almost the entire state political leadership. The initiative had broad support among all voters in the state: 47 percent of Latinos and 42 percent of Democrats voted for it.

PUBLIC BACKLASH

Nationally, a poll in February by Westhill Partners Inc. suggested that the public is growing uneasy with what it sees as too many immigrants getting away with breaking the law. In focus groups, people of all ethnic backgrounds express concerns about losing jobs to illegal immigrants or even having to wait too long at hospital emergency rooms because of people they believe are here illegally. "You've got to address that frustration," says Ed Reilly, Westhill Partners' chief executive officer.

Concern is highest among lower-income households, who face the greatest competition from immigrants. They are less than half as likely to support keeping immigration at the current levels as are high-income voters.

Two California radio talk-show hosts tapped into that rising anger last fall, targeting Republican House member David Dreier, the chairman of the Rules Committee, for what they considered his soft stand on illegal immigration. Dreier, who says his record was distorted, survived, though with his smallest margin of victory in 24 years and the smallest of any Congressional incumbent in the state.

On Capitol Hill, the House has already passed a bill that would create national standards for driver's licenses and require proof of legal status. Supporters of the legislation, sponsored by Wisconsin Republican F. James Sensenbrenner Jr., chairman of the Judiciary Committee, say that allowing illegal immigrants to have driver's licenses threatens homeland security.

But from the perspective of states and localities, the regulations might compound some problems. Opponents say the change is a threat to road safety because it will simply increase the number of unlicensed and uninsured drivers on the road and wind up pushing illegal immigrants further to the edges of society.

Judging by the full parking lot at a Siler City poultry plant that empties out at the end of each shift, simply taking away driver's licenses is unlikely to get undocumented workers off the road. They rely on their cars to get to work because most rural towns such as Siler City have no public transportation.

For now, Marta says her biggest problem is not finding a way to work, but rather finding a job at all. She has been out of work and in debt since doctors diagnosed more kidney stones and a tumor on her liver. Before she can go back to work, she must find a new name and the Social Security number that comes with it. Since the last time she bought one, three years ago, the price has risen 50 percent, to $1,500. In the meantime, all she can do is take care of a few children of other workers inside her trailer.

The long-term cost to federal, state and local governments for illegal immigrants is uncertain. So far, almost all have been adults of working age or their children. Caring for an aging, ailing population has not been a concern. Some experts assume that since illegal immigrants will not qualify for benefits from Social Security or Medicare, even though they help pay for them, large numbers eventually will move back to their home countries, where retirement and health care is cheaper. But that's not necessarily an option for Marta, whose five children have all relocated with her to North Carolina.

"My hope is now my children are moving forward, they'll help me move out of debt," she says. "As a mom, I've done my duty." ■

GOP Quick to Tread Shaky New Ground

Will public see lawmakers' heavy hand in Schiavo case, baseball scandal as leadership or meddling?

DEBATING LIFE: Facing intense pressure from social conservatives, Congress is trying to prolong the life of Terri Schiavo, right, severely brain-damaged in 1990.

BEFORE MARCH 18, the House Government Reform Committee didn't show any great interest in long-term health care. But shortly after midnight that day, the committee announced that it would launch an investigation into the issue.

Why? Because long-term care of incapacitated adults is "an issue of growing importance to the federal government and federal health care policy." Hours later, the Senate Health, Education, Labor and Pensions Committee announced that it, too, would hold a hearing on the subject.

The two committees didn't suddenly decide they had overlooked an urgent national priority. They launched their investigations as a way to keep Terri Schiavo alive. The severely brain-damaged Florida woman, who has been in a vegetative state since 1990, has become an

urgent political priority for Republican leaders and their conservative religious supporters.

Republican leaders even tried to block a court order removing Schiavo's feeding tube by subpoenaing the woman and her husband. The judge in the case rejected the action, and doctors removed Schiavo's feeding tube the afternoon of March 18. Unless it is reinstated, she is expected to live only a week or two.

All of this took place just after Congress inserted itself into another subject it does not usually address: the use of steroids in Major League Baseball. On March 17, the House Government Reform Committee grilled baseball stars such as Mark McGwire and José Canseco over whether they had used steroids in the past, and lawmakers from both parties threatened legislative action if the sport doesn't clean up its act.

The two issues could not be more different. One is a national pastime, the other involves a

woman's life. They don't compare in terms of seriousness. But in both cases, Congress is using its oversight powers to explore issues it doesn't normally tackle.

In doing so, lawmakers are wandering into dangerous territory — gaining support from the people who care most fervently about the issues, perhaps, but at the risk of playing into old stereotypes about members of Congress grandstanding on sensitive issues to generate headlines.

"In both cases, people will want to know why this is an appropriate role for Congress," says Gary W. Copeland, director of the Carl Albert Congressional Research and Studies Center at the University of Oklahoma. That's an easier case to make with the baseball hearing than with the Schiavo case, he says, because baseball enjoys an exemption from antitrust law that might give Congress the right to look into the use of steroids.

EPA PHOTO / PETER MUHLY / LANDOV

"The question is whether they will be able to do the same thing with the Schiavo case," Copeland says.

Congress' energy on the two cases is a contrast to its lethargy on oversight in general. With Republicans controlling the White House and Congress, lawmakers and experts on congressional oversight say the legislative branch has not been eager to investigate the executive branch and its conduct of government programs. Even hearings into the abuse of Iraqi prisoners, which lawmakers said would be tough and unrelenting, quickly sputtered out.

This time, the Bush administration is not the target of the investigations — which makes

feeding tube, an order that the presiding judge refused.

There's a fine line between drawing serious attention to serious issues and exploiting them for political points. With the baseball hearing, nothing more serious than Mark McGwire's reputation was at stake. With Schiavo, the scenarios get much worse. Senate Majority Leader Bill Frist and House Speaker J. Dennis Hastert vowed to work through the weekend in hopes of an agreement on legislation to keep Schiavo alive, an effort they had bungled just before the House adjourned March 18 for its spring recess.

But the fact that House and Senate leaders both ordered the Schiavos to show up at con-

son, a political science professor at the University of California at San Diego, who specializes in congressional elections. "To everyone else, it's going to look like grandstanding politicians interfering in a very difficult and emotional case."

MORALITY VS. POLITICS

On a moral level, Republican leaders say, they have every right to intervene when a woman's life is at stake. Some of the lawmakers involved, including Rick Santorum, the chairman of the Senate Republican Conference, and Rep. Curt Weldon, both of Pennsylvania, are known for their deep convictions about the sanctity of life.

DEFENDING BASEBALL: At a March 17 hearing on steroid use, former star Mark McGwire, left, testified along with current players Rafael Palmeiro and Curt Schilling.

it easier for Congress to go all out. More to the point, they involve high-profile issues that are sure to capture the public's interest. So lawmakers showed no qualms about summoning baseball players to Capitol Hill, questioning them closely and threatening legislative action to keep performance-enhancing drugs from ruining the integrity of the sport.

For the Schiavo case, Republicans used Congress' subpoena powers even more aggressively. The Senate health panel actually ordered Schiavo to show up for a March 28 hearing — along with her husband, Michael, who has been fighting to remove the feeding tube, saying Schiavo had told him she would not want to be kept alive artificially.

The House panel issued subpoenas ordering both to attend a March 25 hearing at Schiavo's Florida hospice. But the committee didn't stop there: It also ordered Michael Schiavo, the doctors and the hospice director not to remove the

gressional hearings raised questions about how far they were prepared to go. Were they actually ready to have Schiavo in a hearing room, under the television lights, in her immobilized state? Would the public see the hearings as a heroic effort to save a life, or as a tasteless exploitation of a human tragedy? And were they really prepared to fine either Schiavo or her husband if they didn't show up?

In the past, Congress has been able to convince the public that it has a legitimate oversight role in areas it had not touched before, says John Hibbing, a professor of political science at the University of Nebraska at Lincoln who specializes in attitudes toward Congress. Where it crosses a line with the public, though, is when it appears to be trying to micromanage an issue rather than just drawing needed attention to it, and that's a real danger with the Schiavo case, Hibbing says.

"It plays well to the base," says Gary C. Jacob-

But others, such as House Majority Leader Tom DeLay of Texas, have not been shy about playing up the politics of the situation. DeLay blamed Democratic senators for the legislative impasse and called their actions "an unprecedented profile in cowardice."

"Right now, murder is being committed against a defenseless American citizen in Florida," DeLay said after Schiavo's feeding tube was removed. "What is happening to her is not compassion — it is homicide."

It's not clear that DeLay's view is widely shared by the public, though. In a Fox News/Opinion Dynamics poll of 900 registered voters conducted March 1-2, only 2 percent said the government should decide whether to keep a patient in Schiavo's condition alive. Instead, 45 percent said it should be the spouse's decision, while 38 percent said the call should be made by the parents or other family members.

Hibbing notes that when Sen. Estes Kefau-

CQ PHOTO / SCOTT J. FERRELL

ver held hearings on organized crime in 1950-51, most of the public thought Congress was "sticking its nose where it didn't belong." Over time, though, people decided it was a legitimate issue for lawmakers to take on.

That's what conservative religious groups say will happen with the Schiavo case. If Congress shows leadership on a moral issue, they say, the public will come along. "Once people understand the issue, I think most people will support Congress' involvement," says Jayd Henricks, a lobbyist for the Family Research Council. "A woman's life is at stake here."

And as much as some baseball fans grumbled about Congress getting involved in their favorite sport, public opinion experts say the hearing was handled so fairly that most of the questions about the legitimacy of the investigation will probably disappear.

"When you listened to the individuals who asked the questions, there was no way to tell if they were Republicans or Democrats," said David Winston, a Republican pollster who advises Senate and House leaders. "It was one of the most nonpartisan hearings I've ever seen, if not the most nonpartisan."

> **"It plays well to the base. To everyone else, it's going to look like grandstanding politicians interfering in a very difficult and emotional case."**
>
> — **Gary C. Jacobson**, political science professor, University of California at San Diego

The bipartisan spirit was jeopardized, however, when GOP leaders announced the Schiavo hearing. Committee Chairman Thomas M. Davis III of Virginia and ranking Democrat Henry A. Waxman of California have a good enough relationship to work together on some issues, including the baseball hearing. But Waxman said the Schiavo subpoenas were "a flagrant abuse of power" and were "issued unilaterally by Tom Davis, acting at the request of the Republican leadership."

There's a practical danger, too. Legal experts say that by using its subpoena powers in such extraordinary ways — especially by issuing orders to physicians, as the House did —. Congress runs the risk of being slapped down by the courts, which would actually reduce its subpoena authority over the long run.

"It is a very reckless act on the part of Congress to push [its] subpoena authority this far," says Jonathan Turley, a professor at the George Washington University law school.

These are all acceptable risks to the social conservatives who want Schiavo kept alive — the same ones who helped re-elect Bush and put more Republicans in Congress.

"There is a risk that it could be seen as bad taste, but the saving of a life trumps all of that," says Jim Backlin, a lobbyist for the Christian Coalition of America. "I think the public will approve of any kind of effort to save a disabled woman who can't speak for herself and seems to have a husband who's determined to put her to death." Republicans will have to hope he's right. ∎

Battle Lines Not So Clear In 'File-Sharing' Debate

Self-interest is proving a tricky call for manufacturers and content producers dependent on one another

IMAGINE A WORLD without any iPods, any TiVo or any DVD burners.

Home electronics and software makers say that many of the gadgets we are coming to take for granted today wouldn't exist without a landmark 1984 Supreme Court ruling that spared Sony from liability for copyright infringement by people who used its Betamax video recorders.

But the technology industry worries that a case now before the high court threatens the Betamax precedent, which they say spawned a generation of innovation. The justices will hear arguments March 29 in the entertainment industry's bid to shut down those Internet services that people can use to illegally swap copyrighted songs and films. Hollywood and the music companies claim that such "file-sharing" services encourage

CQ Weekly March 7, 2005

Internet piracy that costs them billions of dollars a year in uncollected revenue.

"My fear is for the future," says Mark Cuban, an Internet pioneer and owner of the NBA's Dallas Mavericks, who made a fortune selling his digital media company Broadcast.com to Yahoo! Inc.

"If this had happened 15 years ago, e-mail would have been dead before it even got started," he says of the possibility that the justices might reverse their precedent and conclude that companies can be held responsible for the inappropriate use of their products. If that happens, he says, it "will affect applications we don't even know about yet. This has everything to do with stopping technological progress."

Although so much is potentially on the line, the consumer electronics and software companies have been unexpectedly quiet about the file-sharing case, *MGM Studios v. Grokster*, leaving it to their trade associations to do the talk-

ing. Technology companies that never were bashful about speaking out on public issues affecting their bottom lines have a variety of reasons for pulling their punches this time.

Some technology companies are part of conglomerates with conflicting interests. For example, Sony Electronics Inc., a leading maker of videocassette recorders, DVD burners, and other devices that can duplicate and replay unlicensed content, is a unit of Sony Corp. — owner of some of the world's biggest movie studios and record labels. And America Online Inc., which has some subscribers trading unlicensed content on its Internet network, is a unit of Time Warner Inc., owner of film and TV studios and cable television networks.

Then there are software developers such as Microsoft Corp. and Adobe Systems Inc., which make products that can be used to send copyrighted material online — but are them-

Companies In Conflict

Technology and media conglomerates: Time Warner Inc.'s America Online service boasts nearly 30 million users worldwide, but the company's entertainment properties, including Warner Brothers Pictures and New Line Cinema (right), risk substantial losses from online piracy.

Technology firms in business with entertainment firms: Apple Computer Inc. has sold millions of iPods (left), its celebrated portable MP3 player,

leading the company to record profits and stock performance. But Apple relies on the music industry to sell

songs on its iTunes online music store, which helped popularize the iPod. And Apple CEO Steve Jobs also runs Pixar Animation Studios.

Technology firms victimized by piracy: While Microsoft Corp. programs such as Outlook (below) could be seen as vehicles for file-sharing, many of the company's products are themselves pirated on the Internet. The software industry claims $29 billion in losses to piracy last year.

FROM LEFT: APPLE COMPUTER INC.; NEW LINE CINEMA; MICROSOFT CORP.

selves often victims of piracy over the Internet.

Manufacturers of such electronic devices as TiVo Inc.'s digital video recorder and Apple Computer Inc.'s iPod might be vulnerable to any lowering of the liability shield created by the Betamax ruling, but they can ill afford to alienate the entertainment companies that fill their machines with music and video programming. Apple declined to comment, while TiVo said it takes measures to protect intellectual property.

"The computer industry is very dependent on maintaining friendly relations with the entertainment industry because the entertainment industry supplies the content that will be central to the digital media future," says Phil Leigh, a former stock analyst who runs Inside Digital Media Inc., a market research firm.

Technology companies have yet another reason for ambivalence. Some of them agree that the file-sharing services targeted in the entertainment industry's case — Grokster and StreamCast's Morpheus — really do encourage copyright infringement.

"There is a sense among some of the companies involved of being used by entities hiding behind the legal principles," says Markham Erickson, general counsel of NetCoalition, which represents Yahoo, Google Inc. and other Internet companies. "The content industry is trying to stop the technology, and Grokster is trying to hide behind the technology."

In briefs filed with the Supreme Court, the Business Software Alliance, which represents Adobe and Microsoft, and other technology trade groups contend Grokster and Stream-Cast should be held liable for copyright violations if they promote themselves as free music sources — not because they distribute software that can be used for online piracy. The distinction aims to preserve the current precedent by focusing the court on the file-sharing services' behavior, not their technology.

INTERNET PIRACY

The film and music industries — which estimate that they lose more than $7 billion a year to piracy, much of it on the Internet — say they're not trying to weaken or overturn the Betamax precedent, which protects makers of products "capable of substantial non-infringing uses" from liability for infringement.

"We are not opposed to technology," says Fritz Attaway, Washington general counsel for the Motion Picture Association of America. "What we object to is the misuse of technology for infringing purposes and business models based on massive infringement."

Hollywood says file-sharing services encourage and profit from piracy that the services could take steps to prevent.

"Virtually all those who use Grokster and StreamCast are committing unlawful copyright infringement, and they commit millions of acts of infringement each day," the entertainment industry says in a filing with the Supreme Court. "Grokster and StreamCast exploit this massive infringement for profit, and petitioners are suffering extreme harms as a consequence."

But the technology industry fears that the Betamax precedent itself is at risk in the case.

"It's really the technology that's on trial here — and the idea that someone could be held liable for making and marketing a neutral tool like file-sharing software, which can be misused as well as used for legitimate purposes," says Adam Eisgrau, of P2P United, which lobbies for some of the file-sharing services.

Jonathan Zittrain, co-founder of Harvard Law School's Berkman Center for Internet and Society, says the Supreme Court is unlikely to repudiate the doctrine it established two decades ago, but could vastly narrow its scope — turning it into a case about VCRs only.

After winning a court order in 2000 that resulted in shutting down the Napster file-swapping service, the film and music companies in 2001 sued Grokster, StreamCast and Sharman Networks, which offered another file-sharing program, Kazaa. Unlike Napster, the newer file-sharing services permitted people to interact directly and maintained no centralized index of downloadable files.

The argument persuaded the 9th U.S. Circuit Court of Appeals in August to affirm a lower court finding that the Betamax decision protects file-sharing services from liability when their customers misbehave. Members of Congress failed in efforts to reach a legislative compromise last fall; Hollywood appealed, and the Supreme Court agreed to hear the case.

The diverse group asking the court to reverse the 9th Circuit includes former Solicitor General Theodore B. Olson, Baseball Commissioner Bud Selig, the Christian Coalition of America, the Hip-Hop Summit Action Network, and musicians including the Dixie Chicks, Sheryl Crow and Beach Boys founder Brian Wilson. On the same side are lawyers for the film industry, including Kenneth W. Starr, the independent counsel who investigated President Bill Clinton, and David Kendall, who defended Clinton during that inquiry.

Several musicians — including Janis Ian and rapper Chuck D — filed briefs on the other side, arguing that file-sharing services give musicians new ways to distribute their songs and build followings. A long roster of law and computer science professors and consumer groups also filed briefs endorsing the position of Grokster and StreamCast.

Unlike the entertainment industry, however, technology companies and trade groups have taken no united stand on the case.

Intel Corp., Sun Microsystems Inc. and the Consumer Electronics Association filed briefs supporting the lower court ruling, as did a group of Internet service providers, including Verizon Communications Inc. and SBC Internet Services Inc., which are afraid of being held liable for their customers' Internet piracy.

But the Business Software Alliance has come out on the other side, even though popular programs such as Adobe PhotoShop and Microsoft Outlook can be used to send copyrighted files over the Internet — so those software companies could be exposed to new liabilities if the Betamax precedent is weakened. The alliance says software companies lost $29 billion to piracy in 2003.

Other technology industry trade groups and civil liberties organizations filed a neutral brief, asking the justices to instruct the lower courts to examine the behavior — rather than the technology — of the file-sharing services.

ABSENT FROM DEBATE

Largely absent from the debate are the electronics and software makers themselves.

"The technology companies should speak out, because it's their lunch that is being taken from them," says Wendy Seltzer, a lawyer with the Electronic Frontier Foundation, which represents StreamCast. "A lot of technology companies are still dominated by an engineer's sensibility. They still think: 'If we make the coolest products, that's enough.' But if the coolest technology is outlawed, it doesn't matter how good their engineers are."

Whatever the court decides, sticky questions about online piracy are bound to end up before Congress. When that happens, technology companies would be unwise to let Hollywood set the agenda, says Gigi Sohn, president of the public interest group Public Knowledge.

"When Michael Eisner or Rupert Murdoch comes to speak on Capitol Hill and Steve Jobs won't, it has an impact," she says, referring to the heads of Walt Disney Co., News Corp. and Apple. "These CEOs have star power."

Sohn says electronics and software makers are mistaken if they think their interests and those of the entertainment companies are the same. "We've tried to tell them," she says. "You can play nice, but they're still going to go after your machines." ∎

Weighing Nip, Tuck Vs. Total Makeover

Some benefit cuts, revenue increases could mend system

O F ALL THE ADVERTISING created so far to influence the Social Security debate, perhaps no image is so powerful as that of the woman who watches helplessly as her house is smashed to the ground — her plumber's prescription for nothing more serious than a clogged drain.

The message that the AARP, the powerful lobby for the elderly, wants to convey with that television spot is clear: It is overkill in the extreme to address Social Security's financial challenges by diverting trillions of dollars into individual investment accounts that otherwise would flow into the program.

But what are the alternatives? Could the retirement income program's long-term fiscal plight be effectively eliminated without any move toward the introduction of special savings accounts?

The answer is yes. However, since all the options involve cutting benefits or raising taxes, even the most seemingly modest alterations in the program would require significant political pain.

Social Security — as Judd Gregg, R-N.H., the Senate Budget Committee chairman, often says — doesn't have a lot of moving parts. In other words, there is a limited collection of pieces of the program that can be altered in a bid to shore up its future. That is especially so if Social Security is to retain the characteristics that have defined it since its inception in the New Deal, such as its being segregated from the rest of the federal budget or the way it is structured to link what workers pay into the system in taxes to what they receive when they retire.

The options include increasing the payroll taxes that finance the program; raising the cap on the amount of earned income subject to those taxes; slowing the rate of growth in

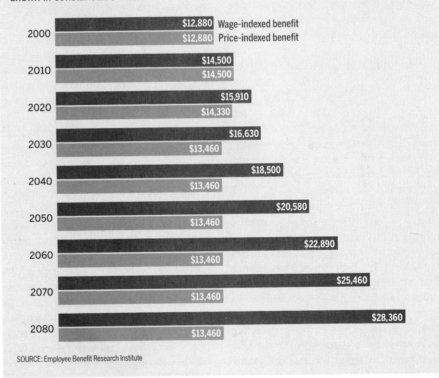

New Index for Benefits Would Cut Payments

This graphic shows the likely result of one proposed change in the way a retiree's initial Social Security benefits are calculated. The red bar shows the current method of adjusting benefits based on the amount by which wages rise during a retiree's working life — known as wage-indexing. The green bar shows what first year benefits would be if they were indexed to changes in consumer prices — known as price-indexing. All figures are shown in constant 2004 dollars.

Year	Wage-indexed benefit	Price-indexed benefit
2000	$12,880	$12,880
2010	$14,500	$14,500
2020	$15,910	$14,330
2030	$16,630	$13,460
2040	$18,500	$13,460
2050	$20,580	$13,460
2060	$22,890	$13,460
2070	$25,460	$13,460
2080	$28,360	$13,460

SOURCE: Employee Benefit Research Institute

benefits by connecting benefit payment to price inflation instead of wage inflation; curtailing the annual cost-of-living increase in benefits; and raising the age at which people may retire with full benefits above the current ceiling of 67 years old.

There are two critical measures of the financial health of the program. The first is the amount being held in its two trust funds. (Technically, there is one for the elderly and a

much smaller one for disabled workers, who also qualify for benefits.)

According to this year's report from the program's trustees, the funds will be depleted of their assets by 2041 if the program continues as is. The balance in the trust funds, which was $1.69 trillion at the end of 2004, has been surging since tweaks were made to the program two decades ago. It is projected to peak at $6 trillion in 2026 and then decline. *(2005*

CQ GRAPHIC / MARILYN GATES-DAVIS

CQ Weekly, Imbalances, p. 835)

These surpluses are invested in federal bonds that will start to be redeemed beginning in about 2017, when a year's worth of payroll tax receipts will fall short of the amount required to pay a year's worth of benefits. Until then, the extra money is being used in essence to help finance the non-Social Security operations of the government. The annual surpluses now reduce the size of the so-called unified budget deficit; in fiscal 2004, for example, the Social Security trust fund surplus was $156 billion, so that much was shaved off the deficit, leaving a final red ink figure of $412 billion.

But the financial health of the program is also measured by how long it will run these surpluses. In other words, in how many more years will payroll tax revenue exceed benefit payments? (The current projection is 12.) After that, while the trust funds are tapped, how large will the gap grow between tax receipts and outlays for benefits? How much cash will be required from the general fund to replace the Treasury bonds held by the trust funds? And how long will it be until the trust funds are empty? (The current projection is that the reserves will be gone in 2041.)

In assessing ideas for shoring up the program, actuaries look at two factors. First, they measure the effect a proposal would have on the long-range solvency of the trust funds — essentially, how many years would be added to the trust funds' current projected depletion date of 2041. Second, they measure how much a proposal could close the long-term gap between tax revenue and benefit payments.

Some ideas, such as a slight increase in payroll taxes, could do much in the short term to enhance Social Security's finances but are less viable options for the long term. (The latest estimate is that 75 years from now, when the trust funds are empty, it would require roughly a 6 percentage-point increase in the payroll tax — to a figure almost 50 percent higher than today's 12.4 percent rate — in order to hold the program at a pay-as-you go annual balance.) On the other hand, benefit reductions generally yield greater savings over the long term.

Payroll tax rate increases are one of the few ideas, moreover, that have been rejected out of hand by the Bush administration. "Payroll taxes have been raised some 20 times since Social Security was established, and it has failed to make the system solvent," Treasury Secretary John W. Snow told an audience in Wilmington, Del., last month.

The basic argument for simultaneously tweaking several of the system's components is that doing so would demand some measure of sacrifice from a broad spectrum of the public. Balancing the program entirely by cutting benefits, for example, would surely be opposed by retirees as unfair. And, of course, wage earners would have the same reaction to an increase in payroll taxes.

Instead, experts in Social Security policy tend to talk about a fix the way they would talk about picking from a Chinese restaurant menu — making a couple of choices from both Column A and Column B. "It's probably going to require some combination to get a compromise," said Steve Goss, chief actuary of the Social Security Administration.

"The only way they're going to get a resolution of this is a balanced package with some revenues and some benefit constraints and that's going to take, I would guess, about four or five of these ideas combined together," said John Rother, director of policy and strategy for AARP, the powerful seniors' lobby, in predicting the eventual outcome of the debate over Social Security's solvency.

OPTIONS FOR RAISING REVENUE

Businesses and their employees each pay 6.2 percent in Social Security payroll taxes on most of each worker's wages — the first $90,000 in 2005 — yielding the overall rate of 12.4 percent.

The two basic ways to increase revenue are increasing that rate — the option Bush has ruled out — and raising the cap on annual earned income subject to the tax. The cap is currently "indexed" to increase with inflation every year; last year, the cap was $87,900.

Bush has hinted he might accept some increase in the cap, and the idea does well in public opinion polls.

Increasing the tax rate 2 percentage points — 1 point each to be covered by employer and employee — would add enough money to the program to keep it in the black for more than 75 years. For the next six years or so, the additional revenue would enhance the trust fund reserves; after that, the extra money would allow the trust funds to be drawn down at a slower rate than is now forecast. Once the trust funds are empty, though, that 2 point increase would not come close to ending the gap between annual receipts and annual payments.

Increasing the cap on income subject to Social Security payroll taxes is popular with the public. It was favored, 60 percent to 33 percent, by respondents in a March 2 poll by the Pew Research Center for the People and the Press.

It also has the advantage of raising lots of money. Doing away with the cap altogether would, by itself, keep the trust funds solvent for about 36 years beyond 2041, Social Security's actuaries say — and longer than that if those who would be paying the higher taxes are not rewarded with increased benefits.

Still, abandoning the cap would delay only into the middle 2020s the point at which Social Security was no longer operating as a pay-as-you-go proposition.

And raising the cap has stirred opposition in some quarters. For starters, an income of $90,000 is not considered especially high in areas of the country with the highest costs of living. And the move could be portrayed as a tax increase for the upper middle class, because taxing income in excess of $90,000 might have the effect of nullifying the benefits of this decade's tax cuts for people with incomes in that range.

In addition, there would surely be a revolt from the self-employed and those owners of small businesses who pay themselves a salary. Both categories of workers must pay the entire 12.4 percent tax.

"Most of the people who would be affected by something like that are in the band between $90,000 and $125,000, and a substantial number of those are small-business people or independent consultants — people who would be paying both ends of the tax. So you're talking about a 12 percent tax," said David John, a research fellow at the conservative Heritage Foundation.

OPTIONS FOR CUTTING BENEFITS

Among Social Security experts, if not yet among lawmakers, there appears to be a widespread agreement that any successful formula for balancing the program's books over the long haul must include benefit cuts of some fashion. The demographic realities of the program — increases in life expectancy and a declining ratio of workers who are paying in to retirees who are taking out — mean that the current rate of annual increases in benefit payments are unsupportable without politically untenable tax increases.

Under current projections, when the trust funds are depleted in 2041, that year's revenues would be sufficient to pay only 74 percent of that year's benefits.

Many of the proposals to reduce benefits involve the concept of "indexing."

At present, each American's benefits are determined using a complicated formula that reflects national wage inflation over most of the person's working life. The idea behind this "wage indexing" is to have a person's retirement benefits reflect improvements in the country's standard of living during the person's working lifetime. Wages generally increase faster than prices.

The obvious alternative, then, is "price indexing," or tying benefit increases to the rate of price inflation over a worker's lifetime. Making such a shift has supporters in the White House, and in Congress it is backed most prominently by Sen. Lindsey Graham, R-S.C., who has positioned himself to be an architect of a bipartisan compromise alternative to Bush's proposals.

One price-indexing plan scored by Social Security's actuaries would make great strides toward returning the system to fiscal health by extending the solvency of the trust fund by about 27 years, to 2068 or so.

Price indexing, however, has already become somewhat politically radioactive. because several nonpartisan analyses have demonstrated that the change would produce sharply lower benefits in the long term. For example, had the system had used price indexing since 1940, the Congressional Research Service found, the average annual Social Security benefit today would be $6,180, less than half the actual benefit of $15,336.

"I can say it out loud," said the AARP's Rother. Price indexing "would only happen over our dead bodies."

As an alternative, some have proposed what has come to be called "progressive price indexing," under which benefits would be linked to price inflation, but workers with the least income would be shielded from cuts in their benefits.

The idea has drawn praise from the president, but it seems almost as controversial as straight price indexing. It is the brainchild of Robert Pozen, a member of the presidential commission that proposed an array of Social Security changes four years ago.

Although it would succeed in closing about three-fourths of the program's projected shortfall over the next 75 years, it would do so by producing a benefit structure that, over time, would flatten the benefits for high earners to levels near those of low earners.

"This raises the question of whether broad political support for Social Security can be sustained if workers pay very different amounts of payroll taxes but most workers receive the same level of benefits," said Jason Furman, a senior fellow at the liberal-leaning Center on Budget and Policy Priorities.

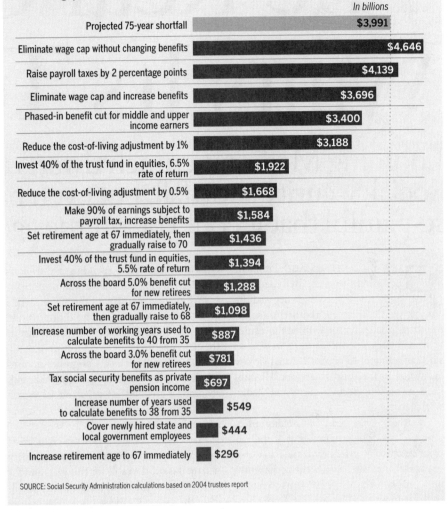

A Few Proposed 'Tweaks'

Social Security faces a shortfall of about $4 trillion over the next 75 years (yellow bar). Below is a partial list of proposals evaluated by the Social Security system that would generate savings, mostly through tax increases and benefit cuts, in a bid to close the gap.

In billions

Projected 75-year shortfall	$3,991
Eliminate wage cap without changing benefits	$4,646
Raise payroll taxes by 2 percentage points	$4,139
Eliminate wage cap and increase benefits	$3,696
Phased-in benefit cut for middle and upper income earners	$3,400
Reduce the cost-of-living adjustment by 1%	$3,188
Invest 40% of the trust fund in equities, 6.5% rate of return	$1,922
Reduce the cost-of-living adjustment by 0.5%	$1,668
Make 90% of earnings subject to payroll tax, increase benefits	$1,584
Set retirement age at 67 immediately, then gradually raise to 70	$1,436
Invest 40% of the trust fund in equities, 5.5% rate of return	$1,394
Across the board 5.0% benefit cut for new retirees	$1,288
Set retirement age at 67 immediately, then gradually raise to 68	$1,098
Increase number of working years used to calculate benefits to 40 from 35	$887
Across the board 3.0% benefit cut for new retirees	$781
Tax social security benefits as private pension income	$697
Increase number of years used to calculate benefits to 38 from 35	$549
Cover newly hired state and local government employees	$444
Increase retirement age to 67 immediately	$296

SOURCE: Social Security Administration calculations based on 2004 trustees report

Similar fairness challenges would surely be raised against proposals to "means test" Social Security benefits so that higher-income retirees would receive a lower benefit. In addition, doing so would probably prove enormously complicated to administer. At the same time, means testing could give future retirees less of an incentive to work into their later years and would generally reward those with assets (but little income) over those with fewer assets and more income.

A less controversial idea is "longevity indexing." Under this alternative, a retiree's annual benefit would be reduced slightly as his or her life expectancy was increased — with the aim of making good on the person's total projected lifetime benefit, but with that amount apportioned over a greater number of years. AARP's Rother said his organization could

probably live with that idea as part of a broader package.

A similar idea is to raise the retirement age at which people qualify for full benefits. The age is increasing gradually — to 67 in 2022, when people born in 1955 will be that old. Accelerating the use of 67 as the "normal" age and then gradually increasing it again, to 70 years old, would extend the viability of the trust fund for about six years, to 2047, according to the Social Security actuaries.

Many analysts say raising the retirement age makes sense, since it both reflects a trend in the workforce and helps compensate for the cost of paying benefits to people living longer, which is one of the cost drivers of the program. But the idea is deeply unpopular with the public. Only 25 percent of respondents favored it in the recent Pew poll. ■

CQ GRAPHIC / JAMIE BAYLIS

The Real Crisis Waits Its Turn

Looming Medicare crunch dwarfs the much-debated Social Security shortfall, but even partial fixes sound so painful that it could be off the agenda for years

FIFTEEN MONTHS AGO, President Bush and Congress fixed Medicare, or at least that is what they told the public. Enacting the new prescription drug benefit and some modest measures to stimulate private competition was so exhausting that both parties declared victory and moved on. Bush and congressional Republicans are tackling Social Security and Medicaid this year.

The reality, though, is that Medicare has not been fixed. The program that 41 million senior citizens rely on for health care is in worse financial shape than Social Security, the retirement program Bush says he wants to rescue from a coming fiscal crunch. Far from trimming Medicare's spending, the legislation that Congress passed in 2003 may have made the program better for seniors, but it piled on bil-

CQ Weekly Feb. 21, 2005

THEN AND NOW: Medicare was designed for a different era. Its first beneficiary, above, was Lillian Grace Avery in 1966.

lions of dollars in new spending and trillions of dollars in long-term liabilities.

"We managed to create the sense in this country that, 'Oh, we did Medicare,' " says Maya MacGuineas, director of fiscal policy at the New America Foundation, a centrist think-tank. Neither Bush nor Congress wants to revisit the program, even though Medicare's spending is growing faster than Social Security's and its reserves are expected to run out sooner.

Medicare faces a larger long-term crisis than any other program in the social safety net, yet it is off the table for this year, and for reasons that speak volumes about the inability of the nation's leaders to solve the biggest problems. Medicare's fixes will be more painful than Social Security's: not just tax increases or payment cuts, but possibly even a halt to certain kinds of care. The repairs will not appeal to younger voters, the way Republicans think Social Security private savings accounts will. The prospect of more changes to the program upsets the powerful health care industry, which is just getting used to the last ones. And a "sweetener" — the one time-honored trick that might make painful changes go down more easily — is no longer available. For Medicare, adding the drug benefit was the sweetener.

"It's so big that no one wants to talk about it," says Peter G. Peterson, a co-founder of The Concord Coalition and author of "Running On Empty: How the Democratic and Republican Parties are Bankrupting Our Future and What Americans Can Do About It."

NO CLEAR ADVANTAGE

Social Security is the largest of the nation's entitlement programs, which automatically provide benefits to anyone who qualifies, but it may be the easiest to restructure. Bush and his advisers are confident that there will be political benefits to tackling Social Security that would offset any backlash from seniors — mainly the chance to remake the most enduring legacy of the New Deal and win the allegiance of younger voters with the idea of personal savings accounts for retirement.

There is no such advantage to be gained from Medicare. Even before the drug benefit was added to the program, it faced the challenges of a 40-year-old system created in a different era, when hospitalizations were more common and before new drugs and disease prevention became the preferred forms of medical care for seniors. The drug benefit was supposed to be, in part, a recognition of how medicine has changed. But it also heaped new spending promises on top of the old ones.

Now, Medicare's liabilities could be as much as eight times greater than Social Security's. With Social Security, there is a $3.7 trillion gap over the next 75 years between the benefits that have been promised and the benefits that can be paid for under the current system. With Medicare, according to the Government Accountability Office, it is a $27.8 trillion gap. That includes $8.1 trillion in liabilities that were added the moment Bush signed the Medicare prescription drug benefit into law.

AP PHOTO FILE PHOTO

Bush's calculations on Social Security's uncertain future are that by 2018, the program will start paying out more than it receives in payroll taxes, and by 2042 its trust funds — which hold the taxes and pay the benefits — will be "exhausted and bankrupt" unless Congress steps in. Medicare has a trust fund too, for the part of the program that covers hospital expenses, but it is projected to run out in 2019. And according to its trustees, the Medicare trust fund started paying out more than it takes in last year.

The prescription drug benefit instantly added hundreds of billions of dollars to the program's cost: up to $724 billion over 10 years, nearly twice as much as the $395 billion price tag that was originally publicized in 2003. Altogether, the costs are about to start escalating faster than ever. By 2024, Medicare is expected to be more expensive than Social Security.

STICKER SHOCK

But all the bickering over how much the drug benefit will cost over 10 years obscures the reality of the more than $8 trillion in long-term expenses it cannot pay for. The reason Congress did not realize how bad the price tag was, according to the Government Accountability Office, is that it looks at everything in 10-year budget windows. A new drug benefit lasts forever.

Not everyone believes Congress needs to take on the biggest problem first. "My own judgment is that the Medicare problem is of course several multiples more difficult than is Social Security," Federal Reserve Board Chairman Alan Greenspan told a Senate committee Feb. 16. But the health care system is in too much flux right now, he said, as researchers develop information technology that could save money by making clinical practices more standard throughout the country. If Congress were to attempt another Medicare overhaul now, Greenspan said, "I'm fearful we would be restructuring an obsolete model and have to come back and undo it."

But others say looking the other way will only make the problems worse. Medicare faces the same demographic trends that trouble Social Security — a wave of retiring baby boomers, people living longer than they did a few decades ago — plus the added complication of runaway increases in medical costs, thanks to the very same advances in medical technologies and treatments that are allowing senior citizens to enjoy longer lives. The cost of keeping them alive is proving to be more than

the entitlement system can bear.

"If the president says it's urgent to address the Social Security crisis. What about Medicare?" says Kent Conrad of North Dakota, the ranking Democrat on the Senate Budget Committee. "My own view is, we need to deal with both, and the sooner the better."

THE COST OF LONGER LIVES

It will not take long for the spending pressures to build up. In 15 years, the government will be using one-fourth of all federal income taxes for Medicare, according to Tom Saving of Texas A&M University, a trustee of the Medicare program who has done the calculation. And if Medicare and Medicaid together grow at just 2 percentage points a year, some estimates predict that by 2040 they will consume 20 percent of the Gross Domestic Product, almost as much as the current federal budget.

Medicare was the landmark accomplishment of Lyndon B. Johnson's Great Society, much as Social Security set the tone for Franklin D. Roosevelt's New Deal. It provides automatic coverage of inpatient hospital expenses for most Americans age 65 and over, voluntary coverage of physician and outpatient hospital expenses, and now the voluntary prescription drug benefit. The hospital insurance is funded by payroll taxes paid by employers and employees, while the physician and prescription drug coverage are funded by beneficiary premiums and general revenues.

On Capitol Hill, conservatives have seized on the new cost estimates to insist that the drug benefit be constrained to fit within the $400 billion limit. Senate Budget Committee Chairman Judd Gregg, R-N.H., who did not support the drug benefit in the first place, says spending more than that would violate Republicans' convictions on fiscal discipline.

There is even talk among some House conservatives of adding another means-testing provision, which would prevent wealthier seniors from qualifying for drug coverage, before the benefit begins next year. The Medicare law requires seniors earning more than $160,000 a year for a couple to pay slightly more in outpatient care monthly premiums. "Just because we created it doesn't mean we have to live with it as it was created," says Tennessee Republican Zach Wamp, who has floated the means-testing idea.

And Democrats are using the new cost estimates to jump-start the arguments for their own priorities, such as reimporting drugs from

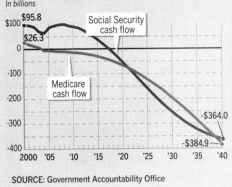

Medicare Trust Fund: Already Running a Deficit

Social Security payroll taxes currently exceed expenses for the program, which is not expected to run a deficit before 2018. But the Medicare Hospital Insurance (Part A) trust fund, which covers the inpatient bills of beneficiaries, already has begun running deficits, and they are projected to get much worse.

In billions

Social Security cash flow

Medicare cash flow

$95.8
$26.3
-$364.0
-$384.9

2000 '05 '10 '15 '20 '25 '30 '35 '40

SOURCE: Government Accountability Office

Canada and using the government's purchasing clout to negotiate better drug prices for Medicare.

Bush on Feb. 11 threatened to veto any attempt to change the drug benefit, and none of the most powerful lawmakers from either party seem willing to tackle Medicare's structural problems.

"Politically, nobody wants to reopen this," says Joseph Antos, a health care expert at the conservative American Enterprise Institute. If any new Medicare legislation comes up, he says, it will "open up the floodgates" to industry lobbyists and result in more spending to health care providers, not less.

It is not just that Congress is tired of the subject. All of the players with an interest in the Medicare drug benefit — health plans, regulatory agencies, the pharmaceutical industry, retail pharmacists — have enough work on their hands adjusting to the rules of the new system. "They want this ship to be steady for a while," Antos says. "They just can't accommodate new changes."

Instead, Bush wants to take on another major entitlement program this year — Medicaid, the health care program for the poor and people with disabilities — with proposed cuts that are controversial themselves, although they are aimed at constituencies with less political power than Medicare's.

The administration says Congress took steps in the Medicare law to lower costs through more private competition and that

CQ GRAPHIC / MARILYN GATES-DAVIS

Drug Benefit Costs Still Unknown

WHEN CONGRESS PASSED a Medicare bill in 2003, the only thing lawmakers knew for sure was that the price tag would be higher than the official estimates. Now, more than a year later, they still do not know how much higher.

President Bush said at the time that the law adding the prescription drug benefit to Medicare would cost $400 billion over a decade, and that the law contained reforms that would reduce its net cost. These changes are modest, however, and most members of Congress knew that the $400 billion figure for the drug benefit was a convenient fiction designed to make the bill politically palatable to fiscal conservatives and an easier sell to the public.

Medicare's chief actuary revealed last year, in fact, that the White House had estimates that the drug benefit would cost about $534 billion over 10 years. But that forecast included two years — 2004 and 2005 — when the drug benefit would not yet exist. On Feb. 8, the administration released a new forecast that the drug benefit would cost at least $724 billion over the first decade of its actual use. The Congressional Budget Office estimated the price at $795 billion.

A Medicare trustees report due in late March may be based on yet another set of estimates. Most analysts agree that these might also be way off, and the true cost will not be clear until the program goes into effect at the start of 2006.

Joseph Antos, a health care expert at the conservative American Enterprise Institute, and Jagadeesh Gokhale, an analyst at the libertarian Cato Institute, have analyzed the available figures and think that the real price tag for 10 years might be significantly higher than the current White House estimate. There are several reasons for this.

The new program may not be as cost-effective as actuaries think. An unexpectedly high number of companies might stop offering drug coverage to their retirees. New blockbuster drugs, which seniors often insist on, may be more costly than expected. Doctors might prescribe more pills than assumed. And finally, drug industry mergers might reduce competition and lead to higher drug costs.

WISHFUL LAWMAKING

It also is not guaranteed that parts of the 2003 law designed to hold down costs will actually do so. The law encourages seniors to use private managed care plans instead of the traditional, fee-for-service program. But in the short run, that does not save money and can actually cost more.

Medicare will pay more for seniors covered by the new plans than for seniors who stay in the old system. And Congress included a $10 billion fund — Democrats labeled it a "slush fund" — that the government can use to encourage private health plans to cover uninsured patients.

"I call it a quiet change," says Mary Grealy, president of the Healthcare Leadership Council, an association of large companies concerned about health care costs. "As [plans] compete with each other, they'll probably do it more efficiently."

The record of managed care plans participating in Medicare is not encouraging, however. The last time Congress expanded the Medicare managed care system, in 1997, managed care plans left the system in droves, complaining of low payments and excessive regulations. Their withdrawal from the program forced millions of seniors to switch coverage.

This time around, managed care plan executives say the new system pays more, requires plans to take on less risk and offers more flexibility. The old system, created during the Clinton administration, was set up to fail, they say, because plans were strangled by regulatory requirements and payment rates that were too low.

The 2003 law includes a demonstration project starting in 2010 in which the traditional, fee-for-service Medicare program in six cities will compete on price with private health plans. The project will gauge whether private insurers can deliver care more efficiently and with better outcomes than the older model. If successful, the model could be expanded to the entire program.

But will it produce any savings? It's not clear that it will, says Paul B. Ginsburg, director of the Center for Health Systems Change, a nonpartisan research organization. The savings, he said, may dissolve if private plans have to pay higher rates and take on the expense of marketing and enrolling beneficiaries.

Some conservatives say that the incentives for seniors to use managed care and the demonstration projects would not bring as much private competition to the system as Republicans originally wanted. Beyond the drug benefit, "we didn't change Medicare at all," says Tom Saving, a health economist and Medicare trustee.

Gail Wilensky, who ran the Medicare and Medicaid programs during the presidency of Bush's father, said that Congress and the administration had done in 2003 as much as they could considering the political realities. The alternative would have been to wait for a better opportunity, she said, and "we may not be serious about wanting to do that for close to a decade."

Going Up With Every Estimate

When Congress created the Medicare drug benefit in 2003, the Bush administration said it would cost less than $400 billion over 10 years. Since then, the forecasted cost has nearly doubled.

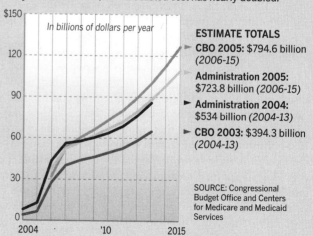

In billions of dollars per year

ESTIMATE TOTALS

► CBO 2005: $794.6 billion (2006-15)

Administration 2005: $723.8 billion (2006-15)

► Administration 2004: $534 billion (2004-13)

► CBO 2003: $394.3 billion (2004-13)

SOURCE: Congressional Budget Office and Centers for Medicare and Medicaid Services

CQ GRAPHIC / MARILYN GATES-DAVIS

they should be given time to work. But few experts think those steps will come close to solving the problem, or even come close to compensating for the added cost of drugs. The White House would also prefer to focus on its other health care proposals for this year, such as limits on medical malpractice lawsuits, better health information technology and an expansion of tax-free health savings accounts. "The most important thing we need to focus on is health care costs overall," says Office of Management and Budget Director Joshua B. Bolten.

Some analysts say Medicare can't be fixed unless the government addresses other aspects of health care that are driving up costs.

"The Medicare issue is so big and broad, it's way beyond the program," said Paul B. Ginsburg, director of the Center for Studying Health System Change, a nonpartisan research organization in Washington. "It's going to cause a revisiting of fiscal policy . . . and a discussion on transforming the entire health care system. There are limits to what can be done in Medicare without influencing the rest of the system."

The most likely scenario is that Medicare's costs will decline significantly only when the nation finds a way to reduce costs for the entire health care system, says Robert D. Reischauer, president of the Urban Institute and a former director of the Congressional Budget Office.

Democrats, who currently control none of the branches of the federal government, have no incentive to propose unpopular changes to Medicare, either — especially since their main criticism of the prescription drug benefit was that it was not big enough.

"It's hard for the president to say, 'We've got a crisis in Medicare and we've got to bring down spending' a year and a half after he signed a prescription drug benefit into law," says Reischauer. And Democrats wanted an even bigger drug benefit, "so that puts them in a bind."

SOCIAL SECURITY FIRST

Bush has a strong partisan incentive to tackle Social Security first. Republican strategists think they can use private savings accounts to help build a permanent government majority by peeling away younger Democrats and possibly African-Americans who might be interested in the accounts. "There's no parallel advantage that they would gain by taking up Medicare first," says David W. Rohde, a professor of political science at Michigan State University. "They'd be squarely up against the wrath of older voters without any offsetting

advantage among younger voters."

Now, Bush is being forced to acknowledge that Medicare's growth is unsustainable. And it will be on the agenda, he says, sometime after Social Security is finished. "There's no question that there is an unfunded liability inherent in Medicare that Congress and the administration is going to have to deal with over time," Bush told reporters Feb. 9. Once the Social Security overhaul is done, "then it'll be time to deal with the unfunded liabilities of Medicare."

A few lawmakers will insist on going further. Republican Bill Thomas of California, chairman of the House Ways and Means Committee, wants to use the Social Security debate as a springboard to take a fresh look at Medicare and other aspects of "an aging society" — possibly exploring ideas, such as more flexible

"My own judgment is that the Medicare problem is of course several multiples more difficult than is Social Security."

— Alan Greenspan, chairman of the Federal Reserve Board

insurance products that would adjust to people's needs as they get older.

Conrad wants to look at options such as better coordination of care for chronically ill patients, who make up only 5 percent of Medicare's beneficiaries but account for the majority of the costs. Many of those costs are unnecessary, he says, such as duplicative medical tests and treatment for adverse drug reactions. He also wants to cut out overpayments to private Medicare plans and eliminate the financial incentives for them to join Medicare.

TOO BIG TO FIX?

Their voices will be a minority in this Congress, however, and their solutions will mostly be on the pain-free side. That is because of the reality that scares both sides: The steps it would

really take to solve the problem would be far more painful than the steps it would take to fix Social Security.

Fixing Social Security's finances will probably require either lower benefits or higher revenues, or both, regardless of what happens with private savings accounts. Most experts say Medicare faces the same types of choices — except that with Medicare, lower benefits could mean politically risky moves such as giving seniors a limited contribution for their health care or gut-wrenching ethical decisions on whether to stop paying for certain kinds of medical care for seniors, particularly at the end of their lives.

There is also the prospect of even lower payments to physicians and hospitals, which could make physicians refuse to treat Medicare patients, just as Medicaid patients often have trouble getting care now. Hospitals are not allowed to turn Medicare patients away, but that means everyone's care would suffer as hospital revenues decline.

"Generally, what they're going to do is cut services, and if they cut services for Medicare patients, they're going to have to cut them for everybody," says Stuart Altman, a professor at the Brandeis University Schneider Institute for Health Policy.

Others, such as David M. Walker, who heads the Government Accountability Office, say a real effort to fix Medicare would have to get into politically touchy subjects, such as who is eligible, what gets covered and how much of the costs patients would have to share. And some experts say there will be no choice but to raise more revenues for Medicare — the conclusion of a 2000 report by the National Academy of Social Insurance.

"No matter what you do to reduce costs, you couldn't do enough," says Bruce Vladeck, a professor of health policy at the Mount Sinai School of Medicine and former administrator of the Health Care Financing Administration. "You wouldn't have anything like a meaningful insurance program."

For seniors, the consequences of a Medicare bankruptcy would be worse than Social Security's insolvency. For the old and sick, it would be easier to find another source of retirement income than it would be to buy better health care.

Walker says both Social Security and Medicare are "unsustainable without major reforms." The difference, he says, is that Medicare "is going to have to be dealt with in stages, it's going to involve much more fundamental reforms than Social Security, and it's

CQ PHOTO / SCOTT J. FERRELL

going to be, believe it or not, much more controversial than Social Security."

IN SEARCH OF PAINLESS SOLUTIONS

Most analysts and politicians would prefer to solve Medicare's financial problems by delivering care more efficiently. But all of the options being discussed — such as cutting payments to doctors and hospitals, basing more treatments on evidence about what works best, managing the care of people with chronic conditions or using electronic instead of paper records — would have but a modest effect on the overall problem.

The Centers for Medicare and Medicaid Services is requiring health care providers to collect and use more data on what treatments are most effective. Agency officials say they can also save money by paying providers to offer better, more efficient care, and they are conducting demonstration projects, including one involving the 10 largest physician groups in the country, that pay doctors more if they improve the quality of the care they deliver. The idea is that pay-for-performance would be cheaper, even after paying doctors bonuses for providing higher-quality care, because patients would avoid costly complications.

Disease management techniques that coordinate the care of chronically ill patients, which are often used by commercial managed care plans, also could save money. Assigning one entity the responsibility of overseeing all the components of a patient's care would probably prevent conflicting treatments — for instance, by having one doctor prescribe a medication that interacts dangerously with medicine that another doctor has ordered. A medical guardian could also pressure patients to follow their regimens as prescribed.

But no one really knows how much these changes could save. And even for those proposals that do have cost estimates, the savings are minor when compared with the overall problem.

Moving to electronic records would save the entire health care system about $78 billion a year, which could produce some savings for Medicare, according to the journal Health Affairs. But that is only 5 percent of the more than $1.6 trillion annual health care bill.

"The dilemma we have is that, of all the ideas on the table or being tried, nobody has a breakthrough solution," says William J. Scan-

lon, a former health analyst for the General Accountability Office.

That is why some say Bush and Congress are right to start with a nice, easy Social Security debate. "In some ways, I look at Social Security as the warm-up" to an even more difficult struggle with the choices facing Medicare, says MacGuineas. And even Republicans who want a broader debate do not fault the president for putting Social Security first.

"You take the opportunities where you can get them," says Thomas. He says he has been talking about better ways to insure against chronic illnesses for more than a decade and is happy to use the Social Security effort as a vehicle to attract more attention to the issue. "Clearly, Social Security is a major component of an aging society," he says, "but it's not the only component."

DOING THE MATH

Just identifying the problem is hard enough. With Social Security projections, the main equation is to multiply the estimated number of beneficiaries by the cost of the benefits.

> ## "The president says it's urgent to address the Social Security crisis. What about Medicare? We need to deal with both, and the sooner the better."

Individual checks vary with an individual's payroll tax contributions and the number of years they have worked.

It is not grammar school math, but it is pretty simple when you compare it with Medicare. First, actuaries have to figure out how many people will be entitled to benefits because of their age or because they become disabled. Then, they have to determine how much medical costs will rise, a factor that is notoriously unpredictable.

Officials have to imagine what new technologies will come on the market or how the nation's health care system might evolve, not only for Medicare but also for other programs

that could affect the way that medical benefits are reimbursed. Some of the uncertainties include the health status of Americans and the demand for treatment of chronic conditions. Other questions include whether the private, employer-sponsored health care system will change, for instance by requiring consumers to pick up more of the costs through consumer-driven plans.

"There so many fewer variables in pensions and Social Security that it's akin to checkers versus multidimensional chess," says Chris Jennings, who was President Bill Clinton's top White House health care adviser.

The costs are even harder to project when the effects of a brand-new program, such as the prescription drug system, must be factored in. And no one knows how health care coverage may change in the future. In 1965, when Medicare was created, outpatient surgery was relatively rare. Now, many procedures can be done without requiring even an overnight stay in the hospital. And new kinds of prescription drugs, as expensive as they are, may be preventing illnesses that would force seniors to go to the hospital in the first place.

None of those developments could have been clearly predicted when the Medicare law was penned, and it is just as likely that the next four decades will hold as many surprises. But it is not just the government that has a tougher time predicting future medical costs than retirement needs. It is also the patients themselves.

People can plan for retirement with some predictability, Jennings says, "but you don't plan to be sick. It could happen anytime, but we tend to deny it and poorly plan for it. This is not just a challenge for policy makers, it's a challenge for people."

FORCING THE ISSUE

At some point, Congress will have to face the ugly Medicare facts. That moment could come sooner than either Bush or Congress would like.

Medicare's hospital coverage gets the most attention because it is the part that has a trust fund that is estimated to go broke in 2019. But two other big parts of the system— outpatient care and now prescription drug coverage — are increasingly important. Outpatient care, paid for by premiums and general tax revenues, is an increasing drain on the treasury.

Under the 2003 Medicare law, each report by the program's trustees must predict whether

CQ PHOTO / SCOTT J. FERRELL

general revenues will make up more than 45 percent of Medicare spending that year or in any of the next six years. If they find that it will, for two reports in a row, the president must propose legislation to Congress to trim Medicare spending until it falls back below 45 percent.

Last year, the trustees reported that Medicare will reach the 45 percent mark in 2012 — just outside the window that would require Congress to act. But if Medicare's condition worsens, some analysts say, this year's report and next year's could both find that general revenues will creep up above 45 percent — triggering a requirement for Bush to propose Medicare-cutting legislation as early as 2006.

"We don't have Medicare on the agenda, but by late spring of 2006, it will be on the agenda," says Reischauer.

And the prescription drug program, which does not even go into effect until Jan. 1, is expected to make up a full 25 percent of Medicare's costs by 2015, according to estimates provided by Gail Wilensky, a former administrator of the Medicare and Medicaid programs.

There may even be some political incentives to take a good, hard look at Medicare. For Republicans, it would be a chance to reassure fiscal conservatives that the party cares about reducing the cost of entitlements. If they do not, some say the Democrats should.

"Democrats need to realize that they're no longer the governing party" and that they need to act more like an insurgent party, says Paul Weinstein Jr., chief operating officer of the Progressive Policy Institute, a centrist Democratic think tank. "If you can't fix the problems on Medicare and Medicaid, how will anyone trust you to expand health care coverage?"

This time, though, no one knows how to make the painful Medicare changes go down easier. Having added the drug benefit, "we've eaten the candy off of the pill," says Antos. "Now, all that's left is the pill." ■

Appendix

The Legislative Process in Brief

Note: Parliamentary terms used below are defined in the glossary.

INTRODUCTION OF BILLS

A House member (including the resident commissioner of Puerto Rico and nonvoting delegates of the District of Columbia, Guam, the Virgin Islands and American Samoa) may introduce any one of several types of bills and resolutions by handing it to the clerk of the House or placing it in a box called the hopper. A senator first gains recognition of the presiding officer to announce the introduction of a bill.

As the usual next step in either the House or Senate, the bill is numbered, referred to the appropriate committee, labeled with the sponsor's name and sent to the Government Printing Office so that copies can be made for subsequent study and action. House and Senate bills may be jointly sponsored and carry several senators' names. A bill written in the executive branch and proposed as an administration measure usually is introduced by the chairman of the congressional committee that has jurisdiction, as a courtesy to the White House.

Bills—Prefixed with HR in the House, S in the Senate, followed by a number. Used as the form for most legislation, whether general or special, public or private.

Joint Resolutions—Designated H J Res or S J Res. Subject to the same procedure as bills, with the exception of a joint resolution proposing an amendment to the Constitution. The latter must be approved by two-thirds of both houses and is then sent directly to the administrator of general services for submission to the states for ratification instead of being presented to the president for his approval.

Concurrent Resolutions—Designated H Con Res or S Con Res. Used for matters affecting the operations of both houses. These resolutions do not become law.

Resolutions—Designated H Res or S Res. Used for a matter concerning the operation of either house alone and adopted only by the chamber in which it originates.

COMMITTEE ACTION

With few exceptions, bills are referred to the appropriate standing committees. The job of referral formally is the responsibility of the Speaker of the House and the presiding officer of the Senate, but this task usually is carried out on their behalf by the parliamentarians of the House and Senate. Precedent, statute and the jurisdictional mandates of the committees as set forth in the rules of the House and Senate determine which committees receive what kinds of bills. Bills are technically considered "read for the first time" when referred to House committees.

When a bill reaches a committee it is placed on the committee's calendar. Failure of a committee to act on a bill is equivalent to killing it and most fall by the legislative roadside. The measure can be withdrawn from the committee's purview only by a discharge petition signed by a majority of the House membership on House bills, or by adoption of a special resolution in the Senate. Discharge attempts rarely succeed and the Senate procedure has not been used for decades.

The first committee action taken on a bill usually is a request for comment on it by interested agencies of the government. The committee chairman may assign the bill to a subcommittee for study and hearings, or it may be considered by the full committee. Hearings may be public, closed (executive session) or both. A subcommittee, after considering a bill, reports to the full committee its recommendations for action and any proposed amendments.

The full committee then votes on its recommendation to the House or Senate. This procedure is called "ordering a bill reported." Occasionally a committee may order a bill reported unfavorably; most of the time a report, submitted by the chairman of the committee to the House or Senate, calls for favorable action on the measure since the committee can effectively "kill" a bill by simply failing to take any action.

After the bill is reported, the committee chairman instructs the staff to prepare a written report. The report describes the purposes and scope of the bill, explains the committee revisions, notes proposed changes in existing law and, usually, includes the views of the executive branch agencies consulted. Often committee members opposing a measure issue dissenting minority statements that are included in the report.

Usually, the committee "marks up" or proposes amendments to the bill. If the amendments are substantial and the measure is complicated, the committee may order a "clean bill" introduced, which will embody the proposed amendments. The original bill then is put aside and the clean bill, with a new number, is reported to the floor.

The chamber must approve, alter or reject the committee amendments before the bill itself can be put to a vote.

FLOOR ACTION

After a bill is reported back to the house where it originated, it is placed on the calendar.

There are five legislative calendars in the House, issued in one cumulative calendar titled *Calendars of the United States House of Representatives and History of Legislation.* The House calendars are:

The Union Calendar to which are referred bills raising revenues, general appropriations bills and any measures directly or indirectly appropriating money or property. It is the Calendar of the Committee of the Whole House on the State of the Union.

The House Calendar to which are referred bills of public character not raising revenue or appropriating money.

The Corrections Calendar to which are referred bills to repeal rules and regulations deemed excessive or unnecessary when the Corrections Calendar is called the second and fourth Tuesday of each month. (Instituted in the 104th Congress to replace the seldom-used Consent Calendar.) A three-fifths majority is required for passage.

The Private Calendar to which are referred bills for relief in the nature of claims against the United States or private immigration bills that are passed without debate when the Private Calendar is called the first and third Tuesdays of each month.

The Discharge Calendar to which are referred motions to discharge committees when the necessary signatures are signed to a discharge petition.

There is only one legislative calendar in the Senate and one "executive calendar" for treaties and nominations submitted to the Senate.

Debate. A bill is brought to debate by varying procedures. In the Senate the majority leader, in consultation with the minority leader and others, schedules the bills that will be taken up for debate. If it is urgent or important it can be taken up in the Senate either by unanimous consent or by a majority vote.

In the House, precedence is granted if a special rule is obtained from the Rules Committee. A request for a special rule usually is made by the chairman of the committee that favorably reported the bill. The request is considered by the Rules Committee in the same fashion that other committees consider legislative measures. The committee proposes a resolution providing for immediate consideration of the bill. The Rules Committee reports the resolution to the House where it is debated and voted on in the same fashion as regular bills.

This graphic shows the most typical way in which proposed legislation is enacted into law. There are more complicated, as well as simpler, routes, and most bills never become law. The process is illustrated with two hypothetical bills, House bill No. 1 (HR 1) and Senate bill No. 2 (S 2). Bills must be passed by both houses in identical form before they can be sent to the president. The path of HR 1 is traced by a gray line, that of S 2 by a black line. In practice, most bills begin as similar proposals in both houses.

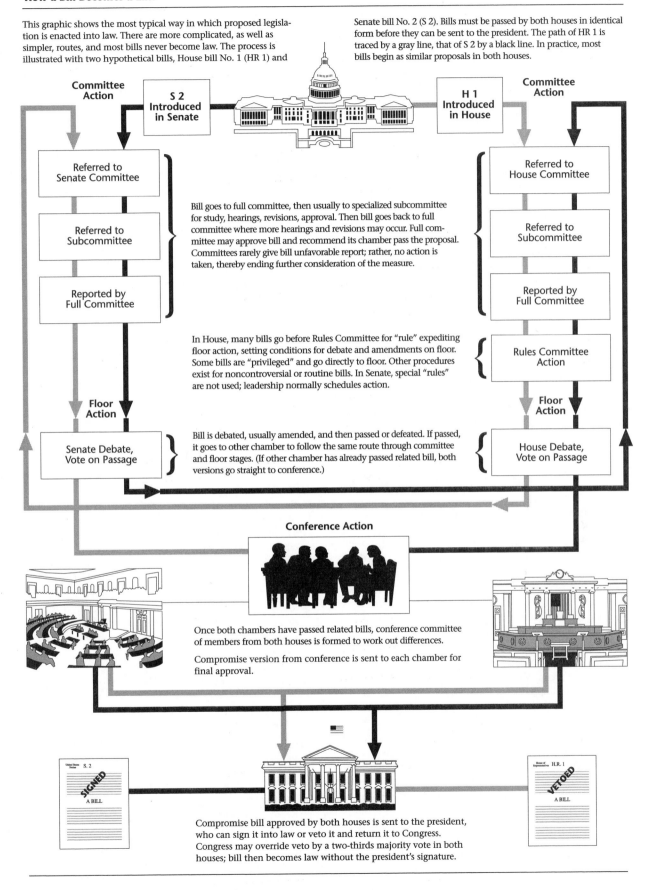

Committee Action

S 2 Introduced in Senate

H 1 Introduced in House

Committee Action

Referred to Senate Committee

Referred to Subcommittee

Reported by Full Committee

Bill goes to full committee, then usually to specialized subcommittee for study, hearings, revisions, approval. Then bill goes back to full committee where more hearings and revisions may occur. Full committee may approve bill and recommend its chamber pass the proposal. Committees rarely give bill unfavorable report; rather, no action is taken, thereby ending further consideration of the measure.

Referred to House Committee

Referred to Subcommittee

Reported by Full Committee

In House, many bills go before Rules Committee for "rule" expediting floor action, setting conditions for debate and amendments on floor. Some bills are "privileged" and go directly to floor. Other procedures exist for noncontroversial or routine bills. In Senate, special "rules" are not used; leadership normally schedules action.

Rules Committee Action

Floor Action

Floor Action

Senate Debate, Vote on Passage

Bill is debated, usually amended, and then passed or defeated. If passed, it goes to other chamber to follow the same route through committee and floor stages. (If other chamber has already passed related bill, both versions go straight to conference.)

House Debate, Vote on Passage

Conference Action

Once both chambers have passed related bills, conference committee of members from both houses is formed to work out differences.

Compromise version from conference is sent to each chamber for final approval.

S 2 SIGNED A BILL

H.R. 1 VETOED A BILL

Compromise bill approved by both houses is sent to the president, who can sign it into law or veto it and return it to Congress. Congress may override veto by a two-thirds majority vote in both houses; bill then becomes law without the president's signature.

The resolutions providing special rules are important because they specify how long the bill may be debated and whether it may be amended from the floor. If floor amendments are banned, the bill is considered under a "closed rule."

When a bill is debated under an "open rule," amendments may be offered from the floor. Committee amendments always are taken up first but may be changed, as may all amendments up to the second degree; that is, an amendment to an amendment to an amendment is not in order.

Duration of debate in the House depends on whether the bill is under discussion by the House proper or before the House when it is sitting as the Committee of the Whole House on the State of the Union. In the former, the amount of time for debate is allocated with an hour for each member if the measure is under consideration without a rule. In the Committee of the Whole the amount of time agreed on for general debate is equally divided between proponents and opponents. At the end of general discussion, the bill is often read section by section for amendment. Debate on an amendment is limited to five minutes for each side; this is called the "five-minute rule." In practice, amendments regularly are debated more than ten minutes, with members gaining the floor by offering pro forma amendments or obtaining unanimous consent to speak longer than five minutes.

Senate debate usually is unlimited. It can be halted only by unanimous consent or by "cloture," which requires a three-fifths majority of the entire Senate except for proposed changes in the Senate rules. The latter requires a two-thirds vote.

The House considers almost all important bills within a parliamentary framework known as the Committee of the Whole. It is not a committee as the word usually is understood; it is the full House meeting under another name for the purpose of speeding action on legislation. Technically, the House sits as the Committee of the Whole when it considers any tax measure or bill dealing with public appropriations. Upon adoption of a special rule, the Speaker declares the House resolved into the Committee of the Whole and appoints a member of the majority party to serve as the chairman. The rules of the House permit the Committee of the Whole to meet when a quorum of 100 members is present on the floor and to amend and act on bills. When the Committee of the Whole has acted, it "rises," the Speaker returns as the presiding officer of the House and the member appointed chairman of the Committee of the Whole reports the action of the committee and its recommendations. The Committee of the Whole cannot pass a bill; instead it reports the measure to the full House with whatever changes it has approved. The full House then may pass or reject the bill — or, on occasion, recommit the bill to committee. Amendments adopted in the Committee of the Whole may be put to a second vote in the full House.

Votes. Voting on bills may occur repeatedly before they are finally approved or rejected. The House votes on the rule for the bill and on various amendments to the bill. Voting on amendments often is a more illuminating test of a bill's support than is the final tally. Sometimes members approve final passage of bills after vigorously supporting amendments that, if adopted, would have scuttled the legislation.

The Senate has three different methods of voting: an untabulated voice vote, a standing vote (called a division) and a recorded roll call to which members answer "yea" or "nay" when their names are called. The House also employs voice and standing votes, but since January 1973 yeas and nays have been recorded by an electronic voting device, eliminating the need for time-consuming roll calls.

After amendments to a bill have been voted upon, a vote may be taken on a motion to recommit the bill to committee. If carried, this vote is usually a death blow to the bill. If the motion is unsuccessful, the bill then is "read for the third time." After the third reading a vote on passage is taken. The final vote may be followed by a motion to reconsider, and this motion

may be followed by a move to lay the motion on the table. Usually, those voting for the bill's passage vote for the tabling motion, thus safeguarding the final passage action. With that, the bill has been formally passed by the chamber.

ACTION IN SECOND CHAMBER

After a bill is passed it is sent to the other chamber. This body may then take one of several steps. It may pass the bill as is — accepting the other chamber's language. It may send the bill to committee for scrutiny or alteration, or reject the entire bill, advising the other chamber of its actions. Or it simply may ignore the bill submitted while it continues work on its own version of the proposed legislation. Frequently, one chamber may approve a version of a bill that is greatly at variance with the version already passed by the other chamber, and then substitute its contents for the language of the other, retaining only the latter's bill number.

Often the second chamber makes only minor changes. If these are readily agreed to by the other chamber, the bill then is routed to the president. However, if the opposite chamber significantly alters the bill submitted to it, the measure usually is "sent to conference." The chamber that has possession of the "papers" (engrossed bill, engrossed amendments, messages of transmittal) requests a conference and the other chamber may agree to it. If the second chamber does not agree, the bill dies.

CONFERENCE ACTION

A conference works out conflicting House and Senate versions of a legislative bill. The conferees usually are senior members from the committees that managed the legislation who are appointed by the presiding officers of the two houses. Under this arrangement the conferees of one house have the duty of trying to maintain their chamber's position in the face of amending actions by the conferees (also referred to as "managers") of the other house.

The number of conferees from each chamber may vary, the range usually being from seven to nine members in each group, depending on the length or complexity of the bill involved. But a majority vote controls the action of each group so that a large representation does not give one chamber a voting advantage over the other chamber's conferees.

Theoretically, conferees are not allowed to write new legislation in reconciling the two versions before them, but this curb sometimes is bypassed. Many bills have been put into acceptable compromise form only after new language was provided by the conferees. Frequently the ironing out of difficulties takes days or even weeks. Conferences on involved, complex and controversial bills sometimes are particularly drawn out.

As a conference proceeds, conferees reconcile differences between the versions, but generally they grant concessions only insofar as they remain sure that the chamber they represent will accept the compromises. Occasionally, uncertainty over how either house will react, or the positive refusal of a chamber to back down on a disputed amendment, results in an impasse, and the bills die in conference even though each was approved by its sponsoring chamber.

When the conferees have reached agreement, they prepare a conference report embodying their recommendations (compromises) and a joint explanatory statement. The report, in document form, must be submitted to each house. The conference report must be approved by each house. Consequently, approval of the report is approval of the compromise bill. In the order of voting on conference reports, the chamber that asked for a conference yields to the other chamber the opportunity to vote first.

FINAL ACTION

After a bill has been passed by both the House and Senate in identical form, all of the original papers are sent to the enrolling clerk of the chamber in which the bill originated. The clerk then prepares an enrolled bill, which is printed on parchment paper.

When this bill has been certified as correct by the secretary of the Senate or the clerk of the House, depending on which chamber originated the bill, it is signed first (no matter whether it originated in the Senate or House) by the Speaker of the House and then by the president of the Senate. It is next sent to the White House to await action.

If the president approves the bill, he signs it, dates it and usually writes the word "approved" on the document. If the president does not sign it within 10 days (Sundays excepted) and Congress is in session, the bill becomes law without his signature.

If Congress adjourns *sine die* at the end of the second session the president can pocket veto a bill and it dies without Congress having the opportunity to override.

A president vetoes a bill by refusing to sign it and, before the ten-day period expires, returning it to Congress with a message stating his reasons.

The message is sent to the chamber that originated the bill. If no action is taken on the message, the bill dies. Congress, however, can attempt to override the president's veto and enact the bill, "the objections of the president to the contrary notwithstanding." Overriding a veto requires a two-thirds vote of those present in each chamber, who must number a quorum and vote by roll call.

If the president's veto is overridden by a two-thirds vote in both houses, the bill becomes law. Otherwise it is dead.

When bills are passed finally and signed, or passed over a veto, they are given law numbers in numerical order as they become law. There are two series of numbers, one for public and one for private laws, starting at the number "1" for each two-year term of Congress. They are then identified by law number and by Congress — for example, Private Law 10, 105th Congress; Public Law 33, 106th Congress (or PL 106-33).

The Budget Process in Brief

Through the budget process, the president and Congress decide how much to spend and tax during the upcoming fiscal year. More specifically, they decide how much to spend on each activity, ensure that the government spends no more than that and spends it only for that activity and report on that spending at the end of each budget cycle.

THE PRESIDENT'S BUDGET

The law requires that, by the first Monday in February, the president submit to Congress his proposed federal budget for the next fiscal year, which begins on October 1. To accomplish this the president establishes general budget and fiscal policy guidelines. Based on these guidelines, executive branch agencies make requests for funds and submit them to the White House's Office of Management and Budget (OMB) nearly a year before the start of a new fiscal year. The OMB, receiving direction from the president and administration officials, reviews the agencies' requests and develops a detailed budget by December. From December to January the OMB prepares the budget documents, so that the president can deliver it to Congress in February.

The president's budget is the executive branch's plan for the next year — but it is just a proposal. After receiving it, Congress has its own budget process to follow from February to October. Only after Congress passes the required spending bills — and the president signs them — has the government created its actual budget.

ACTION IN CONGRESS

Congress first must pass a "budget resolution" — a framework within which the members of Congress will make their decisions about spending and taxes. It includes targets for total spending, total revenues and the deficit, and allocations within the spending target for the two types of spending — discretionary and mandatory.

Discretionary spending, which currently accounts for about 33 percent of all federal spending, is what the president and Congress must decide to spend for the next year through the thirteen annual appropriations bills. It includes money for such activities as the FBI and the Coast Guard, for housing and education, for NASA and highway and bridge construction and for defense and foreign aid.

Mandatory spending, which currently accounts for 67 percent of all spending, is authorized by laws that have already been passed. It includes entitlement spending — such as for Social Security, Medicare, veterans' benefits and food stamps — through which individuals receive benefits because they are eligible based on their age, income or other criteria. It also includes interest on the national debt, which the government pays to individuals and institutions that hold Treasury bonds and other government securities. The only way the president and Congress can change the spending on entitlement and other mandatory programs is if they change the laws that authorized the programs.

Currently, the law requires that legislation that would raise mandatory spending or lower revenues — compared to existing law — be offset by spending cuts or revenue increases. This requirement, called "pay-as-you-go" is designed to prevent new legislation from increasing the deficit.

Once Congress passes the budget resolution, legislators turn their attention to passing the 13 annual appropriations bills and, if they choose, "authorizing" bills to change the laws governing mandatory spending and revenues.

Congress begins by examining the president's budget in detail. Scores of committees and subcommittees hold hearings on proposals under their jurisdiction. The House and Senate Armed Services Authorizing Committees, and the Defense and Military Construction Subcommittees of the Appropriations Committees, for instance, hold hearings on the president's defense budget. The White House budget director, cabinet officers and other administration officials work with Congress as it accepts some of the president's proposals, rejects others and changes still others. Congress can change funding levels, eliminate programs or add programs not requested by the president. It can add or eliminate taxes and other sources of revenue, or make other changes that affect the amount of revenue collected. Congressional rules require that these committees and subcommittees take actions that reflect the congressional budget resolution.

The president's budget, the budget resolution and the appropriations or authorizing bills measure spending in two ways — "budget authority" and "outlays." Budget authority is what the law authorizes the federal government to spend for certain programs, projects or activities. What the government actually spends in a particular year, however, is an outlay. For example, when the government decides to build a space exploration system, the president and Congress may agree to appropriate $1 billion in budget authority. But the space system may take ten years to build. Thus, the government may spend $100 million in outlays in the first year to begin construction and the remaining $900 million during the next nine years as the construction continues.

Congress must provide budget authority before the federal agencies can obligate the government to make outlays. When Congress fails to complete action on one or more of the regular annual appropriations bills before the fiscal year begins on October 1, budget authority may be made on a temporary basis through continuing resolutions. Continuing resolutions make budget authority available for limited periods of time, generally at rates related through some formula to the rate provided in the previous year's appropriation.

MONITORING THE BUDGET

Once Congress passes and the president signs the federal appropriations bills or authorizing laws for the fiscal year, the government monitors the budget through (1) agency program managers and budget officials, including the Inspectors General, who report only to the agency head; (2) the Office of Management and Budget; (3) congressional committees; and (4) the General Accounting Office, an auditing arm of Congress.

This oversight is designed to (1) ensure that agencies comply with legal limits on spending and that agencies use budget authority only for the purposes intended; (2) see that programs are operating consistently with legal requirements and existing policy; and (3) ensure that programs are well managed and achieving the intended results.

The president may withhold appropriated amounts from obligation only under certain limited circumstances — to provide for contingencies, to achieve savings made possible through changes in requirements or greater efficiency of operations or as otherwise provided by law. The Impoundment Control Act of 1974 specifies the procedures that must be followed if funds are withheld. Congress can also cancel previous authorized budget authority by passing a rescissions bill — but it also must be signed by the president.

Glossary of Congressional Terms

AA—(See Administrative Assistant.)

Absence of a Quorum—Absence of the required number of members to conduct business in a house or a committee. When a quorum call or roll-call vote in a house establishes that a quorum is not present, no debate or other business is permitted except a motion to adjourn or motions to request or compel the attendance of absent members, if necessary by arresting them.

Absolute Majority—A vote requiring approval by a majority of all members of a house rather than a majority of members present and voting. Also referred to as constitutional majority.

Account—Organizational units used in the federal budget primarily for recording spending and revenue transactions.

Act—(1) A bill passed in identical form by both houses of Congress and signed into law by the president or enacted over the president's veto. A bill also becomes an act without the president's signature if he does not return it to Congress within ten days (Sundays excepted) and if Congress has not adjourned within that period. (2) Also, the technical term for a bill passed by at least one house and engrossed.

Ad Hoc Select Committee—A temporary committee formed for a special purpose or to deal with a specific subject. Conference committees are ad hoc joint committees. A House rule adopted in 1975 authorizes the Speaker to refer measures to special ad hoc committees, appointed by the Speaker with the approval of the House.

Adjourn—A motion to adjourn is a formal motion to end a day's session or meeting of a house or a committee. A motion to adjourn usually has no conditions attached to it, but it sometimes may specify the day or time for reconvening or make reconvening subject to the call of the chamber's presiding officer or the committee's chairman. In both houses, a motion to adjourn is of the highest privilege, takes precedence over all other motions, is not debatable and must be put to an immediate vote. Adjournment of a house ends its legislative day. For this reason, the House or Senate sometimes adjourns for only one minute, or some other very brief period of time, during the course of a day's session. The House does not permit a motion to adjourn after it has resolved into Committee of the Whole or when the previous question has been ordered on a measure to final passage without an intervening motion.

Adjourn for More Than Three Days—Under Article I, Section 5 of the Constitution, neither house may adjourn for more than three days without the approval of the other. The necessary approval is given in a concurrent resolution to which both houses have agreed.

Adjournment *Sine Die*—Final adjournment of an annual or two-year session of Congress; literally, adjournment without a day. The two houses must agree to a privileged concurrent resolution for such an adjournment. A sine die adjournment precludes Congress from meeting again until the next constitutionally fixed date of a session (Jan. 3 of the following year) unless Congress determines otherwise by law or the president calls it into special session. Article II, Section 3 of the Constitution authorizes the president to adjourn both houses until such time as the president thinks proper when the two houses cannot agree to a time of adjournment. No president, however, has ever exercised this authority.

Adjournment to a Day (and Time) Certain—An adjournment that fixes the next date and time of meeting for one or both houses. It does not end an annual session of Congress.

Administration Bill—A bill drafted in the executive office of the president or in an executive department or agency to implement part of the president's program. An administration bill is introduced in Congress by a member who supports it or as a courtesy to the administration.

Administrative Assistant (AA)—The title usually given to a member's chief aide, political advisor and head of office staff. The administrative assistant often represents the member at meetings with visitors or officials when the member is unable (or unwilling) to attend.

Adoption—The usual parliamentary term for approval of a conference report. It is also commonly applied to amendments.

Advance Appropriation—In an appropriation act for a particular fiscal year, an appropriation that does not become available for spending or obligation until a subsequent fiscal year. The amount of the advance appropriation is counted as part of the budget for the fiscal year in which it becomes available for obligation.

Advance Funding—A mechanism whereby statutory language may allow budget authority for a fiscal year to be increased, and obligations to be incurred, with an offsetting decrease in the budget authority available in the succeeding fiscal year. If not used, the budget authority remains available for obligation in the succeeding fiscal year. Advance funding is sometimes used to provide contingency funding of a few benefit programs.

Adverse Report—A committee report recommending against approval of a measure or some other matter. Committees usually pigeonhole measures they oppose instead of reporting them adversely, but they may be required to report them by a statutory rule or an instruction from their parent body.

Advice and Consent—The Senate's constitutional role in consenting to or rejecting the president's nominations to executive branch and judicial offices and treaties with other nations. Confirmation of nominees requires a simple majority vote of senators present and voting. Treaties must be approved by a two-thirds majority of those present and voting.

Aisle—The center aisle of each chamber. When facing the presiding officer, Republicans usually sit to the right of the aisle, Democrats to the left. When members speak of "my side of the aisle" or "this side," they are referring to their party.

Amendment—A formal proposal to alter the text of a bill, resolution, amendment, motion, treaty or some other text. Technically, it is a motion. An amendment may strike out (eliminate) part of a text, insert new text or strike out and insert — that is, replace all or part of the text with new text. The texts of amendments considered on the floor are printed in full in the Congressional Record.

Amendment in the Nature of a Substitute—Usually, an amendment to replace the entire text of a measure. It strikes out everything after the enacting clause and inserts a version that may be somewhat, substantially or entirely different. When a committee adopts extensive amendments to a measure, it often incorporates them into such an amendment. Occasionally, the term is applied to an amendment that replaces a major portion of a measure's text.

Amendment Tree—A diagram showing the number and types of amendments that the rules and practices of a house permit to be offered to a measure before any of the amendments is voted on. It shows the relationship of one amendment to the others, and it may also indicate the degree of each amendment, whether it is a perfecting or substitute amendment, the order in which amendments may be offered and the order in which they are put to a vote. The same type of diagram can be used to display an actual amendment situation.

Annual Authorization—Legislation that authorizes appropriations for a single fiscal year and usually for a specific amount. Under the rules of the authorization-appropriation process, an annually authorized agency or program must be reauthorized each year if it is to receive appropriations for that year. Sometimes Congress fails to enact the reauthorization but nevertheless provides appropriations to continue the program, circumventing the rules by one means or another.

Appeal—A member's formal challenge of a ruling or decision by the presiding officer. On appeal, a house or a committee may overturn the ruling by majority vote. The right of appeal ensures the body against arbitrary control by the chair. Appeals are rarely made in the House and are even more rarely successful. Rulings are more frequently appealed in the Senate and occasionally overturned, in part because its presiding officer is not the majority party's leader, as in the House.

Apportionment—The action, after each decennial census, of allocating the number of members in the House of Representatives to each state. By law, the total number of House members (not counting delegates and a resident commissioner) is fixed at 435. The number allotted to each state is based approximately on its proportion of the nation's total population. Because the Constitution guarantees each state one representative no matter how small its population, exact proportional distribution is virtually impossible. The mathematical formula currently used to determine the apportionment is called the Method of Equal Proportions. (See Method of Equal Proportions.)

Appropriated Entitlement—An entitlement program, such as veterans' pensions, that is funded through annual appropriations rather than by a permanent appropriation. Because such an entitlement law requires the government to provide eligible recipients the benefits to which they are entitled, whatever the cost, Congress must appropriate the necessary funds.

Appropriation—(1) Legislative language that permits a federal agency to incur obligations and make payments from the Treasury for specified purposes, usually during a specified period of time. (2) The specific amount of money made available by such language. The Constitution prohibits payments from the Treasury except "in Consequence of Appropriations made by Law." With some exceptions, the rules of both houses forbid consideration of appropriations for purposes that are unauthorized in law or of appropriation amounts larger than those authorized in law. The House of Representatives claims the exclusive right to originate appropriation bills — a claim the Senate denies in theory but accepts in practice.

At-Large—Elected by and representing an entire state instead of a district within a state. The term usually refers to a representative rather than to a senator. (See Apportionment; Congressional District; Redistricting.)

August Adjournment—A congressional adjournment during the month of August in odd-numbered years, required by the Legislative Reorganization Act of 1970. The law instructs the two houses to adjourn for a period of at least thirty days before the second day after Labor Day, unless Congress provides otherwise or if, on July 31, a state of war exists by congressional declaration.

Authorization—(1) A statutory provision that establishes or continues a federal agency, activity or program for a fixed or indefinite period of time. It may also establish policies and restrictions and deal with organizational and administrative matters. (2) A statutory provision, as described in (1), may also, explicitly or implicitly, authorize congressional action to provide appropriations for an agency, activity or program. The

appropriations may be authorized for one year, several years or an indefinite period of time, and the authorization may be for a specific amount of money or an indefinite amount ("such sums as may be necessary"). Authorizations of specific amounts are construed as ceilings on the amounts that subsequently may be appropriated in an appropriation bill, but not as minimums; either house may appropriate lesser amounts or nothing at all.

Authorization-Appropriation Process—The two-stage procedural system that the rules of each house require for establishing and funding federal agencies and programs: first, enactment of authorizing legislation that creates or continues an agency or program; second, enactment of appropriations legislation that provides funds for the authorized agency or program.

Automatic Roll Call—Under a House rule, the automatic ordering of the yeas and nays when a quorum is not present on a voice or division vote and a member objects to the vote on that ground. It is not permitted in the Committee of the Whole.

Backdoor Spending Authority—Authority to incur obligations that evades the normal congressional appropriations process because it is provided in legislation other than appropriation acts. The most common forms are borrowing authority, contract authority and entitlement authority.

Baseline—A projection of the levels of federal spending, revenues and the resulting budgetary surpluses or deficits for the upcoming and subsequent fiscal years, taking into account laws enacted to date and assuming no new policy decisions. It provides a benchmark for measuring the budgetary effects of proposed changes in federal revenues or spending, assuming certain economic conditions.

Bells—A system of electric signals and lights that informs members of activities in each chamber. The type of activity taking place is indicated by the number of signals and the interval between them. When the signals are sounded, a corresponding number of lights are lit around the perimeter of many clocks in House or Senate offices.

Bicameral—Consisting of two houses or chambers. Congress is a bicameral legislature whose two houses have an equal role in enacting legislation. In most other national bicameral legislatures, one house is significantly more powerful than the other.

Bigger Bite Amendment—An amendment that substantively changes a portion of a text including language that had previously been amended. Normally, language that has been amended may not be amended again. However, a part of a sentence that has been changed by amendment, for example, may be changed again by an amendment that amends a "bigger bite" of the text — that is, by an amendment that also substantively changes the unamended parts of the sentence or the entire section or title in which the previously amended language appears. The biggest possible bite is an amendment in the nature of a substitute that amends the entire text of a measure. Once adopted, therefore, such an amendment ends the amending process.

Bill—The term for the chief vehicle Congress uses for enacting laws. Bills that originate in the House of Representatives are designated as HR, those in the Senate as S, followed by a number assigned in the order in which they are introduced during a two-year Congress. A bill becomes a law if passed in identical language by both houses and signed by the president, or passed over the president's veto, or if the president fails to sign it within ten days after receiving it while Congress is in session.

Bill of Attainder—An act of a legislature finding a person guilty of treason or a felony. The Constitution prohibits the passage of such a bill by the U.S. Congress or any state legislature.

Bills and Resolutions Introduced—Members formally present measures to their respective houses by delivering them to a clerk in the chamber when their house is in session. Both houses permit any number of members to join in introducing a bill or resolution. The first member listed on the measure is the sponsor; the other members listed are its cosponsors.

Bills and Resolutions Referred—After a bill or resolution is introduced, it is normally sent to one or more committees that have jurisdiction over its subject, as defined by House and Senate rules and precedents. A Senate measure is usually referred to the committee with jurisdiction over the predominant subject of its text, but it may be sent to two or more committees by unanimous consent or on a motion offered jointly by the majority and minority leaders. In the House, a rule requires the Speaker to refer a measure to the committee that has primary jurisdiction. The Speaker is also authorized to refer measures sequentially to additional committees and to impose time limits on such referrals.

Bipartisan Committee—A committee with an equal number of members from each political party. The House Committee on Standards of Official Conduct and the Senate Select Committee on Ethics are the only bipartisan, permanent full committees.

Borrowing Authority—Statutory authority permitting a federal agency, such as the Export-Import Bank, to borrow money from the public or the Treasury to finance its operations. It is a form of backdoor spending. To bring such spending under the control of the congressional appropriation process, the Congressional Budget Act requires that new borrowing authority shall be effective only to the extent and in such amounts as are provided in appropriations acts.

Budget—A detailed statement of actual or anticipated revenues and expenditures during an accounting period. For the national government, the period is the federal fiscal year (Oct. 1 to Sept. 30). The budget usually refers to the president's budget submission to Congress early each calendar year. The president's budget estimates federal government income and spending for the upcoming fiscal year and contains detailed recommendations for appropriation, revenue and other legislation. Congress is not required to accept or even vote directly on the president's proposals, and it often revises the president's budget extensively. (See Fiscal Year.)

Budget Act—Common name for the Congressional Budget and Impoundment Control Act of 1974, which established the basic procedures of the current congressional budget process; created the House and Senate Budget Committees; and enacted procedures for reconciliation, deferrals and rescissions. (See Budget Process; Deferral; Impoundment; Reconciliation; Rescission. See also Gramm-Rudman-Hollings Act of 1985.)

Budget and Accounting Act of 1921—The law that, for the first time, authorized the president to submit to Congress an annual budget for the entire federal government. Before passage of the act, most federal agencies sent their budget requests to the appropriate congressional committees without review by the president.

Budget Authority—Generally, the amount of money that may be spent or obligated by a government agency or for a government program or activity. Technically, it is statutory authority to enter into obligations that normally result in outlays. The main forms of budget authority are appropriations, borrowing authority and contract authority. It also includes authority to obligate and expend the proceeds of offsetting receipts and collections. Congress may make budget authority available for only one year, several years or an indefinite period, and it may specify definite or indefinite amounts.

Budget Enforcement Act of 1990—An act that revised the sequestration process established by the Gramm-Rudman-Hollings Act of 1985, replaced the earlier act's fixed deficit targets with adjustable ones, established discretionary spending limits for fiscal years 1991 through 1995, instituted pay-as-you-go rules to enforce deficit neutrality on revenue and mandatory spending legislation and reformed the budget and accounting rules for federal credit activities. Unlike the Gramm-Rudman-Hollings Act, the 1990 act emphasized restraints on legislated changes in taxes and spending instead of fixed deficit limits.

Budget Enforcement Act of 1997—An act that revised and updated the provisions of the Budget Enforcement Act of 1990, including by extending the discretionary spending caps and pay-as-you-go rules through 2002.

Budget Process—(1) In Congress, the procedural system it uses (a) to approve an annual concurrent resolution on the budget that sets goals for aggregate and functional categories of federal expenditures, revenues and the surplus or deficit for an upcoming fiscal year; and (b) to implement those goals in spending, revenue and, if necessary, reconciliation and debt-limit legislation. (2) In the executive branch, the process of formulating the president's annual budget, submitting it to Congress, defending it before congressional committees, implementing subsequent budget-related legislation, impounding or sequestering expenditures as permitted by law, auditing and evaluating programs and compiling final budget data. The Budget and Accounting Act of 1921 and the Congressional Budget and Impoundment Control Act of 1974 established the basic elements of the current budget process. Major revisions were enacted in the Gramm-Rudman-Hollings Act of 1985 and the Budget Enforcement Act of 1990.

Budget Resolution—A concurrent resolution in which Congress establishes or revises its version of the federal budget's broad financial features for the upcoming fiscal year and several additional fiscal years. Like other concurrent resolutions, it does not have the force of law, but it provides the framework within which Congress subsequently considers revenue, spending and other budget-implementing legislation. The framework consists of two basic elements: (1) aggregate budget amounts (total revenues, new budget authority, outlays, loan obligations and loan guarantee commitments, deficit or surplus and debt limit); and (2) subdivisions of the relevant aggregate amounts among the functional categories of the budget. Although it does not allocate funds to specific programs or accounts, the budget committees' reports accompanying the resolution often discuss the major program assumptions underlying its functional amounts. Unlike those amounts, however, the assumptions are not binding on Congress.

By Request—A designation indicating that a member has introduced a measure on behalf of the president, an executive agency or a private individual or organization. Members often introduce such measures as a courtesy because neither the president nor any person other than a member of Congress can do so. The term, which appears next to the sponsor's name, implies that the member who introduced the measure does not necessarily endorse it. A House rule dealing with by-request introductions dates from 1888, but the practice goes back to the earliest history of Congress.

Byrd Rule—The popular name of an amendment to the Congressional Budget Act that bars the inclusion of extraneous matter in any reconciliation legislation considered in the Senate. The ban is enforced by points of order that the presiding officer sustains. The provision defines different categories of extraneous matter, but it also permits certain exceptions. Its chief sponsor was Sen. Robert C. Byrd, D-W.Va.

Calendar—A list of measures or other matters (most of them favorably reported by committees) that are eligible for floor consideration. The House has five calendars; the Senate has two. A place on a calendar does not guarantee consideration. Each house decides which measures and matters it will take up, when and in what order, in accordance with its rules and practices.

Calendar Wednesday—A House procedure that on Wednesdays permits its committees to bring up for floor consideration nonprivileged measures they have reported. The procedure is so cumbersome and susceptible to dilatory tactics, however, that it is rarely used.

Call Up—To bring a measure or report to the floor for immediate consideration.

Casework—Assistance to constituents who seek assistance in dealing with federal and local government agencies. Constituent service is a high priority in most members' offices.

Caucus—(1) A common term for the official organization of each party in each house. (2) The official title of the organization of House Democrats. House and Senate Republicans and Senate Democrats call their organizations "conferences." (3) A term for an informal group of members who share legislative interests, such as the Black Caucus, Hispanic Caucus and Children's Caucus.

Censure—The strongest formal condemnation of a member for misconduct short of expulsion. A house usually adopts a resolution of censure to express its condemnation, after which the presiding officer reads its rebuke aloud to the member in the presence of his or her colleagues.

Chairman—The presiding officer of a committee, a subcommittee or a task force. At meetings, the chairman preserves order, enforces the rules, recognizes members to speak or offer motions and puts questions to a vote. The chairman of a committee or subcommittee usually appoints its staff and sets its agenda, subject to the panel's veto.

Chamber—The Capitol room in which a house of Congress normally holds its sessions. The chamber of the House of Representatives, officially called the Hall of the House, is considerably larger than that of the Senate because it must accommodate 435 representatives, four delegates and one resident commissioner. Unlike the Senate chamber, members have no desks or assigned seats. In both chambers, the floor slopes downward to the well in front of the presiding officer's raised desk. A chamber is often referred to as "the floor," as when members are said to be on or going to the floor. Those expressions usually imply that the member's house is in session.

Christmas Tree Bill—Jargon for a bill adorned with amendments, many of them unrelated to the bill's subject, that provide benefits for interest groups, specific states, congressional districts, companies and individuals.

Classes of Senators—A class consists of the thirty-three or thirty-four senators elected to a six-year term in the same general election. Because the terms of approximately one-third of the senators expire every two years, there are three classes.

Clean Bill—After a House committee extensively amends a bill, it often assembles its amendments and what is left of the bill into a new measure that one or more of its members introduces as a "clean bill." The revised measure is assigned a new number.

Clerk of the House—An officer of the House of Representatives responsible principally for administrative support of the legislative process in the House. The clerk is invariably the candidate of the majority party.

Cloakrooms—Two rooms with access to the rear of each chamber's floor, one for each party's members, where members may confer privately, sit quietly or have a snack. The presiding officer sometimes urges members who are conversing too loudly on the floor to retire to their cloakrooms.

Closed Hearing—A hearing closed to the public and the media. A House committee may close a hearing only if it determines that disclosure of the testimony to be taken would endanger national security, violate any law or tend to defame, degrade or incriminate any person. The Senate has a similar rule. Both houses require roll-call votes in open session to close a hearing.

Closed Rule—A special rule reported from the House Rules Committee that prohibits amendments to a measure or that only permits amendments offered by the reporting committee.

Cloture—A Senate procedure that limits further consideration of a pending proposal to thirty hours in order to end a filibuster. Sixteen senators must first sign and submit a cloture motion to the presiding officer. One hour after the Senate meets on the second calendar day thereafter, the chair puts the motion to a yea-and-nay vote following a live quorum call. If three-fifths of all senators (sixty if there are no vacancies) vote for the motion, the Senate must take final action on the cloture proposal by the end of the thirty hours of consideration and may consider no other business until it takes that action. Cloture on a proposal to amend the Senate's standing rules requires approval by two-thirds of the senators present and voting.

Code of Official Conduct—A House rule that bans certain actions by House members, officers and employees; requires them to conduct themselves in ways that "reflect creditably" on the House; and orders them to adhere to the spirit and the letter of House rules and those of its committees. The code's provisions govern the receipt of outside compensation, gifts and honoraria and the use of campaign funds; prohibit members from using their clerk-hire allowance to pay anyone who does not perform duties commensurate with that pay; forbids discrimination in members' hiring or treatment of employees on the grounds of race, color, religion, sex, handicap, age or national origin; orders members convicted of a crime who might be punished by imprisonment of two or more years not to participate in committee business or vote on the floor until exonerated or reelected; and restricts employees' contact with federal agencies on matters in which they have a significant financial interest. The Senate's rules contain some similar prohibitions.

College of Cardinals—A popular term for the subcommittee chairmen of the appropriations committees, reflecting their influence over appropriation measures. The chairmen of the full appropriations committees are sometimes referred to as popes.

Comity—The practice of maintaining mutual courtesy and civility between the two houses in their dealings with each other and in members' speeches on the floor. Although the practice is largely governed by long-established customs, a House rule explicitly cautions its members not to characterize any Senate action or inaction, refer to individual senators except under certain circumstances, or quote from Senate proceedings except to make legislative history on a measure. The Senate has no rule on the subject but references to the House have been held out of order on several occasions. Generally the houses do not interfere with each other's appropriations although minor conflicts sometimes occur. A refusal to receive a message from the other house has also been held to violate the practice of comity.

Committee—A panel of members elected or appointed to perform some service or function for its parent body. Congress has four types of committees: standing, special or select, joint, and, in the House, a Committee of the Whole. Committees conduct investigations, make studies, issue reports and recommendations and, in the case of standing committees, review and prepare measures on their assigned subjects for action by their respective houses. Most committees divide their work among several subcommittees. With rare exceptions, the majority party in a house holds a majority of the seats on its committees, and their chairmen are also from that party.

Committee Jurisdiction—The legislative subjects and other functions assigned to a committee by rule, precedent, resolution or statute. A committee's title usually indicates the general scope of its jurisdiction but often fails to mention other significant subjects assigned to it.

Committee of the Whole—Common name of the Committee of the Whole House on the State of the Union, a committee consisting of all members of the House of Representatives. Measures from the union calendar must be considered in the Committee of the Whole before the House officially completes action on them; the committee often considers other major bills as well. A quorum of the committee is 100, and it meets in the House chamber under a chairman appointed by the Speaker. Procedures in the Committee of the Whole expedite consideration of legislation because of its smaller quorum requirement, its ban on certain motions and its five-minute rule for debate on amendments. Those procedures usually permit more members to offer amendments and participate in the debate on a measure than is normally possible. The Senate no longer uses a Committee of the Whole.

Committee Ratios—The ratios of majority to minority party members on committees. By custom, the ratios of most committees reflect party strength in their respective houses as closely as possible.

Committee Report on a Measure—A document submitted by a committee to report a measure to its parent chamber. Customarily, the report explains the measure's purpose, describes provisions and any amendments recommended by the committee and presents arguments for its approval.

Committee Veto—A procedure that requires an executive department or agency to submit certain proposed policies, programs or action to designated committees for review before implementing them. Before 1983, when the Supreme Court declared that a legislative veto was unconstitutional, these provisions permitted committees to veto the proposals. Committees no longer conduct this type of policy review, and the term is now something of a misnomer. Nevertheless, agencies usually take the pragmatic approach of trying to reach a consensus with the committees before carrying out their proposals, especially when an appropriations committee is involved.

Concur—To agree to an amendment of the other house, either by adopting a motion to concur in that amendment or a motion to concur with an amendment to that amendment. After both houses have agreed to the same version of an amendment, neither house may amend it further, nor may any subsequent conference change it or delete it from the measure. Concurrence by one house in all amendments of the other house completes action on the measure; no vote is then necessary on the measure as a whole because both houses previously passed it.

Concurrent Resolution—A resolution that requires approval by both houses but does not need the president's signature and therefore cannot have the force of law. Concurrent resolutions deal with the prerogatives or internal affairs of Congress as a whole. Designated H. Con. Res. in the House and S. Con. Res. in the Senate, they are numbered consecutively in each house in their order of introduction during a two-year Congress.

Conferees—A common title for managers, the members from each house appointed to a conference committee. The Senate usually authorizes its presiding officer to appoint its conferees. The Speaker appoints House conferees, and under a rule adopted in 1993, can remove conferees "at any time after an original appointment" and also appoint additional conferees at any time. Conferees are expected to support the positions of their houses despite their personal views, but in practice this is not always the case. The party ratios of conferees generally reflect the ratios in their houses. Each house may appoint as many conferees as it pleases.

House conferees often outnumber their Senate colleagues; however, each house has only one vote in a conference, so the size of its delegation is immaterial.

Conference—(1) A formal meeting or series of meetings between members representing each house to reconcile House and Senate differences on a measure (occasionally several measures). Because one house cannot require the other to agree to its proposals, the conference usually reaches agreement by compromise. When a conference completes action on a measure, or as much action as appears possible, it sends its recommendations to both houses in the form of a conference report, accompanied by an explanatory statement. (2) The official title of the organization of all Democrats or Republicans in the Senate and of all Republicans in the House of Representatives. (See Party Caucus.)

Conference Committee—A temporary joint committee formed for the purpose of resolving differences between the houses on a measure. Major and controversial legislation usually requires conference committee action. Voting in a conference committee is not by individuals but within the House and Senate delegations. Consequently, a conference committee report requires the support of a majority of the conferees from each house. Both houses require that conference committees open their meetings to the public. The Senate's rule permits the committee to close its meetings if a majority of conferees in each delegation agree by a roll-call vote. The House rule permits closed meetings only if the House authorizes them to do so on a roll-call vote. Otherwise, there are no congressional rules governing the organization of, or procedure in, a conference committee. The committee chooses its chairman, but on measures that go to conference annually, such as general appropriation bills, the chairmanship traditionally rotates between the houses.

Conference Report—A document submitted to both houses that contains a conference committee's agreements for resolving their differences on a measure. It must be signed by a majority of the conferees from each house separately and must be accompanied by an explanatory statement. Both houses prohibit amendments to a conference report and require it to be accepted or rejected in its entirety.

Congress—(1) The national legislature of the United States, consisting of the House of Representatives and the Senate. (2) The national legislature in office during a two-year period. Congresses are numbered sequentially; thus, the 1st Congress of 1789-1791 and the 106th Congress of 1999-2001. Before 1935, the two-year period began on the first Monday in December of odd-numbered years. Since then it has extended from January of an odd-numbered year through noon on Jan. 3 of the next odd-numbered year. A Congress usually holds two annual sessions, but some have had three sessions and the 67th Congress had four. When a Congress expires, measures die if they have not yet been enacted.

Congressional Accountability Act of 1995 (CAA)—An act applying eleven labor, workplace and civil rights laws to the legislative branch and establishing procedures and remedies for legislative branch employees with grievances in violation of these laws. The following laws are covered by the CAA: the Fair Labor Standards Act of 1938; Title VII of the Civil Rights Act of 1964; Americans with Disabilities Act of 1990; Age Discrimination in Employment Act of 1967; Family and Medical Leave Act of 1993; Occupational Safety and Health Act of 1970; Chapter 71 of Title 5, U.S. Code (relating to federal service labor-management relations); Employee Polygraph Protection Act of 1988; Worker Adjustment and Retraining Notification Act; Rehabilitation Act of 1973; and Chapter 43 of Title 38, U.S. Code (relating to veterans' employment and reemployment).

Congressional Budget and Impoundment Control Act of 1974—The law that established the basic elements of the congressional budget process, the House and Senate Budget Committees, the Congressional

Budget Office and the procedures for congressional review of impoundments in the form of rescissions and deferrals proposed by the president. The budget process consists of procedures for coordinating congressional revenue and spending decisions made in separate tax, appropriations and legislative measures. The impoundment provisions were intended to give Congress greater control over executive branch actions that delay or prevent the spending of funds provided by Congress.

Congressional Budget Office (CBO)—A congressional support agency created by the Congressional Budget and Impoundment Control Act of 1974 to provide nonpartisan budgetary information and analysis to Congress and its committees. CBO acts as a scorekeeper when Congress is voting on the federal budget, tracking bills to ensure they comply with overall budget goals. The agency also estimates what proposed legislation would cost over a five-year period. CBO works most closely with the House and Senate Budget Committees.

Congressional Directory—The official who's who of Congress, usually published during the first session of a two-year Congress.

Congressional District—The geographical area represented by a single member of the House of Representatives. For states with only one representative, the entire state is a congressional district. As of 2001 seven states had only one representative each: Alaska, Delaware, Montana, North Dakota, South Dakota, Vermont and Wyoming.

Congressional Record—The daily, printed and substantially verbatim account of proceedings in both the House and Senate chambers. Extraneous materials submitted by members appear in a section titled "Extensions of Remarks." A "Daily Digest" appendix contains highlights of the day's floor and committee action plus a list of committee meetings and floor agendas for the next day's session.

Although the official reporters of each house take down every word spoken during the proceedings, members are permitted to edit and "revise and extend" their remarks before they are printed. In the Senate section, all speeches, articles and other material submitted by senators but not actually spoken or read on the floor are set off by large black dots, called bullets. However, bullets do not appear when a senator reads part of a speech and inserts the rest. In the House section, undelivered speeches and materials are printed in a distinctive typeface. The term "permanent Record" refers to the bound volumes of the daily Records of an entire session of Congress.

Congressional Research Service (CRS)—Established in 1917, a department of the Library of Congress whose staff provide nonpartisan, objective analysis and information on virtually any subject to committees, members and staff of Congress. Originally the Legislative Reference Service, it is the oldest congressional support agency.

Congressional Support Agencies—A term often applied to three agencies in the legislative branch that provide nonpartisan information and analysis to committees and members of Congress: the Congressional Budget Office, the Congressional Research Service of the Library of Congress and the General Accounting Office. A fourth support agency, the Office of Technology Assessment, formerly provided such support but was abolished in the 104th Congress.

Congressional Terms of Office—A term normally begins on Jan. 3 of the year following a general election and runs two years for representatives and six years for senators. A representative chosen in a special election to fill a vacancy is sworn in for the remainder of the predecessor's term. An individual appointed to fill a Senate vacancy usually serves until the next general election or until the end of the predecessor's term, whichever comes first. Some states, however, require their governors to call a special election to fill a Senate vacancy shortly after an appointment has been made.

Constitutional Rules—Constitutional provisions that prescribe procedures for Congress. In addition to certain types of votes required in particular situations, these provisions include the following: (1) the House chooses its Speaker, the Senate its president pro tempore and both houses their officers; (2) each house requires a majority quorum to conduct business; (3) less than a majority may adjourn from day to day and compel the attendance of absent members; (4) neither house may adjourn for more than three days without the consent of the other; (5) each house must keep a journal; (6) the yeas and nays are ordered when supported by one-fifth of the members present; (7) all revenue-raising bills must originate in the House, but the Senate may propose amendments to them. The Constitution also sets out the procedure in the House for electing a president, the procedure in the Senate for electing a vice president, the procedure for filling a vacancy in the office of vice president and the procedure for overriding a presidential veto.

Constitutional Votes—Constitutional provisions that require certain votes or voting methods in specific situations. They include (1) the yeas and nays at the desire of one-fifth of the members present; (2) a two-thirds vote by the yeas and nays to override a veto; (3) a two-thirds vote by one house to expel one of its members and by both houses to propose a constitutional amendment; (4) a two-thirds vote of senators present to convict someone whom the House has impeached and to consent to ratification of treaties; (5) a two-thirds vote in each house to remove political disabilities from persons who have engaged in insurrection or rebellion or given aid or comfort to the enemies of the United States; (6) a majority vote in each house to fill a vacancy in the office of vice president; (7) a majority vote of all states to elect a president in the House of Representatives when no candidate receives a majority of the electoral votes; (8) a majority vote of all senators when the Senate elects a vice president under the same circumstances; and (9) the casting vote of the vice president in case of tie votes in the Senate.

Contempt of Congress—Willful obstruction of the proper functions of Congress. Most frequently, it is a refusal to obey a subpoena to appear and testify before a committee or to produce documents demanded by it. Such obstruction is a misdemeanor and persons cited for contempt are subject to prosecution in federal courts. A house cites an individual for contempt by agreeing to a privileged resolution to that effect reported by a committee. The presiding officer then refers the matter to a U.S. attorney for prosecution.

Continuing Body—A characterization of the Senate on the theory that it continues from Congress to Congress and has existed continuously since it first convened in 1789. The rationale for the theory is that under the system of staggered six-year terms for senators, the terms of only about one-third of them expire after each Congress and, therefore, a quorum of the Senate is always in office. Consequently, under this theory, the Senate, unlike the House, does not have to adopt its rules at the beginning of each Congress because those rules continue from one Congress to the next. This makes it extremely difficult for the Senate to change its rules against the opposition of a determined minority because those rules require a two-thirds vote of the senators present and voting to invoke cloture on a proposed rules change.

Continuing Resolution (CR)—A joint resolution that provides funds to continue the operation of federal agencies and programs at the beginning of a new fiscal year if their annual appropriation bills have not yet been enacted; also called continuing appropriations. Continuing resolutions are enacted shortly before or after the new fiscal year begins and usually make funds available for a specified period. Additional resolutions are often needed after the first expires. Some continuing resolutions have provided appropriations for an entire fiscal year. Continuing resolutions for specific periods customarily fix a rate at which agencies may incur obligations based either on the previous year's appropriations, the president's budget request, or the amount as specified in the agency's regular annual appropriation bill if that bill has already been passed by one or both houses. In the House, continuing resolutions are privileged after Sept. 15.

Contract Authority—Statutory authority permitting an agency to enter into contracts or incur other obligations even though it has not received an appropriation to pay for them. Congress must eventually fund them because the government is legally liable for such payments. The Congressional Budget Act of 1974 requires that new contract authority may not be used unless provided for in advance by an appropriation act, but it permits a few exceptions.

Correcting Recorded Votes—The rules of both houses prohibit members from changing their votes after a vote result has been announced. Nevertheless, the Senate permits its members to withdraw or change their votes, by unanimous consent, immediately after the announcement. In rare instances, senators have been granted unanimous consent to change their votes several days or weeks after the announcement. Votes tallied by the electronic voting system in the House may not be changed. But when a vote actually given is not recorded during an oral call of the roll, a member may demand a correction as a matter of right. On all other alleged errors in a recorded vote, the Speaker determines whether the circumstances justify a change. Occasionally, members merely announce that they were incorrectly recorded; announcements can occur hours, days or even months after the vote and appear in the Congressional Record.

Cosponsor—A member who has joined one or more other members to sponsor a measure.

Credit Authority—Authority granted to an agency to incur direct loan obligations or to make loan guarantee commitments. The Congressional Budget Act of 1974 bans congressional consideration of credit authority legislation unless the extent of that authority is made subject to provisions in appropriation acts.

C-SPAN—Cable-Satellite Public Affairs Network, which provides live, gavel-to-gavel coverage of Senate floor proceedings on one cable television channel and coverage of House floor proceedings on another channel. C-SPAN also televises important committee hearings in both houses. Each house also transmits its televised proceedings directly to congressional offices.

Current Services Estimates—Executive branch estimates of the anticipated costs of federal programs and operations for the next and future fiscal years at existing levels of service and assuming no new initiatives or changes in existing law. The president submits these estimates to Congress with the annual budget and includes an explanation of the underlying economic and policy assumptions on which they are based, such as anticipated rates of inflation, real economic growth and unemployment, plus program caseloads and pay increases.

Custody of the Papers—Possession of an engrossed measure and certain related basic documents that the two houses produce as they try to resolve their differences over the measure.

Dance of the Swans and the Ducks—A whimsical description of the gestures some members use in connection with a request for a recorded vote, especially in the House. When members want their colleagues to stand in support of the request, they move their hands and arms in a gentle upward motion resembling the beginning flight of a graceful swan. When they want their colleagues to remain seated to avoid such a vote, they move their hands and arms in a vigorous downward motion resembling a diving duck.

Dean—Within a state's delegation in the House of Representatives, the member with the longest continuous service.

Debate—In congressional parlance, speeches delivered during consideration of a measure, motion or other matter, as distinguished from speeches in other parliamentary situations, such as one-minute and special order speeches when no business is pending. Virtually all debate in the House of Representatives is under some kind of time limitation. Most debate in the Senate is unlimited; that is, a senator, once recognized, may speak for as long as he or she chooses, unless the Senate invokes cloture.

Debt Limit—The maximum amount of outstanding federal public debt permitted by law. The limit (or ceiling) covers virtually all debt incurred by the government except agency debt. Each congressional budget resolution sets forth the new debt limit that may be required under its provisions.

Deferral—An impoundment of funds for a specific period of time that may not extend beyond the fiscal year in which it is proposed. Under the Impoundment Control Act of 1974, the president must notify Congress that he is deferring the spending or obligation of funds provided by law for a project or activity. Congress can disapprove the deferral by legislation.

Deficit—The amount by which the government's outlays exceed its budget receipts for a given fiscal year. Both the president's budget and the annual congressional budget resolution provide estimates of the deficit or surplus for the upcoming and several future fiscal years.

Degrees of Amendment—Designations that indicate the relationships of amendments to the text of a measure and to each other. In general, an amendment offered directly to the text of a measure is an amendment in the first degree, and an amendment to that amendment is an amendment in the second degree. Both houses normally prohibit amendments in the third degree — that is, an amendment to an amendment to an amendment.

Delegate—A nonvoting member of the House of Representatives elected to a two-year term from the District of Columbia, the territory of Guam, the territory of the Virgin Islands or the territory of American Samoa. By law, delegates may not vote in the full House but they may participate in debate, offer motions (except to reconsider) and serve and vote on standing and select committees. On their committees, delegates possess the same powers and privileges as other members and the Speaker may appoint them to appropriate conference committees and select committees.

Denounce—A formal action that condemns a member for misbehavior; considered by some experts to be equivalent to censure. (See Censure.)

Dilatory Tactics—Procedural actions intended to delay or prevent action by a house or a committee. They include, among others, offering numerous motions, demanding quorum calls and recorded votes at every opportunity, making numerous points of order and parliamentary inquiries and speaking as long as the applicable rules permit. The Senate rules permit a battery of dilatory tactics, especially lengthy speeches, except under cloture. In the House, possible dilatory tactics are more limited. Speeches are always subject to time limits and debate-ending motions. Moreover, a House rule instructs the Speaker not to entertain dilatory motions and lets the Speaker decide whether a motion is dilatory. However, the Speaker may not override the constitutional right of a member to demand the yeas and nays, and in practice usually waits for a point of order before exercising that authority. (See Cloture.)

Discharge a Committee—Remove a measure from a committee to which it has been referred in order to make it available for floor consideration. Noncontroversial measures are often discharged by unanimous consent. However, because congressional committees have no obligation to report measures referred to them, each house has procedures to extract controversial measures from recalcitrant committees. Six discharge procedures are available in the House of Representatives. The

Senate uses a motion to discharge, which is usually converted into a discharge resolution.

District Office—Representatives maintain one or more offices in their districts for the purpose of assisting and communicating with constituents. The costs of maintaining these offices are paid from members' official allowances. Senators can use the official expense allowance to rent offices in their home state, subject to a funding formula based on their state's population and other factors.

District Work Period—The House term for a scheduled congressional recess during which members may visit their districts and conduct constituency business.

Division Vote—A vote in which the chair first counts those in favor of a proposition and then those opposed to it, with no record made of how each member votes. In the Senate, the chair may count raised hands or ask senators to stand, whereas the House requires members to stand; hence, often called a standing vote. Committees in both houses ordinarily use a show of hands. A division usually occurs after a voice vote and may be demanded by any member or ordered by the chair if there is any doubt about the outcome of the voice vote. The demand for a division can also come before a voice vote. In the Senate, the demand must come before the result of a voice vote is announced. It may be made after a voice vote announcement in the House, but only if no intervening business has transpired and only if the member was standing and seeking recognition at the time of the announcement. A demand for the yeas and nays or, in the House, for a recorded vote, takes precedence over a division vote.

Doorkeeper of the House—A former officer of the House of Representatives who was responsible for enforcing the rules prohibiting unauthorized persons from entering the chamber when the House is in session. The doorkeeper was usually the candidate of the majority party. In 1995 the office was abolished and its functions transferred to the sergeant at arms.

Effective Dates—Provisions of an act that specify when the entire act or individual provisions in it become effective as law. Most acts become effective on the date of enactment, but it is sometimes necessary or prudent to delay the effective dates of some provisions.

Electronic Voting—Since 1973 the House has used an electronic voting system to record the yeas and nays and to conduct recorded votes. Members vote by inserting their voting cards in one of the boxes at several locations in the chamber. They are given at least fifteen minutes to vote. When several votes occur immediately after each other, the Speaker may reduce the voting time to five minutes on the second and subsequent votes. The Speaker may allow additional time on each vote but may also close a vote at any time after the minimum time has expired. Members can change their votes at any time before the Speaker announces the result. The House also uses the electronic system for quorum calls. While a vote is in progress, a large panel above the Speaker's desk displays how each member has voted. Smaller panels on either side of the chamber display running totals of the votes and the time remaining. The Senate does not have electronic voting.

Enacting Clause—The opening language of each bill, beginning "Be it enacted by the Senate and House of Representatives of the United States of America in Congress assembled..." This language gives legal force to measures approved by Congress and signed by the president or enacted over the president's veto. A successful motion to strike it from a bill kills the entire measure.

Engrossed Bill—The official copy of a bill or joint resolution as passed by one chamber, including the text as amended by floor action and certified by the clerk of the House or the secretary of the Senate (as appropriate). Amendments by one house to a measure or amendments of the other also are engrossed. House engrossed documents are printed on blue paper; the Senate's are printed on white paper.

Enrolled Bill—The final official copy of a bill or joint resolution passed in identical form by both houses. An enrolled bill is printed on parchment. After it is certified by the chief officer of the house in which it originated and signed by the House Speaker and the Senate president pro tempore, the measure is sent to the White House for the president's signature.

Entitlement Program—A federal program under which individuals, businesses or units of government that meet the requirements or qualifications established by law are entitled to receive certain payments if they seek such payments. Major examples include Social Security, Medicare, Medicaid, unemployment insurance and military and federal civilian pensions. Congress cannot control their expenditures by refusing to appropriate the sums necessary to fund them because the government is legally obligated to pay eligible recipients the amounts to which the law entitles them.

Equality of the Houses—A component of the Constitution's emphasis on checks and balances under which each house is given essentially equal status in the enactment of legislation and in the relations and negotiations between the two houses. Although the House of Representatives initiates revenue and appropriation measures, the Senate has the right to amend them. Either house may initiate any other type of legislation, and neither can force the other to agree to, or even act on, its measures. Moreover, each house has a potential veto over the other because legislation requires agreement by both. Similarly, in a conference to resolve their differences on a measure, each house casts one vote, as determined by a majority of its conferees. In most other national bicameral legislatures, the powers of one house are markedly greater than those of the other.

Ethics Rules—Several rules or standing orders in each house that mandate certain standards of conduct for members and congressional employees in finance, employment, franking and other areas. The Senate Permanent Select Committee on Ethics and the House Committee on Standards of Official Conduct investigate alleged violations of conduct and recommend appropriate actions to their respective houses.

Exclusive Committee—(1) Under the rules of the Republican Conference and House Democratic Caucus, a standing committee whose members usually cannot serve on any other standing committee. As of 2000 the Appropriations, Energy and Commerce (beginning in the 105th Congress), Ways and Means and Rules Committees were designated as exclusive committees. (2) Under the rules of the two party conferences in the Senate, a standing committee whose members may not simultaneously serve on any other exclusive committee.

Executive Calendar—The Senate's calendar for committee reports on its executive business, namely treaties and nominations. The calendar numbers indicate the order in which items were referred to the calendar but have no bearing on when or if the Senate will consider them. The Senate, by motion or unanimous consent, resolves itself into executive session to consider them.

Executive Document—A document, usually a treaty, sent by the president to the Senate for approval. It is referred to a committee in the same manner as other measures. Resolutions to ratify treaties have their own "treaty document" numbers. For example, the first treaty submitted in the 106th Congress would be "Treaty Doc 106-1."

Executive Order—A unilateral proclamation by the president that has a policy-making or legislative impact. Members of Congress have challenged some executive orders on the grounds that they usurped the authority of the legislative branch. Although the Supreme Court has ruled that a particular order exceeded the president's authority, it has upheld others as falling within the president's general constitutional powers.

Executive Privilege—The assertion that presidents have the right to withhold certain information from Congress. Presidents have based their claim on (1) the constitutional separation of powers; (2) the need for secrecy in military and diplomatic affairs; (3) the need to protect individuals from unfavorable publicity; (4) the need to safeguard the confidential exchange of ideas in the executive branch; and (5) the need to protect individuals who provide confidential advice to the president.

Executive Session—(1) A Senate meeting devoted to the consideration of treaties or nominations. Normally, the Senate meets in legislative session; it resolves itself into executive session, by motion or by unanimous consent, to deal with its executive business. It also keeps a separate Journal for executive sessions. Executive sessions are usually open to the public, but the Senate may choose to close them.

Expulsion—A member's removal from office by a two-thirds vote of his or her house; the supermajority is required by the Constitution. It is the most severe and most rarely used sanction a house can invoke against a member. Although the Constitution provides no explicit grounds for expulsion, the courts have ruled that it may be applied only for misconduct during a member's term of office, not for conduct before the member's election. Generally, neither house will consider expulsion of a member convicted of a crime until the judicial processes have been exhausted. At that stage, members sometimes resign rather than face expulsion. In 1977 the House adopted a rule urging members convicted of certain crimes to voluntarily abstain from voting or participating in other legislative business.

Extensions of Remarks—An appendix to the daily Congressional Record that consists primarily of miscellaneous extraneous material submitted by members. It often includes members' statements not delivered on the floor, newspaper articles and editorials, praise for a member's constituents and noteworthy letters received by a member, among other material. Representatives supply the bulk of this material; senators submit very little. "Extensions of Remarks" pages are separately numbered, and each number is preceded by the letter "E." Materials may be placed in the Extensions of Remarks section only by unanimous consent. Usually, one member of each party makes the request each day on behalf of his or her party colleagues after the House has completed its legislative business of the day.

Federal Debt—The total amount of monies borrowed and not yet repaid by the federal government. Federal debt consists of public debt and agency debt. Public debt is the portion of the federal debt borrowed by the Treasury or the Federal Financing Bank directly from the public or from another federal fund or account. For example, the Treasury regularly borrows money from the Social Security trust fund. Public debt accounts for about 99 percent of the federal debt. Agency debt refers to the debt incurred by federal agencies such as the Export-Import Bank but excluding the Treasury and the Federal Financing Bank, which are authorized by law to borrow funds from the public or from another government fund or account.

Filibuster—The use of obstructive and time-consuming parliamentary tactics by one member or a minority of members to delay, modify or defeat proposed legislation or rules changes. Filibusters are also sometimes used to delay urgently needed measures to force the body to accept other legislation. The Senate's rules permitting unlimited debate and the extraordinary majority it requires to impose cloture make filibustering particularly effective in that chamber. Under the stricter rules of the House, filibusters in that body are short-lived and therefore ineffective and rarely attempted.

Fiscal Year—The federal government's annual accounting period. It begins Oct. 1 and ends on the following Sept. 30. A fiscal year is designated by the calendar year in which it ends and is often referred to as FY. Thus, fiscal year 1998 began Oct. 1, 1997, ended Sept. 30, 1998, and is called FY98. In theory, Congress is supposed to complete action on all budgetary measures applying to a fiscal year before that year begins. It rarely does so.

Five-Minute Rule—A House rule that limits debate on an amendment offered in Committee of the Whole to five minutes for its sponsor and five minutes for an opponent. In practice, the committee routinely permits longer debate by two devices: the offering of pro forma amendments, each debatable for five minutes, and unanimous consent for a member to speak longer than five minutes. Consequently, debate on an amendment sometimes continues for hours. At any time after the first ten minutes, however, the committee may shut off debate immediately or by a specified time, either by unanimous consent or by majority vote on a nondebatable motion. The motion, which dates from 1847, is also used in the House as in Committee of the Whole, where debate also may be shut off by a motion for the previous question.

Floor—The ground level of the House or Senate chamber where members sit and the houses conduct their business. When members are attending a meeting of their house they are said to be on the floor. Floor action refers to the procedural actions taken during floor consideration such as deciding on motions, taking up measures, amending them and voting.

Floor Manager—A majority party member responsible for guiding a measure through its floor consideration in a house and for devising the political and procedural strategies that might be required to get it passed. The presiding officer gives the floor manager priority recognition to debate, offer amendments, oppose amendments and make crucial procedural motions.

Frank—Informally, members' legal right to send official mail postage free under their signatures; often called the franking privilege. Technically, it is the autographic or facsimile signature used on envelopes instead of stamps that permits members and certain congressional officers to send their official mail free of charge. The franking privilege has been authorized by law since the first Congress, except for a few months in 1873. Congress reimburses the U.S. Postal Service for the franked mail it handles.

Function or Functional Category—A broad category of national need and spending of budgetary significance. A category provides an accounting method for allocating and keeping track of budgetary resources and expenditures for that function because it includes all budget accounts related to the function's subject or purpose such as agriculture, administration of justice, commerce and housing and energy. Functions do not necessarily correspond with appropriations acts or with the budgets of individual agencies. As of 2000 there were twenty functional categories, each divided into a number of subfunctions.

Gag Rule—A pejorative term for any type of special rule reported by the House Rules Committee that proposes to prohibit amendments to a measure or only permits amendments offered by the reporting committee.

Galleries—The balconies overlooking each chamber from which the public, news media, staff and others may observe floor proceedings.

General Appropriation Bill—A term applied to each of the thirteen annual bills that provide funds for most federal agencies and programs and also to the supplemental appropriation bills that contain appropriations for more than one agency or program.

Germaneness—The requirement that an amendment be closely related — in terms of subject or purpose, for example — to the text it proposes to amend. A House rule requires that all amendments be germane. In the Senate, only amendments offered to general appropriation bills and budget measures or proposed under cloture must be germane.

Germaneness rules can be waived by suspension of the rules in both houses, by unanimous consent agreements in the Senate and by special rules from the Rules Committee in the House. Moreover, presiding officers usually do not enforce germaneness rules on their own initiative; therefore, a nongermane amendment can be adopted if no member raises a point of order against it. Under cloture in the Senate, however, the chair may take the initiative to rule amendments out of order as not being germane, without a point of order being made. All House debate must be germane except during general debate in the Committee of the Whole, but special rules invariably require that such debate be "confined to the bill." The Senate requires germane debate only during the first three hours of each daily session. Under the precedents of both houses, an amendment can be relevant but not necessarily germane. A crucial factor in determining germaneness in the House is how the subject of a measure or matter is defined. For example, the subject of a measure authorizing construction of a naval vessel is defined as being the construction of a single vessel; therefore, an amendment to authorize an additional vessel is not germane.

Gerrymandering—The manipulation of legislative district boundaries to benefit a particular party, politician or minority group. The term originated in 1812 when the Massachusetts legislature redrew the lines of state legislative districts to favor the party of Gov. Elbridge Gerry, and some critics said one district looked like a salamander. (See also Congressional District; Redistricting.)

Government Accountability Office (GAO)—A congressional support agency, often referred to as the investigative arm of Congress. It evaluates and audits federal agencies and programs in the United States and abroad on its initiative or at the request of congressional committees or members.

Gramm-Rudman-Hollings Act of 1985—Common name for the Balanced Budget and Emergency Deficit Control Act of 1985, which established new budget procedures intended to balance the federal budget by fiscal year 1991. (The timetable subsequently was extended and then deleted.) The act's chief sponsors were senators Phil Gramm (R-Texas), Warren Rudman (R-N.H.) Ernest Hollings (D-S.C.).

Grandfather Clause—A provision in a measure, law or rule that exempts an individual, entity or a defined category of individuals or entities from complying with a new policy or restriction. For example, a bill that would raise taxes on persons who reach the age of sixty-five after a certain date inherently grandfathers out those who are sixty-five before that date. Similarly, a Senate rule limiting senators to two major committee assignments also grandfathers some senators who were sitting on a third major committee before a specified date.

Grants-in-Aid—Payments by the federal government to state and local governments to help provide for assistance programs or public services.

Hearing—Committee or subcommittee meetings to receive testimony on proposed legislation during investigations or for oversight purposes. Relatively few bills are important enough to justify formal hearings. Witnesses often include experts, government officials, spokespersons for interested groups, officials of the General Accounting Office and members of Congress.

Hold—A senator's request that his or her party leaders delay floor consideration of certain legislation or presidential nominations. The majority leader usually honors a hold for a reasonable period of time, especially if its purpose is to assure the senator that the matter will not be called up during his or her absence or to give the senator time to gather necessary information.

Hold (or Have) the Floor—A member's right to speak without interruption, unless he or she violates a rule, after recognition by the presiding officer. At the member's discretion, he or she may yield to another member for a question in the Senate or for a question or statement in the House, but may reclaim the floor at any time.

Hold-Harmless Clause—In legislation providing a new formula for allocating federal funds, a clause to ensure that recipients of those funds do not receive less in a future year than they did in the current year if the new formula would result in a reduction for them. Similar to a grandfather clause, it has been used most frequently to soften the impact of sudden reductions in federal grants. (See Grandfather Clause.)

Hopper—A box on the clerk's desk in the House chamber into which members deposit bills and resolutions to introduce them. In House jargon, to drop a bill in the hopper is to introduce it.

Hour Rule—A House rule that permits members, when recognized, to hold the floor in debate for no more than one hour each. The majority party member customarily yields one-half the time to a minority member. Although the hour rule applies to general debate in Committee of the Whole as well as in the House, special rules routinely vary the length of time for such debate and its control to fit the circumstances of particular measures.

House As In Committee of the Whole—A hybrid combination of procedures from the general rules of the House and from the rules of the Committee of the Whole, sometimes used to expedite consideration of a measure on the floor.

House Calendar—The calendar reserved for all public bills and resolutions that do not raise revenue or directly or indirectly appropriate money or property when they are favorably reported by House committees.

House Manual—A commonly used title for the handbook of the rules of the House of Representatives, published in each Congress. Its official title is Constitution, Jefferson's Manual and Rules of the House of Representatives.

House of Representatives—The house of Congress in which states are represented roughly in proportion to their populations, but every state is guaranteed at least one representative. By law, the number of voting representatives is fixed at 435. Four delegates and one resident commissioner also serve in the House; they may vote in their committees but not on the House floor. Although the House and Senate have equal legislative power, the Constitution gives the House sole authority to originate revenue measures. The House also claims the right to originate appropriation measures, a claim the Senate disputes in theory but concedes in practice. The House has the sole power to impeach, and it elects the president when no candidate has received a majority of the electoral votes. It is sometimes referred to as the lower body.

Immunity—(1) Members' constitutional protection from lawsuits and arrest in connection with their legislative duties. They may not be tried for libel or slander for anything they say on the floor of a house or in committee. Nor may they be arrested while attending sessions of their houses or when traveling to or from sessions of Congress, except when charged with treason, a felony or a breach of the peace. (2) In the case of a witness before a committee, a grant of protection from prosecution based on that person's testimony to the committee. It is used to compel witnesses to testify who would otherwise refuse to do so on the constitutional ground of possible selfincrimination. Under such a grant, none of a witness's testimony may be used against him or her in a court proceeding except in a prosecution for perjury or for giving a false statement to Congress. (See also Contempt of Congress.)

Impeachment—The first step to remove the president, vice president or other federal civil officers from office and to disqualify them from any future federal office "of honor, Trust or Profit." An impeachment is a formal charge of treason, bribery or "other high Crimes and Misdemeanors." The House has the sole power of impeachment and the Senate the sole power of trying the charges and convicting. The House impeaches by a simple majority vote; conviction requires a two-thirds vote of all senators present.

Impeachment Trial, Removal and Disqualification—The Senate conducts an impeachment trial under a separate set of twenty-six rules that appears in the Senate Manual. Under the Constitution, the chief justice of the United States presides over trials of the president, but the vice president, the president pro tempore or any other senator may preside over the impeachment trial of another official.

The Constitution requires senators to take an oath for an impeachment trial. During the trial, senators may not engage in colloquies or participate in arguments, but they may submit questions in writing to House managers or defense counsel. After the trial concludes, the Senate votes separately on each article of impeachment without debate unless the Senate orders the doors closed for private discussions. During deliberations senators may speak no more than once on a question, not for more than ten minutes on an interlocutory question and not more than fifteen minutes on the final question. These rules may be set aside by unanimous consent or suspended on motion by a two-thirds vote.

The Senate's impeachment trial of President Clinton in 1999 was only the second such trial involving a president. It continued for five weeks, with the Senate voting not to convict on the two impeachment articles.

Senate impeachment rules allow the Senate, at its own discretion, to name a committee to hear evidence and conduct the trial, with all senators thereafter voting on the charges. The impeachment trials of three federal judges were conducted this way, and the Supreme Court upheld the validity of these rules in Nixon v. United States, 506 U.S. 224, 1993.

An official convicted on impeachment charges is removed from office immediately. However, the convicted official is not barred from holding a federal office in the future unless the Senate, after its conviction vote, also approves a resolution disqualifying the convicted official from future office. For example, federal judge Alcee L. Hastings was impeached and convicted in 1989, but the Senate did not vote to bar him from office in the future. In 1992 Hastings was elected to the House of Representatives, and no challenge was raised against seating him when he took the oath of office in 1993.

Impoundment—An executive branch action or inaction that delays or withholds the expenditure or obligation of budget authority provided by law. The Impoundment Control Act of 1974 classifies impoundments as either deferrals or rescissions, requires the president to notify Congress about all such actions and gives Congress authority to approve or reject them.

Inspector General (IG) In the House of Representatives—A position established with the passage of the House Administrative Reform Resolution of 1992. The duties of the office have been revised several times and are now contained in House Rule II. The inspector general (IG), who is subject to the policy direction and oversight of the Committee on House Administration, is appointed for a Congress jointly by the Speaker and the majority and minority leaders of the House. The IG communicates the results of audits to the House officers or officials who were the subjects of the audits and suggests appropriate corrective measures. The IG submits a report of each audit to the Speaker, the majority and minority leaders and the chairman and ranking minority member of the House Administration Committee; notifies these five members in the case of any financial irregularity discovered; and reports to the Committee on Standards of Official Conduct on possible violations of House rules or any applicable law by any House member, officer or employee. The IG's office also has certain duties to audit various financial operations of the House that had previously been performed by the General Accounting Office.

Instruct Conferees—A formal action by a house urging its conferees to uphold a particular position on a measure in conference. The instruc-

tion may be to insist on certain provisions in the measure as passed by that house or to accept a provision in the version passed by the other house. Instructions to conferees are not binding because the primary responsibility of conferees is to reach agreement on a measure and neither House can compel the other to accept particular provisions or positions.

Investigative Power—The authority of Congress and its committees to pursue investigations, upheld by the Supreme Court but limited to matters related to, and in furtherance of, a legitimate task of the Congress. Standing committees in both houses are permanently authorized to investigate matters within their jurisdictions. Major investigations are sometimes conducted by temporary select, special or joint committees established by resolutions for that purpose.

Some rules of the House provide certain safeguards for witnesses and others during investigative hearings. These permit counsel to accompany witnesses, require that each witness receive a copy of the committee's rules and order the committee to go into closed session if it believes the testimony to be heard might defame, degrade or incriminate any person. The committee may subsequently decide to hear such testimony in open session. The Senate has no rules of this kind.

Item Veto—Item veto authority, which is available to most state governors, allows governors to eliminate or reduce items in legislative measures presented for their signature without vetoing the entire measure and sign the rest into law. A similar authority was briefly granted to the U.S. president under the Line Item Veto Act of 1996. According to the majority opinion of the Supreme Court in its 1998 decision overturning that law, a constitutional amendment would be necessary to give the president such item veto authority.

Jefferson's Manual—Short title of Jefferson's Manual of Parliamentary Practice, prepared by Thomas Jefferson for his guidance when he was president of the Senate from 1797 to 1801. Although it reflects English parliamentary practice in his day, many procedures in both houses of Congress are still rooted in its basic precepts. Under a House rule adopted in 1837, the manual's provisions govern House procedures when applicable and when they are not inconsistent with its standing rules and orders. The Senate, however, has never officially acknowledged it as a direct authority for its legislative procedure.

Johnson Rule—A policy instituted in 1953 under which all Democratic senators are assigned to one major committee before any Democrat is assigned to two. The Johnson Rule is named after its author, Sen. Lyndon B. Johnson, D-Texas, then the Senate's Democratic leader. Senate Republicans adopted a similar policy soon thereafter.

Joint Committee—A committee composed of members selected from each house. The functions of most joint committees involve investigation, research or oversight of agencies closely related to Congress. Permanent joint committees, created by statute, are sometimes called standing joint committees. Once quite numerous, only four joint committees remained as of 2002: Joint Economic, Joint Taxation, Joint Library and Joint Printing. None has authority to report legislation.

Joint Resolution—A legislative measure that Congress uses for purposes other than general legislation. Similar to a bill, it has the force of law when passed by both houses and either approved by the president or passed over the president's veto. Unlike a bill, a joint resolution enacted into law is not called an act; it retains its original title. Most often, joint resolutions deal with such relatively limited matters as the correction of errors in existing law, continuing appropriations, a single appropriation or the establishment of permanent joint committees. Unlike bills, however, joint resolutions also are used to propose constitutional amendments; these do not require the president's signature and become effective only when ratified by three-fourths of the states. The House designates joint resolutions as H.J. Res., the Senate as S.J. Res. Each house numbers its joint resolutions consecutively in the order of introduction during a two-year Congress.

Joint Session—Informally, any combined meeting of the Senate and the House. Technically, a joint session is a combined meeting to count the electoral votes for president and vice president or to hear a presidential address, such as the State of the Union message; any other formal combined gathering of both houses is a joint meeting. Joint sessions are authorized by concurrent resolutions and are held in the House chamber, because of its larger seating capacity. Although the president of the Senate and the Speaker sit side by side at the Speaker's desk during combined meetings, the former presides over the electoral count and the latter presides on all other occasions and introduces the president or other guest speaker. The president and other guests may address a joint session or meeting only by invitation.

Joint Sponsorship—Two or more members sponsoring the same measure.

Journal—The official record of House or Senate actions, including every motion offered, every vote cast, amendments agreed to, quorum calls and so forth. Unlike the Congressional Record, it does not provide reports of speeches, debates, statements and the like. The Constitution requires each house to maintain a Journal and to publish it periodically.

Junket—A member's trip at government expense, especially abroad, ostensibly on official business but, it is often alleged, for pleasure.

Killer Amendment—An amendment that, if agreed to, might lead to the defeat of the measure it amends, either in the house in which the amendment is offered or at some later stage of the legislative process. Members sometimes deliberately offer or vote for such an amendment in the expectation that it will undermine support for the measure in Congress or increase the likelihood that the president will veto it.

King of the Mountain (or Hill) Rule—(See Queen of the Hill Rule.)

LA—(See Legislative Assistant.)

Lame Duck—Jargon for a member who has not been reelected, or did not seek reelection, and is serving the balance of his or her term.

Lame Duck Session—A session of a Congress held after the election for the succeeding Congress, so-called after the lame duck members still serving.

Last Train Out—Colloquial name for last must-pass bill of a session of Congress.

Law—An act of Congress that has been signed by the president, passed over the president's veto or allowed to become law without the president's signature.

Lay on the Table—A motion to dispose of a pending proposition immediately, finally and adversely; that is, to kill it without a direct vote on its substance. Often simply called a motion to table, it is not debatable and is adopted by majority vote or without objection. It is a highly privileged motion, taking precedence over all others except the motion to adjourn in the House and all but three additional motions in the Senate. It can kill a bill or resolution, an amendment, another motion, an appeal or virtually any other matter.

Tabling an amendment also tables the measure to which the amendment is pending in the House, but not in the Senate. The House does not allow the motion against the motion to recommit, in Committee of the Whole, and in some other situations. In the Senate it is the only permissible motion that immediately ends debate on a proposition, but only to kill it.

(The) Leadership—Usually, a reference to the majority and minority leaders of the Senate or to the Speaker and minority leader of the House. The term sometimes includes the majority leader in the House and the majority and minority whips in each house and, at other times, other party officials as well.

Legislation—(1) A synonym for legislative measures: bills and joint resolutions. (2) Provisions in such measures or in substantive amendments offered to them. (3) In some contexts, provisions that change existing substantive or authorizing law, rather than provisions that make appropriations.

Legislation on an Appropriation Bill—A common reference to provisions changing existing law that appear in, or are offered as amendments to, a general appropriation bill. A House rule prohibits the inclusion of such provisions in general appropriation bills unless they retrench expenditures. An analogous Senate rule permits points of order against amendments to a general appropriation bill that propose general legislation.

Legislative Assistant (LA)—A member's staff person responsible for monitoring and preparing legislation on particular subjects and for advising the member on them; commonly referred to as an LA.

Legislative Day—The day that begins when a house meets after an adjournment and ends when it next adjourns. Because the House of Representatives normally adjourns at the end of a daily session, its legislative and calendar days usually coincide. The Senate, however, frequently recesses at the end of a daily session, and its legislative day may extend over several calendar days, weeks or months. Among other uses, this technicality permits the Senate to save time by circumventing its morning hour, a procedure required at the beginning of every legislative day.

Legislative History—(1) A chronological list of actions taken on a measure during its progress through the legislative process. (2) The official documents relating to a measure, the entries in the Journals of the two houses on that measure and the Congressional Record text of its consideration in both houses. The documents include all committee reports and the conference report and joint explanatory statement, if any. Courts and affected federal agencies study a measure's legislative history for congressional intent about its purpose and interpretation.

Legislative Process—(1) Narrowly, the stages in the enactment of a law from introduction to final disposition. An introduced measure that becomes law typically travels through reference to committee; committee and subcommittee consideration; report to the chamber; floor consideration; amendment; passage; engrossment; messaging to the other house; similar steps in that house, including floor amendment of the measure; return of the measure to the first house; consideration of amendments between the houses or a conference to resolve their differences; approval of the conference report by both houses; enrollment; approval by the president or override of the president's veto; and deposit with the Archivist of the United States. (2) Broadly, the political, lobbying and other factors that affect or influence the process of enacting laws.

Legislative Veto—A procedure, declared unconstitutional in 1983, that allowed Congress or one of its houses to nullify certain actions of the president, executive branch agencies or independent agencies. Sometimes called congressional vetoes or congressional disapprovals. Following the Supreme Court's 1983 decision, Congress amended several legislative veto statutes to require enactment of joint resolutions, which are subject to presidential veto, for nullifying executive branch actions.

Limitation on a General Appropriation Bill—Language that prohibits expenditures for part of an authorized purpose from funds provided in a general appropriation bill. Precedents require that the language be phrased in the negative: that none of the funds provided in a pending appropriation bill shall be used for a specified authorized activity. Limitations in general appropriation bills are permitted on the grounds that Congress can refuse to fund authorized programs and, therefore, can refuse to fund any part of them as long as the prohibition does not change existing law. House precedents have established that a limitation does not change existing law if it does not impose additional duties or burdens on executive branch officials, interfere with their discretionary authority or require them to make judgments or determinations not required by existing law. The proliferation of limitation amendments in the 1970s and early 1980s prompted the House to adopt a rule in 1983 making it more difficult for members to offer them. The rule bans such amendments during the reading of an appropriation bill for amendments, unless they are specifically authorized in existing law. Other limitations may be offered after the reading, but the Committee of the Whole can foreclose them by adopting a motion to rise and report the bill back to the House. In 1995 the rule was amended to allow the motion to rise and report to be made only by the majority leader or his or her designee. The House Appropriations Committee, however, can include limitation provisions in the bills it reports.

Line Item—An amount in an appropriation measure. It can refer to a single appropriation account or to separate amounts within the account. In the congressional budget process, the term usually refers to assumptions about the funding of particular programs or accounts that underlie the broad functional amounts in a budget resolution. These assumptions are discussed in the reports accompanying each resolution and are not binding.

Line-Item Veto—(See Item Veto.)

Line Item Veto Act of 1996—A law, in effect only from January 1997 until June 1998, that granted the president authority intended to be functionally equivalent to an item veto, by amending the Impoundment Control Act of 1974 to incorporate an approach known as enhanced rescission. Key provisions established a new procedure that permitted the president to cancel amounts of new discretionary appropriations (budget authority), new items of direct spending (entitlements) or certain limited tax benefits. It also required the president to notify Congress of the cancellation in a special message within five calendar days after signing the measure. The cancellation would become permanent unless legislation disapproving it was enacted within thirty days. On June 25, 1998, in Clinton v. City of New York the Supreme Court held the Line Item Veto Act unconstitutional, on the grounds that its cancellation provisions violated the presentment clause in Article I, clause 7, of the Constitution.

Live Pair—A voluntary and informal agreement between two members on opposite sides of an issue, one of whom is absent for a recorded vote, under which the member who is present withholds or withdraws his or her vote to offset the failure to vote by the member who is absent. Usually the member in attendance announces that he or she has a live pair, states how each would have voted and votes "present." In the House, under a rules change enacted in the 106th Congress, a live pair is only permitted on the rare occasions when electronic voting is not used.

Live Quorum—In the Senate, a quorum call to which senators are expected to respond. Senators usually suggest the absence of a quorum, not to force a quorum to appear, but to provide a pause in the proceedings during which senators can engage in private discussions or wait for a senator to come to the floor. A senator desiring a live quorum usually announces his or her intention, giving fair warning that there will be an objection to any unanimous consent request that the quorum call be dispensed with before it is completed.

Loan Guarantee—A statutory commitment by the federal government to pay part or all of a loan's principal and interest to a lender or the holder of a security in case the borrower defaults.

Lobby—To try to persuade members of Congress to propose, pass, modify or defeat proposed legislation or to change or repeal existing laws. Lobbyists attempt to promote their preferences or those of a group,

organization or industry. Originally the term referred to persons frequenting the lobbies or corridors of legislative chambers in order to speak to lawmakers. In a general sense, lobbying includes not only direct contact with members but also indirect attempts to influence them, such as writing to them or persuading others to write or visit them, attempting to mold public opinion toward a desired legislative goal by various means and contributing or arranging for contributions to members' election campaigns. The right to lobby stems from the First Amendment to the Constitution, which bans laws that abridge the right of the people to petition the government for a redress of grievances.

Lobbying Disclosure Act of 1995—The principal statute requiring disclosure of — and also, to a degree, circumscribing — the activities of lobbyists. In general, it requires lobbyists who spend more than 20 percent of their time on lobbying activities to register and make semiannual reports of their activities to the clerk of the House and the secretary of the Senate, although the law provides for a number of exemptions. Among the statute's prohibitions, lobbyists are not allowed to make contributions to the legal defense fund of a member or high government official or to reimburse for official travel. Civil penalties for failure to comply may include fines of up to $50,000. The act does not include grassroots lobbying in its definition of lobbying activities.

The act amends several other lobby laws, notably the Foreign Agents Registration Act (FARA), so that lobbyists can submit a single filing. Since the measure was enacted, the number of lobby registrations has risen from about 12,000 to more than 20,000. In 1998 expenditures on federal lobbying, as disclosed under the Lobbying Disclosure Act, totaled $1.42 billion. The 1995 act supersedes the 1946 Federal Regulation of Lobbying Act, which was repealed in Section 11 of the 1995 Act.

Logrolling—Jargon for a legislative tactic or bargaining strategy in which members try to build support for their legislation by promising to support legislation desired by other members or by accepting amendments they hope will induce their colleagues to vote for their bill.

Lower Body—A way to refer to the House of Representatives, which is considered pejorative by House members.

Mace—The symbol of the office of the House sergeant at arms. Under the direction of the Speaker, the sergeant at arms is responsible for preserving order on the House floor by holding up the mace in front of an unruly member, or by carrying the mace up and down the aisles to quell boisterous behavior. When the House is in session, the mace sits on a pedestal at the Speaker's right; when the House is in Committee of the Whole, it is moved to a lower pedestal. The mace is forty-six inches high and consists of thirteen ebony rods bound in silver and topped by a silver globe with a silver eagle, wings outstretched, perched on it.

Majority Leader—The majority party's chief floor spokesperson, elected by that party's caucus — sometimes called floor leader. In the Senate, the majority leader also develops the party's political and procedural strategy, usually in collaboration with other party officials and committee chairmen. The majority leader negotiates the Senate's agenda and committee ratios with the minority leader and usually calls up measures for floor action. The chamber traditionally concedes to the majority leader the right to determine the days on which it will meet and the hours at which it will convene and adjourn. In the House, the majority leader is the Speaker's deputy and heir apparent and helps plan the floor agenda and the party's legislative strategy and often speaks for the party leadership in debate.

Managers—(1) The official title of members appointed to a conference committee, commonly called conferees. The ranking majority and minority managers for each house also manage floor consideration of the committee's conference report. (2) The members who manage the initial floor consideration of a measure. (3) The official title of House members appointed to present impeachment articles to the Senate and to act as prosecutors on behalf of the House during the Senate trial of the impeached person.

Mandatory Appropriations—Amounts that Congress must appropriate annually because it has no discretion over them unless it first amends existing substantive law. Certain entitlement programs, for example, require annual appropriations.

Markup—A meeting or series of meetings by a committee or subcommittee during which members mark up a measure by offering, debating and voting on amendments to it.

Means-Tested Programs—Programs that provide benefits or services to low-income individuals who meet a test of need. Most are entitlement programs, such as Medicaid, food stamps and Supplementary Security Income. A few—for example, subsidized housing and various social services—are funded through discretionary appropriations.

Members' Allowances—Official expenses that are paid for or for which members are reimbursed by their houses. Among these are the costs of office space in congressional buildings and in their home states or districts; office equipment and supplies; postage-free mailings (the franking privilege); a set number of trips to and from home states or districts, as well as travel elsewhere on official business; telephone and other telecommunications services; and staff salaries.

Member's Staff—The personal staff to which a member is entitled. The House sets a maximum number of staff and a monetary allowance for each member. The Senate does not set a maximum staff level, but it does set a monetary allowance for each member. In each house, the staff allowance is included with office expenses allowances and official mail allowances in a consolidated allowance. Representatives and senators can spend as much money in their consolidated allowances for staff, office expenses or official mail, as long as they do not exceed the monetary value of the three allowances combined. This provides members with flexibility in operating their offices.

Method of Equal Proportions—The mathematical formula used since 1950 to determine how the 435 seats in the House of Representatives should be distributed among the fifty states in the apportionment following each decennial census. It minimizes as much as possible the proportional difference between the average district population in any two states. Because the Constitution guarantees each state at least one representative, fifty seats are automatically apportioned. The formula calculates priority numbers for each state, assigns the first of the 385 remaining seats to the state with the highest priority number, the second to the state with the next highest number and so on until all seats are distributed. (See Apportionment.)

Midterm Election—The general election for members of Congress that occurs in November of the second year in a presidential term.

Minority Leader—The minority party's leader and chief floor spokesman, elected by the party caucus; sometimes called minority floor leader. With the assistance of other party officials and the ranking minority members of committees, the minority leader devises the party's political and procedural strategy.

Minority Staff—Employees who assist the minority party members of a committee. Most committees hire separate majority and minority party staffs but they also may hire nonpartisan staff. Senate rules state that a committee's staff must reflect the relative number of its majority and minority party committee members, and the rules guarantee the minority at least one-third of the funds available for hiring partisan staff. In the House, each committee is authorized thirty professional staff, and the minority members of most committees may select up to ten of these staff (subject to full committee approval). Under House rules, the minority party is to be "treated fairly" in the apportionment of additional staff resources. Each House committee determines the portion of its additional staff it allocates to the minority; some committees allocate one-third; and others allot less.

Modified Rule—A special rule from the House Rules Committee that permits only certain amendments to be offered to a measure during its floor consideration or that bans certain specified amendments or amendments on certain subjects.

Morning Business—In the Senate, routine business that is to be transacted at the beginning of the morning hour. The business consists, first, of laying before the Senate, and referring to committees, matters such as messages from the president and the House, federal agency reports and unreferred petitions, memorials, bills and joint resolutions. Next, senators may present additional petitions and memorials. Then committees may present their reports, after which senators may introduce bills and resolutions. Finally, resolutions coming over from a previous day are taken up for consideration. In practice, the Senate adopts standing orders that permit senators to introduce measures and file reports at any time, but only if there has been a morning business period on that day. Because the Senate often remains in the same legislative day for several days, weeks or months at a time, it orders a morning business period almost every calendar day for the convenience of senators who wish to introduce measures or make reports.

Morning Hour—A two-hour period at the beginning of a new legislative day during which the Senate is supposed to conduct routine business, call the calendar on Mondays and deal with other matters described in a Senate rule. In practice, the morning hour very rarely, if ever, occurs, in part because the Senate frequently recesses, rather than adjourns, at the end of a daily session. Therefore the rule does not apply when the senate next meets. The Senate's rules reserve the first hour of the morning for morning business. After the completion of morning business, or at the end of the first hour, the rules permit a motion to proceed to the consideration of a measure on the calendar out of its regular order (except on Mondays). Because that normally debatable motion is not debatable if offered during the morning hour, the majority leader may, but rarely does, use this procedure in anticipating a filibuster on the motion to proceed. If the Senate agrees to the motion, it can consider the measure until the end of the morning hour, and if there is no unfinished business from the previous day it can continue considering it after the morning hour. But if there is unfinished business, a motion to continue consideration is necessary, and that motion is debatable.

Motion—A formal proposal for a procedural action, such as to consider, to amend, to lay on the table, to reconsider, to recess or to adjourn. It has been estimated that at least eighty-five motions are possible under various circumstances in the House of Representatives, somewhat fewer in the Senate. Not all motions are created equal; some are privileged or preferential and enjoy priority over others. Some motions are debatable, amendable or divisible, while others are not.

Multiple and Sequential Referrals—The practice of referring a measure to two or more committees for concurrent consideration (multiple referral) or successively to several committees in sequence (sequential referral). A measure may also be divided into several parts, with each referred to a different committee or to several committees sequentially (split referral). In theory this gives all committees that have jurisdiction over parts of a measure the opportunity to consider and report on them.

Before 1975, House precedents banned such referrals. A 1975 rule required the Speaker to make concurrent and sequential referrals "to the maximum extent feasible." On sequential referrals, the Speaker could set deadlines for reporting the measure. The Speaker ruled that this provision authorized him to discharge a committee from further consideration of a measure and place it on the appropriate calendar of the House if the committee fails to meet the Speaker's deadline. The Speaker also used combinations of concurrent and sequential referrals. In 1995 joint referrals were prohibited. Now each measure is referred to a primary committee and also may be referred, either concurrently or sequentially, to one or more other committees, but usually only for consideration of portions of the measure that fall within the jurisdiction of each of those other committees.

In the Senate, before 1977 concurrent and sequential referrals were permitted only by unanimous consent. In that year, a rule authorized a privileged motion for such a referral if offered jointly by the majority and minority leaders. Debate on the motion and all amendments to it is limited to two hours. The motion may set deadlines for reporting and provide for discharging the committees involved if they fail to meet the deadlines. To date, this procedure has never been invoked; multiple referrals in the Senate continue to be made by unanimous consent.

Multiyear Appropriation—An appropriation that remains available for spending or obligation for more than one fiscal year; the exact period of time is specified in the act making the appropriation.

Multiyear Authorization—(1) Legislation that authorizes the existence or continuation of an agency, program or activity for more than one fiscal year. (2) Legislation that authorizes appropriations for an agency, program or activity for more than one fiscal year.

Nomination—A proposed presidential appointment to a federal office submitted to the Senate for confirmation. Approval is by majority vote. The Constitution explicitly requires confirmation for ambassadors, consuls, "public Ministers" (department heads) and Supreme Court justices. By law, other federal judges, all military promotions of officers and many high-level civilian officials must be confirmed.

Oath of Office—Upon taking office, members of Congress must swear or affirm that they will "support and defend the Constitution...against all enemies, foreign and domestic," that they will "bear true faith and allegiance" to the Constitution, that they take the obligation "freely, without any mental reservation or purpose of evasion," and that they will "well and faithfully discharge the duties" of their office. The oath is required by the Constitution, and the wording is prescribed by a statute. All House members must take the oath at the beginning of each new Congress. Usually, the member with the longest continuous service in the House swears in the Speaker, who then swears in the other members. The president of the Senate or a surrogate administers the oath to newly elected or reelected senators.

Obligation—A binding agreement by a government agency to pay for goods, products, services, studies and the like, either immediately or in the future. When an agency enters into such an agreement, it incurs an obligation. As the agency makes the required payments, it liquidates the obligation. Appropriation laws usually make funds available for obligation for one or more fiscal years but do not require agencies to spend their funds during those specific years. The actual outlays can occur years after the appropriation is obligated, as with a contract for construction of a submarine that may provide for payment to be made when it is delivered in the future. Such obligated funds are often said to be "in the pipeline." Under these circumstances, an agency's outlays in a particular year can come from appropriations obligated in previous years as well as from its current-year appropriation. Consequently, the money Congress appropriates for a fiscal year does not equal the total amount of appropriated money the government will actually spend in that year.

Off-Budget Entities—Specific federal entities whose budget authority, outlays and receipts are excluded by law from the calculation of budget totals, although they are part of government spending and income. As of early 2001, these included the Social Security trust funds (Federal Old-Age and Survivors Insurance Fund and the Federal Disability Insurance Trust Fund) and the Postal Service. Government-sponsored enterprises are also excluded from the budget because they are considered private rather than public organizations.

Office of Management and Budget (OMB)—A unit in the Executive Office of the President, reconstituted in 1970 from the former Bureau of the Budget. The Office of Management and Budget (OMB) assists the president in preparing the budget and in formulating the government's fiscal program. The OMB also plays a central role in supervising and controlling implementation of the budget, pursuant to provisions in appropriations laws, the Budget Enforcement Act and other statutes. In addition to these budgetary functions, the OMB has various management duties, including those performed through its three statutory offices: Federal Financial Management, Federal Procurement Policy and Information and Regulatory Affairs.

Officers of Congress—The Constitution refers to the Speaker of the House and the president of the Senate as officers and declares that each house "shall chuse" its "other Officers," but it does not name them or indicate how they should be selected. A House rule refers to its clerk, sergeant at arms and chaplain as officers. Officers are not named in the Senate's rules, but Riddick's Senate Procedure lists the president pro tempore, secretary of the Senate, sergeant at arms, chaplain and the secretaries for the majority and minority parties as officers. A few appointed officials are sometimes referred to as officers, including the parliamentarians and the legislative counsels. The House elects its officers by resolution at the beginning of each Congress. The Senate also elects its officers, but once elected Senate officers serve from Congress to Congress until their successors are chosen.

Omnibus Bill—A measure that combines the provisions of several disparate subjects into a single and often lengthy bill.

One-Minute Speeches—Addresses by House members that can be on any subject but are limited to one minute. They are usually permitted at the beginning of a daily session after the chaplain's prayer, the pledge of allegiance and approval of the Journal. They are a customary practice, not a right granted by rule. Consequently, recognition for one-minute speeches requires unanimous consent and is entirely within the Speaker's discretion. The Speaker sometimes refuses to permit them when the House has a heavy legislative schedule or limits or postpones them until a later time of the day.

Open Rule—A special rule from the House Rules Committee that permits members to offer as many floor amendments as they wish as long as the amendments are germane and do not violate other House rules.

Order of Business (House)—The sequence of events prescribed by a House rule during the meeting of the House on a new legislative day that is supposed to take place, also called the general order of business. The sequence consists of (1) the chaplain's prayer; (2) reading and approval of the Journal; (3) the pledge of allegiance; (4) correction of the reference of public bills to committee; (5) disposal of business on the Speaker's table; (6) unfinished business; (7) the morning hour call of committees and consideration of their bills; (8) motions to go into Committee of the Whole; and (9) orders of the day. In practice, the House never fully complies with this rule. Instead, the items of business that follow the pledge of allegiance are supplanted by any special orders of business that are in order on that day (for example, conference reports; the corrections, discharge or private calendars; motions to suspend the rules) and by other privileged business (for example, general appropriation bills and special rules) or measures made in order by special rules or unanimous consent. The regular order of business is also modified by unanimous consent practices and orders that govern recognition for one-minute speeches (which date from 1937) and for morning-hour debates, begun in 1994. By this combination of an order of business with privileged interruptions, the House gives precedence to certain categories of important legislation, brings to the floor other major legislation from its calendars in any order it chooses and provides expeditious processing for minor and noncontroversial measures.

Order of Business (Senate)—The sequence of events at the beginning of a new legislative day, as prescribed by Senate rules and standing orders. The sequence consists of (1) the chaplain's prayer; (2) the pledge of allegiance; (3) the designation of a temporary presiding officer if any; (4) Journal reading and approval; (5) recognition of the majority and minority leaders or their designees under the standing order; (6) morning business in the morning hour; (7) call of the calendar during the morning hour (largely obsolete); and (8) unfinished business from the previous session day.

Organization of Congress—The actions each house takes at the beginning of a Congress that are necessary to its operations. These include swearing in newly elected members, notifying the president that a quorum of each house is present, making committee assignments and fixing the hour for daily meetings. Because the House of Representatives is not a continuing body, it must also elect its Speaker and other officers and adopt its rules.

Original Bill—(1) A measure drafted by a committee and introduced by its chairman or another designated member when the committee reports the measure to its house. Unlike a clean bill, it is not referred back to the committee after introduction. The Senate permits all its legislative committees to report original bills. In the House, this authority is referred to in the rules as the "right to report at any time," and five committees (Appropriations, Budget, House Administration, Rules and Standards of Official Conduct) have such authority under circumstances specified in House Rule XIII, clause 5.

(2) In the House, special rules reported by the Rules Committee often propose that an amendment in the nature of a substitute be considered as an original bill for purposes of amendment, meaning that the substitute, as with a bill, may be amended in two degrees. Without that requirement, the substitute may only be amended in one further degree. In the Senate, an amendment in the nature of a substitute automatically is open to two degrees of amendment, as is the original text of the bill, if the substitute is offered when no other amendment is pending.

Original Jurisdiction—The authority of certain committees to originate a measure and report it to the chamber. For example, general appropriation bills reported by the House Appropriations Committee are original bills, and special rules reported by the House Rules Committee are original resolutions.

Other Body—A commonly used reference to a house by a member of the other house. Congressional comity discourages members from directly naming the other house during debate.

Outlays—Amounts of government spending. They consist of payments, usually by check or in cash, to liquidate obligations incurred in prior fiscal years as well as in the current year, including the net lending of funds under budget authority. In federal budget accounting, net outlays are calculated by subtracting the amounts of refunds and various kinds of reimbursements to the government from actual spending.

Override a Veto—Congressional enactment of a measure over the president's veto. A veto override requires a recorded two-thirds vote of those voting in each house, a quorum being present. Because the president must return the vetoed measure to its house of origin, that house votes first, but neither house is required to attempt an override, whether immediately or at all. If an override attempt fails in the house of origin, the veto stands and the measure dies.

Oversight—Congressional review of the way in which federal agencies implement laws to ensure that they are carrying out the intent of Congress and to inquire into the efficiency of the implementation and the effectiveness of the law. The Legislative Reorganization Act of 1946 defined oversight as the function of exercising continuous watchfulness over the execution of the laws by the executive branch.

Oxford-Style Debate—The House held three Oxford-style debates in 1994, modeled after the famous debating format favored by the Oxford Union in Great Britain. Neither chamber has held Oxford-style debates since then. The Oxford-style debates aired nationally over C-SPAN television and National Public Radio. The organized event featured eight participants divided evenly into two teams, one team representing the Democrats (then holding the majority in the chamber) and the other the Republicans. Both teams argued a single question chosen well ahead of the event. A moderator regulated the debate, and began it by stating the resolution at issue. The order of the speakers alternated by team, with a debater for the affirmative speaking first and a debater for the opposing team offering a rebuttal. The rest of the speakers alternated in kind until all gained the chance to speak.

Parliamentarian—The official advisor to the presiding officer in each house on questions of procedure. The parliamentarian and his or her assistants also answer procedural questions from members and congressional staff, refer measures to committees on behalf of the presiding officer and maintain compilations of the precedents. The House parliamentarian revises the House Manual at the beginning of every Congress and usually reviews special rules before the Rules Committee reports them to the House. Either a parliamentarian or an assistant is always present and near the podium during sessions of each house.

Party Caucus—Generic term for each party's official organization in each house. Only House Democrats officially call their organization a caucus. House and Senate Republicans and Senate Democrats call their organizations conferences. The party caucuses elect their leaders, approve committee assignments and chairmanships (or ranking minority members, if the party is in the minority), establish party committees and study groups and discuss party and legislative policies. On rare occasions, they have stripped members of committee seniority or expelled them from the caucus for party disloyalty.

Pay-as-You-Go (PAYGO)—A provision first instituted under the Budget Enforcement Act of 1990 that applies to legislation enacted before Oct. 1, 2002. It requires that the cumulative effect of legislation concerning either revenues or direct spending should not result in a net negative impact on the budget. If legislation does provide for an increase in spending or decrease in revenues, that effect is supposed to be offset by legislated spending reductions or revenue increases. If Congress fails to enact the appropriate offsets, the act requires presidential sequestration of sufficient offsetting amounts in specific direct spending accounts. Congress and the president can circumvent this requirement if both agree that an emergency requires a particular action or if a law is enacted declaring that deteriorated economic circumstances make it necessary to suspend the requirement.

Permanent Appropriation—An appropriation that remains continuously available, without current action or renewal by Congress, under the terms of a previously enacted authorization or appropriation law. One such appropriation provides for payment of interest on the public debt and another the salaries of members of Congress.

Permanent Authorization—An authorization without a time limit. It usually does not specify any limit on the funds that may be appropriated for the agency, program or activity that it authorizes, leaving such amounts to the discretion of the appropriations committees and the two houses.

Permanent Staff—Term used formerly for committee staff authorized by law, who were funded through a permanent authorization and also called statutory staff. Most committees were authorized thirty permanent staff members. Most committees also were permitted additional staff, often called investigative staff, who were authorized by annual or biennial funding resolutions. The Senate eliminated the primary distinction between statutory and investigative staff in 1981. The House eliminated the distinction in 1995 by requiring that funding resolutions authorize money to hire both types of staff.

Personally Obnoxious (or Objectionable)—A characterization a senator sometimes applies to a president's nominee for a federal office in that senator's state to justify his or her opposition to the nomination.

Pocket Veto—The indirect veto of a bill as a result of the president withholding approval of it until after Congress has adjourned sine die. A bill the president does not sign but does not formally veto while Congress is in session automatically becomes a law ten days (excluding Sundays) after it is received. But if Congress adjourns its annual session during that ten-day period the measure dies even if the president does not formally veto it.

Point of Order—A parliamentary term used in committee and on the floor to object to an alleged violation of a rule and to demand that the chair enforce the rule. The point of order immediately halts the proceedings until the chair decides whether the contention is valid.

Pork or Pork Barrel Legislation—Pejorative terms for federal appropriations, bills or policies that provide funds to benefit a legislator's district or state, with the implication that the legislator presses for enactment of such benefits to ingratiate himself or herself with constituents rather than on the basis of an impartial, objective assessment of need or merit. The terms are often applied to such benefits as new parks, post offices, dams, canals, bridges, roads, water projects, sewage treatment plants and public works of any kind, as well as demonstration projects, research grants and relocation of government facilities. Funds released by the president for various kinds of benefits or government contracts approved by him allegedly for political purposes are also sometimes referred to as pork.

Postcloture Filibuster—A filibuster conducted after the Senate invokes cloture. It employs an array of procedural tactics rather than lengthy speeches to delay final action. The Senate curtailed the postcloture filibuster's effectiveness by closing a variety of loopholes in the cloture rule in 1979 and 1986.

Power of the Purse—A reference to the constitutional power Congress has over legislation to raise revenue and appropriate monies from the Treasury. Article I, Section 8 states that Congress "shall have Power To lay and collect Taxes, Duties, Imposts and Excises, [and] to pay the Debts." Section 9 declares: "No Money shall be drawn from the Treasury, but in Consequence of Appropriations made by Law."

Preamble—Introductory language describing the reasons for and intent of a measure, sometimes called a whereas clause. It occasionally appears in joint, concurrent and simple resolutions but rarely in bills.

Precedent—A previous ruling on a parliamentary matter or a long-standing practice or custom of a house. Precedents serve to control arbitrary rulings and serve as the common law of a house.

President of the Senate—One constitutional role of the vice president is serving as the presiding officer of the Senate, or president of the Senate. The Constitution permits the vice president to cast a vote in the Senate only to break a tie, but the vice president is not required to do so.

President Pro Tempore—Under the Constitution, an officer elected by the Senate to preside over it during the absence of the vice president of the United States. Often referred to as the "pro tem," this senator is usually a member of the majority party with the longest continuous service in the chamber and also, by virtue of seniority, a committee chairman. When attending to committee and other duties the president pro tempore appoints other senators to preside.

Presiding Officer—In a formal meeting, the individual authorized to maintain order and decorum, recognize members to speak or offer motions and apply and interpret the chamber's rules, precedents and practices. The Speaker of the House and the president of the Senate are the chief presiding officers in their respective houses.

Previous Question—A nondebatable motion which, when agreed to by majority vote, usually cuts off further debate, prevents the offering of additional amendments and brings the pending matter to an immediate vote. It is a major debate-limiting device in the House; it is not permitted in Committee of the Whole in the House or in the Senate.

Private Bill—A bill that applies to one or more specified persons, corporations, institutions or other entities, usually to grant relief when no other legal remedy is available to them. Many private bills deal with claims against the federal government, immigration and naturalization cases and land titles.

Private Calendar—Commonly used title for a calendar in the House reserved for private bills and resolutions favorably reported by committees. The private calendar is officially called the Calendar of the Committee of the Whole House.

Private Law—A private bill enacted into law. Private laws are numbered in the same fashion as public laws.

Privilege—An attribute of a motion, measure, report, question or proposition that gives it priority status for consideration. Privileged motions and motions to bring up privileged questions are not debatable.

Privilege of the Floor—In addition to the members of a house, certain individuals are admitted to its floor while it is in session. The rules of the two houses differ somewhat but both extend the privilege to the president and vice president, Supreme Court justices, cabinet members, state governors, former members of that house, members of the other house, certain officers and officials of Congress, certain staff of that house in the discharge of official duties and the chamber's former parliamentarians. They also allow access to a limited number of committee and members' staff when their presence is necessary.

Pro Forma Amendment—In the House, an amendment that ostensibly proposes to change a measure or another amendment by moving "to strike the last word" or "to strike the requisite number of words." A member offers it not to make any actual change in the measure or amendment but only to obtain time for debate.

Pro Tem—A common reference to the president pro tempore of the Senate or, occasionally, to a Speaker pro tempore. (See President Pro Tempore; Speaker Pro Tempore.)

Procedures—The methods of conducting business in a deliberative body. The procedures of each house are governed first by applicable provisions of the Constitution, and then by its standing rules and orders, precedents, traditional practices and any statutory rules that apply to it. The authority of the houses to adopt rules in addition to those specified in the Constitution is derived from Article I, Section 5, clause 2, of the Constitution, which states: "Each House may determine the Rules of its Proceedings...." By rule, the House of Representatives also follows the procedures in Jefferson's Manual that are not inconsistent with its standing rules and orders. Many Senate procedures also conform with Jefferson's provisions, but by practice rather than by rule. At the beginning of each Congress, the House uses procedures in general parliamentary law until it adopts its standing rules.

Proxy Voting—The practice of permitting a member to cast the vote of an absent colleague in addition to his or her own vote. Proxy voting is prohibited on the floors of the House and Senate, but the Senate permits its committees to authorize proxy voting, and most do. In 1995, House rules were changed to prohibit proxy voting in committee.

Public Bill—A bill dealing with general legislative matters having national applicability or applying to the federal government or to a class of persons, groups or organizations.

Public Debt—Federal government debt incurred by the Treasury or the Federal Financing Bank by the sale of securities to the public or borrowings from a federal fund or account.

Public Law—A public bill or joint resolution enacted into law. It is cited by the letters "PL" followed by a hyphenated number. The digits before the hyphen indicate the number of the Congress in which it was enacted; the digits after the hyphen indicate its position in the numerical sequence of public measures that became law during that Congress. For example, the Budget Enforcement Act of 1990 became PL 101-508 because it was the 508th measure in that sequence for the 101st Congress. (See also Private Law.)

Qualification (of Members)—The Constitution requires members of the House of Representatives to be twenty-five years of age at the time their terms begin. They must have been citizens of the United States for seven years before that date and, when elected, must be "Inhabitant[s]" of the state from which they were elected. There is no constitutional requirement that they reside in the districts they represent. Senators are required to be thirty years of age at the time their terms begin. They must have been citizens of the United States for nine years before that date and, when elected, must be "Inhabitant[s]" of the states in which they were elected. The "Inhabitant" qualification is broadly interpreted, and in modern times a candidate's declaration of state residence has generally been accepted as meeting the constitutional requirement.

Queen of the Hill Rule—A special rule from the House Rules Committee that permits votes on a series of amendments, especially complete substitutes for a measure, in a specified order, but directs that the amendment receiving the greatest number of votes shall be the winning one. This kind of rule permits the House to vote directly on a variety of alternatives to a measure. In doing so, it sets aside the precedent that once an amendment has been adopted, no further amendments may be offered to the text it has amended. Under an earlier practice, the Rules Committee reported "king of the hill" rules under which there also could be votes on a series of amendments, again in a specified order. If more than one of the amendments was adopted under this kind of rule, it was the last amendment to receive a majority vote that was considered as having been finally adopted, whether or not it had received the greatest number of votes.

Quorum—The minimum number of members required to be present for the transaction of business. Under the Constitution, a quorum in each house is a majority of its members: 218 in the House and 51 in the Senate when there are no vacancies. By House rule, a quorum in Committee of the Whole is 100. In practice, both houses usually assume a quorum is present even if it is not, unless a member makes a point of no quorum in the House or suggests the absence of a quorum in the Senate. Consequently, each house transacts much of its business, and even passes bills, when only a few members are present. For House and Senate committees, chamber rules allow a minimum quorum of one-third of a committee's members to conduct most types of business.

Quorum Call—A procedure for determining whether a quorum is present in a chamber. In the Senate, a clerk calls the roll (roster) of senators. The House usually employs its electronic voting system.

Ramseyer Rule—A House rule that requires a committee's report on a bill or joint resolution to show the changes the measure, and any committee amendments to it, would make in existing law. The rule requires the report to present the text of any statutory provision that would be repealed and a comparative print showing, through typographical devices such as stricken-through type or italics, other changes that would be made in existing law. The rule, adopted in 1929, is named after its sponsor, Rep. Christian W. Ramseyer, R-Iowa. The Senate's analogous rule is called the Cordon Rule.

Rank or Ranking—A member's position on the list of his or her party's members on a committee or subcommittee. When first assigned to a committee, a member is usually placed at the bottom of the list, then moves up as those above leave the committee. On subcommittees, however, a member's rank may not have anything to do with the length of his or her service on it.

Ranking Member—(1) Most often a reference to the minority member with the highest ranking on a committee or subcommittee. (2) A reference to the majority member next in rank to the chairman or to the highest ranking majority member present at a committee or subcommittee meeting.

Ratification—(1) The president's formal act of promulgating a treaty after the Senate has approved it. The resolution of ratification agreed to by the Senate is the procedural vehicle by which the Senate gives its consent to ratification. (2) A state legislature's act in approving a proposed constitutional amendment. Such an amendment becomes effective when ratified by three-fourths of the states.

Reapportionment—(See Apportionment.)

Recess—(1) A temporary interruption or suspension of a meeting of a chamber or committee. Unlike an adjournment, a recess does not end a legislative day. Because the Senate often recesses from one calendar day to another, its legislative day may extend over several calendar days, weeks or even months. (2) A period of adjournment for more than three days to a day certain, especially over a holiday or in August during odd-numbered years.

Recess Appointment—A presidential appointment to a vacant federal position made after the Senate has adjourned sine die or has adjourned or recessed for more than thirty days. If the president submits the recess appointee's nomination during the next session of the Senate, that individual can continue to serve until the end of the session even though the Senate might have rejected the nomination. When appointed to a vacancy that existed thirty days before the end of the last Senate session, a recess appointee is not paid until confirmed.

Recommit—To send a measure back to the committee that reported it; sometimes called a straight motion to recommit to distinguish it from a motion to recommit with instructions. A successful motion to recommit kills the measure unless it is accompanied by instructions.

Recommit a Conference Report—To return a conference report to the conference committee for renegotiation of some or all of its agreements. A motion to recommit may be offered with or without instructions.

Recommit with Instructions—To send a measure back to a committee with instructions to take some action on it. Invariably in the House and often in the Senate, when the motion recommits to a standing committee, the instructions require the committee to report the measure "forthwith" with specified amendments.

Reconciliation—A procedure for changing existing revenue and spending laws to bring total federal revenues and spending within the limits established in a budget resolution. Congress has applied reconciliation chiefly to revenues and mandatory spending programs, especially entitlements. Discretionary spending is controlled through annual appropriation bills.

Recorded Vote—(1) Generally, any vote in which members are recorded by name for or against a measure; also called a record vote or roll-call vote. The only recorded vote in the Senate is a vote by the yeas and nays and is commonly called a roll-call vote. (2) Technically, a recorded vote is one demanded in the House of Representatives and supported by at least one-fifth of a quorum (forty-four members) in the House sitting as the House or at least twenty-five members in Committee of the Whole.

Recorded Vote by Clerks—A voting procedure in the House where members pass through the appropriate "aye" or "no" aisle in the chamber and cast their votes by depositing a signed green (yea) or red (no) card in a ballot box. These votes are tabulated by clerks and reported to the chair. The electronic voting system is much more convenient and has largely supplanted this procedure. (See Committee of the Whole; Recorded Vote; Teller Vote.)

Redistricting—The redrawing of congressional district boundaries within a state after a decennial census. Redistricting may be required to equalize district populations or to accommodate an increase or decrease in the number of a state's House seats that might have resulted from the decennial apportionment. The state governments determine the district lines. (See Apportionment; Congressional District; Gerrymandering.)

Referral—The assignment of a measure to committee for consideration. Under a House rule, the Speaker can refuse to refer a measure if the Speaker believes it is "of an obscene or insulting character."

Report—(1) As a verb, a committee is said to report when it submits a measure or other document to its parent chamber. (2) A clerk is said to report when he or she reads a measure's title, text or the text of an amendment to the body at the direction of the chair. (3) As a noun, a committee document that accompanies a reported measure. It describes the measure, the committee's views on it, its costs and the changes it proposes to make in existing law; it also includes certain impact statements. (4) A committee document submitted to its parent chamber that describes the results of an investigation or other study or provides information it is required to provide by rule or law.

Representative—An elected and duly sworn member of the House of Representatives who is entitled to vote in the chamber. The Constitution requires that a representative be at least twenty-five years old, a citizen of the United States for at least seven years and an inhabitant of the state from which he or she is elected. Customarily, the member resides in the district he or she represents. Representatives are elected in even-numbered years to two-year terms that begin the following January.

Reprimand—A formal condemnation of a member for misbehavior, considered a milder reproof than censure. The House of Representatives first used it in 1976. The Senate first used it in 1991. (See also Censure; Code of Official Conduct; Denounce; Ethics Rules; Expulsion; Seniority Loss.)

Rescission—A provision of law that repeals previously enacted budget authority in whole or in part. Under the Impoundment Control Act of 1974, the president can impound such funds by sending a message to Congress requesting one or more rescissions and the reasons for doing so. If Congress does not pass a rescission bill for the programs requested by the president within forty-five days of continuous session after receiving the message, the president must make the funds available for obligation and expenditure. If the president does not, the comptroller general of the United States is authorized to bring suit to compel the release of those funds. A rescission bill may rescind all, part or none of an amount proposed by the president, and may rescind funds the president has not impounded.

Reserving the Right To Object—Members' declaration that at some indefinite future time they may object to a unanimous consent request. It is an attempt to circumvent the requirement that members may prevent such an action only by objecting immediately after it is proposed.

Resident Commissioner from Puerto Rico—A nonvoting member of the House of Representatives, elected to a four-year term. The resident commissioner has the same status and privileges as delegates. Like the delegates, the resident commissioner may not vote in the House or Committee of the Whole.

Resolution—(1) A simple resolution; that is, a nonlegislative measure effective only in the house in which it is proposed and not requiring concurrence by the other chamber or approval by the president. Simple resolutions are designated H. Res. in the House and S. Res. in the Senate. Simple resolutions express nonbinding opinions on policies or issues or deal with the internal affairs or prerogatives of a house. (2) Any type of resolution: simple, concurrent or joint. (See Concurrent Resolution; Joint Resolution.)

Resolution of Inquiry—A resolution usually simple rather than concurrent calling on the president or the head of an executive agency to provide specific information or papers to one or both houses.

Resolution of Ratification—The Senate vehicle for agreeing to a treaty. The constitutionally mandated vote of two-thirds of the senators present and voting applies to the adoption of this resolution. However, it may also contain amendments, reservations, declarations or understandings that the Senate had previously added to it by majority vote.

Revenue Legislation—Measures that levy new taxes or tariffs or change existing ones. Under Article I, Section 7, clause 1 of the Constitution, the House of Representatives originates federal revenue measures, but the Senate can propose amendments to them. The House Ways and Means Committee and the Senate Finance Committee have jurisdiction over such measures, with a few minor exceptions.

Revise and Extend One's Remarks—A unanimous consent request to publish in the Congressional Record a statement a member did not deliver on the floor, a longer statement than the one made on the floor or miscellaneous extraneous material.

Revolving Fund—A trust fund or account whose income remains available to finance its continuing operations without any fiscal year limitation.

Rider—Congressional slang for an amendment unrelated or extraneous to the subject matter of the measure to which it is attached. Riders often contain proposals that are less likely to become law on their own merits as separate bills, either because of opposition in the committee of jurisdiction, resistance in the other house or the probability of a presidential veto. Riders are more common in the Senate.

Roll Call—A call of the roll to determine whether a quorum is present, to establish a quorum or to vote on a question. Usually, the House uses its electronic voting system for a roll call. The Senate does not have an electronic voting system; its roll is always called by a clerk.

Rule—(1) A permanent regulation that a house adopts to govern its conduct of business, its procedures, its internal organization, behavior of its members, regulation of its facilities, duties of an officer or some other subject it chooses to govern in that form. (2) In the House, a privileged simple resolution reported by the Rules Committee that provides methods and conditions for floor consideration of a measure or, rarely, several measures.

Rule Twenty-Two—A common reference to the Senate's cloture rule. (See Cloture)

Second-Degree Amendment—An amendment to an amendment in the first degree. It is usually a perfecting amendment.

Secretary of the Senate—The chief financial, administrative and legislative officer of the Senate. Elected by resolution or order of the Senate, the secretary is invariably the candidate of the majority party and usually chosen by the majority leader. In the absence of the vice president and pending the election of a president pro tempore, the secretary presides over the Senate. The secretary is subject to policy direction and oversight by the Senate Committee on Rules and Administration. The secretary manages a wide range of functions that support the administrative operations of the Senate as an organization as well as those functions necessary to its legislative process, including record keeping, document management, certifications, housekeeping services, administration of oaths and lobbyist registrations. The secretary is responsible for accounting for all funds appropriated to the Senate and conducts audits of Senate financial activities. On a semiannual basis the secretary issues the Report of the Secretary of the Senate, a compilation of Senate expenditures.

Section—A subdivision of a bill or statute. By law, a section must be numbered and, as nearly as possible, contain "a single proposition of enactment."

Select or Special Committee—A committee established by a resolution in either house for a special purpose and, usually, for a limited time. Most select and special committees are assigned specific investigations or studies but are not authorized to report measures to their chambers. However, both houses have created several permanent select and special committees and have given legislative reporting authority to a few of them: the Ethics Committee in the Senate and the Intelligence Committees in both houses. There is no substantive difference between a select and a special committee; they are so called depending simply on whether the resolution creating the committee calls it one or the other.

Senate—The house of Congress in which each state is represented by two senators; each senator has one vote. Article V of the Constitution declares that "No State, without its Consent, shall be deprived of its equal Suffrage in the Senate." The Constitution also gives the Senate equal legislative power with the House of Representatives. Although the Senate is prohibited from originating revenue measures, and as a matter of practice it does not originate appropriation measures, it can amend both. Only the Senate can give or withhold consent to treaties and nominations from the president. It also acts as a court to try impeachments by the House and elects the vice president when no candidate receives a majority of the electoral votes. It is often referred to as "the upper body," but not by members of the House.

Senate Manual—The handbook of the Senate's standing rules and orders and the laws and other regulations that apply to the Senate, usually published once each Congress.

Senator—A duly sworn elected or appointed member of the Senate. The Constitution requires that a senator be at least thirty years old, a citizen of the United States for at least nine years and an inhabitant of the state from which he or she is elected. Senators are usually elected in even-numbered years to six-year terms that begin the following January. When a vacancy occurs before the end of a term, the state governor can appoint a replacement to fill the position until a successor is chosen at the state's next general election or, if specified under state law, the next feasible date for such an election, to serve the remainder of the term. Until the Seventeenth Amendment was ratified in 1913, senators were chosen by their state legislatures.

Senatorial Courtesy—The Senate's practice of declining to confirm a presidential nominee for an office in the state of a senator of the president's party unless that senator approves.

Seniority—The priority, precedence or status accorded members according to the length of their continuous service in a house or on a committee.

Seniority Loss—A type of punishment that reduces a member's seniority on his or her committees, including the loss of chairmanships. Party caucuses in both houses have occasionally imposed such punishment on their members, for example, for publicly supporting candidates of the other party.

Seniority Rule—The customary practice, rather than a rule, of assigning the chairmanship of a committee to the majority party member who has served on the committee for the longest continuous period of time.

Seniority System—A collection of long-standing customary practices under which members with longer continuous service than their colleagues in their house or on their committees receive various kinds of preferential treatment. Although some of the practices are no longer as rigidly observed as in the past, they still pervade the organization and procedures of Congress.

Sequestration—A procedure for canceling budgetary resources — that is, money available for obligation or spending — to enforce budget limitations established in law. Sequestered funds are no longer available for obligation or expenditure.

Sergeant at Arms—The officer in each house responsible for maintaining order, security and decorum in its wing of the Capitol, including the chamber and its galleries. Although elected by their respective houses, both sergeants at arms are invariably the candidates of the majority party.

Session—(1) The annual series of meetings of a Congress. Under the Constitution, Congress must assemble at least once a year at noon on Jan. 3 unless it appoints a different day by law. (2) The special meetings of Congress or of one house convened by the president, called a special session. (3) A house is said to be in session during the period of a day when it is meeting.

Severability (or Separability) Clause—Language stating that if any particular provisions of a measure are declared invalid by the courts the remaining provisions shall remain in effect.

Sine Die—Without fixing a day for a future meeting. An adjournment sine die signifies the end of an annual or special session of Congress.

Slip Law—The first official publication of a measure that has become law. It is published separately in unbound, single-sheet form or pamphlet form. A slip law usually is available two or three days after the date of the law's enactment.

Speaker—The presiding officer of the House of Representatives and the leader of its majority party. The Speaker is selected by the majority party and formally elected by the House at the beginning of each Congress. Although the Constitution does not require the Speaker to be a member of the House, in fact, all Speakers have been members.

Speaker Pro Tempore—A member of the House who is designated as the temporary presiding officer by the Speaker or elected by the House to that position during the Speaker's absence.

Speaker's Vote—The Speaker is not required to vote, and the Speaker's name is not called on a roll-call vote unless so requested. Usually, the Speaker votes either to create a tie vote, and thereby defeat a proposal or to break a tie in favor of a proposal. Occasionally, the Speaker also votes to emphasize the importance of a matter.

Special Session—A session of Congress convened by the president, under his constitutional authority, after Congress has adjourned sine die at the end of a regular session. (See Adjournment Sine Die; Session.)

Spending Authority—The technical term for backdoor spending. The Congressional Budget Act of 1974 defines it as borrowing authority, contract authority and entitlement authority for which appropriation acts do not provide budget authority in advance. Under the Budget Act, legislation that provides new spending authority may not be considered unless it provides that the authority shall be effective only to the extent or in such amounts as provided in an appropriation act.

Spending Cap—The statutory limit for a fiscal year on the amount of new budget authority and outlays allowed for discretionary spending. The Budget Enforcement Act of 1997 requires a sequester if the cap is exceeded.

Split Referral—A measure divided into two or more parts, with each part referred to a different committee.

Sponsor—The principal proponent and introducer of a measure or an amendment.

Staff Director—The most frequently used title for the head of staff of a committee or subcommittee. On some committees, that person is called chief of staff, clerk, chief clerk, chief counsel, general counsel or executive director. The head of a committee's minority staff is usually called minority staff director.

Standing Committee—A permanent committee established by a House or Senate standing rule or standing order. The rule also describes the subject areas on which the committee may report bills and resolutions and conduct oversight. Most introduced measures must be referred to one or more standing committees according to their jurisdictions.

Standing Order—A continuing regulation or directive that has the force and effect of a rule, but is not incorporated into the standing rules. The Senate's numerous standing orders, like its standing rules, continue from Congress to Congress unless changed or the order states otherwise. The House uses relatively few standing orders, and those it adopts expire at the end of a session of Congress.

Standing Rules—The rules of the Senate that continue from one Congress to the next and the rules of the House of Representatives that it adopts at the beginning of each new Congress.

Standing Vote—An alternative and informal term for a division vote, during which members in favor of a proposal and then members opposed stand and are counted by the chair.

Star Print—A reprint of a bill, resolution, amendment or committee report correcting technical or substantive errors in a previous printing; so called because of the small black star that appears on the front page or cover.

State of the Union Message—A presidential message to Congress under the constitutional directive that the president shall "from time to time give to the Congress Information of the State of the Union, and recommend to their Consideration such Measures as he shall judge necessary and expedient." Customarily, the president sends an annual State of the Union message to Congress, usually late in January.

Statutes at Large—A chronological arrangement of the laws enacted in each session of Congress. Though indexed, the laws are not arranged by subject matter nor is there an indication of how they affect or change previously enacted laws. The volumes are numbered by Congress, and the laws are cited by their volume and page number. The Gramm-Rudman-Hollings Act, for example, appears as 99 Stat. 1037.

Straw Vote Prohibition—Under a House precedent, a member who has the floor during debate may not conduct a straw vote or otherwise ask for a show of support for a proposition. Only the chair may put a question to a vote.

Strike From the *Record*—Expunge objectionable remarks from the Congressional Record, after a member's words have been taken down on a point of order.

Subcommittee—A panel of committee members assigned a portion of the committee's jurisdiction or other functions. On legislative committees, subcommittees hold hearings, mark up legislation and report measures to their full committee for further action; they cannot report directly to the chamber. A subcommittee's party composition usually reflects the ratio on its parent committee.

Subpoena Power—The authority granted to committees by the rules of their respective houses to issue legal orders requiring individuals to appear and testify, or to produce documents pertinent to the committee's functions, or both. Persons who do not comply with subpoenas can be cited for contempt of Congress and prosecuted.

Subsidy—Generally, a payment or benefit made by the federal government for which no current repayment is required. Subsidy payments may be designed to support the conduct of an economic enterprise or activity, such as ship operations, or to support certain market prices, as in the case of farm subsidies.

Sunset Legislation—A term sometimes applied to laws authorizing the existence of agencies or programs that expire annually or at the end of some other specified period of time. One of the purposes of setting specific expiration dates for agencies and programs is to encourage the committees with jurisdiction over them to determine whether they should be continued or terminated.

Sunshine Rules—Rules requiring open committee hearings and business meetings, including markup sessions, in both houses, and also open conference committee meetings. However, all may be closed under certain circumstances and using certain procedures required by the rules.

Supermajority—A term sometimes used for a vote on a matter that requires approval by more than a simple majority of those members present and voting; also referred to as extraordinary majority.

Supplemental Appropriation Bill—A measure providing appropriations for use in the current fiscal year, in addition to those already provided in annual general appropriation bills. Supplemental appropriations are often for unforeseen emergencies.

Suspension of the Rules (House)—An expeditious procedure for passing relatively noncontroversial or emergency measures by a two-thirds vote of those members voting, a quorum being present.

Suspension of the Rules (Senate)—A procedure to set aside one or more of the Senate's rules; it is used infrequently, and then most often to suspend the rule banning legislative amendments to appropriation bills.

Task Force—A title sometimes given to a panel of members assigned to a special project, study or investigation. Ordinarily, these groups do not have authority to report measures to their respective houses.

Tax Expenditure—Loosely, a tax exemption or advantage, sometimes called an incentive or loophole; technically, a loss of governmental tax revenue attributable to some provision of federal tax laws that allows a special exclusion, exemption or deduction from gross income or that provides a special credit, preferential tax rate or deferral of tax liability.

Televised Proceedings—Television and radio coverage of the floor proceedings of the House of Representatives has been available since 1979 and of the Senate since 1986. They are broadcast over a coaxial cable system to all congressional offices and to some congressional agencies on channels reserved for that purpose. Coverage is also available free of charge to commercial and public television and radio broadcasters. The Cable-Satellite Public Affairs Network (C-SPAN) carries gavel-to-gavel coverage of both houses.

Teller Vote—A voting procedure, formerly used in the House, in which members cast their votes by passing through the center aisle to be counted, but not recorded by name, by a member from each party appointed by the chair. The House deleted the procedure from its rules in 1993, but during floor discussion of the deletion a leading member stated that a teller vote would still be available in the event of a breakdown of the electronic voting system.

Third-Degree Amendment—An amendment to a second-degree amendment. Both houses prohibit such amendments.

Third Reading—A required reading to a chamber of a bill or joint resolution by title only before the vote on passage. In modern practice, it has merely become a pro forma step.

Three-Day Rule—(1) In the House, a measure cannot be considered until the third calendar day on which the committee report has been available. (2) In the House, a conference report cannot be considered until the third calendar day on which its text has been available in the Congressional Record. (3) In the House, a general appropriation bill cannot be considered until the third calendar day on which printed hearings on the bill have been available. (4) In the Senate, when a committee votes to report a measure, a committee member is entitled to three calendar days within which to submit separate views for inclusion in the committee report. (In House committees, a member is entitled to two calendar days for this purpose, after the day on which the committee votes to report.) (5) In both houses, a majority of a committee's members may call a special meeting of the committee if its chairman fails to do so within three calendar days after three or more of the members, acting jointly, formally request such a meeting.

In calculating such periods, the House omits holiday and weekend days on which it does not meet. The Senate makes no such exclusion.

Tie Vote—When the votes for and against a proposition are equal, it loses. The president of the Senate may cast a vote only to break a tie. Because the Speaker is invariably a member of the House, the Speaker is entitled to vote but usually does not. The Speaker may choose to do so to break, or create, a tie vote.

Title—(1) A major subdivision of a bill or act, designated by a roman numeral and usually containing legislative provisions on the same general subject. Titles are sometimes divided into subtitles as well as sections. (2) The official name of a bill or act, also called a caption or long title. (3) Some bills also have short titles that appear in the sentence immediately following the enacting clause. (4) Popular titles are the unofficial names given to some bills or acts by common usage. For example, the Balanced Budget and Emergency Deficit Control Act of 1985 (short title) is almost invariably referred to as Gramm-Rudman (popular title). In other cases, significant legislation is popularly referred to by its title number (see definition (1) above). For example, the federal legislation that requires equality of funding for women's and men's sports in educational institutions that receive federal funds is popularly called Title IX.

Track System—An occasional Senate practice that expedites legislation by dividing a day's session into two or more specific time periods, commonly called tracks, each reserved for consideration of a different measure.

Transfer Payment—A federal government payment to which individuals or organizations are entitled under law and for which no goods or services are required in return. Payments include welfare and Social Security benefits, unemployment insurance, government pensions and veterans benefits.

Treaty—A formal document containing an agreement between two or more sovereign nations. The Constitution authorizes the president to make treaties, but the president must submit them to the Senate for its approval by a two-thirds vote of the senators present. Under the Senate's rules, that vote actually occurs on a resolution of ratification. Although the Constitution does not give the House a direct role in approving treaties, that body has sometimes insisted that a revenue treaty is an invasion of its prerogatives. In any case, the House may significantly affect the application of a treaty by its equal role in enacting legislation to implement the treaty.

Trust Funds—Special accounts in the Treasury that receive earmarked taxes or other kinds of revenue collections, such as user fees, and from which payments are made for special purposes or to recipients who meet the requirements of the trust funds as established by law. Of the more than 150 federal government trust funds, several finance major entitlement programs, such as Social Security, Medicare and retired federal employees' pensions. Others fund infrastructure construction and improvements, such as highways and airports.

Unanimous Consent—Without an objection by any member. A unanimous consent request asks permission, explicitly or implicitly, to set aside one or more rules. Both houses and their committees frequently use such requests to expedite their proceedings.

Uncontrollable Expenditures—A frequently used term for federal expenditures that are mandatory under existing law and therefore cannot be controlled by the president or Congress without a change in the existing law. Uncontrollable expenditures include spending required under entitlement programs and also fixed costs, such as interest on the public debt and outlays to pay for prior-year obligations. In recent years, uncontrollables have accounted for approximately three-quarters of federal spending in each fiscal year.

Unfunded Mandate—Generally, any provision in federal law or regulation that imposes a duty or obligation on a state or local government or private sector entity without providing the necessary funds to comply. The Unfunded Mandates Reform Act of 1995 amended the Congressional Budget Act of 1974 to provide a mechanism for the control of new unfunded mandates.

Union Calendar—A calendar of the House of Representatives for bills and resolutions favorably reported by committees that raise revenue or directly or indirectly appropriate money or property. In addition to appropriation bills, measures that authorize expenditures are also placed on this calendar. The calendar's full title is the Calendar of the Committee of the Whole House on the State of the Union.

Upper Body—A common reference to the Senate, but not used by members of the House.

U.S. Code—Popular title for the United States Code: Containing the General and Permanent Laws of the United States in Force on.... It is a consolidation and partial codification of the general and permanent laws of the United States arranged by subject under 50 titles. The first six titles deal with general or political subjects, the other forty-four with subjects ranging from agriculture to war, alphabetically arranged. A supplement is published after each session of Congress, and the entire Code is revised every six years.

User Fee—A fee charged to users of goods or services provided by the federal government. When Congress levies or authorizes such fees, it determines whether the revenues should go into the general collections of the Treasury or be available for expenditure by the agency that provides the goods or services.

Veto—The president's disapproval of a legislative measure passed by Congress. The president returns the measure to the house in which it originated without his signature but with a veto message stating his objections to it. When Congress is in session, the president must veto a bill within ten days, excluding Sundays, after the president has received it; otherwise it becomes law without his signature. The ten-day clock begins to run at midnight following his receipt of the bill. (See also Committee Veto; Item Veto; Line Item Veto Act of 1996; Override a Veto; Pocket Veto.)

Voice Vote—A method of voting in which members who favor a question answer aye in chorus, after which those opposed answer no in chorus, and the chair decides which position prevails.

Voting—Members vote in three ways on the floor: (1) by shouting "aye" or "no" on voice votes; (2) by standing for or against on division votes; and (3) on recorded votes (including the yeas and nays), by answering "aye" or "no" when their names are called or, in the House, by recording their votes through the electronic voting system.

War Powers Resolution of 1973—An act that requires the president "in every possible instance" to consult Congress before committing U.S. forces to ongoing or imminent hostilities. If the president commits them to a combat situation without congressional consultation, the president must notify Congress within forty-eight hours. Unless Congress declares war or otherwise authorizes the operation to continue, the forces must be withdrawn within sixty or ninety days, depending on certain conditions. No president has ever acknowledged the constitutionality of the resolution.

Well—The sunken, level, open space between members' seats and the podium at the front of each chamber. House members usually address their chamber from their party's lectern in the well on its side of the aisle. Senators usually speak at their assigned desks.

Whip—The majority or minority party member in each house who acts as assistant leader, helps plan and marshal support for party strategies, encourages party discipline and advises his or her leader on how colleagues intend to vote on the floor. In the Senate, the Republican whip's official title is assistant leader.

Yeas and Nays—A vote in which members usually respond "aye" or "no" (despite the official title of the vote) on a question when their names are called in alphabetical order. The Constitution requires the yeas and nays when a demand for it is supported by one-fifth of the members present, and it also requires an automatic yea-and-nay vote on overriding a veto. Senate precedents require the support of at least one-fifth of a quorum, a minimum of eleven members with the present membership of 100.

Index